For Amy and Zachary,
my family, my world

Manhood in America

Manhood in America

A CULTURAL HISTORY

Second Edition

MICHAEL S. KIMMEL

New York   Oxford
OXFORD UNIVERSITY PRESS
2006

Oxford University Press, Inc., publishes works that further Oxford University's
objective of excellence in research, scholarship, and education.

Oxford   New York
Auckland   Cape Town   Dar es Salaam   Hong Kong   Karachi
Kuala Lumpur   Madrid   Melbourne   Mexico City   Nairobi
New Delhi   Shanghai   Taipei   Toronto

With offices in
Argentina   Austria   Brazil   Chile   Czech Republic   France Greece
Guatemala   Hungary   Italy   Japan Poland   Portugal   Singapore
South Korea   Switzerland   Thailand   Turkey   Ukraine   Vietnam

Copyright © 2006 by Michael S. Kimmel

Published by Oxford University Press, Inc.
198 Madison Avenue, New York, New York 10016
http://www/oup.com

Oxford is a registered trademark of Oxford University Press.

Library of Congress Cataloging-in-Publication Data

Kimmel, Michael S.
    Manhood in America—2nd ed.
      p. cm.
    Includes bibliographical references and index.
    ISBN-13: 978-0-19-518113-5 (alk. paper)

    1. Men—United States—Psychology.   2. Masculinity—United States.   I. Title.

    HQ1090.3.K553 2005
    305.31′0973—dc22
                                                         2005047346
ISBN: 0-19-518113-1 (paper)
      (9780195181135)

Printed in the United States of America
on acid-free paper.

Contents

Preface to the Second Edition

The publication of a second edition of a book is usually a mixed blessing: it means that the book has been successful enough to warrant a new edition, but that there are parts of it that need fixing—either by updating old material or by revising some of the ideas. In this case, I've done little of either. Since *Manhood in America* is a cultural history, I will stand by the assessments of the historical development of masculinity I sketched out in the first edition. While I have tried to add a few historical references to buttress the original claims, the work remains pretty much as I first wrote it.

I have, however, attempted to add by subtraction: I've cut back the supporting reference materials dramatically, especially pruning away much of the additional commentary that I had earlier carried out in the footnotes. The reference materials should be slimmer and more navigable for the reader.

I have also added a new chapter, updating the book from 1994, when I finished the first draft, through the end of 2004. While writing this, I began to notice a shift in American men's attitudes. If the history of middle-class white American masculinity that I trace here has been a history of a self-made man "restless in the midst of abundance" as de Tocqueville so eloquently observed, anxious, driven to prove his masculinity at every turn, the past decade has seen that anxiety morph into anger, that restlessness drift inexorably into rage. While many American men drift toward greater gender equality—sharing childcare, developing cross-sex friendships, accepting women's equality in the workplace and in the professions—there is also a growing vitriolic chorus of defensively unapologetic regression. American men have probably never been more equal with women, and many American men have never been angrier.

Do I think there's a connection? Yes and no. I think the tide of gender equality is rising inexorably, despite the efforts of what Spiro Agnew would have called these "nattering nabobs of negativism." They're two different groups. As the pundits yearn nostalgically for some anterior moment when men's privileges were intact and unchallenged, others howl with derision at the prospect of gender equality, claiming men as the victims of reverse discrimination. Others declare that Neanderthal masculinity is our birthright or genetic inheritance, ordained via divine or evolutionary imperatives.

And while fewer men seem to be trooping off to the woods these days for mythopoetic gatherings, many are still searching for authenticity in their relationships to their work, their families, and their friends, and are finding depth, resonance, and fulfillment far closer to home than they ever expected. Middle-class men say they are more likely to spend weekends with their families than pursuing all other activities—hanging out with friends, playing golf, watching sports, etc.—combined.

At the same time, men still use the same strategies to anchor their identities and achieve a secure masculinity in an increasingly insecure world. The three patterns I initially discerned—self-control, exclusion, and escape—are all in evidence today. Fitness regimens, steroid scandals, and the emergence of a virtual pharmacy of potions and elixirs ministering to men's physical and sexual problems and insecurities offer ample evidence that the drive for self-control as a quest for physical perfection remains potent. The increased virulence of the men's rights movement, the categorical denials of gender inequality—indeed, the assertions that men are the victims of reverse discrimination—suggest that even as women's equality proceeds inexorably both at home and in the workplace, there are many men who see their hope for manhood hinging upon women's return to dependent mother or luscious sexpot. Much of their leaders' rhetoric about gender is reminiscent of contemporary white supremacists' rhetoric about race: contrary to all evidence, they argue that it is the privileged who are really the oppressed. In this Orwellian rhetorical reversal, they claim to promote equality and to oppose "sexism" or "racism," while their view of equality sounds like the 50s—the 1850s. New organizations have developed to organize their efforts and sustain those impulses.

This book is about the development of an idea—manhood—over the course of American history. I try to show the forces that shaped the cultural definition of manhood, how it changed over time, and the ways in which cultural prescriptions about the meaning of manhood were bound up with those social and cultural forces. I stress this because the single negative review of my book was confused about this; the reviewer seemed incapable of understanding the distinction between *men* and *manhood*, and thus accused me of writing a one-dimensional history of men.

My hopes for this edition of the book remain the same as before: that by understanding the history of the idea of masculinity, its contours and shifts over the past two centuries, we can also begin to tease apart those strands that constrain and confuse us—draw or distract us from the fabric of meaning and authenticity that we crave—from those that enrich and fulfill us, and would anchor us securely in a harbor both safe and deep.

Acknowledgments

When the first edition of this book was published a decade ago, I acknowledged those whose work had inspired me to undertake what seemed a formidable project—extracting the history of the idea of masculinity over the course of American history. Professional inspiration and institutional support came from many places, and I remain grateful to all those I credited earlier.

A decade later, I want to acknowledge those who also have sustained me, intellectually and personally: Harry Brod, Scott Coltrane, Bob Connell, Martin Duberman, Krin Gabbard, Jeff Hearn, Michael Kaufman, Terry Kupers, Mike Messner, Joe Pleck, Tony Rotundo, and Don Sabo. I am grateful that many of them have become my friends, as well as intellectual collaborators in defining a new field within Gender Studies: the Critical Studies on Men and Masculinities. I am glad to acknowledge them, as much for their companionship as for their fine work.

Oxford University Press has become a haven for my work. Peter Labella's been an ideal editor, friend and baseball companion for more than a decade; Shiwani Srivastava and Sean Mahoney have been both responsive and consistent. And I'm glad to acknowledge the Department of Sociology at SUNY Stony Brook, which has nurtured my research and supported my efforts to build this new field.

My family of origin, therapists and healers all, probably gave me a head start on understanding the anxiety that lies at the heart of American masculinity, and some of the tools with which to deal with it.

The love of friends—Mitchell Tunick and Pam Hatchfield, Michael Kaufman, Mary Morris and Larry O'Connor, Lillian and Hank Rubin—keeps me afloat; my family keeps me buoyant.

One friend deserves special mention. Lillian Rubin has read every word and argued every point with sharpness and clarity, coupled with grace and a generosity of spirit that is rare and precious.

Virtually every baseball fan of a certain age has Lou Gehrig's farewell speech imprinted indelibly in his or her mind. Standing on the field of a packed Yankee Stadium, his record-setting streak of consecutive games played ending as he struggled against ALS, his voice booms into the cavernous stadium, and the echo booms back nearly as loudly. (It is impossible to write without including the echo; it's how I hear it): "Today (today), I consider myself (I consider myself), the luckiest man (the luckiest man) on the face of the earth (on the face of the earth)."

I say those same words, more quietly and without the echo, every single day, living with Amy and Zachary.

—M. S. K.
Brooklyn, NY
July, 2005

Manhood in America

Introduction

Toward a History of Manhood in America

And what is our Ideal Man? On what grand and luminous mythological figure does contemporary humanity attempt to model itself? The question is embarrassing. Nobody knows.
—Aldous Huxley *Texts and Pretexts*

A man would never get the notion of writing a book on the peculiar situation of the human male.
—Simone de Beauvoir *The Second Sex* (1953)

American men have no history. Sure, we have libraries filled with the words of men about the works of men—stacks of biographies of the heroic and famous, and historical accounts of events in which men took part, like wars, strikes, or political campaigns. We have portraits of athletes, scientists, and soldiers, histories of unions and political parties. And there are probably thousands of histories of institutions that were organized, staffed, and run entirely by men.

So how can I claim that men have no history? Isn't virtually every history book a history of men? After all, as we have learned from feminist scholars, it's been *women* who have had, until recently, no history. In fact, if the book doesn't have the word *women* in the title, it's a good bet that the book is largely about men. Yet such works do not explore how the experience of being a man, of *manhood,* structured the lives of the men who are their subjects, the organizations and institutions they created and staffed, the events in which they participated. American men have no history of themselves *as men.*[1]

What does it mean, then, to write of men *as men*? It requires two things: first, to chart how the definition of masculinity has changed over time; second, to explore how the experience of manhood has shaped the activities of American men. When we do that, we find some startling news—that the sources of the current confusion, defensiveness, and malaise among American men lie deep in our nation's past. Beginning in the early part of the nineteenth century, the idea of testing and proving one's manhood became one of the defining experiences in American men's lives. The long-term causes of the idea of proving one's manhood were structural—change in the work world, the political arena, and the family. The consequences of those changes, however, have been both social and psychological, carried out both in the relationships between different groups throughout our history as well as in men's sense of themselves as men. And the idea of proving one's manhood continues to reverberate to the present day.

That's not to say that charting the history of manhood will become a catchall cornucopia, that by injecting gender into the standard historical narrative, we will suddenly, magically, illuminate the entire American historical pageant. We cannot understand manhood without understanding American history. But I believe we also cannot fully understand American history without understanding masculinity. How has American history been shaped by the efforts to test and prove manhood—the wars we Americans have waged, the frontier we have tamed, the work we have done, the leaders we admire? Why do so many contemporary American men feel that they have to "prove it" all the time? These are big questions, and in this book I hope only to suggest some of the larger patterns that such a detailed historical inquiry into the meaning of manhood might observe.

American men still have no history in part, I believe, because we haven't known what questions to ask. In the past twenty-five years the pioneering work of feminist scholars, both in traditional disciplines and in women's studies, has made us increasingly aware of the centrality of gender in shaping social life. By gender I mean the sets of cultural meanings and prescriptions that each culture attaches to one's biological sex. And these meanings become one of the poles around which our experiences revolve.[2]

The women's movement made gender visible—at least to women. Courses on gender in the universities are populated largely by women, as if the term only applied to them. "Woman alone seems to have 'gender' since the category itself is defined as that aspect of social relations based on difference between the sexes in which the standard has always been man," writes the historian Thomas Lacquer.[3] Consider the evolution of women's studies, which originally focused on what Catharine Stimpson, one of the field's founders, called the "omissions, distortions, and trivializations" of women's experiences.[4] Women's Studies rescued from obscurity the lives of notable women who had been ignored or whose work had been minimized by traditional scholarship and also examined the everyday lives of women in the past—the efforts, for example, of laundresses, factory workers, pioneer homesteaders, or housewives to carve out lives of meaning and dignity in a world controlled by men. Only gradually have scholars seen the patterns among these female subjects and realized the different meanings that being a woman has taken throughout our history.

Eventually, it will be time to go further, to explore the history of both women and men. "We should not be working on the subjected sex any more than a historian of class can focus exclusively on peasants," writes the historian Natalie Zemon Davis. "Our goal is to understand the significance of the *sexes*, of gender groups in the historical past."[5] Such a perspective understands the relations among men or among women, or the relationships between women and men as gendered relationships, not simply relationships in which men and/or women happen to be participating.

But first we must make gender visible to men. We continue to treat our male military, political, scientific, or literary figures as if their gender, their masculinity, had nothing to do with their military exploits, policy decisions, scientific experiments, or writing styles and subjects. As the Chinese proverb has it, the fish are the last to discover the ocean.

This problem was made clear to me in a seminar on Feminist Theory I attended several years ago. There, in a discussion between two women, I first confronted the invisibility of gender to men. During one meeting, a white woman and a black woman were discussing whether all women were, by definition, "sisters" because they all had essentially the same experiences and because all women faced a common oppression by men. The white woman asserted that the fact that they were both women bonded them, in spite of racial differences. The black woman disagreed.

"When you wake up in the morning and look in the mirror, what do you see?" she asked.

"I see a woman," replied the white woman.

"That's precisely the problem," responded the black woman. "I see a *black* woman. To me, race is visible every day, because race is how I am *not* privileged in our culture. Race is invisible to you, because it's how you are privileged. It's a luxury, a privilege, not to see race all the time. It's why there will always be differences in our experience."

As I witnessed this exchange, I was startled, and groaned—more audibly, perhaps, than I had intended. Someone asked what my response meant.

"Well," I said, "when I look in the mirror, I see a human being." I'm universally generalizable. As a middle-class white man, I have no class, no race, no gender. I'm the generic person!

Sometimes I like to think it was on that day that I *became* a middle-class white man. Sure, I had been a member of all those groups before, but they had not meant much to me. That was, itself, a form of privilege. Since then, I've begun to understand that race, class, and gender do not refer only to the marginalized "others"; they also describe me.

Writing a history of men in America, I have placed gender in the center of my historical analysis. I argue that the quest for manhood—the effort to achieve, to demonstrate, to prove our masculinity—has been one of the formative and persistent experiences in men's lives. That we remain unaware of the centrality of gender in our lives only helps to perpetuate gender inequality.

Even when we do acknowledge gender, we often endow manhood with a transcendental, almost mythic set of properties that still keep it invisible. We think of manhood as eternal, a timeless essence that resides deep in the heart of every man. Either we think of manhood as innate, residing in the particular anatomical organization of the human male, or we think of manhood as a transcendent tangible property that each man manifests in the world, the reward presented with great ceremony to a young novice by his elders for having successfully completed an arduous initiation ritual. In the words of Robert Bly, "the structure at the bottom of the male psyche is still as firm as it was twenty thousand years ago."[6]

Putting manhood in historical context presents it differently, as a constantly changing collection of meanings that we construct through our relationships with ourselves, with each other, and with our world. Manhood is neither static nor timeless. Manhood is not the manifestation of an inner essence; it's socially constructed. Manhood does not bubble up to consciousness from our biological constitution; it is created in our culture. In fact, the search for a transcendent, timeless definition of manhood is itself a sociological phenomenon—we tend to search for the timeless and eternal during moments of crisis, those points of transition when the old definitions no longer work and the new definitions are yet to be firmly established.

Manhood means different things at different times to different people. Some cultures encourage a manly stoicism we might find familiar. Many men in many cultures seem preoccupied with demonstrating sexual prowess. But some cultures prescribe a more relaxed definition of masculinity, a more emotional and familial man. Nor are all American men alike. What it means to be a man in America depends heavily on one's class, race, ethnicity, age, sexuality, region of the country. To acknowledge these differences among men, we must speak of *masculinities*. At the same time, though, all American men must also contend with a singular vision of masculinity, a particular definition that is held up as the model against which we all measure ourselves. As the sociologist Erving Goffman once wrote:

> In an important sense there is only one complete unblushing male in America: a young, married, white, urban, northern, heterosexual, Protestant, father, of college education, fully employed, of good complexion, weight, and height, and a recent record in sports. . . . Any male who fails to qualify in any one of these ways is likely to view himself—during moments at least—as unworthy, incomplete, and inferior.[7]

A history of manhood must, therefore, recount two histories: the history of the changing "ideal" version of masculinity and the parallel and competing versions that coexist with it.[8]

It is this tension between the multiplicity of masculinities that collectively define American men's actual experiences and this singular "hegemonic" masculinity that is prescribed as the norm that forms one of the organizing dynamics of this book. In a sense, this is a history of that "complete" male that Goffman describes—straight, white, middle class, native-born—the story of his great accomplishments and his nagging anxieties. Yet in another sense, it is at least indirectly the story of the marginalized "others"—working-class men, gay men, men of color, immigrant men—how these different groups of men and, of course, women were used as a screen against which those "complete" men projected their fears and, in the process, constructed this prevailing definition of manhood. I do not tell the story of these "others" from their point of view nor in their own voices; rather, I trace the ways that they were set up as everything that "straight white men" were not, so as to provide public testimony and private reassurance that those "complete" men were secure in their gender identity. Thus, this book describes only one version of "Manhood in America"—albeit the dominant version.

There have been some attempts to tell the story of American manhood—by women. But many feminist analyses failed to resonate with men's own experiences. Not a surprise, since women theorized about masculinity from *their* point of view, from the way women experienced masculinity. And women theorized that men's relationships with women were the pivotal relationship in the lives of both women and men. Masculinity, we were told, was defined by the drive for power, for domination, for control.

I began the historical research for this book guided by that feminist perspective. But the historical record has revealed a somewhat different picture. Manhood is less about the drive for domination and more about the fear of others dominating us, having power or control over us. Throughout American history American men have been afraid that others will see us as less than manly, as weak, timid, frightened. And men have been afraid of not measuring up to some vaguely defined notions of what it means to be a man, afraid of failure. Here's how novelist John Steinbeck put it in *Of Mice and Men* (1937):

> "Funny thing," [Curley's wife] said. "If I catch any one man, and he's alone, I get along fine with him. But just let two of the guys get together an' you won't talk. Jus' nothin' but mad." She dropped her fingers and put her hands on her hips. "You're all scared of each other, that's what. Ever'one of you's scared the rest is goin' to get something on you."[9]

Curley's wife sees clearly what we've often missed: In large part, it's other men who are important to American men; American men define their masculinity, not as much in relation to women, but in relation to each other. Masculinity is largely a homosocial enactment. "Women have, in men's minds, such a low place on the social ladder of this country that it's useless to define yourself in terms of a woman," noted playwright David Mamet. "What men need is men's approval."[10]

Such a bold claim does not mean that women are incidental to men's efforts to prove their manhood. Far from it. As I will show in the pages that follow, men often go to elaborate lengths and take extraordinary risks to prove their manhood in the eyes of women. Women are not incidental to masculinity, but they are not always its central feature, either. At times, it is not women as corporeal beings but the "idea" of women, or femininity—and most especially a perception of effeminacy by other men—that animates men's actions. Femininity, separate from actual women, can become a negative pole against which men define themselves. Women themselves often serve as a kind of currency that men use to improve their ranking with other men.

The historical record underscores this homosociality. From the early nineteenth century until the present day, much of men's relentless effort to prove their manhood contains this core element of homosociality. From fathers and boyhood friends to teachers, coworkers, and bosses, the evaluative eyes of other men are always upon us, watching, judging. As one Army general put it, every soldier fears "losing the one thing he is likely to value more highly than life—his reputation as *a man among other men*."[11] Our real fear, writes the literary critic David Leverenz, "is not fear of women but of being ashamed or humiliated in front of other men, or being dominated by stronger men."[12]

Masculinity defined through homosocial interaction contains many parts, including the camaraderie, fellowship, and intimacy often celebrated in male culture. It also includes homophobia. Homophobia is more than the irrational fear of homosexuals, more than the fear that we might (mistakenly) be perceived as gay. It is these, of course, but it is also something deeper. Homophobia is the fear of other men—that other men will unmask us, emasculate us, reveal to us and the world that we do not measure up, are not real men, that we are, like the young man in a poem by Yeats, "one that ruffles in a manly pose for all his timid heart." "The word 'faggot' has nothing to do with homosexual experience or even with fears of homosexuals," writes David Leverenz. "It comes out of the depths of manhood: a label of ultimate contempt for anyone who seems sissy, untough, uncool."[13]

My task in this book is to set these constant efforts to prove manhood, the burdens of proof, within the context of American history and to do so by holding American history up to the prism of gender. Like all prisms, this works in two ways. First, I take the disparate strands of economic, political, social, cultural, and literary events, focus them into one beam, and shed the brightest light possible on one aspect of American society—men. But the prism will also refract that light to fragment what seems to be a unitary vision of masculinity in a rainbow of different colors, shades, and hues.

The history of American manhood is many histories at once. It is the story of spectacular technological and military triumphs and of the sobering dullness of everyday life. It is the inspiring story of heroic efforts to overcome adversity through feats of dazzling brilliance, astonishing physical strength, or remarkable courage and the story of ordinary men in ordinary circumstances shouldering the responsibilities of quotidian routine, seeking moments of comfort and solace in the face of their personal daily grind. It is a history of energy and excitement, of sadness and silences.

And always also a history of fears, frustration, and failure. At the grandest social level and the most intimate realms of personal life, for individuals and institutions, American men have been haunted by fears that they are not powerful, strong, rich, or successful enough. And many of our actions, on both the public and private stages, have been efforts to ward off these demons, to silence these fears. I argue that there have been certain patterns to these actions: American men try to *control themselves*; they project their fears onto *others*; and when feeling too pressured, they attempt an *escape*. These three themes recur frequently in the following pages, as men return to self-control, exclusion, and escape in their efforts to ground a secure sense of themselves as men.

In rough outline my argument will look something like this: At the turn of the nineteenth century, American manhood was rooted in landownership (the Genteel Patriarch) or in the self-possession of the independent artisan, shopkeeper, or farmer (the Heroic Artisan). In the first few decades of the nineteenth century, though, the Industrial Revolution had a critical effect on those earlier definitions. American men began to link their sense of themselves as men to their position in the volatile marketplace, to their economic success—a far less stable yet far more exciting and potentially rewarding peg upon which to hang one's identity. The Self-Made Man of American mythology was born anxious and insecure, uncoupled from the more stable anchors of landownership or workplace autonomy. Now manhood had to be proved. This "*self-maker*, self-improving, is always a construction in progress," writes cultural historian Garry Wills. "He must ever be tinkering, improving, adjusting; starting over, fearful his product will get out of date, or rot in the storehouse."[14] This book is a history of the Self-Made Man—ambitious and anxious, creatively resourceful and chronically restive, the builder of culture and among the casualties of his own handiwork, a man who is, as the great French thinker Alexis de Tocqueville wrote in 1832, "restless in the midst of abundance."

In the first part of this book (Chapters 1 and 2), I describe the fitful birth of the Self-Made Man and observe how he sought to secure his sense of himself in the years before the Civil War. In Part Two (Chapters 3, 4, and 5), I trace his experiences from the end of the Civil War to the first decades of the twentieth century as he confronted new challenges in an increasingly industrialized, urban, and crowded society. His working life became too precarious to provide a firm footing, so the Self-Made Man turned to leisure activities, such as sports, to give his manhood the boost he needed and strove to develop some all-male preserves where he could both be alone with other men and teach his sons to become Self-Made Men themselves. Part Three (Chapters 6 and 7) traces his efforts during the first half of the twentieth century, following him through two world wars, one Depression, and adding the new media of film and television, while Part Four (Chapters 8, 9, and 10) follows his move to postwar suburbia and brings his saga up to the present day.

To map the meanings of manhood over the past two centuries, I've relied upon an eclectic reading of a variety of sources—advice books for young parents, and for anxious young men about to go off and seek their fortunes; records of public displays of manly prowess and recollections of private moments in masculine preserves; novels and popular fiction in magazines and comic books; film and television; political pamphlets engaged with questions raised by the women's movement, as well as from electoral campaigns and union struggles; and finally, more conventional political and economic history. I'm interested especially in moments of crisis when masculinity was seen as threatened and people worked hard to try and salvage, revitalize, and resurrect it. These crisis points in the meaning of manhood were also crisis points in economic, political, and social life— moments when men's relationships to their work, to their country, to their families, to their visions, were transformed.

The advice of experts, the claims of politicians, and the flights of literary or cinematic fantasy—these are the materials from which I construct a history of the changing ideals of American manhood. This book is less about what boys and men actually *did* than about what they were told that they were *supposed* to do, feel, and think and what happened in response to those prescriptions. America and American masculinity evolved together, each in relation to the other, a dynamic that has made this country the wealthiest and most powerful that the world has ever known and laid the possibilities for unlimited personal success, strength, power, and achievement on the shoulders of every Self-Made Man. Such possibilities have been both our freedom and our imprisonment, propelling us forward toward new horizons, and keeping us racing on treadmills, unable to stop.

PART ONE

The Making of the Self-Made Man in America, 1776–1865

CHAPTER 1

The Birth of the Self-Made Man

Nothing conceivable is so petty, so insipid, so crowded with paltry interests—in one word, so anti-poetic—as the life of a man in the United States.
—Alexis de Tocqueville *Democracy in America* (1832)

On April 16, 1787, a few weeks before the opening of the Constitutional Convention, the
first professionally produced play in American history opened in New York. *The Contrast*,
a five-act comedy by Royall Tyler, centered around two men—one, a disingenuous
womanizing fop, and the other, a courageous American army officer—and the woman for
whose affections they competed.[1] Tyler parodied the dandy's pretensions at the same
time that he disdained the superficial vanities of women, contrasting both with an ideal
of chaste and noble love. A patriotic play, *The Contrast* offered a kind of Declaration of
Independence of Manners and Morals a decade after the original Declaration had spelled
out political and economic rights and responsibilities.

The Contrast posed the most challenging question before the newly independent
nation: What kind of nation were we going to be? The sharply drawn differences between
the two leading male characters, Billy Dimple and Colonel Manly, allowed the playwright
to set (in names worthy of Dickens) the Old World against the New. Dimple was a
feminized fop, an Anglophilic, mannered rogue who traveled to England and returned
a dandy. "The ruddy youth, who washed his face at the cistern every morning, and swore
. . . eternal love and constancy, was now metamorphosed into a flippant, pallid, polite
beau, who devotes the morning to his toilet, reads a few pages of Chesterfield's letters [on
the art of seduction], and then minces out to put the infamous principles in practice on
every woman he meets."[2] His rival, the virtuous Colonel Manly, is a former military
officer, modeled after George Washington, fresh from the victory over the British—a
man loyal to his troops and to honor and duty. Dimple and Manly compete for the hand
of Maria, daughter of Mr. Van Rough, a successful urban businessman who is looking
to solidify his newly prosperous economic position with a marriage to the well-positioned
Dimple. Van Rough's motto is "Money makes the mare go; keep your eye upon the
main chance."[3]

While audiences were quick to see the political choices before them—pitting ill-gained
wealth and dubious morality against hard work and civic virtue—Tyler was also presenting another contrast, the answer to a different set of questions: What kind of men would
populate this new nation? What vision of manhood would be promoted? What would
it mean to be a man in the newly independent United States? Dimple, Manly, and Van

Rough offered the audience a contrast among three types of men, three versions of manhood; each embodied different relationships to his work, to his family, to his nation. The signal work in the history of American theater is also one of the earliest meditations on American manhood.

When we first meet Maria Van Rough in the play's opening scene, she is disconsolate, extolling the manly virtues that her fiancé, Dimple, lacks:

> The manly virtue of courage, that fortitude which steels the heart against the keenest misfortunes, which interweaves the laurel of glory amidst the instruments of torture and death, displays something so noble, so exalted, that in despite of the prejudices of education I cannot but admire it, even in a savage.

Maria sees Dimple as "a depraved wretch, whose only virtue is a polished exterior; who is actuated by the unmanly ambition of conquering the defenseless; whose heart, insensible to the emotions of patriotism, dilates at the plaudits of every unthinking girl; whose laurels are the sighs and tears of the miserable victims of his specious behavior."[4]

Enter Colonel Manly. When he and Maria meet by accident in the second act, they are smitten, but Manly's virtue precludes any action on his part. As the play builds to the inevitable confrontation between Dimple and Manly, Tyler provides brief exchanges between the two men (and their manservants) to maintain the audience's interest. In one exchange they parry over the question of whether aristocratic wealth saps virility. Manly warns that no one "shall convince me that a nation, to become great, must first become dissipated. Luxury is surely the bane of a nation: Luxury! which enervates both soul and body, . . . which renders a people weak at home and accessible to bribery, corruption and force from abroad."

Dimple responds by describing the pleasures of seduction. "There is not much pleasure when a man of the world and a finished coquette meet, who perfectly know each other; but how delicious it is to excite the emotions of joy, hope, expectation, and delight in the bosom of a lovely girl who believes every tittle of what you say to be serious!" (We learn later that Dimple's disquisition was more than theoretical, as he has seduced all three of the play's leading women.) Manly's retort is angry and virtuous. "The man who, under pretensions of marriage, can plant thorns in the bosom of an innocent, unsuspecting girl is more detestable than a common robber, in the same proportion as private violence is more despicable than open force."[5]

Finally, Dimple is exposed as a phony and denounced by all. Even in defeat, though, he asks that those assembled consider "the contrast between a gentleman who has read Chesterfield and received the polish of Europe and an unpolished, untravelled American." Manly gets Maria's hand and also has the last word, closing the play with what he has learned, that "probity, virtue, honour, though they should not have received the polish of Europe, will secure to an honest American the good graces of his fair countrywomen."[6]

Maria's father, Mr. Van Rough, presents still another masculine archetype; indeed, each of the three—Dimple, Manly, and Van Rough—embodies one of the three dominant ideals of American manhood available at the turn of the nineteenth century.[7] Despite the play's focus on the other two, it is Van Rough who would come to dominate the new country in a new century. Dimple represents what I will call the Genteel Patriarch. Though Tyler's critical characterization sets Dimple out as a flamboyant fop, the Genteel Patriarch was a powerful ideal through the early part of the nineteenth century. It was, of course, an ideal inherited from Europe. At his best, the Genteel Patriarch represents a dignified aristocratic manhood, committed to the British upper-class code of honor and to well-rounded character, with exquisite tastes and manners and refined sensibilities. To the Genteel Patriarch, manhood meant property ownership and a benevolent patriarchal authority at home, including the moral instruction of his sons. A Christian gentleman, the Genteel Patriarch embodied love, kindness, duty, and compassion, exhibited through philanthropic work, church activities, and deep involvement with his family. For an illustration of the Genteel Patriarch, think of Thomas Jefferson at Monticello, George Washington, John Adams, or James Madison.

Colonel Manly embodies a second type of manhood—the Heroic Artisan. This archetype was also inherited from Europe, despite Royall Tyler's attempt to Americanize him. Independent, virtuous, and honest, the Heroic Artisan is stiffly formal in his manners with women, stalwart and loyal to his male comrades. On the family farm or in his urban crafts shop, he was an honest toiler, unafraid of hard work, proud of his craftsmanship and self-reliance. With a leather apron covering his open shirt and his sleeves rolled up, Boston silversmith Paul Revere, standing proudly at his forge, well illustrates this type.

The newcomer to this scene is Mr. Van Rough, the wealthy entrepreneur, whose newly acquired financial fortune leads to his social aspirations of marrying his daughter to the well-placed aristocratic Dimple. Van Rough represents the Self-Made Man, a model of manhood that derives identity entirely from a man's activities in the public sphere, measured by accumulated wealth and status, by geographic and social mobility. At the time, this economic fortune would have to be translated into permanent social standing—Van Rough must try to become Mr. Smooth. Since a man's fortune is as easily unmade as it is made, the Self-Made Man is uncomfortably linked to the volatile marketplace, and he depends upon continued mobility. Of course, Self-Made Men were not unique to America; as the natural outcome of capitalist economic life, they were known as *nouveaux riches* in revolutionary France (and also known as *noblesse de robe*, as well as other, less pleasant, terms, in the preceding century), and they had their counterparts in every European country. But in America, the land of immigrants and democratic ideals, the land without hereditary titles, they were present from the start, and they came to dominate much sooner than in Europe.

In the growing commercial and, soon, industrial society of the newly independent America, the Self-Made Man seemed to be born at the same time as his country. A man on the go, he was, as one lawyer put it in 1838, "made for action, and the bustling scenes of moving life, and not the poetry or romance of existence."[8] Mobile, competitive, aggressive in business, the Self-Made Man was also temperamentally restless, chronically insecure, and desperate to achieve a solid grounding for a masculine identity.

Royall Tyler hoped that the republican virtue of the Heroic Artisan would triumph over the foppish Genteel Patriarch, just as democratic America defeated the aristocratic British. But it was not to be: It was the relatively minor character, Van Rough, who would emerge triumphant in the nineteenth century, and the mobility and insecurity of the Self-Made Man came to dominate the American definition of manhood.

This book is the story of American manhood—how it has changed over time and yet how certain principles have remained the same. I believe some of its most important characteristics owe their existence to the timing of the Revolution—the emergence of the

Self-Made Men at that time and their great success in the new American democracy have a lot to do with what it is that defines a "real" man even today.

Let's look at the Self-Made Man's first appearance on the historical stage, which will help us limn the shifts in the definitions of manhood in the first half of the nineteenth century. An old standard rooted in the life of the community and the qualities of a man's character gave way to a new standard based on individual achievement, a shift in emphasis "from service to community and cultivation of the spirit to improvement of the individual and concern with his body."[9] From a doctrine of "usefulness" and "service" to the preoccupation with the "self," American manhood got off to a somewhat disturbing start.

Part of this start, the American Revolution, brought a revolt of the sons against the father—in this case, the Sons of Liberty against Father England.[10] And this introduced a new source of tension in the act of resolving an old one. The relatively casual coexistence of the Genteel Patriarch and the Heroic Artisan had been made possible by the colonies' relationship with England. Many Genteel Patriarchs looked to England not just for political and economic props but also for cultural prescriptions for behavior. Patriarchs had the right to lead their country by virtue of their title. The American colonies had few noblemen, like Sir William Randolph, but they had plenty of substitutes, from upper-class political elites to Dutch landed gentry in New York and the large plantation owners in Virginia and around Chesapeake Bay. There was little tension between them and the laborers who worked for or near them. The real problem was that as long as the colonies remained in British hands, it seemed to all that manly autonomy and self-control were impossible. Being a man meant being in charge of one's own life, liberty, and property.

Being a man meant also not being a boy. A man was independent, self-controlled, responsible; a boy was dependent, irresponsible, and lacked control. And language reflected these ideas. The term *manhood* was synonymous with "adulthood." Just as black slaves were "boys," the white colonists felt enslaved by the English father, infantilized, and thus emasculated.

The American Revolution resolved this tension because in the terms of the reigning metaphor of the day, it freed the sons from the tyranny of a despotic father. The Declaration of Independence was a declaration of manly adulthood, a manhood that was counterposed to the British version against which American men were revolting. Jefferson and his coauthors accused the king of dissolving their representative assemblies because they had opposed "with manly firmness, his invasions on the rights of the people." (Of course, the rebellion of the sons did not eliminate the need for patriarchal authority. George Washington was immediately hailed as the Father of our Country, and many wished he would become king.)

By contrast, British manhood and, by extension, aristocratic conceptions of manhood (which would soon come to include the Genteel Patriarch) were denounced as feminized, lacking manly resolve and virtue, and therefore ruling arbitrarily. Critiques of monarchy and arisocracy were tainted with a critique of aristocratic luxury as effeminate. John Adams posed the question about how to prevent the creation of a new aristocracy in a letter to Thomas Jefferson in December 1819. "Will you tell me how to prevent riches becoming the effects of temperance and industry? Will you tell me how to prevent riches from producing luxury? Will you tell me how to prevent luxury from producing effeminacy, intoxication, extravagance, vice and folly?"[11]

Works of fiction and essays exploited the Lockean theme of America as the state of nature in which individual morality could emerge, a contrast between virtue born of nature and vice born of luxury and refinement. In the preface to *Edgar Huntley*, the first work of fiction written by an American specifically about the American experience, novelist Charles Brockden Brown claimed that he had replaced the "puerile superstitions and exploded manner, Gothic castles and chimeras" of the European novel with "the incidents of Indian hostility and the perils of the Western wilderness." And Washington Irving echoed these themes a few decades later, writing that "[w]e send our youth abroad to grow luxurious and effeminate in Europe; it appears to me, that a previous tour on the Prairies would be more likely to produce that manliness, simplicity and self-dependence, most in unison with our political institutions." In politics and in culture, in both fiction and fact, American men faced a choice between effeminacy and manliness, between aristocracy and republicanism.[12]

To retrieve their manhood from its British guardians, the Sons of Liberty carried out a symbolic patricide. "Having left the British parent as a child, America miraculously becomes capable of its own nurturing; independence transforms the son into his own parent, a child into an adult."[13] The American man was now free to invent himself. The birth of the nation was also the birth of a New Man, who, as Hector St. John de Crèvecoeur put it in his marvelous *Letters from an American Farmer* (1782), "leaving behind him all his ancient prejudices and manners, receives new ones from the new mode of life he has embraced, the new government he obeys, and the new rank he holds. The American is a new man who acts upon new principles. . . . Here individuals of all nations are melted into a new race of men."[14]

At first, the American new man at the turn of the nineteenth century cautiously tried to fit in, either as a Genteel Patriarch, Heroic Artisan, or even Van Roughian Self-Made Man. In the early American magazines, for example, heroism was defined by a man's usefulness and service, his recognition of responsibilities. Between 1810 and 1820, the term *breadwinner* was coined to denote this responsible family man. The breadwinner ideal would remain one of the central characteristics of American manhood until the present day. At its moment of origin, it meant that a man's "great aim" was "to fill his station with dignity, and to be useful to his fellow beings"; in another magazine, a man's death was lamentable because of "his desire of usefulness—his wish to be one of those by whom society is enlightened and made better."[15]

This is well illustrated in *The Farmer's Friend*, an advice book written by the Reverend Enos Hitchcock in 1793. In recounting the story of the well-named Charles Worthy, Hitchcock describes the Heroic Artisan as young farmer and recounts his gradual rise as he diligently pursues his calling. Worthy, Hitchcock writes, "never felt so happy as when conscious of industriously following his occupation. . . . In order to merit the esteem of others, we must become acquainted with the duties of our particular professions, occupations, or stations in life, and discharge the duties of them in the most useful and agreeable manner." Virtue inheres in the work virtuously performed, the calling followed, not in the financial rewards that accrue to the virtuous worker. Benjamin Franklin, perhaps the first American prototype of the Self-Made Man, underscored this theme. "In order to secure my credit and character as a tradesman," he wrote in his *Autobiography*, first published in 1791, "I took care not only to be in *reality* industrious and frugal, but to avoid all appearances to the contrary." To Franklin, as to many other early Self-Made Men, image may not have been everything, but it was of importance.[16]

But patricide has significant costs, including the loneliness of the fatherless son and the burden of adult responsibilities placed upon his shoulders. American men's chief fear at the time was that the overthrown effeminate aristocracy would return to haunt them. Samuel Adams articulated this fear in an article in the *Massachusetts Sentinel* in January 1785. "Did we consult the history of Athens and Rome, we should find that so long as they continued their frugality and simplicity of manners, they shone with superlative glory; but no sooner were effeminate refinements introduced amongst them, than they visibly fell from whatever was elevated and magnanimous, and became feeble and timid, dependent, slavish and false." In other words, aristocratic luxury and effeminacy threatened the Revolution's moral edge. The post-Revolutionary American man had to be constantly vigilant against such temptation, eternally distancing himself from feminized indulgence.[17]

A few years later, Benjamin Rush saw the threat to the newly emerging republican manhood as coming from both sides—from effeminate aristocrats as well as from lazy laborers. In his "Address to the Ministers of the Gospel of Every Denomination in the United States upon Subjects Interesting to Morals" (1788), Rush advocated that American men turn themselves into "republican machines." He called for the elimination of fairs, racehorses, cockfighting, and clubs of all kinds, argued that all forms of play be banned on Sundays, and that all intoxicating spirits, including liquor and wine, the "parents of idleness and extravagance," be prohibited.

But Adams and Rush, like Royall Tyler, were wrong. Neither effeminate aristocrats nor lazy laborers were the real threats. Billy Dimple's time was slowly passing, and Colonel Manly could never be as dominant as Cincinnatus. Instead, the economic boom of the new country's first decades produced the triumph of the Self-Made Men, the Van Roughs, men who were neither aristocratic fops nor virtuous drones—far from it. These Self-Made Men built America.

Between 1800 and 1840 the United States experienced a market revolution. Freed from colonial dependence, mercantile capitalism remade the nation. America undertook the construction of a national transportation system and developed extensive overseas and domestic commerce. Between 1793 and 1807 American exports tripled, while between 1800 and 1840 the total amount of free labour outside the farm sector rose from 17 to 37 percent.[18] The fiscal and banking system expanded rapidly, from eighty-nine banks in 1811 to 246 five years later, and 788 by 1837. The economic boom meant westward expansion as well as dramatic urban growth.

Such dramatic economic changes were accompanied by political, social, and ideological shifts. Historian Nancy Cott notes that the period 1780–1830 witnessed a demographic transition to modern patterns of childbirth and childcare, development of uniform legal codes and procedures, expansion of primary education, the beginning of the democratization of the political process, and the "invention of a new language of political and social thought." Democracy was expanding, and with it, by the end of the first half of the century, America was "converted to acquisitiveness," a conversion that would have dramatic consequences for the meanings of manhood in industrializing America. In the third decade of the century, between 1825 and 1835, a bourgeoisie worthy of the name came into being in the Northeast, a self-consciously self-made middle class.[19]

The emerging capitalist market in the early nineteenth century both freed individual men and destabilized them. No longer were men bound to the land, to their estates, to Mother England, or to the tyrannical father, King George. No longer did their manhood rest on their craft traditions, guild memberships, or participation in the virtuous republic of the New England small town. America was entering a new age, and men were free to create their own destinies, to find their own ways, to rise as high as they could, to write their own biographies. God had made man a "moral free agent," according to revivalist minister Charles Finney in a celebrated sermon in 1830. The American Adam could fashion himself in his own image. This new individual freedom was as socially and psychologically unsettling as it was exciting and promising. To derive one's identity, and especially one's identity as a man, from marketplace successes was a risky proposition.

Yet that is precisely what defined the Self-Made Man: success in the market, individual achievement, mobility, wealth. America expressed political autonomy; the Self-Made Man embodied economic autonomy. This was the manhood of the rising middle class. The flip side of this economic autonomy is anxiety, restlessness, loneliness. Manhood is no longer fixed in land or small-scale property ownership or dutiful service. Success must be earned, manhood must be proved—and proved constantly.

Contemporary observers of early nineteenth-century American life noticed the shift immediately. One of the most popular tracts of the 1830s was Thomas Hunt's *The Book of Wealth* (1836), which went through several printings while proving to its readers that the Bible mandates that men strive for wealth. "No man can be obedient to God's will as revealed in the Bible without, as the general result, becoming wealthy," Hunt wrote. The drive for wealth penetrated everything. "Nearly all Americans trade and speculate," observed Thomas Nichols in 1837. "They are ready to swap horses, swap watches, swap farms; and to buy and sell anything. . . . Money is the habitual measure of all things." One English traveler in 1844 remarked that Americans used the phrase "I calculate" as a synonym for "I believe" or "I think." "Things are in the saddle, and ride mankind," quipped Ralph Waldo Emerson in an 1847 ode, which commented on the reversal of priorities encouraged by the emerging capitalist market.[20]

In the early republic, as today, equal opportunity meant equal opportunity to either succeed or to fail. "True republicanism requires that every man shall have an equal chance—that every man shall be free to become as unequal as he can," was the way one advice manual, *How to Behave*, expressed it. "Some are sinking, others rising, others balancing, some gradually ascending toward the top, others flamingly leading down," wrote a young Daniel Webster. In his 1837 book *The Americans*, Francis Grund commented on the "endless striving," the "great scramble in which all are troubled and none are satisfied." "A man, in America, is not despised for being poor in the outset . . . but every year which passes, without adding to his prosperity, is a reproach to his understanding of industry" and, he might have added, a stain on his sense of manliness.[21]

The contrast with European manhood was a constant theme, and one that European observers noted with special relish. The Frenchman Michel Chevalier wrote, after a visit to Jacksonian America, of its "universal instability." "Here is all circulation, motion, and boiling agitation. . . . Men change their houses, their climate, their trade, their laws, their officers, their constitutions."[22] Even after ten years as a resident of Boston, the Viennese immigrant Francis Grund still couldn't figure it out:

> There is probably no people on earth with whom business constitutes pleasure, and industry amusement, in an equal degree with the inhabitants of the United States of America. Active participation is not only the principal source of their happiness, and the foundation of their national greatness, but they are absolutely wretched without it. . . . Business is the very soul of an American: he pursues it, not as a means of procuring for himself and his family the necessary comforts of life, but as the fountain of all human felicity.[23]

The acclaimed British novelist Charles Dickens expected to be delighted when he visited the United States in 1842 but found himself increasingly disappointed with the American people both for their self-congratulatory myopia and defensiveness and for their energy and restlessness. As he chronicled in his rambling work *American Notes for General Circulation* (1842), Dickens was awestruck in this "great emporium of commerce" as much by the "national love of trade" as by the "universal distrust" that accompanied it, which Americans "carry into every transaction of public life." Dickens told the American people,

> It has rendered you so fickle, and so given to change, that your inconstancy has passed into a proverb; for you no sooner set up an ideal firmly, than you are sure to pull it down and dash it into fragments: and this, because directly you reward a benefactor, or a public servant, you distrust him, merely because he *is* rewarded; and immediately apply yourselves to find out, either that you have been too bountiful in your acknowledgements, or he remiss in his deserts.[24]

Dickens found Americans "dull and gloomy," without either joy or humor, and found himself "oppressed by the prevailing seriousness and melancholy air of business" among these strange people, "restless and locomotive, with an irresistible desire for change."[25]

The era's most perceptive visitor—perhaps the most observant visitor in our history—was a young French nobleman, Alexis de Tocqueville. When Tocqueville arrived in America in 1830, he was instantly struck by the dramatically different temperament of the American, a difference he attributed to the difference between aristocracies and democracies. Unlike his European counterpart, Tocqueville observed, the American man was a radical democrat—equal and alone, masterless and separate, autonomous and defenseless against the tyranny of the majority. Each citizen was equal, and "equally impotent, poor and isolated." In Europe caste distinctions between nobles and commoners froze social positions but also connected them; "aristocracy links everybody, from peasant to king, in one long chain." Democracy meant freedom but disconnection; it "breaks the chain and frees every link." American democracy also meant a great sliding toward the center; all Americans tended to "contract the ways of thinking of the manufacturing and trading classes."[26]

Tocqueville's dissection of the double-edged quality of the democratic personality remains as incisive today as it was in the early nineteenth century. The middle-class man was an anxious achiever, constantly striving, casting his eyes nervously about as he tried, as Mr. Van Rough put it in *The Contrast*, to "mind the main chance." The American man was "restless in the midst of abundance." In a passage that eloquently defines this restlessness of the Self-Made Man, Tocqueville writes:

An American will build a house in which to pass his old age and sell it before the roof is on; he will plant a garden and rent it just as the trees are coming into bearing; he will clear a field and leave others to reap the harvest; he will take up a profession and leave it, settle in one place and soon go off elsewhere with his changing desires. . . . [H]e will travel five hundred miles in a few days as a distraction from his happiness.[27]

Like Dickens, Tocqueville also found the American marked by a "strange melancholy"; every American "is eaten up with a longing to rise, but hardly any of them seem to entertain very great hopes or to aim very high." The American man was a man in a hurry but with not very far to go.[28]

Even the term *self-made man* was an American neologism, first coined by Henry Clay in a speech in the U.S. Senate in 1832. Defending a protective tariff that he believed would widen opportunities for humble men to rise in business, he declared that in Kentucky "almost very manufactory known to me is in the hands of enterprising, self-made men, who have whatever wealth they possess by patient and diligent labor."[29]

The term immediately caught on. Rev. Calvin Colton noted in 1844 that America "is a country where men start from a humble origin, and from small beginnings gradually rise in the world, as the reward of merit and industry. . . . One has as good a chance as another, according to his talents, prudence, and personal exertions. . . . [T]his is a country of *self-made men* [in which] work is held in the highest respect [while] the idle, lazy, poor man gets little pity in his poverty."[30] By the 1840s and 1850s a veritable cult of the Self-Made Man had appeared, as young men devoured popular biographies and inspirational homilies to help future Self-Made Men create themselves. John Frost's *Self Made Men in America* (1848), Charles Seymore's *Self-Made Men* (1858), and Freeman Hunt's *Worth and Wealth* (1856) and *Lives of American Merchants* (1858) provided self-making homilies, packaged between brief biographies of poor boys who had made it rich.

The central characteristic of being self-made was that the proving ground was the public sphere, specifically the workplace. And the workplace was a man's world (and a native-born white man's world at that). If manhood could be proved, it had to be proved in the eyes of other men. From the early nineteenth century until the present day, most of men's relentless efforts to prove their manhood contain this core element of homosociality. From fathers and boyhood friends to our teachers, coworkers, and bosses, it is the evaluative eyes of other men that are always upon us, watching, judging. It was in this regime of scrutiny that such men were tested. "Every man you meet has a rating or an estimate of himself which he never loses or forgets," wrote Kenneth Wayne in his popular turn-of-the-century advice book, *Building the Young Man* (1912). "A man has his own rating, and instantly he lays it alongside of the other man." Almost a century later, another man remarked to psychologist Sam Osherson that "[b]y the time you're an adult, it's easy to think you're always in competition with men, for the attention of women, in sports, at work."[31]

In the early decades of the nineteenth century, the Self-Made Man competed with the two other archetypes from Tyler's play. The Genteel Patriarch had to be displaced, and the Heroic Artisan had to be uprooted and brought into the new industrial marketplace. In the rush of the new century, Self-Made Men did indeed triumph, but neither the patriarch nor the laborer disappeared overnight.

First, the Genteel Patriarch. While the richest tenth of all Americans held slightly less (49.6 percent) than half the wealth in 1774, they held 73 percent in 1860, and the richest 1 percent more than doubled their share of the wealth, from 12.6 to 29 percent, and then to about 50 percent by mid-century. The period 1820–1860 was "probably the most unequal period in American history."[32] But these new wealthy were no longer the landed aristocracy but the new merchants and industrialists. Economically, Van Rough simply blew away Billy Dimple.

American culture followed suit. Gone were the powder, wigs, and richly ornamented and colorfully patterned clothing that had marked the old gentry; the new man of commerce wore plain and simple clothing "to impart trust and confidence in business affairs."[33] Countless pundits recast the Genteel Patriarch as a foppish dandy as they railed against Europe, against traditional feudal society, against historical obligation.[34] Even older, venerated Genteel Patriarchs were not immune to the feminization of the landed gentry. Jefferson himself was castigated as dandified, the product of aristocratic and chivalric Virginia, "America's Athens." He was accused of "timidity, whimsicalness," "a wavering of disposition," and a weakness for flattery, a man who "took counsel in his feelings and imagination," and the Jeffersonians were condemned for their "womanish resentment" against England and their "womanish attachment to France."[35]

Leading the charge against the Genteel Patriarch was Ralph Waldo Emerson, who signaled the shifting taste in his seminal essay "The American Scholar" (1837). Emerson "enshrined psychic self-sovereignty as the essential manly virtue," according to literary critic T. Walter Herbert, and the theme of his essays "of self-reliant struggle from humble origins to high position became the ruling narrative of manly worth, supplanting that of the well-born lad demonstrating his superior breeding in the exercise of responsibilities, that were his birthright."[36] Nathaniel Hawthorne even suggested that a young man could be crippled by inheriting "a great fortune." Here was a "race of non-producers," warned S. C. Allen in 1830, a "new sort of aristocracy, of a more uncompromising character than the feudal, or any landed aristocracy can ever be."[37]

Such efforts were not altogether successful, but certainly indicated a trend. Even in the mid-nineteenth century, cultural observers venerated a "romantic consumptiveness" as the preferred male body type—composed of a thin physique, pale complexion, and languid air. (Muscular bodies were snubbed as artisanal, a sign of a laborer.) "An American exquisite must not measure more than 24 inches round the chest; his face must be pale, thin and long; and he must be spindle-shanked," wrote the venerable observer Francis Grund in 1839. "There is nothing our women dislike so much as corpulency; weak and refined are synonymous." (Even then there was a difference between a manhood constructed for women's approval and the masculinity of a man's man.) It was in the Old South where the Genteel Patriarch made his last stand, at least until the Civil War. While southern manhood was increasingly caricatured as effeminate and dandified in the northern press, even in the South the old cavalier's time was passing.

Meanwhile, the Heroic Artisan was losing his independence, which he so dearly prized. He "looks the whole world in the face/For he owes not any man," as Henry Wadsworth Longfellow put it in "The Village Blacksmith" (1844).[38] Disciplined and responsible, the Heroic Artisan believed that "independent men of relatively small means were both entitled to full citizenship and best equipped to exercise it." A firm believer in self-government, the Heroic Artisan was the embodiment of Jeffersonian liberty; the virtuous "yeoman of the city," as he had called them. Before the Civil War nine of every ten American men owned their own farm, shop, or small crafts workshop. About half of all workmen were employed in shops of ten or fewer; four-fifths worked in shops of no more than twenty. His body was his own, his labor a form of property.[39]

The independence of the Heroic Artisan did not mean that he was isolated, reclusive, nor, on the other hand, overly competitive; both in his daily interactions in the workplace and as he strolled through the city or town, the Heroic Artisan saw himself as deeply embedded within a community of equals, a "shirtless democracy," in the words of Mike Walsh. On the occasion of the dedication of the Apprentice's Library in 1820, Thomas Mercein said that "[e]very man looks with independent equality in the face of his neighbor; those are exalted whose superior virtues entitle them to confidence; they are revered as legislators, obeyed as magistrates, but still considered as equals." One bit of verse used equality before God as another foundation for political equality:

Of rich and poor the difference what?—
In working or in working not
Why then on Sunday we're as great
As those who own some vast estate.

Sure, the Heroic Artisan wanted to get ahead in the market, and he was not immune to its rewards or temptations. Even Tocqueville remarked that the craftsman's goal was not "to manufacture as well as possible" but to "produce with great rapidity many imperfect commodities." But he was just as determined to retain his independence and protect the independence of the community of equals in the republic of virtue.[40]

The cement of this republican virtue was the coupling of economic autonomy to political community and workplace solidarity. This combination is the essence of *producerism*, an ideology that claimed that virtue came from the hard work of those who produce the world's wealth. Producerism held that there was a deep-rooted conflict in society between the producing and the nonproducing classes and that work was a source of moral instruction, economic success, and political virtue. "We ask that every man become an independent proprietor, possessing enough of the goods of this world, to be able by his own moderate industry to provide for the wants of his body," wrote Orestes Brownson in his tract "The Laboring Classes" (1840). The doctrines of producerism resurface constantly through the century as rural and urban workingmen, from the Populists to the Knights of Labor and early union organizers, cast their resistance to proletarianization in terms of preservation of economic autonomy and political community.[41]

The British historian E. P. Thompson's explorations of the emergence of the British working class revealed an easy flow between the workplace and leisure in the British villages of the pre-Industrial Revolution, even in the actual length and organization of the working day. In their workshops, apprentices, journeymen, and master craftsmen integrated work and leisure. Customers would appear, contract for specific tasks, and socialize and wait while it was being done; when no customers appeared, masters and journeymen would continue to train young apprentices while jugs of hard cider were constantly passed around. At leisure the Heroic Artisan was communitarian, participating regularly in "evenings of drink, merriment, and ceremony that were part of longstanding premodern traditions" and that provided ample opportunities for artisans to meet in a mood of "mutual self-esteem and exaltation."[42]

Workplace solidarity and ease of movement between work and leisure also spilled over into the organization of the trades. Many trades resembled fraternal orders in which artisans developed modest welfare systems for their sick and needy brethren or for the families of deceased brethren. Each volunteer fire department, for example, was its own fraternal society with its own insignias, mottoes, "freshly minted traditions," "fiercely masculine rituals," and sacred emblems like the fire hose, company crest, and fire chief's trumpet.[43]

These independent artisans, craftsmen, and small shopkeepers were on the defensive throughout the first half of the century. Each of the periodic economic crises had struck these artisans especially hard. Older skills became obsolete and factory employment grew—from an average of eight women and men to anywhere between fifty and five hundred men.[44] Masters increased the scale, pace, and routine of production, hiring young strangers, with whom they shared only contractual relations, rather than the sons of their neighbors.[45] Real wages of skilled workers declined, and workplace autonomy seemed to be disappearing everywhere. New forms of labor control, including the putting-out system, sweated labor, and wages, all eroded the virtuous republic.

In Philadelphia in 1819, three of four workers were idle, and nearly two thousand were jailed for unpaid debts. By 1836 ten major strikes hit the skilled trades, and convulsive strikes took place on the waterfront and the building sites. In June of that year, thirty thousand men showed up for a demonstration in New York, the single largest protest gathering in American history to that point. Also in New York six thousand masons and carpenters were discharged in April 1837 alone.[46]

The sons of the Sons of Liberty were fast becoming, as they put it in a letter of protest to President John Tyler, "mere machines of labor." Ironically, the same experiences that cemented their solidarity and underscored their autonomy now left them isolated and defensive. While, politically, democracy had "hastened the destruction of onerous forms of personal subordination to masters, landlords, and creditors that American working people had historically faced," writes the labor historian David Montgomery, it also left them unprotected from unscrupulous masters and conniving employers and disconnected from others who shared a similar fate.[47]

Many workingmen tried to combat this trend by organizing the nation's first workingmen's political parties, there to redress their economic and political grievances in parties like the Mechanics Union of Trade Associations (1827), the Workingmen's Party (1828), and the Equal Rights Party (1833). These organizations' rhetoric was saturated with equations of autonomy and manhood. Loss of autonomy was equated with emasculation; economic dependence on wages paid by an employer was equivalent to social and sexual dependency. The factory system was "subversive of liberty," according to one worker in the fledgling National Trades Union in 1834, "calculated to change the character of a people from bold and free to enervated, dependent and slavish." Under such circumstances, held an editorialist in the union newspaper *The Man*, it would have been "unmanly" and undignified, "an abdication of their responsibilities as citizens" if they did *not* organize.[48]

Newspapers like *The Man* inveighed regularly against three groups: women, immigrants, and black slaves. Women had earlier been excluded (of course) from craft guilds and apprenticeships, but the emerging working class supported women's complete exclusion from the public sphere, even though only around 2 percent of all females over the age of ten worked in any type of industry. These formerly independent small shopkeepers and craftsmen opposed women's rights to education, property ownership, and suffrage.[49] It was as if workplace manhood could only be retained if the workplace had only men in it.

And only native-born men at that. Immigration had increased rapidly through the first half of the century, from 140,439 in the 1820s to 599,125 in the 1830s. During the 1840s immigration more than tripled to 1,713,251, and 2,598,214 more immigrants arrived during the 1850s. Anti-immigrant demonstrations and riots followed as the native-born artisans felt increasingly threatened by these less-skilled workers, who were willing to work longer hours for lower wages.[50] In antebellum America Irish immigrants were especially stamped with a problematic masculinity. Imagined as rough and primitive, uncivilized and uncivilizable, the Irish were ridiculed as a subhuman species, born to inferiority and incapable of being true American men.[51]

Of course, not all native-born men were real men. In an arresting book the historian David Roediger argues that, from the moment of its origins, the white working class used black slaves as the economic and moral "other," whose economic dependency indicated emasculation and moral degeneracy. Whiteness, Roediger argues, served as a secondary "wage" for white workers who were resisting the view of wage labor as a form of wage slavery. By asserting their whiteness, workers could compensate for their loss of autonomy; the "status and privileges conferred by race could be used to make up for alienating and exploitative class relationships."[52]

What Roediger describes economically, social historian Eric Lott discusses symbolically in his analysis of blackface minstrel shows in antebellum America. Minstrel shows performed a double mimesis; the minstrel show was, Lott argues, both love and theft. The projection of white men's fears onto black men was simultaneously for "whites insecure about their whiteness" and for men insecure about their manhood. "Mediating white men's relations with other white men, minstrel acts certainly made currency out of the black man himself," he writes. The "pale gaze" of the white audience faced with a caricatured black identity paralleled the "male gaze" of this now conscious audience of men reasserting their manhood through the symbolic appropriation of the black man's sexual potency.[53]

In these literal and symbolic ways the American working class that emerged in the decades before the Civil War was self-consciously white, native-born, and male, rooted as much in racism, sexism, and xenophobia as in craft pride and workplace autonomy—a combination that has haunted its efforts to retrieve its lost dignity and organize successfully against industrial capitalists throughout American history. The rage of the dying class of Heroic Artisans took many forms.

In the 1830s, however, something remarkable happened. The working class saw its salvation in the presidential campaign of one of its own. Andrew Jackson was both the last gasp of Jeffersonian republican virtue and the first expression of the politics of class-based resentment.

Andrew Jackson was not the first American leader to combine virulent hypermasculinity with vengeful, punitive political maneuvers nor, certainly, was he (nor will he be) the last. But he was one of the most colorful and charismatic of such, and he embodied the hopes and fears of many men. The emotions that seem to have animated Jacksonian America were fear and rage. When Jackson first arrived in the Senate, he was unable to speak because of "the rashness of his feelings," then–Vice President Thomas Jefferson recalled. "I have seen him attempt it repeatedly and as often choke with rage." A "choleric, impetuous" man, according to turn-of-the-century historian Frederick Jackson Turner, Jackson was a "tall, lank, uncouth-looking personage, with long locks of hair hanging over his face and a cue [ponytail] down his back tied in an eel skin; his dress singular, his manners those of a rough backwoodsman."[54]

It is difficult not to see Jackson and the men he stood for in starkly Freudian terms. Here was the fatherless son, struggling without guidance to separate from the mother and, again, for adult mastery over his environment. Terrified of infantilization, of infantile dependency, his rage propelled the furious effort to prove his manhood against those who threatened it, notably women and infantilized "others." It was as if America found an adolescent leader to preside over its own adolescence as a nation. Here was "the nursling of the wilds," a "pupil of the wilderness," according to George Bancroft, a man, as Tocqueville put it, "of violent character and middling capacities." Andrew Jackson was the consummate schoolyard bully.[55]

The hero of the War of 1812 and the Creek War of 1813–14, Jackson saw his military exploits as an effort to overcome his own "indolence" and achieve republican purification through violence. He came to power as the champion of the Heroic Artisan, whether rural yeoman farmer or urban artisan, against the effete aristocracy of the Eastern urban entrepreneur and the decadent Europeanized landed gentry. One laudatory biography of Jackson from 1820 began with alarm over the "voluptuousness and effeminacy" that was attendant upon the sudden rise of new wealth in America, characteristics that were "rapidly diminishing that exalted sense of national glory."[56]

The Heroic Artisans embraced Jackson. He campaigned in 1828, in the words of a campaign song, as one "who can fight" against John Quincy Adams, "who can write," pitting "the plowman" against "the professor."[57] As president, his hostility toward paper currency, his opposition to corporate charters, his deep suspicion of public enterprise and public debt—all elements of American producerism—appealed to small planters, farmers, mechanics, and laborers, the "bone and sinew of the country." His administration was saturated with the rhetoric of the violent, short-tempered, impulsively democratic artisanate, especially in his struggle against the savage nature of primitive manhood (Indians) and the effete, decadent institutions that signaled Europeanized overcivilization (the Bank).

In his brilliant, psychoanalytically informed biography and cultural history of Jackson and his historical era, Michael Rogin focuses on these twin peaks of the Jacksonian landscape. Jackson projected his own and the nation's fears of dependency onto the Indians, who were cast as the passive, helpless children that the Heroic Artisan was attempting to avoid becoming. A simple pattern emerged: Appropriate their land and abridge their freedom because you see them as passive and helpless. This makes them passive and helpless, which then allows you to justify the whole thing by referring to the passivity and helplessness you have just caused.

It was as if, by making these independent Indian tribes dependent upon the benevolent paternalism of a centralizing state, white artisans and farmers could avoid becoming dependent. "Like a kind father," James Gadsden said to the Seminoles in Florida, "the

President says to you, there are lands enough for both his white and his red children. His white are strong, and might exterminate his red, but he will not permit them. He will preserve his red children." And Jackson told three chiefs that the bad counsel they had heeded "compelled your Father the President to send his white children to chastise and subdue you, and thereby give peace to his children both red and white." Now, Jackson continued, it was necessary for the Indians to come under the President's care, where "your Father the President may be enabled to extend to you his fatherly care and assistance." No sooner had the sons of liberty thrown off their own tyrannical monarchical father than they set themselves up as the benevolent fathers they had never had and, tragically, were utterly unable to become.[58]

If the Indian symbolized the savage brute transformed into a helpless dependent child, the Bank symbolized the devouring mother from whose grasp the adolescent nation was trying to escape. The "Mother Bank," was a "monster Hydra," a "hydra of corruption," as Jackson himself put it, and it became a symbol of corporate power—paper money, monopoly privilege, complex credit—that turned men from "the sober pursuits of honest industry." The Bank represented centralized economic and political power, which threatened to overwhelm the virtue of the republic. If the Bank was able to consolidate credit, control a single paper currency, and control all business transactions, the independence of the Heroic Artisan would be compromised, and he would be returned to helpless childhood dependency. As Vice President Martin Van Buren warned, the Bank would "produce throughout society a chain of dependence . . . in preference to the manly virtues that give dignity to human nature, a craving desire for luxurious enjoyment and sudden wealth [and] substitute for republican simplicity and economical habits a sickly appetite for effeminate indulgence." The freeborn sons of liberty would be turned into the dependent daughters of the Mother Bank.[59]

Jackson's flight from feminizing influences illustrates a psychodynamic element in the historical construction of American manhood. Having killed the tyrannical father, American men feared being swallowed whole by an infantilizing and insatiable mother— voluptuous, voracious, and terrifyingly alluring. Jackson projected those emotions onto "others" so that by annihilating or controlling them, his own temptations to suckle helplessly at the breast of indolence and luxury could be purged. Jackson's gendered rage at weakness, feminizing luxury, and sensuous pleasure resonated for a generation of symbolically fatherless sons, the first generation of American men born after the Revolution.

Historically, such flight from feminization produced its opposite as the Heroic Artisan became wedded to exclusionary policies that left him increasingly defenseless against unscrupulous capitalist entrepreneurs, just as Jackson's effort to reconcile simple yeoman values with the free pursuit of economic interest ultimately cleared the path for the expansion of laissez-faire capitalist development. The heroic resistance of the artisan against the feminizing Bank was ironically the mechanism by which he was eventually pushed aside and transformed into a proletarian.

That process was begun in the 1830s but by no means quickly completed. In the presidential campaign of 1836, Jackson had picked his vice president, Martin Van Buren, as his successor to continue the struggle against the forces of feminization and proletarianization. The son of an innkeeper, Van Buren was praised by Jackson as "frank, open, candid, and manly . . . *able and prudent*." But after one term in office, Van Buren was outmasculinized in the campaign of 1840 by his Whig opposition as they seized upon the very sentiments that Jackson and Van Buren had aroused. The rhetoric of that campaign, which pitted William Henry Harrison, the hero of Tippecanoe, against Van Buren, was a political masterpiece of gendered speech. Harrison's manly virtues and log cabin birth were contrasted with Van Buren's ruffled shirts and his cabinet composed of "eastern officeholder pimps." In a sense, the presidential campaign of 1840 was the first—but certainly not the last—national presidential campaign characterized by dirty tricks, race-baiting, and the promotion of form over substance, and it continued the great American tradition of using manhood as political currency.[60]

Rather than articulate Harrison's position on specific issues, the Whigs chose to denigrate his opponent and promote their man by attaching to him two symbols of the Heroic Artisan: the log cabin, symbolizing the humble birth of a self-made man of the people—Harrison was labeled the "Cincinnatus of the West"—and the hard cider jug, symbolizing his alliance with the traditional artisanal work world and his opposition to the new discipline of the market. Images of log cabins were everywhere—"hung on watches, earrings, in parlor pictures and shop windows, mounted on wheels, decorated with coon-skins, and hauled in magnificent parades."[61]

The chief task for the Whigs was to dissociate Van Buren from his predecessor. Congressman Charles Ogle's speech, "The Regal Splendor of the Presidential Palace," delivered in April 1840, signaled the beginning of perhaps the most gendered rhetorical barrage in the history of American politics. Ogle freely mixed gender and class in his effort to discredit Van Buren. In vain imitation of European aristocratic tastes, Ogle observed, the president's table was not "provided with those old and unfashionable dishes *hog and hominy, fried meat and gravy, schnitz, kneop and sourcrout* with a mug of *hard cider*." Instead, Van Buren's "French cooks" furnished the president's table in "massive gold plate and French sterling silver services." Van Buren was, moreover, the first president who insisted upon "the pleasures of the warm or tepid bath." Perhaps most shocking was Ogle's contention that a recent appropriation of $3,665 for alterations and repairs to the president's home "may be expended in the erection of a *throne* within the 'Blue Elliptical Saloon' [the Oval Office] and for the purchase of a *crown, diadem, sceptre* and *royal jewels*" so that this president, "although deprived of the *title* of royalty, will be invested, not only with its *prerogatives* but with its *trappings* also."[62]

The tone for the campaign was set, and pundits quickly fell into step. The *Louisville Journal* reported that when Van Buren read this outrageous attack, "he actually *burst his corset*." Davy Crockett penned an incendiary faux biography of Van Buren, damning the president as traveling in "an English coach" with liveried "English servants." "He is laced up in corsets, such as women in town wear, and, if possible, tighter than the best of them," wrote Crockett, so that "[i]t would be difficult to say from his personal appearance, whether he was man or woman, but for his large *red* and *gray* whiskers."[63]

As the log cabin dwellers and drinkers of hard cider campaigned against "Vanocracy," they sang newly penned campaign songs. (This campaign marked the political songbook's first appearance.) Like the journalists, songwriters went after his physical appearance and his manner and style, chastising "little Van" as a "used up man," a man "who wore corsets, put cologne on his whiskers, slept on French beds, rode in a British coach, and ate from golden spoons from silver plates when he sat down to dine in the White House." According to the song lyrics, Van Buren "had no taste for fighting" but adored "scheming" and "intrigue."[64] Of Harrison, by contrast, they sang:

No ruffled shirt, no silken hose
No airs does TIP display
But like the "pith of worth" he goes
In homespun "hoddin-grey."

Upon his board there ne'er appeared
The costly "sparkling wine"
But plain "hard cider" such as sheered
In days of old lang syne.

The strategy paid off handsomely, sending an incumbent to defeat for only the third time in American history. Over 80 percent of the eligible white male voters turned out for the election—a turnout rarely, if ever, equaled before or since. And it set a dubious precedent: Since 1840 the president's manhood has always been a question, his manly resolve, firmness, courage, and power equated with the capacity for violence, military virtues, and a plain-living style that avoided cultivated refinement and civility.

The campaign of 1840 had a sad, if well-known, coda. Harrison apparently believed his own hype. Taking the oath of office on one of the most bitterly cold days on record in Washington, Harrison refused to wear a topcoat lest he appear weak and unmanly. He caught pneumonia as a result, was immediately bedridden, and died one month later—the shortest term in office of any president in our history.

But gender had become political currency, and subsequent campaigns continued to trade in manly rhetoric. Of Zachary Taylor, Old Rough and Ready, for example, it was said that his education on the frontier had developed his manly character, while Taylor's supporters castigated his opponent, Lewis Cass, for his service as Jackson's ambassador to France. Cass was a "common man" if ever there was one—the son of a New Hampshire blacksmith who had fought in the Revolution, he rose to fame as a soldier and frontiersman, fought the British at Detroit, and made peace with the Indians. Yet even he could be smeared by the association with France. In the following election, General Winfield Scott attempted to "clothe military aristocracy in frontier buckskin."[65] By 1860 one newspaper chastised James Buchanan for his "shrill, almost female voice, and wholly beardless cheeks," while the bearded and deep-voiced Abraham Lincoln parlayed his plain-spoken humble origins into a national myth of probity, economy, and virtue that come from a log cabin president.[66] Our president could never be some Europeanized dandy who dreamed of aristocracy or monarchy; he would, for many years, claim the mantle of the artisanate, a descendent of the agrarian yeoman farmer.

In the last decade before the outbreak of the Civil War, it was still unclear which model of manhood would emerge as triumphant. Already the Heroic Artisans were in retreat though they still exerted significant influence in local urban politics. And though Genteel Patriarchs had been discredited politically, at least as a political symbol, they still controlled a significant proportion of the nation's property. Their decline and the Self-Made Man's ascendancy were still in question, as was made abundantly clear in a shocking series of events that took place in May 1849. As with Royall Tyler's *The Contrast*, the stage was set, literally, in the New York City theater. Or rather in the Opera House at Astor Place and the surrounding square and city streets.

In May the celebrated British actor William Macready was preparing to perform *Macbeth* at the tony Astor Place Opera House. At the same time, Edwin Forrest, perhaps the most acclaimed American actor of his era, was taking up theatrical residence at the Broadway Theater for a run of his own. What might have begun as a personal squabble between the two premier actors of their respective countries turned into a clash between the patriotic, xenophobic nationalism of the New York working classes and the contemptuous elitism of the powerful. To the emerging urban elite, the working classes were nothing but gutter rabble, "sanguinary ruffians," filthy and uncouth; those same working-men branded the bankers and merchants as "the dandies of Uppertendom."[67]

The actors themselves had squared off before. Macready was pompous, elegant, and extraordinarily gifted; an "actor autocrat," according to one critic. Forrest was a man of the people, "born in humble life," who "worked his way up from poverty and obscurity." In short, the man hailed as "the American Tragedian" was a self-made man and as the *Boston Mail* put it in 1848:

> he is justly entitled to that honor—he has acquired it by his own labors; from a poor boy
> in a circus he has arisen to be a man of fame and wealth, all of which he has lastingly
> gained by enterprise and talent, and secured both by economy and temperance.[68]

Stylistically and sartorially, the two men were as different as a leather-aproned artisan and a liveried aristocrat. When Macready played Hamlet, one critic observed, he "wore a dress, the waist of which nearly reached his arms; a hat with a sable plume big enough to cover a hearse; a pair of black silk gloves, much too large for him; a ballet shirt of straw coloured satin," which, combined with his angular facial features, made him appear "positively hideous." Forrest's rugged appearance and muscular acting style stood in sharp contrast; Forrest had, in the words of one London reviewer, "shot up like the wild mountain pine and prairie sycamore, amid the free life and spontaneous growths of the west, not rolled in the garden-bed of cities to a dead level, nor clipped of all proportion by too careful husbandry." The two actors captured the contrast of national cultures and of versions of manhood, pitting, as one critic put it, "the unsophisticated energy of the daring child of nature" against the "more glossy polish of the artificial European civilian."[69]

The two played their parts superbly. Neither especially liked the other, either as an actor or as a man. Macready was struck by the "vehemence and rude force" of Forrest's performances, which favorable critics attributed to Forrest's manly vigor and oracular power. Macready was criticized as a "high-hatted" player, "craven-hearted, egotistical, cold, selfish, inflated," and obsessed with his "aristocratic importance."[70] Forrest had earlier hissed at Macready's performance of *Hamlet* ostensibly because the Englishman, castigated as a "superannuated driveller," had tinkered with the play somewhat, introducing into one scene a "fancy dance" that was excoriated by Forrest as a "pas de mouchoir —dancing and throwing up his handkerchief across the stage."

When Macready and Forrest were each booked to perform in New York in May 1849, both stages were set for an explosive confrontation. The opening night performance of Macready's *Macbeth* was punctuated by noisy demonstrations and efforts by the rowdy throngs in the balconies to disrupt the performance. Tossing rotten eggs, "pennies, and other missiles" and eventually throwing a few chairs, they succeeded in driving Macready from the stage of that "aristocratic, kid-glove Opera House."[71] Disgusted, the stalwart

English actor determined to cancel his performances and sail the next night for England. The plebeian crowds were jubilant in their assumed victory. The next day, though, Macready changed his mind after being entreated by several New York notables, including bankers, merchants, and writers like Washington Irving and Herman Melville.

The next night, May 10, thousands of workingmen and young working-class teenagers, known colloquially as B'hoys and renowned for their "virtuous contempt" for all things aristocratic, gathered in front of the Opera House.[72] Ned Buntline, the organizer of the infamous nativist organizations the United Sons of America and the Patriotic Order of Sons of America, whipped the "mobbish nativism" of the crowds to a fever pitch; the group now intended to prevent the performance or at least to disrupt its conclusion. Meanwhile the New York City police, joined by the local battalions of the state militia, were determined to keep the enormous crowd in check. By the end of the performance, as the crowds were whisked away via side exits, tempers were flaring. There was the expected shouting back and forth and even a few projectiles launched in the direction of the police and soldiers. Suddenly and unexpectedly the soldiers opened fire on the crowd. Twenty-two were killed, thirty more wounded, and over sixty more arrested.[73]

The Astor Place riot marked the first time in American history that American troops had ever opened fire on American citizens. To some it signaled the beginning of the great class struggle. A year after Marx and Engels had published *The Communist Manifesto* in Germany, one eyewitness saw the Astor Place riots in these terms:

> [I]t was the rich against the poor—the aristocracy against the people; and this hatred of wealth and privilege is increasing all over the world, and ready to burst out whenever there is the slightest occasion. The rich and well bred are too apt to despise the poor and ignorant; and they must not think it strange if they are hated in return.[74]

Those killed and arrested were all local artisans or small shopkeepers, including printers, clerks, grocers, ship joiners, butchers, plumbers, sailmakers, carpenters, and gunsmiths.[75] And their opponents were the newly moneyed urban entrepreneurs, flexing their political muscles, able to harness military and police power for their side and able to fend off efforts to taint them as aristocratic dandies.

It had taken scarcely twenty years for the Self-Made Man to establish a foothold in the consciousness of American men and to stake a claim for dominance in American politics and culture. He had gone from being the new kid on the block to owning the street. Avoiding the taint of aristocracy and subduing the working classes, the Self-Made Man was now, at mid-century, the dominant American conception of manhood. And in the decades following the Civil War, he would transform the nation.

CHAPTER 2

Born to Run

Self-Control and Fantasies of Escape

The mass of men lead lives of quiet desperation. What is called resignation is confirmed desperation. From the desperate city you go to the desperate country. . . . A stereotyped but unconscious despair is concealed even under what are called the games and amusements of mankind. There is no play in them, for this comes after work. But it is a characteristic of wisdom not to do desperate things.

—Henry David Thoreau *Walden* (1854)

Where lies the final harbor, whence we unmoor no more?

—Herman Melville *Moby Dick* (1851)

In the middle of the nineteenth century, the Self-Made Man began to remake America in his own image—restless, insecure, striving, competitive, and extraordinarily prosperous. Thrown into the anarchy of the marketplace, a place Thoreau had described as a "site of humiliation," American men's economic, political, and social identity was no longer fixed. If social order, permanence, could no longer be taken for granted and a man could rise as high as he aspired, then his sense of himself as a man was in constant need of demonstration. Everything became a test—his relationships to work, to women, to nature, and to other men.

No wonder Thoreau penned his now-famous line that the "mass of men lead lives of quiet desperation" when he took off for Walden Pond.[1] As such a relentless test, civilization can be unbearable. One must be completely self-controlled, since in the new democracy there was no one else to look to for such control. Society was chock-full of equals—which is another way of saying it was full of *competitors*. Two choices seemed possible: Stay and compete, or try to escape.

American men chose both. They struggled to build themselves into powerful, impervious machines, capable of victory in any competition. And they ran away to the frontier, to the West, to start over, to make their fortunes and thus to remake themselves, to escape the civilizing constraints of domestic life represented by the Victorian woman.

More than these, though, American men also tried to stack the decks in their favor. Although America has been from its birth a multicultural society, American manhood has often been built on the exclusion of others from equal opportunity to work, to go to school, to vote—to do any of the things that allow people to compete equally. It seemed as though men believed that by keeping the public worlds of work, education, or politics as the homosocial preserves of native-born white men, they could more reliably prove their manhood. Exclusion also allowed men a kind of domestic version of escape; everytime they went off to work, they ran away from women to prove themselves with other men. These solutions—self-control, exclusion, and escape—have been the dominant themes in the history of American masculinity until the present day.

The Doctrine of Self-Control

The drive for control, for order, stems from experiencing the world as *dis*ordered, as out of control. And to middle-class American men the mid-nineteenth century world often felt like it was spinning out of control, rushing headlong toward an industrial future. For a young man seeking his fortune in such a free and mobile society, identity was no longer fixed, and there was no firm patriarchal lineage to ground a secure sense of himself as a man. For the first time in American history, young men experienced "identity crises." "Sons had to compete for elusive manhood in the market rather than grow into secure manhood by replicating fathers. Where many could never attain the self-made manhood of success, middle-class masculinity pushed egotism to extremes of aggression, calculation, self-control and unremitting effort."[2] The Self-Made Man was a control freak.

First, he had to gain control over himself. In the 1830s and 1840s a spate of advice manuals counseled young men on how to do just that. This mania for self-control focused, perhaps not surprisingly, on sexual appetites and how to avoid the temptation of masturbation.[3] Concerns about "self-abuse" were not new—as early as 1724, an anonymous work was published in Boston entitled *Onania*; it carried a self-explanatory subtitle, "The Heinous Sin of Self-Pollution, and all its Frightful Consequences, in both Sexes, Considered. With Spiritual and Physical Advice to Those who have already injur'd themselves by this Abominable Practice." But in the mid-nineteenth century, the scope and scale of these works was unprecedented, as was the basis for their advice. Earlier, writers had stressed the immoral causes of sinful sexual behaviors; now they were more concerned with the secular effects of those behaviors, the debility, enervation, and sapping of vigor. When an English translation of S. A. Tissot's classic French work, *A Treatise on the Diseases Produced by Onanism*, appeared in 1832, it was an instant hit.[4]

To the medical experts of the time, the willful sexual control of a body was the ultimate test of mind over matter. Conservation of sperm was the single best way to conserve energy for other, more productive uses. It was believed that a body's total energy was finite, and the world of work demanded a full measure of it.[5] The link between economic and sexual behavior was so explicit, in fact, that a recent writer coined the phrase "spermatic economy" to describe the fusion of sexual and marketplace activities. "Sturdy manhood," one mid-century writer claimed, "loses its energy and bends under too frequent expenditure of this important secretion."[6]

The body was a well of carnal desires and diffuse energies. Advice-manual writers sought to control these desires and harness the energy toward productive activity. If some of their prescriptions sound silly to modern ears, they nonetheless sprang from an admirable impulse. The new, self-made man in the newly formed democracy was embarking on an experiment in social anarchy. With no birthrights, no one "knew his place." In such a self-made world, control must come from *somewhere*, and it could only come from within.

By the 1850s several advice books—among them William Alcott's *The Young Man's Guide* (1846), George Burnap's *Lectures to Young Men* (1848), George Peck's *The Formation of a Manly Character* (1853), and Timothy Arthur's *Advice to Young Men* (1855)—addressed men's need for self-control over passion, temptation, and masturbation, which would sap their vital energies and leave "effeminated" men's bodies, as Sophia Hawthorne worried, and thus render them unfit for the tasks ahead.

Among the most successful of these advice books were Sylvester Graham's *A Lecture to Young Men* (1834), his later *Lectures on Science and Human Life* (1839), and John Todd's *The Student's Manual* (1835). Todd, a New England minister who became one of the nation's foremost campaigners against women's rights, and Graham, a health reformer and the inventor of the cracker that bears his name, were the preeminent experts who addressed themselves to the problems of becoming and remaining a successful man in the mid-nineteenth century. In his autobiographical work, *John Todd, The Story of His Life, Told Mainly by Himself* (1876), Todd claimed to have been "an orphan, shelterless, penniless" as a boy; he was, therefore, a prime example of the Self-Made Man. (Except that it was not entirely true. Todd had been raised by his mother and two aunts after his father had died.) *The Student's Manual* struck a nerve among American youth; by 1854 it had gone through twenty-four editions. Todd claimed that masturbation enfeebled the mind, debased and polluted the heart and feelings; the so-called "solitary vice" was, as he saw it, "almost inseparable from the habit of revery"—the province of the idle. As far as he could see, masturbation had claimed more healthy lives than war.[7]

Graham laid out an elaborate plan for dietary and behavioral reforms that would allow men to live secure, upright, productive, and healthy lives. Desire, he believed, "disturbs and disorders all the functions of the system," so Graham offered a set of bodily dos and don'ts, a prescription of dietary and sexual temperance. He advocated a diet of farinaceous foods, properly prepared, like "good bread, made of coarsely ground, unbolted wheat, or rye-meal, and hominy, made of cracked wheat, or rye, or Indian corn." Young men should avoid full and large suppers and should eat no animal meat whatever, since he was convinced that one is more susceptible to sins of the flesh if one eats another's flesh. (For this, Graham was twice attacked by a mob of Boston butchers, who claimed that he was ruining their business.)

Graham advocated strenuous exercise, the avoidance of "every kind of stimulating and heating substances," and sleeping on a hard wood bed, since feather beds would wrap the sleeper in indolent luxury and thereby enervate him. Graham warned that socializing boys to bad habits of "luxury, indolence, voluptuousness and sensuality" would lead them to surrender their "nobleness, dignity, honor, and manhood" and reenact the fall from grace into a debased near devilry, becoming:

> the wretched transgressor [who] sinks into a miserable fatuity, and finally becomes a confirmed and degraded idiot, whose deeply sunken and vacant, glossy eye, and livid shrivelled countenance, and ulcerous, toothless gums, and fetid breath, and feeble, broken voice, and emaciated and dwarfish and crooked body, and almost hairless head—covered perhaps with suppurating blisters and running sores—denote a premature old age! a blighted body—and a ruined soul![8]

Sexual relations between husbands and wives also needed to be regulated and their frequency curtailed—Graham suggested no more than once a month—lest a variety of illnesses befall the husband. Even sexual fantasies—"those lascivious day-dreams and amorous reveries"—must be suppressed.[9]

There were many other members of this antebellum vice squad. Dr. Augustus Kingsley Gardner advised parents that even if their children attempt to hide their practice of the solitary vice, sooner or later, "hysterias, epilepsies, spinal irritations, and a train of symptoms" would give them away. Another writer counseled parents to employ several innovative treatments for sexual intemperance and especially masturbation to help boys keep their hands to themselves. These included using a straitjacket and tying the feet such that the thighs would remain apart. If these methods didn't work, he contrived "cork cushions," which could be placed inside the thighs to pry them apart, and a "genital cage," a metal truss of silver or tin in which the boy's penis and scrotum were placed and held by springs. R. J. Culverwell invented a chair that served as a kind of bidet for the sexually tempted. An armchair was fitted with an open seat, beneath which a pan of cold water, or "medicated refrigerant fluid," would be placed. By means of a pump, a young man could direct this cold water to his genitals, thus "cooling" his sexual urges and making himself more capable of self-control.[10]

Some advice manuals took up some of Graham's nonsexual counsel and dietary regimens.[11] Even Charles Dickens suggested a few healthful reforms Americans might adopt, including greater personal cleanliness and exercise, as well as changing "the custom of hastily swallowing large quantities of animal food, three times a day, and rushing back to sedentary pursuits after each meal."[12] G. W. Docine's *Manners Maketh Man* (1852) and Eliza W. R. Farrar's *The Young Man's Own Book* (1832) advised men to avoid "anything which brings weariness and exhaustion, and fatigue," including dancing, theatrical performances, gambling, and alcohol.[13]

Alcohol was perhaps the second greatest challenge for the new ethic of self-control since, by today's standards, American men of the early national period were hopeless sots. Men would routinely wash down meals with hard cider (or peach brandy in the South), and frequent drams in the shop or in the field fortified young men for bursts of heavy labor in the cold or in the heat. In the South men took a break from work in midmorning for what they called "eleveners," the antebellum version of the coffee break, during which they drank a mixture of whiskey and berry flavorings. Workingmen, historians Paul Johnson and Sean Wilentz write, "liked to drink, at all times of the day, in stupefying quantities." Traditionally, the successful drank wine, while the unambitious or unsuccessful drank cider or, later, beer. One itinerant minister, James Finley, wrote in his *Autobiography* in 1854 that "a house could not be raised, a field of wheat cut down, nor could there be a log rolling, a husking, a quilting, a wedding, or a funeral without the aid of alcohol." Alcohol was a way of life; even the Founding Fathers drank heavily. "Neighborhood sociability centered on taverns," writes historian Charles Sellers, "and strong waters cheered funerals, ministerial ordinations, militia musters, elections, corn huskings, and houseraisings." Drink "made them men," they thought, and "gave them strength."[14]

In the first decades of the nineteenth century, though, American men went on a national bender, especially imbibing hard liquor. Historian William Rorabaugh surveys the scene in this way:

Figure 2.1 Annual Consumption of Distilled Spirits (i.e., rum, whiskey, gin, brandy) per Capita, in U.S. Gallons

Source: William Rorabaugh, *The Alcoholic Republic* (New York: Oxford University Press, 1979), p. 28.

> A western husbandman tarried at the tavern until drunk; an eastern harvest laborer received daily a half pint or pint of rum; a southern planter was considered temperate enough to belong to the Methodist Church if he restricted his daily intake of alcohol to a quart of peach brandy. A city mechanic went directly from work to the public house where he stayed late and spent his day's wages. Alcohol was such an accepted part of American life that in 1829 the secretary of war estimated that three-quarters of the nation's laborers drank daily at least 4 ounces of distilled spirits.[15]

All that drinking signaled more than workplace conviviality and smalltown democracy. Americans drank more—far more—hard alcoholic beverages between 1790 and 1830 than at any other time in our history before or since. (See Figures 2.1 and 2.2.) This was "the great American whiskey binge." By 1830 hard liquor consumption had climbed to 9.5 gallons a year for every American over fourteen, and over 5 gallons per capita overall, plus 30.3 gallons of hard cider and other intoxicants. Rorabaugh speculates that the reason for such constant intoxication was that Americans' economic aspirations were so high that they were constantly warding off feelings of failure. The volatility of the marketplace, the fortunes to be won and lost, and the general economic uncertainty of the early Industrial Revolution left this generation of working Americans fretting constantly over their plight. As Edward Bourne noted at mid-century, American men's drinking habits "grew out of the anxiety of their condition."[16]

Advice manuals bravely promoted temperance in the face of this tradition. Following the founding of the American Society for the Promotion of Temperance in 1826, begun largely by clergymen opposed to Andrew Jackson, writers like Henry Ward Beecher and health reformers like Graham railed against the dangers of drink and frequently peppered their tales of woe by contrasting two friends who embark on the path of life together. When one succumbs to drink and the other doesn't, their lives diverge, but not before the drunkard steals from or otherwise harms the temperate young man. In the end the

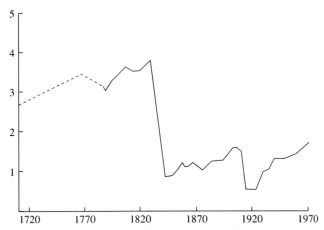

Figure 2.2 Annual Consumption of Alcohol Contained in All Alcoholic Beverages per Capita, in U.S. Gallons
Source: William Rorabaugh, *The Alcoholic Republic* (New York: Oxford University Press, 1979), p. 29.

drunkard is either lying dissolute by the side of the road or is dead of his own cause, while the pure young man continues on, his fortune assured.

Other social reformers promoted temperance as part of larger reforms. Abolitionists William Lloyd Garrison and Theodore Weld, for example, linked intemperance and slavery; each, they argued, was economically wasteful as well as immoral. Fueled by ministerial leaders and followers of the Second Great Awakening, temperance advocates sought to stem the tide. They had their work cut out for them, especially since so many of the reformers were women; drinking became an expression of masculine protest against feminization at the same time as it was an artisanal protest against proletarianization.

The urge for self-control and the need for social control were easily fused in the new republic—and with serious social consequences. Beyond sexual and alcoholic temperance there was also the possibility that those "repressed middle-class sexual energies were channeled into a xenophobic hostility toward the immigrant and the black, then projected into fantasies incorporating the enviable and fully expressed sexuality of these alien groups" and projected onto women, who were cast as seductive temptresses, brimming with carnal desires they were unable to control, and at the same time, as pious, asexual angels who, at the merest mention of the body and its desires, would faint straight away.[17] These projections led to what was perhaps the most significant development in the relations between the sexes prior to the birth of feminism.

The Separation of Spheres

When Tocqueville came to the United States in the early 1830s, he was amazed by the way this new democratic society had affected relations within the family. In particular, he noticed startling differences between Europe and America in the treatment of women and the relationship between fathers and sons. He observed that what begins as greater freedom and intimacy in the New World actually soon changes into its opposite. In Europe women were far more dependent before marriage, unable to move about freely beyond the boundaries of the home, whereas in America unmarried women were relatively independent as girls. Marriage changed all that—"the independence of woman is irrecoverably lost in the bonds of matrimony: if an unmarried woman is less constrained [in America] than elsewhere, a wife is subjected to stricter obligations." She "never leaves her domestic sphere, and is in some respects very dependent within it."[18]

A similar paradox could be seen in the relationship between fathers and sons. American democracy dramatically reduced the distance between them, relaxing filial bonds of obedience, as "relations between father and sons become more intimate and gentle; there is less of rule and authority, often more of confidence and affection." Sons addressed their fathers "with a tang of freedom, familiarity and tenderness all at once." And yet these tender and intimate relations ended quickly as the sons grew up. Preparation for manhood required that the son become independent quickly, "master of his thoughts" and soon "master of his conduct." He was raised to shed his familial dependence like a snake sheds its old skin.[19]

Tocqueville was thus among the first of many commentators to confront the American separation of spheres. "In America, more than anywhere else in the world," he wrote, "care has been taken to constantly trace clearly the distinct spheres of action of the two sexes and both are required to keep in step, but along paths that are never the same."[20] It is significant that the doctrine of separate spheres was "a male creation," first promoted by male writers of advice books and said to "serve men's needs."[21] Only later was it picked up, embraced, and elaborated by women writers celebrating domesticity. Separate spheres allowed insecure middle-class men to feel like men, both in the homosocial workplace and when they returned to their homes.

There had always been, of course, a division of labor between the sexes, from hunting and gathering to agricultural to these early industrial societies, on both sides of the Atlantic. What was new—and distinctly American—were the strictness and the degree to which women and men were now seen as having a separate sphere. The home became entirely the domain of wives; husbands were even less involved than before. Men ceded both responsibility and authority over household management. In the early part of the century, men performed some work around the home—gathering fuel, leather work, grain processing—that could not be done elsewhere. "Virtually all the stereotypically male household occupations were eliminated by technological and economic innovations," writes historian Ruth Schwartz Cowan. This was not so for women, who saw their work "either untouched or augmented." Advice manuals once written primarily to fathers were now geared exclusively to mothers.[22]

And some services and functions that husbands and wives had performed together could now be delegated elsewhere. Middle-class children had once been educated at home but now increasingly went to school, and to a lesser degree the new asylums served a caretaking function that had earlier fallen on the family.[23] To modern eyes, of course, the family still had lots to do: early childhood socialization and the shaping of emotion and morality, acting like a "shrine for upholding and examplifying all the softer virtues—love, generosity, tenderness, altruism, harmony, repose."[24] But at the time, this represented a significant retrenchment.

Thus the separation of spheres: The workplace became harder, the home softer. The casual conviviality of the workplace was fast disappearing in the new world of the factory system and mass production. Time and work discipline increasingly ruled. Outside the home was the "turmoil and bustle of an active, selfish world," explained Thomas Drew, where a man has to "encounter innumerable difficulties, hardships and labors,"[25] The home would be a balm to soothe men from the roughness of the working day. The workplace was masculinized, the home feminized.

Whenever men have felt threatened by social change, some of them have resorted to arguments based on the natural distinctions between women and men as the justification for the newly endangered status quo. In the early nineteenth century men resorted to religious doctrine and scientific and medical evidence that "proved" that women were neither theologically nor biologically capable of moving into the public sphere. Religious fanatics, such as the Prophet Matthias, who drew zealous followers during the Second Great Awakening, preached the imminent restoration of a kind of "divine patriarchy" which utterly excluded women as God's plan. Other, more mainstream, ministers agreed that women were ordained by God and their bodies to remain at home.[26]

Women got the message. "If you are thinking of entering the matrimonial state," wrote Rebeccah Root Buell to her friend Weltha Brown in 1822, "you had better come [visit] while you can, as there is no certainty attending [marriage] but confinement."[27] Advice manuals for these newly domesticated women flooded the market in Jacksonian America; historian Nancy Cott lists dozens of these books published in New England between 1830 and 1840 alone, by both male and female authors, including *The Mother at Home, The Mother's Book, The Young Mother, Domestic Education, Familiar Letters on Subjects Interesting to the Minds and Hearts of Females*, and *Letters to Young Ladies*.[28] "Because women remain out of the world, men can safely enter into it," writes one historian, while another observes that "by making the women and children of the society the guardians of virtue, the male was released to act amorally in the world outside the home." The separation of spheres thus bolstered men's identities on both the home front and in the workplace.[29]

To justify this spatial and emotional segregation, writers of advice manuals invented the Cult of True Womanhood.[30] Women were not to be excluded from participation in the public sphere as much as exempted from participation in such a competitive and ugly world. Delicate and fragile, women were not subservient but "chosen vessels" requiring protection from the world, said Henry Harrington in *Ladies Companion* in 1838. Woman was a "moral, a sexual, a germiferous, gestative, and parturient creature" whose head is "almost too small for intellect but just big enough for love," declared Philadelphia gynecologist Dr. Charles Meigs. And Dr. William Acton's *Functions and Disorders of the Reproductive System* taught that "love of home, children and domestic duties are the only passions [women] feel."[31]

It was a woman's job to act as moral restraint, since men, alone, were not capable of restraining their baser emotions, their violence, their aggressive, competitive, acquisitive edge. "There is but little of the genuine emotion in our [sex]," observed Sylvester Judd in 1839. "The habits of men are too commercial and restrained, too bustling and noisy, too ambitious and repellent." The world outside the home was "a vast wilderness" fueled by the "rage of competitive battle," wrote one minister in 1827. Home, then, became the place where man "seeks a refuge from the vexation and embarrassments of business."[32] If men were going to be able to exercise any self-control and yet take necessary risks in the work world, then women were going to have to help. Women were the "moralizers," who would elicit moral behavior from men. "The purity of women is the everlasting barrier against which the tides of man's sensual nature surge," was how Eliza Farnham put it in 1864.[33]

The strictures of Self-Made Manhood filtered down to younger and younger men, making their boyhoods appear increasingly to be little manhoods. No wonder Tocqueville lamented how quickly and sadly Americans are forced to renounce their boyhoods. What historian E. Anthony Rotundo calls "boy culture" came increasingly to imitate adult male culture as young boys were taught the "aggressive, self-reliant qualities needed for men's work" so that each one could "assert himself and stand emotionally alone while away from his family." Such prescriptions transformed the carefree tenderness of male friendships in the nineteenth century as the carefree play of youth was renounced for more instrumental relationships. The transition to manhood, then, was a sustained loss as the "crude aggressions and the raw boisterousness of boyhood" were transformed into the "refined self-assertion and purposeful self-discipline of manhood."[34]

This loss continued through the American man's adult life. Although industrialization pushed more and more men together in the workplace, it also increased the distance they each felt from one another. Gone were the casual intimacies of boyhood. Gone too was a view that other men—coworkers and friends—could act as moral constraints on excessive behavior. Instead, other men were potential economic rivals. "Between man and man," wrote Nathaniel Hawthorne in *The Marble Faun*, "there is always an insuperable gulf. They can never quite grasp each other's hands; and therefore man never derives any intimate help, any heart sustenance, from his brother man, but from woman—his mother, his sister, or his wife."[35] Men's reliance on women to meet all their emotional needs is a sad product of the separation of spheres.

The widening chasm between men produced a deep yearning for the intimacies that had earlier marked men's lives. "As networks of mutual trust and support among males gave way to individualist self-reliance, a prohibition was placed on physical intimacies between men that had earlier been accepted without qualm," writes literary critic T. Walter Herbert in a perceptive aside to his revealing portrait of Nathaniel and Sophia Hawthorne.[36] Such tenderness and intimacy were now tainted by fears of dependency; by the end of the century, those fears would be more fully sexualized into a fear of homosexuality.

The separation of spheres also affected the laboring classes, although these groups stressed female virtue less and male authority more than the middle class. "In their labor organizations they spoke in behalf of a rejuvenated patriarchal family, with men in the workplace and women in their rightful and natural place—the home."[37] The National Trades Union elaborated an artisanal version of separate spheres when it took up the question of female labor in the mid-1830s. Women, they argued, were incapable of pressing the demands of unionized labor. "The natural weakness of the sex—their modesty and bashfulness—their ignorance of the forms and conduct of public meetings and of the measures necessary to enable them to resist the oppression under which they labor—will ever prevent them from obtaining any melioration or improvement of their conditions," observed one report in July 1835. The next year the report of the Committee on Female Labor noted how women's "hysterical organization, the natural responsibilities and the moral sensibility . . . prove conclusively that her labors should be only of a domestic nature."[38]

What these male workers also realized was that women workers would suppress wages and make it harder for men to find jobs. "When the females are found capable of performing duties generally performed by the men, as a natural consequence, from the cheapness of their habits and dependent situation, they acquire complete control of that particular branch of labor." Ironically, the National Trade Union advocated equal wages for women, in part so that men's wages would remain high. Equal wages were "the only means of curtailing or arresting the evil" of female labor in the first place—curious and circuitous logic to reach a position of support for women's rights.[39]

Most men followed a less circuitous route to arrive at more antifeminist conclusions. Women's brains, they argued, were neither large nor strong enough to handle the enormity of the intellectual challenge of the collegiate curriculum. Education "would only confuse these feebleminded creatures, bring them into contact with polluting ideas whose misunderstood complexity would contaminate the virginal purity of their minds, and hence interfere with their role as soul-keepers." According to the Reverend John Todd, a Calvinist minister who became one of the best-selling advice-book authors of the mid-century, "the great danger of our day is forcing the intellect of woman beyond what her physical organization will possibly bear."[40]

Efforts by women to educate themselves met with no better reception. When Emma Willard opened her seminary, one man remarked that "[t]hey'll be educating the cows next." E. A. Andrews attacked the founding of Mount Holyoke in 1837, warning of gender inversion: "[I]n place of all which is most attractive in female manners, we see characters expressly formed for acting a *manly* part upon the theater of life. Under such influences, the female character is fast becoming masculine." In 1854 a young James Garfield, then an Ohio schoolteacher, listened to a speech by Antoinette Brown, who had been ordained into the ministry a year earlier. Garfield wrote that "there is something about a woman speaking in public that unsexes her in my mind, and how much soever I might admire the talent, yet I could never think of the female speaker as the gentle sister, the tender wife, or the loving mother."[41]

Reverend John Todd also used gender inversion as a theme in the fight against woman suffrage, especially after the First Woman's Rights Convention was held in Seneca Falls, New York, in 1848. Suffrage is a civil right, which cannot contravene women's natural right "to be exempted from certain things which men must endure." Thus, he argued, woman suffrage is a "rebellion against God's law of the sexes, against marriage . . . and against the family organization, the holiest thing that is left from Eden." James Long went further, to naturalize the continuing power of white men: "How did woman first become subject to man as she now is all over the world? By her nature, her sex, just as the negro is and always will be, to the end of time, inferior to the white race, and therefore, doomed to subjection; but happier than she would be in any other condition, just because it is the law of her nature."[42]

Finally, the separation of spheres between women and men had enormous consequences for the relations between men and their families. If, as contemporary feminist writers would have it, women had become prisoners in the home, then men were increasingly exiled from the home, unable to return without fear of feminization. And so American fathers were increasingly estranged from the lives of their children, just as the workplace demanded an increasing amount of time and energy. "Most men are so entirely engrossed by business as to have but little opportunity of fully understanding the characters of their children," complained Sarah Pierce in 1818. Just as motherhood was advancing, "fatherhood was in retreat." The term *father* no longer had unequivocally positive connotations. Charles Francis Adams yearned to "know" his father but never did and confessed that he "suffered from it all through life." Theodore Dwight's *The Father's Book* (1834) tried to persuade fathers to resume their responsibilities in the home. "Paternal neglect at the present time is one of the most abundant sources of domestic sorrow," wrote the Reverend John S. C. Abbott in an article in *Parents Magazine* in 1842. The father, "eager in the pursuit of business, toils early and late, and finds no time to fulfill . . . duties to his children."[43] If a man's home was his castle, by the mid-1800s he was becoming an absentee landlord.

American manhood had been born as the Sons of Liberty threw off the yoke of a tyrannical father. In but one generation the sons had grown to manhood and had turned themselves into fathers without sons:

> In terms of male-male interaction, the old unity was shattered. Sons found themselves within a world neither they nor their fathers understood. The young man stood alone. The men of Jacksonian America experienced themselves both as sons loosed from the fathers' ways, and as fathers increasingly troubled as to how to provide for, control, or even to understand the experiences of their sons.[44]

The Self-Made Man's constant drive for self-control helped to create what we think of as the modern nuclear family: the Breadwinner Father and Homemaker Mother and children who remained under their mother's immediate charge. If life in the public sphere left him battered and bruised and his efforts to assert his manly will over both his body and his fortune left him exhausted, these domestic arrangements could provide a needed balm, a haven in a heartless world. "It is at home where man . . . seeks a refuge from the vexation and embarrassments of business," claimed New Hampshire minister Charles Burroughs in a sermon in 1827.[45]

Many men chafed at what they felt was a loss—of freedom, of casual homosocial intimacies, of authority. These Self-Made Men longed to make themselves all over again; they yearned for a place where they could reestablish their manhood and replace market competition with male camaraderie. In both fiction and fact, they ran away.

On the Road

In the last lines of the novel that bears his name, Huckleberry Finn anxiously plans an escape. "I reckon I got to light out for the territory ahead of the rest, because Aunt Sally she's going to adopt me and sivilize me, and I can't stand it. I been there before." Huck eloquently expresses the sentiments of many young American men. Women constrained manhood—through temperance, Christian piety, sober responsibility, sexual fidelity. Women set the tone of those institutions that restrained masculine excess—schoolroom, parlor, church. "Woman" meant mother, the one responsible for curtailing boyish rambunctiousness; later, "woman" meant wife, the wellspring of emotional and moral strength. If men wanted relief from the demands for self-control, they had to "light out for the territory."

Part of the struggle was simply to get out of the middle-class house, now a virtual feminine theme park, where well-mannered and well-dressed children played quietly in heavily draped and carpeted parlors and adults chatted amiably over tea served from porcelain services. This contrast with the frantic and aggressive business world made men feel uneasy in their own homes. A man's house "is a prison, in which he finds himself oppressed and confined, not sheltered and protected," wrote Thoreau. "His muscles are never relaxed. It is rare that he overcomes the house, and learns to sit at home in it."[46]

Women were not only domestic, they were domesticators, expected to turn their sons into virtuous Christian gentlemen—dutiful, well-mannered, and feminized. Orestes Brownson growled about "female religion" as well as male ministers who were the domesticated pets of widows and spinsters, "fit only to balance teacups and mouth platitudes." It fell increasingly to women to teach their sons how to be men.[47]

Thus did a portion of the definition of American manhood become the repudiation of the feminine, a resistance to mothers' and wives' efforts to civilize men. Part of the struggle was one of appearance. Beards and moustaches proliferated in the 1840s and 1850s, while critics lampooned feminized styles among urban men.[48] Preachers during the Second Great Awakening excluded "men who wear spectacles" from their lists of Americans scheduled to enter the Kingdom of Heaven (as well as those merchants who hire women to work). Walt Whitman chastised the painted urban male who "looks like a doll," and a writer in *Harper's Monthly* described the human "poodles" who paraded in the cities with their "velvet tunics" and "long glossy locks." And Oliver Wendell Holmes foresaw the end of our race in 1858, convinced that a "set of black-coated, stiff-jointed, soft-muscled, paste-complexioned youth as we can boast from our Atlantic cities never before sprang from loins of Anglo-Saxon lineage."[49]

The ultimate relief was simply to get out of town. When Horace Greeley gave his famous advice in 1837—the full text of which was "Go West, young man, and grow up with the country"—men perked up their ears and followed in droves. The West was a safety valve, siphoning off excess population, providing an outlet for both the ambitious and the unsuccessful. "All the past we leave behind," Walt Whitman wrote in "Pioneers! O Pioneers!" in 1865. As Frederick Jackson Turner put it:

> To the peasant and artisan of the Old World, bound by the chains of social class, as old as custom and as inevitable as fate, the West offered an exit into a free life and greater well-being among the bounties of nature, into the midst of resources that demanded manly exertion and that gave in return the chance for indefinite ascent in the scale of social advance.[50]

Timothy Flint suggested, in 1831, that these "shrinking and effeminate spirits, the men of soft hands and fashionable life" ought to follow the pioneers, for "there is a kind of moral sublimity in the contemplation of the adventures and daring of such men" with their "manly hardihood." This was a far cry from Yale president Timothy Dwight's four-volume *Travels in New England and New York* (1821–22), in which the author regretted that as the pioneer pushed further and further into the wilderness, he became "less and less a civilized man," or J. Hector St. John Crèvecoeur's lament that on the frontier, men "degenerated altogether into the hunting state" and became, ultimately, "no better than carnivorous animals of a superior rank."[51]

Reports from the field of this westward rush all celebrated the return to manly virtues. Francis Parkman's *The Oregon Trail: Sketches of Prairie and Rocky Mountain Life* (1849) was an immediate best-seller, as was his later *Discovery of the Great West* (1869). A scrawny, feeblebodied rich boy, Parkman saw his masculine salvation in the repudiation

of all things civilized. Rejecting his own class as a bunch of "soft hearted philanthropists," Parkman sought out Indians and frontiersmen as manly examples to hold up to effete Bostonians. The "vigorous life of the nation springs from the deep soil at the bottom of society," he wrote from the trail.[52] And Parkman wasn't alone in repudiating the educated elite and idealizing the rough-hewn working classes in their ability to confront life's "incessant battle." Ruling-class weakling Richard Henry Dana penned a masculinist escape memoir, *Two Years Before the Mast*, in 1840. Charles Webber's *Old Hicks, the Guide; or, Adventures in the Comanche Country in Search of a Gold Mine* (1848) also celebrated the "philosophy of the savage life."[53]

The rush westward reached its apotheosis with the California Gold Rush of 1849. Never before or since have men created such a homosocial preserve on such a scale. Nearly 200,000 men came to California in 1849 and 1850 alone, composing 93 percent of the state's population, 71 percent of whom were younger men, aged twenty to forty.[54] Though they had been lured by the exciting possibilities of sudden and exorbitant wealth, money alone did not keep them there. It was the homosocial life, a world of "rude freedom" outside the conventional boundaries of civilization and away from wives. "There was no female society," wrote Reverend John Todd, "no homes to soften and restrain." "The condition of the mining population, especially their carelessness in regard to appearances, mode of life, and habits in general," observed C. W. Haskins, "showed conclusively that man, when alone, and deprived of that influence which the presence of woman only can produce, would in a short time degenerate into a savage and barbarous state." With women scarcer than gold, one doctor explained that in California, "all the *restrictive influence* of fair women is lost, and the ungoverned tempers of men run wild."[55]

And they looked and acted the part. Forty-niners cast off the cultural baggage they brought from the East. They took new names, manly and rough, like Texas Jack, Whiskey Tom, French Flat Pete, Buckeye, and Sawbones (a doctor); they neither bathed nor changed their clothes, but they gambled, drank incessantly, swore, and attended bare-knuckle prizefights more often than they attended church services. A deck of cards was called the "California prayer book." Three years after leaving home, one prospector informed his family that he was now a "bull necked, horny handed, whiskered backwoodsman" unable to function "under the eye and hand of a boss." The forty-niners may have found what they were really looking for in those gold mines: they discovered a "pure" manhood—even if they didn't find any gold.[56]

Of course, one needn't go to all the trouble of traveling across the country to confront nature. One could find it in one's own backyard, the way Henry David Thoreau did. Thoreau, too, rejected a definition of masculinity that pushed men into "such desperate haste to succeed and in such desperate enterprises" that their lives are "frittered away by detail." The fear of failure suffocated urban businessmen and left workingmen with neither time nor inclination to develop their manly integrity. Men, Thoreau believed, needed liberation.[57] "We should come home from far, from adventures, and perils, and discoveries every day, with new experience and character." In short, we need the "tonic of the wilderness," as an antidote to the lockstep inanity of civilization.[58]

So Thoreau set out to live at Walden Pond in 1845, shunning the company of women in order to create himself, to become a Self-Made Man in the wilderness. In a sense, Thoreau conducted his own initiation into this new version of manhood. First, he rejected as model the old aristocratic father, England. "I look on England today as an old gentleman who is travelling with a great deal of baggage, trumpery which has accumulated from long housekeeping, which he has not the courage to burn." Then he baptized himself. "I got up early and bathed in the pond; that was a religious exercise, and one of the best things which I did." And finally, he took communion, in a rather brutal fashion. "I caught a glimpse of a woodchuck stealing across my path, and felt a strange thrill of savage delight, and was strongly tempted to seize and devour him raw; not that I was hungry then, except for that wildness which he represented." Ingesting the wildness, Thoreau suggests, allows middle-class men to free themselves.

If middle-class men were unable to venture to the West, or even to the local pond, the tonic virtues of the wilderness could be brought to their homes; they could escape through fantasy. In the first half of the century, two forms of fantasy were available—popular biographies of pioneers and backwoodsmen, elevated to the level of national myths, and general fiction, both of which allowed men to escape through fantasies of identification. For example, although Kit Carson and Daniel Boone were each active in the first two decades of the century and Davy Crockett active in the 1830s, all became mythic heroes in the 1840s and especially in the 1850s, when their biographies were rewritten as primitivist narratives of innate, instinctual manhood. All three were in constant retreat from advancing civilization.

Boone was the "natural man," uninterested in accumulation of wealth, always on the move, never weighted down. "Boone used to say to me," declared one backwoodsman, who claimed to be Boone's hunting buddy, "that when he could not fell the top of a tree near enough to his door for firewood, it was time to move to a new place." Another legend held that when Boone heard that someone was clearing a farm twelve miles west of him, he declared the area "too thickly settled" and prepared his next move. Lionizing such misanthropic grumpiness seems to be a peculiarly American trait.[59]

Equally distinctive was the creation of the American myth of mobility and especially the link between geographic mobility, social mobility, and self-re-creation as men. The Heroic Artisan here returns in the guise of the pioneer, the masculine primitive, but he is still humble and beholden to his origins. As Richard Slotkin, who has traced what he calls the "frontier fable" as a dominant theme in American culture, writes:

> The protagonist is usually represented as having marginal connections to the Metropolis and its culture. He is a poor and uneducated borderer or an orphan lacking the parental tie to anchor him to the Metropolis and is generally disinclined to learn from book culture when the book of nature is free to read before him. His going to the wilderness breaks or attenuates the Metropolitan tie, but it gives him access to something far more important than anything the Metropolis contains—the wisdom, morality, power, and freedom of Nature in its pure wild form.[60]

This myth contains an obvious irony—the very activity in moving west to escape civilization transforms the protagonists into culture's advance guard as they tame the West for future settlement. Yet even today, with little admission of irony, it remains a most potent myth. When one historian dared, in 1989, to debunk aspects of the myth about how and when Crockett died at the Alamo, he was berated by irate writers as a "wimp," fit for nothing better than the lowly profession of college teaching. In the 1992 presidential campaign Republican challenger Pat Buchanan donned a coonskin cap as he campaigned in Crockett's native Tennessee.[61]

These real-life historical figures were transformed into mythic heroes within a decade or two of their deaths; early nineteenth-century American novelists made them up as they went along. Heroic men, to be sure, populated their pages, but antebellum fiction by men is also marked by the startling absence of sexuality, of marriage, of families—the virtual absence of women entirely. American novels were about "adventure and isolation plus an escape at one point or another, or a flight from society to an island, a woods, the underworld, a mountain fastness—some place, at least, where mothers do not come."[62]

Take Washington Irving's famous story "Rip Van Winkle" (1820). What appears to be a surface treatment of progress—Van Winkle sleeps for twenty years and comes back to find everything changed—is also the story of poor Rip's escape from his shrewish wife. "Morning, noon, and night her tongue was incessantly going, and everything he did or said was sure to produce a torrent of household eloquence." Usually, Rip simply "shrugged his shoulders, shook his head, and cast up his eyes" in response. But finally he had to get away. "Poor Rip was at last reduced almost to despair; and his only alternative, to escape from the labor of the farm and clamor of his wife, was to take gun in hand and stroll away into the woods." Rip's musket-laden stroll culminates in a twenty-year alcoholic reverie and confrontation with the homosocial world of the mountain trolls. Upon his return Rip is most struck by the changes in the gender order that his absence—and his wife's death—has elicited:

> Rip, in fact, was no politician; the changes of states and empires made but little impression on him; but there was one species of despotism under which he had long groaned, and that was—petticoat government. Happily that was at an end; he had got his neck out of the yoke of matrimony, and could in and out whenever he pleased, without dreading the tyranny of Dame Van Winkle. Whenever her name was mentioned, however, he shook his head, shrugged his shoulders, and cast up his eyes; which might pass either for an expression of resignation to his fate, or joy at his deliverance.

The story's last line extends Irving's fable to the "common wish of all hen-pecked husbands in the neighborhood, when life hangs heavy on their hands, that they might have a quieting draught of Rip Van Winkle's flagon." Rip is the first of this fictional American archetype of the man in flight—he is the fugitive, born to run.[63]

By the mid-nineteenth century this new American male hero began to encounter another man, usually a man of color, as a sort of spirit guide to this world without women. From Natty Bumppo and Chingachgook, Huck and Jim, Ishmael and Queequeg, Billy Budd and Claggart, all the way to the Lone Ranger and Tonto, Captain Kirk and Mr. Spock, Lt. John Dunbar and Kicking Bird in *Dances with Wolves*, and Murtaugh and Riggs in the *Lethal Weapon* series, American fiction has celebrated male bonding, "a love between males, more enduring and purer than any heterosexual passion," which culminates in an asexual countermarriage "in which the white refugee from society and the dark skinned primitive are joined till death do them part."[64]

Literary critic Leslie Fiedler attributes this tradition of cross-race male bonding to a search for redemption for white guilt, but I believe it is also a way to present screens against which white manhood is projected, played out, and defined.[65] The nonwhite male stands in for women—as dependent child (Jim), male mother (Chingachgook, Tonto), spiritual guide and moral instructor (Queequeg, Chingachgook)—sometimes all at once. Their homoerotic passion is never the passion of equals; the nonwhite is either the guide and exemplar or the Rousseauian "noble savage" who, in his childlike innocence, is more susceptible to the wiles of civilization. Murtaugh and Riggs are the only ones who seem to play against type, as Danny Glover plays a stable sober policeman, a mature and responsible black family man, in contrast to Mel Gibson's Riggs, who plays the masculine primitive in whiteface. This is not as inverted, however, as it might at first appear. Chingachgook, Tonto, Jim, Queequeg—all of them are closer to both nature and nurture. They are male mothers, nurturing their younger, wilder white charges into the deeply spiritual world of the primitive. One must be sane, sober, and soulful to remain so close to nature; one must be tame to be primitive and wild to be so tame.

Sexuality—succumbing to the lustful temptations of the body—would ruin everything. Transforming homoerotic bonding into homosexual union would destroy the charged but chaste basis for the bond. Nowhere is this more clear than in the five-novel saga of the *Leatherstocking Tales* by James Fenimore Cooper, certainly among the most popular male novelists of antebellum America. In Natty Bumppo—the hero of *The Pioneers* (1823), *The Last of the Mohicans* (1826), *The Prairie* (1827), *The Pathfinder* (1840), and *The Deerslayer* (1841)—Cooper created the prototype of masculinist flight and "showed how the solitary hunter, unencumbered by social responsibilities, utterly self-sufficient, uncultivated but endowed with a spontaneous appreciation of natural beauty, could become the central figure in the great American romance of the West."[66] "And Natty, what sort of man is he?" asked D. H. Lawrence. "Why, he is a man with a gun. He is a killer, a slayer. Patient and gentle, as he is, he is a slayer. Self-effacing . . . still he is a killer." Natty Bumppo is the first "last real man in America," created, ironically, by an author who was a leading Manhattan socialite.[67]

When we first meet Natty, he and his Indian companion Chingachgook are engaged in a debate about whether whites have any rights to take the Indians' land. At first, Natty says that whites are only doing to the Indians what the Indians used to do to each other, although he acknowledges that it does seem a bit unfair to be using bullets. But then Natty launches into a critique of feminization that seems to come out of nowhere. Modern white men no longer publicly shame the "cowardly" and applaud bravery; nowadays they "write in books" instead of telling their deeds in the villages, "where the lie can be given to the face of a cowardly boaster, and the brave soldier can call on his comrades to witness for the truth of his words." As a result, "a man who is too conscientious to misspend his days among the women, in learning the names of black marks [reading], may never hear of the deeds of his fathers, nor feel a pride in striving to outdo them."[68]

Women are but helpless and frail creatures in this telling. Throughout the novel, men spend a lot of time in the forests, risking all manner of danger, to rescue women who they believe cannot survive without male protection. Enemies are also feminized: "The Delawares are women!" exclaims Hawkeye (Natty). "The Yengeese, my foolish countrymen, have told them to take up the tomahawk, and strike their fathers in the Canada, and they have forgotten their sex. Does my brother wish to hear Le Cerf Agile ask for his petticoats, and see him weep before the Hurons, at the stake?"[69] Though Hawkeye delivers the masculinist attacks on effeminate mama's boys and disdains women, it falls to Chingachgook, the Indian, to deliver the most stinging critique of Self-Made Manhood in the guise of a critique of the white man:

> Some [The Great Spirit] made with faces paler than the ermine of the forests: and these he ordered to be traders; dogs to their women and wolves to their slaves. He gave this people the nature of the pigeon; wings that never tire: young, more plentiful than the leaves on the trees, and appetites to devour the earth. He gave them tongues like the false call of the wildcat: hearts like rabbits; the cunning of the hog . . . and arms to fight his battles; his cunning tells him how to get together the goods of the earth; and his arms inclose the land from the shore of the salt water to the islands of the great lake. His gluttony makes him sick. God gave him enough, and yet he wants all. Such are the palefaces.[70]

Such was the masculinity expressed by the urban entrepreneur, against which Cooper was rebelling; he celebrated, in his sentimental style, the return of the virtuous hunter, the Heroic Artisan in the wilderness. Cooper's strength lies in his ability to combine an elegy for the fast-receding state of nature (and its native inhabitants) with the tragic irony of the white men, whose very idealizing of the natives was part of the process of their disappearance.

Other antebellum writers were similarly more ambivalent about the triumph of the Self-Made Man. Walt Whitman celebrated the Heroic Artisan's vibrant sensuality and the nation's "athletic Democracy" as a counterpoint to the stoic self-control of the Self-Made Man, as in his homoerotic adulation of artisanal comradeship—both physical and spiritual:

> I will plant companionship thick as trees along the rivers of America, and along the
>   shores of the Great Lakes, and all over the prairies.
> I will make inseparable cities with their arms about each other's necks,
> By the love of comrades
> By the manly love of comrades.[71]

Some observers were suspicious of masculine escape. Charles Russell Lowell questioned the celebration of the West, writing in 1858 that "the West may make a man strong, massy, rock-like—never large and generous and manly."[72] Nathaniel Hawthorne was especially critical of the Self-Made Man's drive to dominate. His novels, especially *Blithedale Romance* (1852), equate competitive manhood with demonic possession (as did Sylvester Graham earlier) but make it clear that neither the yeoman ideal nor Genteel Patriarch offered much alternative.

More perhaps than any other single work, Herman Melville's *Moby Dick* reveals men's uncomfortable ambivalence about the possibilities of escape, while providing a compelling analysis of the mid-century crisis of masculinity. Captain Ahab's "desperate narcissistic rage" and "mesmerizing coerciveness" are the marks of "a man obsessed with avenging his shattered manhood."[73] In Ahab, Melville provides a portrait of gendered madness, a blind rage fueled by sexualized obsession, the self-destruction of the Self-Made Man. Here is a man driven to dominate, compulsively competitive, obsessively insecure —in short, the archetypal capitalist man, a nineteenth-century type A power broker. His monomania, that obsession with domination that is the disease of the driven, is the nineteenth-century male version of hysteria.

The great whale is both the more powerful man against which masculinity is measured and, simultaneously, the archetypal woman—carnal, sexually insatiable, other. What are we to make, after all, of the fact that Ahab, who had lost his "leg" trying to plunge his "six inch blade" into the whale, is now engaged in a "crazed flight to prove his manhood"? *Moby Dick* is "the most extravagant projection of male penis envy" in American litera-ture.[74] Ahab's inevitable failure is both economic and sexual; the Self-Made Man is no match for the forces of nature, and so the relations are inverted, revealing the terror of being dominated that lies beneath the drive to dominate. Ahab is the male Dora, seducing and seduced, rapist and raped, willing to partake of the savage butchery of his entire crew to avoid humiliation at the hands of his rival. Like Andrew Jackson, the fictional Ahab is finally hysterically mute, incapable of speech. He dies strangled in the harpoon's ropes, choking—voiceless and terrified.

These violent passions offer a startling contrast to the tender artisanal homoeroticism between the narrator, Ishmael, and the harpoonist, Queequeg, who discover, as they lie asleep in bed, wrapped in each other's arms, that chaste, yet eroticized, homosocial fraternalism that characterizes the purified male bond. To Melville those bonds were impossible if one adopted the competitive drive of the marketplace. When Ishmael, alone, survives, he has become, as the book's final words tell us, "another orphan." But buoyed by Queequeg's coffin and eventually saved by the "feminized" sailing ship, the *Rachel*, this orphan finally understands the seductive fatal trappings of the Self-Made Man and knows how to remake himself. He sails for home.

Was There an Alternative?

American men were uncertain which model of masculinity would emerge triumphant in the second half of the century. As America drifted slowly toward Civil War and the con-trasts between North and South sharpened, the national debates about slavery and woman suffrage also allowed a small group of men to articulate an alternative to the strategies that had been the stock responses to the antebellum masculine identity crisis. Instead of self-control, exclusion, and escape, these men proposed a broadly democratic vision, a manhood based on inclusion and self-expression. Such men were to be found among the abolitionists, especially those who also advocated women's rights. By advocating abolition and suffrage, several of these men also advanced an alternative vision of American manhood.

Some of them challenged the separation of spheres and supported women's entry into the public sphere.[75] Others championed women's sexual autonomy and men's responsibil-ity. Several founders of spiritual communes in the 1830s and 1840s, for example, included women as spiritual or even sexual equals. John Humphrey Noyes, founder of the Oneida commune, promoted sexual equality between women and men and male continence as a form of birth control.[76] Robert Dale Owen's *Moral Physiology* (1831) and Thomas Gove Nichols's *Esoteric Anthropology* (1853) provided counterweights to the many advice manuals that supported the separation of spheres and sexual self-control.

Still others supported male bonding and homosocial intimacies but eschewed the fantasies of escape from women. Though Walt Whitman sang of the "muscular urge" of manly comradeship and friendship as a counter to "limber tongued lawyers, very fluent but empty, feeble old men, professional politicians, dandies, dyspeptics, and so forth," he also insisted that women were "not one jot less" than he was.[77]

The debates over the abolition of slavery offer a fascinating window into the antebellum debate about masculinity. Abolitionists—like Wendell Phillips, William Lloyd Garrison, Thomas Wentworth Higginson, Martin Delany, Theodore Tilton, Parker Pillsbury—extended their antislavery vision to women's position and thus entered a debate about manhood as well. For Garrison, founder of the New England Anti-Slavery Society in 1831 and the American Anti-Slavery Society in 1833 and publisher of the *Liberator*, an imperious definition of manhood was indissolubly linked to women's subordination. In his speech to the Fourth Woman's Rights Convention in Cleveland in 1853, Garrison railed against sexist injustice. "I believe that man has done this through calculation, accentuated by a spirit of spite, *a desire for domination which has made him degrade woman* in her own eyes, and thereby tend to make her a mere vassal."[78]

Frederick Douglass linked his struggle to claim his manhood as a free black man to the struggles of women for full equality. To be a man meant autonomy and meant denying full autonomy to no one. His critics, however, believed that support of women's rights indicated a failure of manhood. The Syracuse papers called Douglass an "Aunt Nancy Man" in an editorial the week after his speech at the Seneca Falls Convention, and other supporters were vilified as "manmilliners" and "Miss-Nancys." The next year the *Syracuse Daily Star* opined in an editorial:

> The poor creatures who take part in the silly rant of "brawling women" and Aunt Nancy men, are most of the "ismizers" of the rankest stamp, Abolitionists of the most frantic and contemptible kind, and Christian sympathizers with such heretics as Wm. Lloyd Garrison, Parker Pillsbury, C. C. Burleigh, and S. S. Foster. These men are all Woman's Righters, and preachers of such damnable doctrines and accursed heresies, as would make demons of the pit shudder to hear.[79]

Support for women's rights and opposition to slavery had brought their manhood into question. For example, a defense of slavery by James Gordon Bennett, editor of the *New York Herald*, was saturated with gendered language. Bennett feared that middle-class pieties would feminize the nation. "They would snatch the convivial tankard from the honest toiler, close down the dance halls and theaters, shut up the Post Offices and railroad depots on Sundays, encourage blacks to seek white mates, and bring on a return to the theocratic tyrannies of puritan New England." The *New York Daily World* lampooned male supporters as "crack-brained, rheumatic, dyspeptic, henpecked men, vainly striving to achieve the liberty to open their heads in the presence of their wives." And the *Baltimore Patriot* declared that abolitionist lecturers had to be escorted to their lecterns by "a life guard of elderly ladies, and protected by a rampart of whale bones and cotton padding," i.e., a hoop skirt.[80]

For their part, abolitionists defended their manhood against such slanders; slavery's supporters were "cringing wretches," according to Wendell Phillips, while Garrison promoted a virile Christian manliness against slavery. "Men of natural softness and timidity, of a sincere and effeminate virtue, will be apt to look on these bolder, hardier spirits" of the antislavery crusade as "violent, perturbed, and uncharitable."[81] John Brown's raid on Harpers Ferry was experienced by many abolitionists as redemptive of their manhood.

Such a debate illustrates a theme we encounter again and again throughout American history. Support for feminism or civil rights has been seen as an indication that a man is less than manly—as if support for inequality somehow made one *more* of a man.

The Civil War propelled that debate into the nation's consciousness. To be sure, the Civil War centered around the morality of slavery, political questions of states' rights, economic struggles between industrial capitalism and agrarian slave-based economies, and the rending of American families in fratricidal struggle. But the Civil War was also a gendered war in which the meanings of manhood were bitterly contested.

All wars, of course, are meditations on masculinity. And the Civil War was no different. Take, for example, the metaphors we use to describe it. The American Revolution was a rebellion of the Sons of Liberty against the tyrannical Father; in the Civil War brother fought against brother in "the house divided." Those fatherless sons had grown out of their Jacksonian adolescence and now faced each other to determine which vision of manhood would dominate for the rest of the century.

Four different groups of men pressed their case, each plagued by different questions about their manhood. For the northern upper classes the war provided an opportunity to reclaim a manhood that had been dismissed as enervated and effete. Some even prescribed war as an antidote for the overcivilized indolent luxury of the eastern educated elite. Emerson snarled at his age "of fops and toys / Wanting Wisdom, void of right" as he began his poem "Voluntaries"; he believed that the war would "restore intellectual and moral power to these languid and dissipated populations." The editor of *Harper's Monthly* promised in 1861 that the "discipline of the camp is a wonderful check upon effeminacy and self-indulgence." A Philadelphia minister claimed:

> this war promises to arrest in a measure the extravagance and parade, the epicurianism and effeminacy into which we are fast running. It puts our young men upon a training which will nourish their manly virtues. It inculcates, as no moralist could, lessons of economy, of moderation, of patience, of self-control.

And one editor heralded the substitution of a purer manhood for the "commercial estimate of virtue now existing," while another chided upper-class Bostonians who lived "in safe and cowardly ease."[82]

The Civil War also represented a claim for manhood on the part of black men. Many abolitionists, both white and black, saw the struggle against slavery, as the governor of Wisconsin put it in 1859, "a question of manhood, not of color."[83] "The negro is a man, and has all the elements of manhood, like other men," claimed H. Ford Douglass. What's more, he added, "he has the *highest* elements of manhood."[84] Frederick Douglass (no relation) explicitly linked his critique of manhood to his experience as a black man. The turning point in Douglass's powerful autobiography comes when he finds himself a free man, "my own master," capable of self-respect earned through freedom and hard work. "Personal independence is the soul out of which comes the sturdiest manhood," he wrote.[85] Independence from slavery provided the material foundation, but it was violent physical confrontation that added the mortar to that foundation. After he beats a slavebreaker named Covey, Douglass claims that he "was a changed being." He had been "*nothing* before; I was A MAN NOW," he writes in *My Bondage and My Freedom*. Later, in his *Narrative of the Life . . .* , he looks back at the fight almost nostalgically, recognizing that it "revived within me a sense of my own manhood." Douglass reveled in his discovery. In a speech entitled "Self-Made Men," he placed himself in a long line of men who owe little or nothing to birth, relationship, friendly surroundings; to wealth inherited or to early approved means of education; who are what they are, without the aid of any of the favoring conditions by which other men usually rise in the world and achieve great results.[86]

For both black men and the northern upper classes, the deployment of the 54th Massachusetts regiment, the famed all-black Union army regiment under the command of Boston Brahmin Robert Gould Shaw, was heroically redemptive. Shaw represented the innate heroism of the aristocratic *noblesse oblige*, which assuaged a "deep seated anxiety among the members of the cultivated classes about their own ability . . . to meet some undefined challenge," according to the historian George Frederickson. And free black men also sensed this reclamation of manhood. "This was the biggest thing that ever happened in my life," said one former slave. "I feel like a man with a uniform on and a gun in my hand."[87]

At the war's end black manhood had been formally established via emancipation, though asserting their manhood would continue to be a central struggle for black American men throughout American history. Black poet Albery A. Whitman celebrated that moment in his epic poem *Not a Man, and Yet a Man* (1877):

> This was the day when Southern chivalry
> Beheld black manhood clothed in liberty,
> Step from the shadow of his centuries
> Of bondage, shake dejection from his eyes,
> And to the awful verge of valor rise.
> The day that heard the negro, scarred and maimed,
> Of sovereign battle's lips a man proclaimed.

"When God made me I wasn't much," said a former slave. "But I's a man now."[88]

In addition, northern and southern men questioned each other's manhood, both on the battlefield and in rhetorical skirmishes. The Civil War pitted Confederate chivalry against Self-Made Yankees and signaled the triumph of the urban industrial entrepreneur over the genteel southern patrician. Contemporaries saw northerners and southerners as distinctly different species, different expressions of manhood. Georgian William Lowndes Yancey explained in 1855 that

> The Creator has beautified the face of this Union with sectional features. Absorbing all minor subdivisions, He has made the North and the South; the one the region of frost, ribbed with ice and granite; the other baring its generous bosom to the sun and ever smiling under its influence. The climate, soil, and productions of these two grand divisions of the land, have made the character of their inhabitants. Those who occupy the one are cool, calculating, enterprising, selfish, and grasping; the inhabitants of the other are ardent, brave, and magnanimous, more disposed to give than to accumulate, to enjoy ease rather than to labor.[89]

Southern planters represented a "doomed aristocrat," free of any taint of "new wealth or old European corruption." "Each planter is in fact a Patriarch—his position compels him to be a ruler in his household," noted G. Memminger in a lecture in Georgia in 1852. As Daniel Huntley, a southerner with extensive experience in the North put it in 1860, some northerners believed

> that the citizens of our Southern States are so many Chevalier Bayards, *sans peur et sans reproche*; living upon their broad estates in all baronial splendor and hospitality, but, being nevertheless—like the slave-holding Catos and Brutuses of republican Rome, and the equally slave-holding Solons and Leonidases of democratic Greece—still true to the Constitution, the Commonwealth, and the Laws.

As southerners saw it, the legend of the Old South was a world where:

> gesturing gentlemen moved soft-spokenly against a background of rose gardens and dueling grounds, through always gallant deeds, and lovely ladies, in farthingales, never for a moment lost that exquisite remoteness which has been the dream of all men and the possession of none. Its social pattern was manorial, its civilization that of the Cavalier, its ruling class an aristocracy coextensive with the planter group.[90]

Southern conservative men offered a profound challenge to Self-Made Manhood, perhaps, as the historian Eugene Genovese wrote, "the only politically powerful challenge to liberal capitalism to emanate from within the United States." Only men like John C. Calhoun and the lawyer and journalist George Fitzhugh "questioned the assumptions of liberal society, denounced the hypocrisy and barbarism of the marketplace, and advanced a vision of an organic society and a collective community."[91] Southerners saw northerners as crassly commercial, avaricious, unscrupulous, aggressive, and mercenary; "Yankee" was a decidedly negative term, denoting unethical business practices and concern only for the bottom line.[92] Northern men had abandoned honor for money, morality for nobility, community values for self-improvement. Southerners saw themselves as a doomed aristocracy, falling in the wake of the triumph of the Self-Made Man, who, it turns out, was a northerner. Sarah Hale wrote:

> It is not the love of pleasure, the taste for amusements, that constitute the love of the world. It is the love of money, the craving desire to accumulate property, the entire devotion of the heart and soul, mind, might, and strength, to the one object of increasing or preserving an estate, that bows down to lofty intellect of men, and makes their sordid souls as grovelling as the appetites of the brutes that perish. This inordinate thirst for riches is the besetting sin of Americans' situation, institutions, education, all combine to foster it.[93]

For southerners the Civil War represented the last stand of the Genteel Patriarch, now cast as a Confederate cavalier.

The war's denouement offers a particularly interesting example of this vilification of southern manhood as feminized. At the end of the war, it was believed that Jefferson Davis, president of the Confederacy, sought to escape from his capital in Richmond disguised in a woman's clothing. Northern cartoonists and popular songwriters immediately set to work, producing dozens of illustrations and lampoons of Davis. One popular song, "Jeff in Petticoats," recounted the story like this:

> Jeff Davis was a warrior bold,
> And vowed the Yanks should fall;
> He jumped into his pantaloons
> And swore he'd rule them all.
> But when he saw the Yankees come
> To hang him if they could
> He jumped into a petticoat
> And started for the wood.

By lampooning "Jeffie" Davis, the "Belle of Richmond," as one cartoon had it , the victorious northerners could ridicule southern manhood, its feminized Genteel Patriarchal pretense, and the "Petticoat Confederacy" at the same time.[94]

The Union triumph ensured that American men would ground their identities in the shifting sands of the marketplace. It was a Pyrrhic victory. This intrafamilial squabble between brothers led to an unprecedented mobilization of resources and manpower, and left the nation drenched in the blood of those brothers—over 600,000 of them, with over $15 billion gone up in smoke.

What did it mean for American manhood? Instead of resolving the antebellum anxieties of American men, the Civil War only seemed to keep them momentarily at bay. "Instead of purging the nation once and for all of self-seeking materialism and corruption, the war opened the floodgates for the greatest tide of personal and political selfishness the nation had ever seen," writes the historian George Frederickson.[95] More than ever, self-making men would find the going tough; they still had something to prove.

For southern men, defeat meant a kind of gendered humiliation—the southern gentleman was discredited as a "real man." Southern soldiers returned to a barren and broken land of untilled farms, broken machinery, gutted and burned buildings, and a valueless currency. Schools, banks, and businesses were closed, unemployment was high, and inflation crippling. For the rest of the century and well into the twentieth century, southern manhood would continually attempt to assert itself against debilitating conditions, northern invaders (from carpetbaggers to civil rights workers), and newly freed blacks. The southern rebel, waving the Confederate flag at collegiate football games, is perhaps his most recent incarnation.

The forces transforming the meanings of manhood lay beyond class and region. The last decades of the century witnessed the unleashing of forces that had taken shape in the Civil War years, now given free reign to flourish. Three coincident processes shifted the terrain upon which manhood had been traditionally grounded—an unprecedented level of industrialization; the entry into the public sphere of large numbers of women, newly freed blacks, and immigrants; and the closing of the frontier—and the meanings of manhood were once again uncertain. The combined impact of these processes led many men to feel frightened, cut loose from the traditional moorings of their identities, adrift in some anomic sea. By the last decades of the century, manhood was widely perceived to be in crisis.

This fin de siécle crisis of masculinity was a popular theme for critics and experts.[96] All agreed that it was increasingly difficult to be a real man. Who was a man? What did manhood mean? How could one tell that he was a real man? As experts dedated, American men still struggled to carve out a world in which they could successfully experience their manhood. Such a large-scale loss of control as a civil war, the new political and social claims of women and freed blacks, and failed attempts at escape all signaled the inadequacy of the various strategies American men had developed upon which to ground a secure sense of themselves as men. Something had forever changed. Mark Twain captured this in his eloquent eulogy for lost manhood as Tom Sawyer and his band of young men searched for their lost boyhoods. "The boys dressed themselves, hid their accoutrements, and went off grieving that there were no outlaws anymore, and wondering what modern civilization could claim to have done to compensate them for their loss."[97]

PART TWO

The Unmaking of the Self-Made Man at the Turn of the Century

CHAPTER 3

Men at Work

Captains of Industry, White Collars, and the Faceless Crowd

A man's business makes him,—it hardens his muscle . . . wakes up his inventive genius, puts his wits to work, arouses ambition, makes him feel that he is a man, and must show himself a man by taking a man's part in life.
—Madison Peters *The Strenuous Career* (1908)

In this fiercely competitive age, when the law of the survival of the fittest acts with seemingly merciless rigor, no one can afford to be indifferent to the smallest detail of dress, or manner, or appearance, that will add to his chance of success.
—Orison Swett Marden *Power of Personality* (1899)[1]

The end of the Civil War ushered in an era of unprecedented economic transformation. Between 1870 and 1900 industrial output in the United States increased by 500 percent. The demands of war had been "technology forcing"; the growth of the steel industry, the laying of a railroad and transportation infrastructure, and the substitution of petroleum for whale oil were spurred by the war and in turn fueled this enormous growth.

Both agriculture and industry were jolted by what the historian Alan Trachtenberg calls "the incorporation of America." In 1800 over 80 percent of American men had been farmers; by 1880 only one-half the nation's labor force was in agriculture. Although four of every five American men were self-employed in the first decades of the century, by 1870 only one-third were self-employed.[2] Large factories, not small shops, now dominated the industrial landscape. On the eve of the Civil War, the McCormick factory employed three hundred to four hundred workers and was the largest factory of its kind in the world. In 1870 Best and Company (which eventually became the Pabst Brewing Company) was the nation's second largest brewery and employed no more than a hundred workers. Even in the early 1880s only the railroads and the New England textile mills employed more than a thousand workers. But within the decade all this had changed markedly. By 1884 Best Brewery had fourteen hundred workers, and by 1899 more than four thousand. Carnegie Steel employed more than four thousand at its Homestead works alone. Edison Electric, precursor to General Electric, employed one thousand workers in the early 1880s, two thousand four hundred by 1890, and over ten thousand by 1892.[3]

Most importantly, perhaps, America was increasingly an urban society. In 1830 about one American in fifteen lived in a city of over eight thousand. Between 1860 and 1890 the proportion of Americans living in municipalities with more than two thousand five hundred doubled to about 30 percent; by 1900 one-third of Americans lived in cities of at least eight thousand people; and by 1910 one-half lived there.[4] In short, the great new fact in American life was the crowd. And crowds created a new problem for self-made, self-controlled men.

For one thing, changes in scale, location, and level of technology transformed men's working lives. Workers increasingly seemed to lose control of their labor and the production process, which was transferred upward to a new class of managers and supervisors. New technological advances sped up production but invaded men's sphere of control. "Machinery has advanced, apprenticeship has declined," lamented a carpentry union official in 1886.[5] The application of military discipline to production, epitomized by Frederick Winslow Taylor's "scientific management" based on the "soldiering" of workers, led to standardization of tools and jobs, increased use of semiskilled and unskilled workers, and fragmentation of jobs into minute and discrete tasks. Taylor's famous time-and-motion studies, using time clocks, reduced jobs into their principal components to determine the minimum amount of time for each task. Workers were becoming human machines. The new managers were elated since these shifts, as two observers gloated in their report to the Ford Motor Company in 1915, tended to

> make the workmen absolutely docile. New regulations, important or trivial, are made almost daily; workmen are studied individually and changed from place to place with no cause assigned, as the bosses see fit, and not one word of protest is ever spoken, because every man knows the door to the street stands open for any man who objects in any way, shape, or manner to instant and unquestioning obedience to any directions whatsoever.

Workers, of course, were far less sanguine. "There are men standing over you all the time, and of course you are almost drove to it. You have got to keep pegging at it and working," commented one worker at the Watertown strike in 1911. Such conditions, he observed, were "getting down to slavery."[6]

Rapid industrialization, technological transformation, capital concentration, urbanization, and immigration—all of these created a new sense of an oppressively crowded, depersonalized, and often emasculated life. Manhood had meant autonomy and self-control, but now fewer and fewer American men owned their own shops, controlled their own labor, owned their own farms. More and more men were economically dependent, subject to the regime of the time clock. By the turn of the century, less-skilled workers began to out-number the highly skilled and more self-ruling members of the labor force. In these impersonal factories former apprentices and journeymen were placed alongside semiskilled workers, and by the end of the century, no one spoke of mechanics, artisans, journeymen, or master craftsmen anymore. Family farmers were, of course, far from extinct, but their decline was dramatic.

These changes had gender consequences. Samuel Eliot, writing in the *Journal of Social Science* in 1871, observed that to "put a man upon wages is to put him in the position of a dependent" and that the longer he holds that position, the more his capacities atrophy and "the less of a man . . . he becomes." Horace Greeley claimed that the separation of wage work from management reversed traditional craftsman-apprentice relations, further humiliating adult men. "I dislike to see men in advanced years working for salaries in places where perhaps they are ordered about by boys." And Anthony Ludovici observed the "steady degeneration of men" brought on by the "spectacle of men working at tasks which every woman knows she could easily undertake." "It was different then," one wage worker looked back nostalgically while testifying before a U.S. Senate panel on the relations between labor and capital in 1885. "A mechanic was considered somebody and he felt he was somebody." The era of the Heroic Artisan was over.[7]

The world of the merchant would likewise never be the same. "The one-man ownership stage of capitalism" was disappearing, noted a professor at the newly founded (1908) Harvard Business School. What was needed now was training in administrative organization, investment banking, large sales organization—thus the need for the nation's first business school.[8] The postbellum world, Henry Adams argued, was a crowded "banker's world," and one's place in it was both less valuable and more competitive than before. A man in this world knew what that meant:

> He was for sale, in the open marked. So were many of his friends. All the world knew it, and knew too that they were cheap; to be bought at the price of a mechanic. . . . The young man was required to impose himself, by the usual business methods, as a necessity on his elders, in order to compel them to buy him as an investment.[9]

And just as he himself became a marketable commodity, the pressure to make good increased markedly. "Life is a sharp conflict of man with man, a remorseless struggle for existence . . . in which the men of greatest skill and perseverance still defeat their fellows," wrote James Platt in 1889, in the seventy-fifth edition of his book *Business*. It is "your duty to get rich," Rev. Russell Conwell admonished his listeners. His best-seller *Acres of Diamonds*, was drafted as a sermon in 1870 and delivered over six thousand times, reaching an audience of millions. He preached that every man's worth was entirely up to him. "There is not a poor person in the United States who was not made so by his own shortcomings."[10]

The possibilities for self-making were also complicated by dramatic social changes. As new groups entered the public arena, the competitive field became increasingly crowded. In the last decades of the century, unprecedented numbers of immigrants and recently freed blacks poured into northern industrializing cities, demanding recognition and rights, challenging native-born white men for dominance on what had been their turf. The war's end catapulted the country into the position of world economic power, full of economic opportunity and a beacon of hope for the "huddled masses, yearning to breathe free," as Emma Lazarus's poem, inscribed on the Statue of Liberty, put it in 1886. This resulted in the most massive immigration of Europeans in U.S. history. In 1870, of the nearly one million people living in New York City, almost half were foreign-born (mostly Irish and German). More than a half-million immigrants came to New York City alone in 1902. In the 1870s 115,000 Chinese arrived on the West Coast, joined by another fifty thousand in 1881 and 1882, until Congress passed the Chinese Exclusion Act. Over 130,000 Japanese arrived in the United States between 1891 and 1907. A total of nine million immigrants came to the United States between 1880 and 1900, and fourteen million more arrived by 1914.[11]

Postbellum black migration also swelled northern and eastern cities and changed the complexion of America's urban population. Between 1870 and 1890, 156,000 came north, and another 185,000 came north in the 1890s. The Great Migration was to come later, after 1914, when the combination of wartime industrial opportunity in the North and Midwest and a devastating boll weevil attack on southern cotton in 1914 pressed many to seek their fortunes elsewhere. Between 1910 and 1920 the black population of the North increased from 850,000 to 1.4 million; it reached 2.3 million by 1930. In the first few decades of the twentieth century, the black population of Chicago and New York grew at approximately five times the rate of the white population: from 43,103 to 109,458 in Chicago and from 91,709 to 152,467 in New York City, a 66 percent increase between 1910 and 1920. In the next decade the black population grew another 115 percent to 327,706, while the white population grew 20 percent.[12]

Black men saw their new lives in terms of economic opportunity and survival, and also in gender terms, as they escaped the emasculation of Jim Crow laws, first enacted in the 1880s. And they escaped the literal emasculation of despicably gendered torture, in which many victims of lynching were first castrated. Between 1900 and 1917 more than eleven hundred black men were lynched in the South. Escape from such conditions meant the opportunity to be a real man as well as a free man. One man commented that he left because he wanted to "go anywhere you want to go . . . [and you] don't have to look up to the white man, get off the street for him, and go to the buzzard roost at shows." Another told a journalist, "I want to be a free man, come when I please, and nobody say nothing to me, nor order me around." And still another put it most simply and eloquently; in the North, he said, "a man could feel more like a man."[13]

It was hard enough that America was more urban, more heavily populated, more diverse, and more bureaucratized at work. The additional postbellum surge of women into the public arena was almost too much to bear. The first wave of the women's movement really picked up momentum after the Civil War, with concurrent campaigns for entry into the workplace, university, and voting booth. The opening of several women's colleges, notably Vassar (1865), Wellesley (1872), Bryn Mawr (1885), Smith (1875), and Mount Holyoke (1837), provided new opportunities for women's education.[14] In 1870, 21 percent of all enrolled college students were women. By 1890, 36 percent were women; by 1920 the number was over 47 percent, and women received one-third of all graduate degrees.[15] The passage of the Morrill Act in 1862 established many public universities as coeducational institutions, prompting new political and ideological struggles about the virtues and vices of coeducation.

Women were also entering the workforce. Between 1870 and 1900 the female percentage of the workforce edged up from 16 percent to 20 percent (1.8 million women in 1870, 5.3 million in 1900). Ten years later one-fourth of all workers were women; by 1920 the percentage was closer to 40 percent, and by 1930, nearly 50 percent of the workforce. The number of married white women in the labor force rose from about 4 percent in 1900 to about 10 percent by the end of the 1920s.[16] In the expanding world of white-collar offices, this increase was startling and rapid. In 1870 women made up 2.5 percent of the clerical labor force and 5 percent of all stenographers and typists. By 1930 women accounted for 52.5 percent of the total clerical workforce and 96 percent of all stenographers and typists. Other working women campaigned for entry into the growing labor unions and proved dedicated and fierce unionists, leading the famous strikes in Paterson and Lawrence; one Philadelphia newspaper warned that the "governor may have to call out the militia to prevent a gynecocracy."[17]

Men no longer worried only about controlling their own passions; now they were fretting that the new crowds surrounding them would put them in a straitjacket. And sadly, at least to many of them, escape was increasingly difficult. For two centuries the ever-receding frontier had been a place where men could achieve their manhood or re-prove it after failure. The frontier had offered "perennial rebirth" to both men and nation, according to Frederick Jackson Turner. In this midwestern-educated Harvard professor the frontier found its historian and its most enthusiastic booster. Turner "discovered" the frontier's significance in American history at the moment of its disappearance, the turn of the century.[18]

Turner's original thesis was actually quite progressive, articulated as a corrective to his mentor Herbert Baxter Adams's "germ theory," which explained American culture by reference to its Germanic and Anglo-Saxon antecedents, or "germs." According to Turner, too much attention had been paid to European antecedents, and too little to the distinctive shaping influence of the American continent itself. Echoing Ralph Waldo Emerson's arguments in *Nature* (1836), Turner claimed that it was the frontier that had provided American democracy's literal grounding, liberating men from European influence, and imbued a "forest philosophy" that was anti-intellectual, anticonsumerist, and anti–European refinement.[19]

The late nineteenth century was full of commentary on how the frontier made men. If the workplace could not inspire the "manly independence" of the earlier Heroic Artisan, escape to the primitive conditions of existence on the frontier might do the trick. In a magazine essay, General Horace Porter invited his audience to compare two men:

> Let one remain in a quiet city, playing the milksop . . . leading to an unambitious namby-pamby life, . . . while the other goes out on the frontier, runs his chance in encounters with wild animals, finds that to make his way he must take his life in his hands, and assert his rights, if necessary with deadly weapons. . . .

Porter's conclusion was unavoidable. He "will become the superior of the lad who has remained at home." "The wilderness will take hold of you," added George Evans. "It will give you good red blood; it will turn you from a weakling into a man."[20]

Commentators also recognized that the frontier provided a cultural safety valve, siphoning off potentially rebellious young men whose economic futures were clouded or stymied. Geographic mobility might compensate for failed social mobility—if one couldn't rise in the economic system, one could at least head west. "For more than a half century, the outlet toward the free lands of the West has been the escape valve of social discontent in the great cities of America," wrote Hamlin Garland, in 1892. "Whenever the conditions of his native place pressed too hard on him, the artisan or the farmer has turned his face toward the prairies and forests of the West."[21]

The same commentators who were championing the virtues of the frontier were also lamenting its passing. Francis Parkman, who had earlier celebrated frontier manhood, now wrote mournfully:

> The buffalo is gone, and of all his millions nothing is left but bones. Tame cattle and fences of barbed wire have supplanted his vast herds and boundless grazing grounds. The wild Indian is turned into an ugly caricature of his conqueror; and that which made him

romantic, terrible, and hateful is in large measure scourged out of him. The slow cavalcade of horsemen armed to the teeth have disappeared before parlor cars and the effeminate comforts of modern travel.[22]

An article in the *North American Review* in 1906 noted that

the old cabins and dugouts are replaced by modern dwellings. The great ranges are fast passing into orderly farms, where cultivated crops take the place of wild grasses. Steadily is man's rational selection directing the selection of nature. Even the cowboy, the essential creation of Western conditions, is rapidly passing away. Like the buffalo, he has had his place in the drama of civilization. The Indian of the plain must yield to civilization or pass away. Custer, Cody, Bridger, and Carson did their work and passed on. Pioneers of the old school are giving place to a young and vigorous group of men of intellect, will and ceaseless activity, who are turning the light of scientific discovery on plain and mountain.[23]

The Self-Made Man had tamed the wilderness, and so it could no longer be relied upon to make him wild.

Exclusion as Masculine Retreat

In the rush of the new at the turn of the century, the old way of life was passing quickly from view—and with it the possibilities to test and prove manhood in the time-honored ways that American men had historically used. But that didn't stop them from trying. The turn-of-the-century city was overcrowded and bustling, and men were overwhelmed by the changes. After all, aristocratic honor was unreachable, and moral self-control didn't help explain a gilded age in which some men's success was so visibly the result of other skills, like self-promotion, avarice, or outright theft. And yet sheer economic worth neither seemed very scientific nor very fair—most Americans ranked well below the captains of industry.

For many men, resistance meant retreat to a bygone era. To some, the restorative tonic would be found in a return to earlier historical notions of masculine virtue. To others, that era could only be restored by stemming what one writer called "the rising tide of color." To that writer, it meant both the masses of immigrants flooding America's cities and the streams of blacks migrating north at the same time. But to many men, that tide that threatened to wash over American manhood and dash their hopes for self-making included other groups as well, among them women and homosexuals.

Racism, antifeminism, and nativism fed off these fears, as though by excluding the "others," gender identity could be preserved. American manhood had earlier been grounded upon the exclusion of blacks and women, the non-native-born (immigrants) and the genuinely native-born (Indians), each on the premise that they weren't "real" Americans and couldn't, by definition, be real men. The ideas of Social Darwinism provided the perfect ideological justification for such exclusion. No sooner had Darwin's *Origin of the Species* been published in 1859 than social thinkers on both sides of the Atlantic attempted to apply his theories of natural selection and the survival of the fittest to human societies— something Darwin himself had been hesitant to do. Herbert Spencer in England and Yale's William Graham Sumner in the United States developed Social Darwinism as a doctrine that explained social inequality as evidence of natural superiority. "Let it be understood that we cannot go out of this alternative," wrote Sumner, "liberty, inequality, survival of the fittest; non-liberty, equality, survival of the unfittest. The former carries society forward and favors all its best members; the latter carries society downwards and favors all its worst members."[24]

It has often been noted that such principles were applied to the racial and ethnic diversity of the crowded nation. What has been ignored is how they were also linked to gender, to the greater or lesser degrees of manhood among different peoples. For example, opposing the Emancipation Proclamation in 1862, Ohio Congressman Samuel Sullivan Cox argued:

> Our statistician boasts that Ohio has men of greater height . . . than England, Belgium or Scotland, and in breadth of chest nearly equal to that of Scotland, and above all others. I do not offer myself as a specimen [laughter]. But how long before the manly, warlike people of Ohio of fair hair and blue eyes, in a large preponderance, would become, in spite of Bibles and morals, degenerate under the wholesale emancipation and immigration [of black slaves]?

Francis Parkman believed that white Anglo-Saxons were "peculiarly masculine," while in *Democracy and the Overman* (1910) Charles Zueblin fused Social Darwinism and a bastardized Nietzschean evocation of the Overman when he argued that the survival of the fittest resulted in the "raw, sturdy Saxon of primitive England." The danger would be to dilute it by diffusion to those below.[25]

Survival of the most manly was also used against blacks. Georges Clemenceau, the future French prime minister, commented on a visit to the United States in 1869 that blacks "must gird up their loins and struggle for their existence, in Darwin's phrase, for their physical as well as their moral existence. In a word, they must become men."[26] But Social Darwinian hierarchies implied that some groups were more manly than others. Self-Made Men were supposed to be "frugal and productive"; it was argued that black men represented "laziness and license."[27]

Intermarriage was particularly terrifying because it would dilute the purity of the race and, hence, pure manhood. Lathrop Stoddard's *The Rising Tide of Color* (1920), Homer Lea's *The Day of the Saxon* (1912), and Madison Grant's *The Passing of the Great Race* (1916) bordered on hysteria. "The whole white race is exposed . . . to the possibility of social sterilization and final replacement or absorption by the teeming colored races," which would be an "unspeakable catastrophe," wrote Stoddard. "The white man is being rapidly bred out by negroes," Grant echoed, resulting in an "ever thinning veneer of white culture." Racial mixing leads to "disintegration and dissolution," wrote Lea, which will result in an "apocalypse of the white man's ignorance." Grant's terrors were grounded in racialist ideas that "the cross between a white man and a Negro is a Negro" and between a "European and a Jew is a Jew."[28] Here, too, groupthink was a form of gender-think.

Grant's anti-Semitism added a new group to the ranks of the less manly. The Jew was effeminate, bookish, and conniving; he got his way insidiously by passing himself off as a real man, and thereby sabotaging the purity of the race. And what was this pure race? The men "of the old stock" comprised a "race of soldiers, sailors, adventurers and explorers, but above all, of rulers, organizers, and aristocrats." Perhaps, if Grant had been less focused on genetics, he would not have feared that urbane, bookish Jews could have any impact on those men of action. But the new Darwinian world was one of racial bloodlines, not behavior.

There were two ways in which the new pseudoscientific doctrines of racial superiority were cloaked as comparative levels of masculinity. Many believed that men were at a higher stage of Darwinian evolution than women. Thus, one common strategy was to link the men of other races to women and children, to make them Darwinian throwbacks, lower down the evolutionary ladder from white Anglo-Saxon or Teutonic men. The Negro was "next below man in the zoological scale," noted one St. Louis physician in 1882. One anatomist argued that the adult Negro men are intellectually the equals of "the child, the female and the senile white."[29] One method to demonstrate innate intelligence was the weighing of brains, which became a booming business during the 1880s and 1890s. One anatomist "proved" conclusively that black men "have a brain scarcely heavier than that of white women"; while other scientists compared men's and women's brains to demonstrate that in men's heavier brain weight lay the justification for exclusion of women from education and voting.[30]

The perceived—or, just as frequently, projected—effeminacy of nonwhite men was a standard racialist theme. Ignatius Donnelly railed, in his novel *Caesar's Column* (1890), against those "wretched yellow under-fed coolies, with women's garments over their effeminate limbs, [who] will not have the courage or the desire or the capacity to make soldiers and defend their oppressors." Samuel Gompers had contempt for the Chinese because they would "allow themselves to be barbarously tyrannized over in their own country," without the gumption to fight back. Harvard zoologist Louis Agassiz was alarmed at the possibility that "the manly populations" descended from Nordic stock would be replaced by the "effeminate progeny of mixed races, half Indian, half Negro, sprinkled with white blood." Mexican acquiescence to U.S. domination was attributed to Mexicans' lack of "all the manlier virtues," which made them "perfectly accustomed to being conquered," wrote an editor of the *New York Sun*.[31]

Yet there was a noteworthy confusion in this group assignment of virtue, a confusion that has remained to this day. Black men and immigrants were seen simultaneously as less manly than native-born whites and as *more* manly, especially as more sexually voracious and potent. Some Social Darwinists who claimed that blacks and immigrants were lower on the evolutionary scale placed them alongside primitive beasts rather than women and children. And these beasts sounded a lot like the hypermasculine men of the old frontier. The Chinese were depicted as "invariably degenerate," a "savage, vicious, idol-worshiping and barbarous race" against which "every man in America should be at work." Dr. William English noted that blacks' instinctual composition was toward "bestiality and gratification" and the "innate tendency to sex appetite."[32] Immigration, one advice book warned, "tends to lower the standards of morality," because

> year after year Europe pours into the United States multitudes of degenerate human beings [including Italians, Germans, Huns, Poles, Frenchmen, and Austrians] who, incited by the freedom of American institutions, and without the deterrent fear of summary punishment, immediately give free reign to their atavistic imaginations, and whenever they think that the favorable moment has arrived, plunge into anarchy and lawlessness.[33]

One critic wanted it both ways, drawing on images of both hyper-masculinity and effeminacy when he labeled the Chinese "a barbarous race, devoid of energy."[34]

Two groups of men were singled out as especially threatening. "Indians," of course, had to be continually pushed aside in the headlong scramble toward the receding frontier. In the last decades of the nineteenth century, Native-American life was completely and finally transformed. The Homestead Act (1862) brought large numbers of settlers to claim free land, while the completion of the railroads and the annihilation of the great buffalo herds obliterated the traditional Native-American economy. Through the 1870s tribes were forcibly consolidated, removed, and destroyed, acts justified because they were no longer fierce men, men whose virility could rival that of the settlers, but were now, in the words of one editorialist in the *New York Daily Graphic*, "a degraded relic of a decayed race." It was unclear, the writer continued,

> whether he is worth civilizing, even if he is capable of civilization. . . . Were the money and effort wasted in trying to civilize the Indians wisely expended in reclaiming and educating the savages in our cities the world would be vastly better off in the end. The globe is none too large for the civilized races to occupy, and all others are doomed by a law that is irrevocable and that it is folly to resist.

Now that the "Indian" had been stripped of his dignity and manhood, he was on his own.[35]

For themselves, Native Americans developed new, symbolic ways to ease the pain of emasculation at the hand of the white man. Increasing alcoholism and the growth of the peyote cult provided a kind of temporary anesthesia for these men, and the Ghost Dance and Sun Dance religions allowed hope and enthusiasm, especially the possibility of spiritual transcendence of depraved temporal life. One ritual in the Sun Dance religion (popularized in the 1970s movie *A Man Called Horse*) is particularly striking in its efforts to retrieve a sense of power and virility. Sun Dance festivals consisted of days of fasting and dancing after which rituals of self-mutilation by the men would begin. Warriors would slice open the skin on their chests, pass rawhide skewers through these cuts, and then tie the rawhide to poles. At a signal, they would step back forcefully from the poles until the skewers ripped through their skin. These rituals of individual heroism—the ability to withstand self-initiated torture in the hope of experiencing some form of transcendence—were all that was left for these men who had been stripped of the traditional expressions of their manhood by white society.

Such rituals seemed to confirm the Darwinists' notions that nonwhite men were primitive beasts. Black men, too, were a screen against which white men projected their own fears of emasculation. In the South, recall, military defeat was experienced as the emasculation of southern white manhood, the chivalrous and gallant southern cavalier, although those ideals of honor continued to dominate. The organization of the Ku Klux Klan and other fraternal orders, the founding of and expansion of military schools designed to produce "officers and gentlemen," and a revival of dueling to preserve personal honor all temporarily gave southern white men a respite from this perceived assault on their manhood.

The Klan's goal was the reclamation of southern manhood, whose principles included "all that is chivalric in conduct, noble in sentiment, generous in manhood, and patriotic in purpose" and whose purpose, according to the *Prescript of the Order of the Ku Klux Klan* (1868), was

> to protect the weak, the innocent, and the defenseless, from the indignities, wrongs and
> outrages of the lawless, the violent and the brutal; to relieve the injured and oppressed;
> to succor the suffering and unfortunate, and especially the widows and orphans of Con-
> federate soldiers.[36]

Klan rhetoric was saturated with images of heroic and chivalrous southern manhood.
Members were required to demonstrate "manly" character and courage, and initiation
rituals were punctuated by prayers that "God, give us Men!"[37] Playing on traditional
images of the emasculated southern gentleman and his fears of rapacious blacks and
conniving northern reformers, the Klan mobilized southern white men into its "invisible
empire" for many decades. At its peak, in 1926, the Klan numbered over five million
members, and with other groups, like the American Protective Association and the
American Super-Race Foundation, it was memorialized in, among others, Thomas
Dixon's novel *The Clansman* (1905) and the film based on it, D. W. Griffiths's *Birth of a
Nation* (1915).

The new and powerful fear of the black rapist revealed more about southern white
men's fears of lost manhood than about any propensity on the part of black men. George
Lydston's 1904 study of vice and crime attributed the frequency of rape in the South to the
"primitive impulses of the black race," for which he proposed what was conceived of as a
"progressive" solution: castration—"the total ablation of the sexual organs." The criminal
would be "incapacitated," prevented from repeating the crime or perpetuating his kind, as
well as becoming a walking deterrent to other would-be rapists. Others' solutions were
more conventional, simply advocating lynching and murder.[38]

Social Darwinists also lent new force to biological arguments about the differences
between women and men. They had plenty of opportunities to make their case in reaction
to the first wave of feminism, from Seneca Falls in 1848 to the ratification of woman
suffrage in 1920. In 1880 one speaker claimed:

> I am opposed to woman's sufferage [*sic*] on account of the burden it will place on her. Her
> delicate nature has already enough to drag it down. Her slender frame, naturally weakened
> by the constant strain attendant upon her nature is too often racked by the diseases that
> are caused by a too severe tax upon her mind. The presence of passion, love, ambition
> is all too potent for her enfeebled constitution and wrecked health and early death are all
> too common.[39]

Here was a heightened reliance on biological difference, complete with disease and fears
of extinction. Women should not be deprived of the vote, opponents argued, as much as
exempted from it. Antisuffrage organizations abounded, such as the national Man Suffrage
Association and state-level associations.

Antifeminists argued that college-educated women had already lost their delicate
feminine virtue. The publication of Edward Clarke's *Sex in Education* in 1873 galvanized
the opposition to higher education for women. Clarke rehearsed biological arguments
in the guise of protecting women from the injurious effects of education beyond their
biological capacities. The result of college education, Clarke argued, was that women were
losing their ability to breed, developing "monstrous brains and puny bodies" with "flowing
brains and constipated bowels." Wombs and brains seemed in direct competition; as

women's brains grew heavier and larger due to education, their wombs would atrophy and they would cease to reproduce.[40]

All participation in the public sphere would harm women by "masculinizing" them so that women would "feebly imitate" men in their social clubs, on the streets, in the school-rooms, and in the workplace. "The number of women in business who lose their gentleness and womanliness is far greater than those who retain what, after all, are woman's best and chief qualities," warned Edward Bok, editor of the *Ladies' Home Journal* in 1893.[41] Another writer claimed that women's independence would make men lose interest in them. "A state of independence always begets more or less of jealous rivalry and hostility. A man loves his children because they are weak, help-less, and dependent. He loves his wife for similar reasons. When his children grow up and assert their independence, he is apt to transfer his affection to his grand-children. He ceases to love his wife when she becomes masculine or rebellious."[42]

What men seemed to fear at least as much was that "the newly civilized worker had lost his manhood in the gendered office." And many men believed that they could retrieve it only by pushing women back out of the labor force, that "the sense of subordination and vulnerability endemic to corporate work could only be overcome by reasserting their position relative to women—by attempting to reinforce a traditional gender hierarchy by separating themselves from women and behaviors ascribed to women."[43] Thus, it appears that other sentiments motivated such apparent concern for women's protection. For one thing, manhood was seen as noble sacrifice. Work is unpleasant, painful, difficult, and cruel—a dirty job that someone has to do. Women should be placed on a pedestal glorifying feminine delicacy, for which men must sacrifice themselves. This was a new twist on the definition of manhood: It was no picnic of power and privilege; it was dirty and demanding, and men went through it because they loved their wives and children.

However defensive such arguments were, it was through them that masculinity became an "issue." Men wanted to be taken into consideration *as men*. "We hear so much about the rights of women, that just for the sake of variety it ought not to be displeasing to hear a little something about the rights of men," suggested Harry Thurston Peck in 1899. And the editor of *Harper's* magazine added that, given all the women's magazines "devoted to the aspirations and the wants of women alone," it was time to consider a Men's Journal, "which should try to keep his head above water in the struggle for social supremacy."[44]

That struggle was increasingly difficult as so many newcomers demanded recognition. As Sojourner Truth had earlier demanded inclusion into the women's struggle with the ringing cry of "Ain't I a Woman," a growing chorus of black and immigrant men asked angrily if they, too, weren't men. One of the more revealing moments of this struggle came in 1893 at Chicago's Columbian Exposition. The organizers of the exposition planned a glorious White City to celebrate the progress of civilization and promoted a "vision of Strong Manhood and Perfection of Society." Outside the White City, down the midway, exposition organizers placed exhibits of other cultures with "authentic" reproductions of Egyptian, Dahoman, and Turkish villages—ostensibly to demonstrate how far modern white American civilization had come. These other races were uncivilized and "unmanly" compared with the White City, and the layout allowed visitors, as the *Chicago Tribune* enthused, to trace "humanity in its highest phases down almost to its animalistic origins." Black reformers Ida Wells and Frederick Douglass demanded that black Americans be included in the White City, instead of on the midway. "We are men and our aim is perfect manhood, to be men among men," wrote Douglass in a flyer handed to exposition atten-dees. The organizers refused, and black men thus remained excluded from full manhood, both in reality and in the nation's representation of itself to itself.[45]

The emergence of another group of men—homosexuals—onto the public stage at the turn of the century further fueled men's anxieties. A visible gay subculture had already emerged in the nation's cities as early as the 1850s; by the end of the century, gay men had "resorts in every large city," places "where the 'queens' hung out." George Beard had noted "great numbers" of gay men in New York City in 1884; by 1911 the Chicago Vice Commission observed "whole colonies" of them.[46] In his impressive study *Gay New York*, historian George Chauncey described "an organized, multilayered, and self-conscious gay subculture, with its own meeting places, language, folklore and moral codes." At the turn of the twentieth century, he writes:

> an extensive gay world took shape in the streets, cafeterias, saloons, and apartments of New York, and gay men played an integral role in the social life of certain neighborhoods. Fairies drank with sailors and other workingmen at waterfront dives and entertained them at Bowery resorts; "noted faggots" mixed with other patrons at Harlem's rent parties and basement cabarets; and lesbians ran speakeasies where Greenwich Village Bohemians—straight and queer alike—gathered to read their verse.[47]

Gay men were defined almost entirely in terms of their masculinity, or rather, in terms of its absence. Homosexuality involved a "comprehensive gender role inversion (or reversal)," writes Chauncey. These men—called "fairies" or "queers" at that time—"act effeminately; most of them are painted and powdered . . . [and] ape the female character," noted one police investigator in 1899. Psychiatrists routinely diagnosed men as homosex-ual if they exhibited traits that were seen as less than manly—an "abnormal dread of dust and dirt," for example, or a finicky attention to clothing and personal appearance. On the streets, too, gay men's "irrepressible desire to act the part of the opposite sex" resulted in "effeminacy of voice, dress, and manner"; they could thus be easily spotted by their imitation of women. "He acted sort of peculiar, walking around with his hands on his hips," noted one sailor at a criminal trial. "His manner was not masculine." One fairy con-fessed that he had "never been one who felt like taking a man's place among men."[48]

Chauncey argues that such flagrant flouting of traditional masculinity came less from some internal drive to express innate effeminacy; gay effeminacy was more a behavioral strategy to signal other homosexual men. "Effeminacy was one of the few sure means they had to identify themselves to others," he writes. Thus, it may have been that a man "chose to be effeminate precisely because he wanted to identify himself to other men."[49] Ironically, such overt repudiation of traditional masculine behaviors permitted a more casual relationship between many heterosexual and homosexual men at the turn of the century. Gay male effeminacy simultaneously exaggerated the differences between them-selves and "normals" and between women and men and thus "served to confirm rather than threaten the masculinity of other men."[50] For many straight men, then, homosexuality did not threaten their masculinity but reinforced it.

Such casual coexistence was relatively short-lived. As the nature of work changed and as women, immigrants, and black men "invaded" men's spheres, masculinity was experienced as increasingly difficult to prove. Sexuality emerged as a central element of

American manhood. "Middle class men increasingly conceived of their sexuality—their heterosexuality, or exclusive desire for women—as one of the hallmarks of a real man," writes Chauncey. "It was as if they had decided that no matter how much their gender comportment might be challenged as unmanly, they were normal men because they were heterosexual." Homosexuality and effeminacy were thus added to the repertoire of men's anxieties. Terms like "pussyfoot" and "sissy" became increasingly prominent, and negative. "Sissy," for example, had originally been coined in the 1840s as an affectionate term for "sister." By the 1880s the term had become a derisive description for spineless boys and men and by 1900 had become clearly associated with effeminacy, cowardice, and lack of aggression. Heterosexual men had begun to define themselves in opposition to all that was soft and womanlike.[51]

With such definitions came campaigns of exclusion, concerted attacks on homosexuals for gender deviance. Health reformer Bernarr Macfadden, for example, praised men who practiced turn-of-the-century gay-bashing; in 1904 he denounced "the shoals of painted, perfumed, Kohl-eyed, lisping, mincing youths that at night swarm on Broadway in the Tenderloin section, or haunt the parks and 5th Avenue, ogling every man that passes and—it is pleasant to relate—occasionally getting a sound thrashing or an emphatic kicking."[52] Even though the larger social debates about homosexuality were still some decades away, the association between masculinity and heterosexuality was now firmly embedded in public perception. "If a man was walking around and did not act real masculine, I would think he was a cocksucker," observed a sailor who was testifying in a criminal trial. Such an observation illustrates my central themes about American manhood at the turn of the twentieth century: that masculinity was increasingly an act, a form of public display; that men felt themselves on display at virtually all times; and that the intensity of the need for such display was increasing. To be considered a real man, one had better make sure to always be walking around and acting "real masculine."

The Problem of Business Civilization

The reassertion of this version of masculinity, whether through Social Darwinism or some other ideology, was a conservative reaction against real and perceived threats to increasingly anxious Self-Made Men, as if pushing others out could reassure those who were left that they were, in fact, real men. There were other responses as well. Former Heroic Artisans asserted manly pride in workmanship as they united to fight against becoming faceless workers. And they were backed by liberal theorists who celebrated both the virility and the dignity of craftsmanship. Others sought to accommodate anxious men to the crowd, and thereby both soothe their insecurities and redefine manhood away from marketplace success.

Of course, some men didn't buy the idea of Self-Made Masculinity at all and simply dropped out the struggle, resigned to workplace failure. For example, new social problems emerged in decaying urban neighborhoods—problems such as chronic alcoholism among the "bums" who lived on Seattle's Skid Row or New York's Bowery. Here were men who had given up in their work or family lives, who were now creating a community of failed men. Itinerant hobos who rode the rails and lived by the sides of the tracks were not only escaping economic dislocation but running away from Self-Made Manhood, away from the settled responsibility of a boring, unpleasant job that such a gender ideal seemed to require. There was also a peculiar solace among them, a collective nursing of wounds, as if having been declared failures as men had suddenly freed these men from having to maintain the social and physical distance and the emotional neutrality that masculinity required. On the margins, on the skids, men held one another, wept openly, and shared their momentary pleasures and their constant despair. Out of the rat race, they had no one to turn to but themselves.[53]

Other men were ambivalent about the entire project of being Self-Made Men. Why should manhood require having power over other men and over women? And if so many men were casualties of these relentless efforts to prove their manhood in the marketplace, then perhaps something was wrong with American culture itself. Throughout the nineteenth century there were men who were less sanguine about the virilizing effects of the market and urged a redefinition of success so that it would be possible for ordinary men to grasp. Henry Ward Beecher's popular *Twelve Lectures to Young Men* (1888) argued that industry, not wealth, was the real key to manhood, that one should strive for "the applause of conscience, the self-respect of pride, the consciousness of independence, the manly joy of usefulness, the consent of every faculty of the mind to one's occupation"—these were the emotions that should animate men. The blind pursuit of money was a blind alley. Another advice book counseled that "money getting under competitive conditions is by no means the indispensable motive power that impels men to their best activity," while another observed that "no matter how much a man has, when he comes to a point where he stops getting richer, he is scared."[54]

In place of the scramble for wealth, men were advised to return to more stately and Protestant virtues, such as industry, usefulness, and thrift; to substitute virtues of personality for success; and do a good job. "Manhood is greater than wealth, grander than fame," wrote Orison Swett Marden. His *Pushing to the Front* (1894) was a collection of homey platitudes, designed to help men who feel like failures feel like successes by returning to the antebellum value of character. (It went through twelve editions in its first year of publication alone.) His other books—including *Success* (1897), *The Secrets of Achievement* (1898), *Character, the Greatest Thing in the World* (1899), *The Power of Personality* (1899), *The Young Man Entering Business* (1903), *He Who Can Thinks He Can* (1908), and *How to Get What You Want* (1917)—made Marden perhaps the era's most successful self-help writer.[55]

Marden himself was a self-made success story. He was originally invited to Harvard to establish a dining service on campus and later admitted to the college. After the enormous success of *Pushing to the Front*, he founded a magazine, *Success*, in which he preached a gospel of hard work, dedication, and relentless sublimation. Men, he argued in *The Optimistic Life* (1907), had to be healthy and strong and develop "manly qualities" such as vigor, energy, and enthusiasm. But ultimately, Marden preached a gospel of individual achievement through acceptance of limited possibilities. It was far better to know one's place, he counseled, to be the "Napoleon of bootblacks, the Alexander the Great of chimney sweeps," and do a great job there. "It matters not whether the boy is born in a log cabin or in a mansion; if he is dominated by resolute purpose and upholds himself, neither men nor demons can keep him down." Every business opportunity, win or lose, was an opportunity "to be polite . . . to be manly . . . to be honest . . . to make friends."[56] Standing out was a matter of fitting in.

Middle-class men found the going tough; managers and white-collar salaried employees were particularly hard hit by these newly gendered anxieties. For them the question was how to participate in the business world, find their rung upon the ladder, and still maintain a sense of their manhood. One writer defined a government clerk in 1873 as someone who "has no independence while in office, no manhood . . . he must openly avow his implicit faith in all his superiors, on pain of dismissal, and must cringe and fawn upon them." By 1910 about 20 percent of the adult male population was working in such white-collar jobs in large companies, banks, and retail firms. But they remained dependent upon the corporation as paternal authority, and just as much in need of manly validation.[57]

With office work increasingly feminized, aspiring white-collar men were counseled to enter the newly expanding field of sales. Salesmen were heralded as the self-made men of the new century. Sales reinforced "independence and individuality," wrote one salesman. Life insurance was described as a "manly calling." The Equitable Company recruited would-be salesmen to a world in which their possibilities for success were "almost limitless," in which an ambitious young man could "reach the top if he have but the requisite ability and energy." America became "a nation of salesmen," and what those salesmen sold was themselves, their winning personalities, their smiles and shoeshines.[58]

Two of the more prescient observers of these changes in American business life were the stolid German economist and sociologist Max Weber, and Thorstein Veblen, an irascible economist from the midwestern American heartland. Weber's observations on American society at the turn of the century offer a chilling portrait of men's psyches. In *The Protestant Ethic and the Spirit of Capitalism*, written in 1902 after a visit to the United States, Weber looked deeply into the heart of modern society and into the anxious soul of modern American manhood. Like Tocqueville seventy years earlier, Weber saw the Americans' frantic scramble for wealth as a kind of proof of salvation, an insatiable quest that both animated American life and left individual Americans feeling bewildered and trapped. One would have thought that the material wealth produced by advanced capitalist economic organization would have brought great happiness. But the most successful, he observed, "were characterized by the exact opposite of the joy of living." Borrowing heavily from Benjamin Franklin's epigrams, Weber decried the perversion of the Protestant work ethic into "the earning of more and more money, combined with the strict avoidance of all spontaneous enjoyment of life," so that a man would be "dominated by the making of money, by acquisition as the ultimate purpose of his life."[59]

This corruption of the work ethic traps us in an "iron cage." Devoid of meaning, bereft of hope, we scurry about in "economic compulsion," unable to make sense of the world. We become, Weber argues, "specialists without spirit, sensualists without heart"—a condemnation of characterological emptiness that rings as true today as at the beginning of the century. Thus, "the pursuit of wealth, stripped of its religious and ethical meaning, tends to become associated with purely mundane passions, which often actually give it the character of sport." Or, in the words of a bumper sticker from the Reagan era: He who has the most toys when he dies, wins.[60]

The grandsons of those antebellum Self-Made Men now found themselves trapped in that iron cage. The very strategies they had used to resolve the earlier identity crisis now led them to scramble relentlessly to grasp that elusive ideal. To Veblen this signaled an endless cycle of "conspicuous consumption"—the frenzied and competitive consumption of expensive items that demonstrate high status. His controversial book *The Theory of the Leisure Class* (1899) revealed the shift—from the realm of production to the realm of consumption—of the arena in which men proved their worth. Men consume conspicuously to demonstrate "that the wearer can afford to consume freely and uneconomically," that money is no object. Beneath his satiric view of consumerist culture lay a bitter antipathy to parasitic upper-class men. Veblen claimed that traditional ideals of producerism, ideals of thrift and hard work and dedication that had earlier animated the Heroic Artisan, were now in too short supply. American manhood required a return to artisanal values of republican virtue, simplicity, and hard work.[61]

For others, though, it was the achievement of wealth and success by American men that was proving to be their undoing, producing the very effeminacy that was eroding manhood. "No nation becomes rich and prosperous without becoming also luxurious and debilitated," noted Edward Hitchcock, a professor at Amherst College. In *Democratic Vistas* (1876) Walt Whitman warned against "extreme business energy" leading to an "almost maniacal appetite for wealth." Luxury and wealth "produces national effeminacy and effeteness," warned Homer Lea, which produces "whole tribes of theorists, feminists," and other examples of "opulent decadence."[62] In an astonishing inversion of his own position, Andrew Carnegie joined the chorus of those who warned that wealth leads to feminization; in a 1902 article in *Success* magazine, he scorned the genteel aristocrat as an object of pity:

> The youth who is reared in a luxurious home, who, from the moment of his birth is waited on by an army of servants, pampered and indulged by overfond parents, and deprived of every incentive . . . is more to be pitied than the poorest, most humbly born boy or girl in the land. Unless he is gifted with an unusual mind, he is in danger of becoming a degenerate, a parasite, a creature who lives on the labor of others, whose powers ultimately atrophy from disuse.[63]

And Dr. James Weir warned that such luxury leaves the door open for the less highly evolved working class. "The rich become effeminate, weak and immoral," Weir wrote, "and the lower classes, taking advantage of this moral lassitude, and led on by their savage inclinations, undertake strikes, mobs, boycotts, and riots."[64] All the more reason to slam that door shut again.

Workingmen, for their part, used manhood to turn upper-class ideals on their heads. Frank James, the celebrated outlaw, put it like this:

> If there is ever another war in this country, which may happen, it will be between capital and labor, I mean between greed and manhood, and I'm as ready to march now in defense of American manhood as I was when a boy in defense of the south.[65]

Workers must "stand erect in the full majesty of our manhood" observed the writer of a letter to *Miner's Magazine* in 1904, and against the "effeminate monopolistic system" and "effete methods of tyranny," as another correspondent had written in 1887.[66]

Some workers' organizations considered the plight of the wage laborer to be analogous to that of a feudal serf. "We claim, that although the masses have advanced towards independence, they will never be completely free from vassalage until they have thrown off the system of working for hire," observed the Knights of St. Crispin, a shoemakers' union, in 1870. Other workers used prostitution as a metaphor for wage labor, as men were forced to sell their bodies to the capitalist in the same way that a prostitute sells her body to her well-heeled customer. Unemployment emasculated men who could not support their families. "I have no more desire to be idle," commented one iron puddler, "than I do to wear women's clothes." Thus, women (as prostitutes), blacks (as slaves), and European peasants (as indentured serfs) served as the screens against which late nineteenth-century "artisans" sought to reconfigure their claims to independent manhood.[67]

The development of the labor movement in the United States was built on such contrapuntal images of masculinity. Within the ranks of organized labor, the Heroic Artisan returned as a vision of resistance to the workers' degradation into a proletariat, a form of symbolic resistance to their emasculation as independent, self-made men. The artisanal community of the Jeffersonian yeoman's republic resurfaced as the basis for the American working-class movement. The appeal of socialism, observed one worker in 1899, was that it promised to instill a sympathetic solidarity in the face of that "wasteful war of competition between man and his brother in the wilderness of anarchical production in which people blindly wander."[68]

Of course, organizing these fiercely independent men proved difficult, since groups each held onto their craft or skill as the mark of autonomy and were often indifferent to the claims of other groups in perilously similar positions. (This prevented the much-sought-after worker-farmer alliance in the last decades of the century.) Exclusion remained a potent organizing principle in many developing unions. Blacks were a "scab race," and were therefore not to be admitted. At a meeting of the Bricklayers National Union in 1871, for example, a heated argument developed about the incorporation of black workers. "I wouldn't let a nigger into our union, and if he came in I would go out," one delegate remarked. "We will not recognize a nigger bricklayer in Baltimore," he roared, to great approval of the assembled. The making of the American working class was the making of a distinctly white, male, and native-born class.[69]

A surprising exception to grounding working-class masculinity on racist, sexist, and nativist foundations was also one of the most successful organizations of the era. In the 1870s and 1880s the Knights of Labor took up where earlier, smaller unions left off. Organized in 1869 as a secret society by Philadelphia garment workers, the Noble and Holy Order of the Knights of Labor grew to become America's first mass-membership labor organization, counting between two and three million members over its twenty-year life and numbering over 750,000 at its peak in 1886. The Knights harkened back to an era in which labor was dignified, chivalric, and even heroic. Their language was the language of the Jeffersonian yeoman transplanted into the industrial sphere. Wage earners were "producers," and factory owners were "accumulators" or "monopolists." Their goal was to uphold "the dignity of labor"—the abolition of "wage slavery," not the overthrow of capitalism. In short, the Knights sought to return America to the virtuous republic of producerism, a true "workingman's democracy" of the "noblest and bravest of our race."[70]

Apparently, these "noblest and bravest" knew neither race, skill, nor gender; all workers could take pride in honest and useful work. Free blacks were welcome, as were women. "The rights of the sexes are co-equal, their privileges should be the same, and I can see no reason why women should not be entitled to giving to the world its products as well as men," commented Knights' president Terrence Powderly. Unfortunately, the

Knights were not so inclusionary for nonnative workers, as they encouraged and participated in anti-Chinese riots and supported the Chinese Exclusion Act in 1882.

Among rural yeomen, those independent small family farmers, the consolidation of American capitalism and industrial development was no less serious a threat. As the railroads created a national market, these small farmers were increasingly squeezed between falling farm prices and rising costs of transportation and machinery, and many were transformed into tenants and hired laborers. "Once the domain of yeomen freeholders," the Georgia up-country was fast becoming a "territory of the dispossessed."[71]

The Populist movement—a broad-based agrarian resistance to rural proletarianization—organized these rural discontents into local producer cooperatives to set transport and grain prices. Populism's backbone was "the yeomanry of the country," as the *People's Party Paper* put it in 1892—"the small landed proprietors, the working farmers, the intelligent artisans, the wage workers, men who own homes and want a stable government." And these independent farmers expressed the Jeffersonian republicanism of small-scale producers seeking the restoration of the cooperative commonwealth with its noble vision of manhood. At their mass meetings and rallies, wagon trains and encampments, Populists expressed their belief that the farmer wasn't a peasant but rather a "peer of the realm," "as much of a business man as his employer," as William Jennings Bryan put it—and that his contribution was fundamental to society. In the presidential campaign of 1896, the Populists, as the People's Party, mounted "the largest and most threatening third party movement" since the Civil War for candidate Bryan. His thundering orations chastising aggressive, rapacious finance capitalists—the "idle holders of idle capital"—and his pleas in defense of rural innocence "against the encroachments of organized wealth," revealed a vision of the rural Heroic Artisan, the independent farmer as autonomous worker and family man, virtuous and virile.[72]

This vision of republican, artisanal manhood was also expressed in fiction, particularly in one of America's best-loved children's stories. Although L. Frank Baum's *The Wizard of Oz* (1900) has long been understood as a Populist parable as well as a beloved children's tale, this distinctly American story can also be read as a parable on the meanings of manhood at the turn of the century. Each of the men in the story undertakes a quest to reclaim his manhood.

When we first meet them, Dorothy's relatives are as cold and gray as the dreary Kansas landscape where they still try to eke out a living as independent farmers before a cyclone literally dispossesses them of their house. Dorothy's companions on her odyssey are initially losers, too—particularly losers as men. The Scarecrow (farmer) is incapable of doing his job, scaring away the crows, and is down on himself because he has no brains. The Tin Woodsman (the industrial worker) is the literal embodiment of alienated labor. Under the spell of the Wicked Witch of the East (manufacturers and bankers), he has been hacking himself to bits, cutting off each of his limbs, and replacing them with tin. His labor is literally alienated. A formerly independent craftsman, he now has no control over his work, which is turned against him in graphic self-mutilation. He has been transformed into a machine that needs a heart, without which he will not have the compassion to make common cause with the farmer. And the Cowardly Lion (the well-known symbol of Bryan's presidential campaign) lacks only the courage to be powerful.

Off they go down the Yellow Brick Road (the gold standard) to Oz (abbreviation for "ounce") to seek redemption from the Wizard of Oz, a carnival confidence man, a humbug who stands in for all the U.S. presidents since the Civil War. "I think you are a very bad man," says Dorothy to the wizard as he is unmasked as a fraud. "Oh no, my dear; I'm really a very good man; but I'm a very bad wizard, I must admit."

Through the course of the story, each of these symbolic representations proves himself as a real man. The Tin Woodsman kills a swarm of bees and a pack of wolves sent by the Wicked Witch of the West to kill the stalwart troop and later chops off the branches of trees that grab those who seek to enter the forest. The Scarecrow finally scares off some crows, and the Lion decapitates a gigantic spider which had terrified the entire forest. And so each of them receives the validation of his virility that he seeks from the Wizard, who gives them, as Baum puts it, "exactly what they thought they wanted." In the end, they each return to the scenes of their respective triumphs to become the ruler over the local residents. As political allegory, Baum's *The Wizard of Oz* represents hope that Bryan's Populist campaign would restore the manhood of these symbolic characters; as a meditation on gender, it is a tale of that masculine revival, set in motion by a protofeminist heroine.[73]

One last effort to retrieve a form of manhood for the heroic toiler came from the Arts and Crafts Movement. Originally a British movement following art critic John Ruskin and, later, William Morris, the Arts and Crafts Movement in the United States also damned industrialization for eliminating the hearty fellowship and craft pride among working men. Factory production had "reduced the workman to such a skinny and pitiful existence that he scarcely knows how to frame a desire for any life much better than that which he now endures," wrote Morris. He argued that work should be "pleasurable as well as useful" with the product a "joy to the maker and the owner."[74] In the arts and crafts workshop independent craftsmen would enjoy both the process and the product of their labor; work would be a "calling" whose outcome would be, as Horace Traubel put it in 1906, "manhood."[75] For some leading figures of the movement, such as C. R. Ashbee, the workshop was also an eroticized homosocial Eden where vigorous young men worked, played, and lived together. Influenced by Edward Carpenter and Walt Whitman, Ashbee fused a critique of modernity's enervating effects on manhood with an exploration of homosexuality. Ashbee promised to keep "the sacred lamp of the New Socialism always before me . . . making the bulwarks of real human love so strong in the hearts of our men and boys that no castrated affection shall dare face it."[76]

While the British wing of the movement was sympathetic to women's dissatisfaction with their role in society (arts and crafts workshops became staging grounds for British feminism), the American wing launched a critique of "the feminization of American culture." Syracuse-based Gustav Stickley, guild organizer, furniture maker, and editor of the *Craftsman* (begun in 1901), saw his mission as providing the homes for men who embraced Theodore Roosevelt's "strenuous life." Stickley despised the typical American home—"built to meet the needs of women, whose tendency is still to emphasize emotion —to minimize reason"—and his designs, with their disciplined geometry, generous proportions, and sturdiness offered men the possibility of return to their castles. "It is the place to which a man comes home when his day's work is done and where he expects to find himself comfortable and at ease in surroundings that are in harmony with his daily life, thought and pursuits." The message to women was equally clear: "Place Craftsman furniture in your parlor or sitting room and men will remain at home instead of leaving for the club or the saloon."[77]

Turn-of-the-century designers carved out a distinctly male space in the home as an antidote to feminized Victorian parlors—the den, "the man's special room." By 1905 Montgomery Ward offered a Morris chair for "manly comfort," and others suggested furniture and paneling of solid oak—"a robust, manly sort of wood," wrote Stickley. Brown leather seat covers, smoking paraphernalia on the well-wrought tables, and perhaps a few hunting trophies on the walls—all made it clear that man was not in the least feminized by returning to his lair, his den, after hunting in the corporate jungle all day.[78]

Finally, other men sought to revive manhood in the real jungle. If the frontier was closed, some reasoned, why not extend its boundaries beyond the borders of the continental United States and create new frontiers where men could test and prove their manhood? No sooner was there no frontier left on the continent than Alfred Thayer Mahan argued that America should develop overseas colonies to serve as coaling stations for the navy and to increase the nation's commerce. In *The Influence of Sea Power upon History* (1890), Mahan's idea of "race patriotism" linked a desire for frontier manhood to racial terrors of the Asian countries whose conquest he was urging.

Imperialist expansion could create the new frontier. The annexation of Hawaii, the Philippine Islands, Puerto Rico, and Guam (all in 1898), the division of the Samoan Islands with the Germans (1899), and the suppression of the Boxer Rebellion (1900) all signaled a new imperial strategy. Others believed that decades of peace had made American men effeminate and effete; only by being constantly at war could frontier masculinity be retrieved. General Homer Lea—short, physically deformed, and nearly blind—was one of the most virulent warmongers; his books *The Valor of Ignorance* (1909) and *The Day of the Saxon* (1912) made the analogy between man and nation explicit. "As manhood marks the height of physical vigor among mankind, so the militant successes of a nation mark the zenith of its physical greatness," he wrote.[79] After the sinking of the *Maine*, one journalist wrote that "a nation needs a war from time to time to prevent it from becoming effeminate, to shake it up from demoralizing materialism, and to elevate the popular heart by awakening heroic emotions and the spirit of patriotic self-sacrifice."[80]

For William James militarism was "the greatest preserver of our ideals of hardihood, and human life with no use for hardihood would be contemptible"; his search was, therefore, for the "moral equivalent" of war—"something heroic that will speak to men as universally as war does." In his landmark book *The Varieties of Religious Experience* (1902), James argued that the martial virtues "must be the enduring cement; intrepidity, contempt for softness, surrender of private interest, obedience to command, must still remain the rock upon which states are built." He found such a moral equivalent in the person of the ascetic monk, whose voluntary poverty was an example of the "strenuous life."[81]

The celebration of the military spirit was more than an attempt to redraw the boundaries of the frontier—it was an attempt to re-create the experience of the frontier, a virulent reaction against the perceived feminization of American manhood by the deadening routine of office work or the loss of autonomy and other craft values among the growing proletariat. But the costs were great. When Joyce Kilmer, the poet best known for "Trees," was killed in battle in the First World War, a eulogy in a magazine indicated how he had redeemed his manhood. "Kilmer was young, only 32, and the scholarly type of man," it read. "One did not think of him as a warrior. And yet from the time he entered the war, he could think of but one thing—that he must, with his own hands, strike a blow at the Hun. He was a man."[82]

A Profeminist Alternative

Several of these liberal efforts to challenge the rise of both the corporation and the crowd ended up unintentionally reinforcing them—in part because their proponents linked their challenge to restoring masculinity by exclusion, or by retrieving outmoded definitions. One liberal thinker at the turn of the century daringly tried to use conservative Darwinian arguments in the service of a redefinition of masculinity. Using evolutionism, anthropology, and sociology, Lester Ward expounded a theory he called "gynecocracy," claiming that the female sex was both the primary and the original sex in evolutionary development. The origins of human life were matriarchal and matrilineal; woman "is the unchanging trunk of the great genealogic tree." The origins of male domination lay in women's selection of larger and stronger men for mates, who had then usurped political and social power by virtue of their strength, thus ushering in an era defined by patriarchy and monogamous sexual relations. Male domination and monogamy were not some divinely sanctioned moral law, Ward reasoned, but simply a temporary stage of evolution—a stage out of which we were, fortunately, beginning to pass.[83]

Ward also argued that the state should regulate family and marriage to ensure equality between women and men and that sexual relationships should be free of all political, social, or moral encumbrances. Women's position was both morally insupportable and unnatural. "Throughout all human history," he wrote in *Pure Sociology* (1903), "woman has been powerfully discriminated against and held down by custom, law, literature and public opinion." Sexism—not biology, not evolutionary inferiority—held women back. "The universal prevalence of the androcentric world view acts as a wet blanket on all the genial fire of the female sex," he argued in *Applied Sociology* (1906). "Let this be at once removed and woman's true relation to society will be generally perceived, and all this will be changed."[84]

Ward would have few takers, even in our own times, although a recent popularity of feminist anthropologists in search of prehistoric matriarchies, not to mention feminists who attack the gender biases of sciences generally, suggests that Ward's model of redefinition is still very much with us.

At the time, though, Ward's reliance on evolutionary biology was an oddity among the liberal wing of respondents to the crisis of masculinity. Most of his fellow travelers were decidedly unscientific, and some were eager to try to practice what they preached. The Greenwich Village radicals of the turn of the century developed a new vision of masculinity that in many ways set the stage for the new century; what's more, they tried to implement their ideas in the lives they were living. Unlike earlier male supporters of feminism, the Greenwich Village radicals drew less on abstract conceptions of justice or on women's putative monopoly on morality as the basis for their support of feminism.[85] Both feminist and socialist, this group embraced feminist ideas as much for self-interest as anything else; they saw their potential to liberate men as their importance to the liberation of women.

The Bohemian radicals who clustered around Greenwich Village attempted to create new relationships while they promoted and supported feminist causes. In this "moral health resort," as Floyd Dell called it, they confronted issues of monogamy and sexual fidelity, women's sexual autonomy, and women's rights to birth control and abortion while they supported women's entry into the economic sphere, increased educational opportunities, and of course, suffrage. Feminism wasn't threat; it was an exciting challenge. The New Woman of the century was about to meet the New Man—a man who could thrill to woman's sexual autonomy, who was outraged at economic and political discrimination, and who worked in both public and private spheres to bring about a system of sexual equality and gender justice.

Men like the young Max Eastman, Floyd Dell, Hutchins Hapgood, William Sanger, and Randolph Bourne. Eastman, the editor of *Masses* and secretary and organizer of the Men's League for Woman Suffrage, was (in his early years) an exemplary figure, organizing other men around feminist issues and struggling toward equality in his personal life. Eastman and his wife, Ida Rauh, caused a scandal when, on their return from a trip to Europe in the fall of 1911, they began a Village custom by posting Rauh's full name on their mailbox. Eastman linked his support for feminism with his understanding of masculinity. "There was nothing harder for a man with my mamma's-boy complex to do than stand up and be counted as a 'male suffragette'," he wrote in *Enjoyment of Living*. "It meant not only that I had asserted my manhood, but that I had passed beyond the need of asserting it."[86]

In the political sphere the Greenwich Village radicals were very visible in their campaigns for women's equality. Officers of the Men's League for Woman Suffrage (founded by Eastman in 1910) included Oswald Garrison Villard, publisher of the *New York Evening Post*, Columbia professor John Dewey, and Rabbi Stephen Wise. The Men's League was the first organized profeminist men's organization in the United States; its purpose was to organize men's contingents in suffrage marches and parades and to visibly support, as men, woman suffrage. An editorial in *La Follette's* in May 1911 praised the eighty-five "courageous and convinced men" who had marched in a recent demonstration; one marcher counted being "booed and hissed down the Avenue a very thrilling experience" and indicated his determination that "if I can help to that end, there shall be a thousand men in line next year." He wasn't very far off. An editorial in the *New York Times* one year later predicted that eight hundred men would march the next day in a suffrage demonstration.

Many of these men saw the social revolution offered by feminist demands for personal autonomy as the personal complement to the socialist revolution. And such personal autonomy required sexual freedom; Greenwich Village radicals linked socialist economic critiques of American capitalism with a feminist critique of sexual repression. Thus, Floyd Dell argued in "Feminism for Men" (1914), an article in *The Masses*, that capitalism is opposed to feminism because "it wants men with wives and children who are dependent on them for support." But feminism will allow men to rediscover women as equals, which means to discover women all over again; the home, he argues is "a little dull":

> When you have got a woman in a box, and you pay rent on the box, her relationship to you insensibly changes character. It loses the fine excitement of democracy. It ceases to be companionship, for companionship is only possible in a democracy. It is no longer a sharing of life together—it is a breaking of life apart. Half a life—cooking, clothes, and children; half a life—business, politics, and baseball. . . . It is in the great world that a man finds his sweetheart, and in that narrow little box outside of the world that he loses her. When she has left that box and gone back into the great world, a citizen and a worker, then with surprise and delight he will discover her again, and never let her go.[87]

Eastman claimed a similar motive for supporting feminism and was equally certain that feminism held an important message for men. In one short item in *The Masses*, Eastman recounted a brief (and possibly apocryphal) exchange with a new stenographer:

"Are you a feminist?" we asked the stenographer.
She said she was.
"What do you mean by Feminism?"
"Being like men," she answered.
"Now you are joking!"
"No, I'm not. I mean real independence. And emotional independence too—living in relation to the universe rather than in relation to some other person."
"All men are not like that," we said sadly.
"Then they should join the Feminist movement!"[88]

For all their contradictory arguments and eventual abandonment of the feminist cause, Dell, Eastman, and other Greenwich Village radicals had discovered the fusion of the personal and the political. And what's more, some men had come to see that the success of feminism contained within it both a critique of traditional masculinity and the seeds of male liberation. Men had come to understand that feminism, as Dell wrote, "is going to make it possible for the first time for men to be free."[89]

Possible, perhaps, but not likely—at least for another century. Not even the Greenwich Village bohemians could fully implement their vision of feminism and socialism as building blocks of a new masculinity. In the meantime, conservatives would continue to use race, sex, and place of birth as criteria for exclusion from the masculine testing ground and extol the virtues of the Heroic Artisan even as he receded into historical memory. And new strategies would develop in the new century—strategies that relied on the growing culture of consumption to enable American men to re-create their masculinity at their leisure.

CHAPTER 4

Playing for Keeps

Masculinity as Recreation and the Re-Creation of Masculinity

The curse of our age is its femininity, its lack, not of barbarism, but of virility.
—Orestes Brownson (1884)

In his popular novel *The Bostonians* (1885), Henry James captured the anger and resentment many men had come to feel at the turn of the century. After pursuing the young feminist visionary Verena Tarrant for what seems like an eternity, Basil Ransome explodes in a rhetorical torrent:

> The whole generation is womanized; the masculine tone is passing out of the world; it's a feminine, nervous, hysterical, chattering, canting age, an age of hollow phrases and false delicacy and exaggerated solicitudes and coddled sensibilities, which, if we don't soon look out, will usher in the reign of mediocrity, of the feeblest and flattest and most pretentious that has ever been. The masculine character, the ability to dare and endure, to know and yet not fear reality, to look the world in the face and take it for what it is . . . that is what I want to preserve, or rather . . . recover; and I must tell you that I don't in the least care what becomes of you ladies while I make the attempt![1]

Through Ransome, James here expresses a powerful current of malaise and resentment felt by turn-of-the-century American men, railing against what they perceived as the feminization of American culture.[2] Something had happened to American society that had led to a loss of cultural vitality, of national virility. That spirit had to be retrieved and revived for a new century.

But not in the workplace, now a site of uneasiness. What had formerly been the central arena in which self-making men had made themselves had now become unreliable, tenuous. Changes in the nature of work itself and changes in the composition of the workforce combined to make these self-making men uncertain of their futures. As historian Elliot Gorn recently asked:

> Where would a sense of maleness come from for the worker who sat at a desk all day? How could one be manly without independence? Where was virility to be found in increasingly faceless bureaucracies? How might clerks or salesmen feel masculine doing

"women's work"? What became of rugged individualism inside intensively rationalized corporations? How could a man be a patriarch when his job kept him away from home for most of his waking hours?[3]

With so many breadwinners faced with becoming breadlosers, what was a man to do?

One answer, as we've seen, was to try and clear away those newcomers to the workplace and to thus reestablish marketplace success as still possible. Another answer was to pretend. "As men felt their real sense of masculinity eroding, they turned to fantasies that embodied heroic physical action, reading novels of the Wild West and cheering the exploits of baseball and football players."[4] If manhood could no longer be directly experienced, then perhaps it could be vicariously enjoyed by appropriating the symbols and props that signified earlier forms of power and excitement.

Such attempts played out the well-worn psychological axiom that what we lose in reality we re-create in fantasy. In our psychological development, the theory goes, those relationships and experiences that give life meaning, that make us feel full, satisfied, secure, are snatched from us, leaving us insecure, frightened, and desperate. Part of the normal, garden-variety neurosis that is the human condition is the creation of a stockpile of symbols that remind us of those lost objects, a secret symbolic treasure chest we can occasionally raid to re-create those earlier moments of fulfillment. As individuals struggling to find meaning in the world, we create those symbols to help us return to those earlier experiences so that we can again feel secure and without anxiety.

The analogy between individual development and cultural development holds—and at no time more clearly than the turn of the century. Just as the realm of production had been so transformed that men could no longer anchor their identity in their position in the market, we created new symbols, the consumption of which "reminded" men of that secure past, evoking an age before identity crises, before crises of masculinity—a past when everyone knew what it meant to be a man and achieving one's manhood was a given. In the culture of consumption, identity was based less on what one did and who one was and more upon how one appeared and lived. In his classic study *The Lonely Crowd*, sociologist David Riesman discerned the shift in identities and ethics from the "inner directed" nineteenth-century man—a man of strong character animated by an inner sense of morality, fixed principles by which he grounded his identity—to the twentieth-century "other directed" man—a sensitive personality, animated by a need to fit in, to be liked. Inner-directed men went their own way, could stand alone, tuned to the hum of an internal gyroscope; other-directed men scanned a mental radar screen for fluctuations in public opinion. For the other-directed man, having a good personality was the way to win friends and influence people.[5]

Such a shift was reflected in the terms men used to describe themselves. *Manhood* had been understood to define an inner quality, the capacity for autonomy and responsibility, and had historically been seen as the opposite of *childhood*. Becoming a man was not taken for granted; at some point the grown-up boy would demonstrate that he had become a man and had put away childish things. At the turn of the century, *manhood* was replaced gradually by the term *masculinity*, which referred to a set of behavioral traits and attitudes that were contrasted now with a new opposite, *femininity*. Masculinity was something that had to be constantly demonstrated, the attainment of which was forever in question—lest the man be undone by a perception of being too feminine.

Masculinity required proof, and proof required serious effort, whether at the baseball park, the gymnasium, or sitting down to read *Tarzan* or a good western novel. Suddenly, books about the urban "jungle" or "wilderness" appeared, which allowed men to experience manly risk and excitement without ever leaving the city—books like Upton Sinclair's classic muckraking exposé of the Chicago meatpacking industry, *The Jungle* (1906), or Robert Wood's work on settlement houses, *The City Wilderness* (1898). Or they could flip through *National Geographic* (1888 on) to encounter the primitive "other."

One could replace the inner experience of manhood—a sense of manly confidence radiating outward from the virtuous self into a sturdy and muscular frame that had taken shape from years of hard physical labor—and transform it into a set of physical character- istics obtainable by persistent effort in the gymnasium. The ideal of the Self-Made Man gradually assumed increasingly physical connotations so that by the 1870s the idea of "inner strength" was replaced by a doctrine of physicality and the body. By the turn of the century, a massive, nationwide health and athletics craze was in full swing as men compulsively attempted to develop manly physiques as a way of demonstrating that they possessed the interior virtues of manhood. The self-made man of the 1840s "shaped himself by acting upon the material world and [testing] himself in the crucible of compe- tition"; by century's end he was making over his physique to *appear* powerful physically, perhaps to replace the lost real power he imagined that he—or at least his father or grandfather—once felt. If the body revealed the virtues of the man, then working on the body could demonstrate the appearance of the possession of the very virtues that one was no longer certain one possessed.[6]

What had caused such anxiety and insecurity among American men? Why were they so afraid of being feminized? And what could they do to combat such physical, psychological, and spiritual erosion? Some writers believed that cultural feminization was the natural consequence of the invasion of cultural outsiders, the "others," whose manhood was suspect to begin with. Fears of cultural degeneration were fueled by the entry of supposedly weaker and less virile races and ethnicities into the growing northern industrial city. To some commentators it was the city itself that bred feminization, with its con- formist masses scurrying to work in large bureaucratic offices, which sapped innate masculine vitality and harnessed it to the service of the corporation. The great architect Frank Lloyd Wright had excoriated the urban world as an "enormity *devouring manhood.*" "Our cities are populated by weaklings," complained health reformer Bernarr Macfadden in a letter to President Theodore Roosevelt a few years later.[7]

Many men believed that cultural feminization was the direct result of the feminization of American boyhood, the predominance of women in the lives of young boys—mothers left alone at home with their young sons and teachers in both elementary and Sunday schools. In 1910 four of every five elementary-school teachers were women, up from three-fourths in 1900 and two-thirds in 1870.[8] The "preponderance of women's influence in our public schools," warned Rabbi Solomon Schindler in 1892, is feminizing our boys; a "vast horde of female teachers" were teaching boys how to become men, added psychologist J. McKeen Cattell. A 1904 report of a British group that was sent to the United States to observe American education and head off a similar problem in Britain concluded that the preponderance of women teachers meant that "the boy in America is not being brought up to punch another boy's head; or to stand having his own punched in an healthy and proper manner."

Observers were alarmed about the effect of so many women teaching young boys. One writer posed two unpleasant outcomes, the "effeminate babyish boy" and "the bad boy," and suggested that masculine influence "is necessary for the proper development" of young boys. Another writer in the *Educational Review* in 1914 complained that women teachers had created "a feminized manhood, emotional, illogical, non-combative against public evils." This psychic threat to "masculine nature," he argued, was beginning to "warp the psyches of our boys and young men into femininity."[9]

To others the problem wasn't women but the demands of the culture itself that made men "weak, effeminate, decaying and almost ready to expire from sheer exhaustion and decrepitude," as an 1867 editorial in the *North Carolina Presbyterian* had earlier put it. Overcivilization had made men "over-sophisticated and effete"; their energies had been spent, not saved, their manhood dissipated. Suddenly, new words, such as "pussyfoot" and "stuffed shirt," entered into common parlance. Women "pity weakly men," O. S. Fowler warned, but they love and admire those "who are red faced, not white livered; right hearty feeders, not dainty; sprightly, not tottering; more muscular than exquisite, and powerful than effeminate, in mind and body."[10]

Most terrifying to men was the specter of the sissy. As we have seen, by the last decade of the century the term had come to mean weakness, dependency, and helplessness—all the qualities that men were not. The sissy was outwardly feminine in demeanor, comportment, and affect. If manhood is defined by courage, generosity, modesty, dignity, wrote Rafford Pyke in his 1902 diatribe against sissies in *Cosmopolitan* magazine, then the sissy was "flabby, feeble, mawkish . . . chicken-hearted, cold and fearful." He was "a slender youthful figure, smooth faced, a little vacuous in the expression of the countenance, with light hair and rather pale eyes a little wide apart; a voice not necessarily weak, but lacking timbre, resonance, carrying power." Real men, Pyke argued, "laugh at him," while women rightfully shun him, as he causes a general "moral nausea" among observers, "a vague yet insurmountable feeling of malaise." Dr. Alfred Stillé, president of the American Medical Association, weighed in with a claim that "a man with feminine traits of character, or with the frame and carriage of a female, is despised by both the sex he ostensibly belongs to, and that of which he is at once a caricature and a libel."[11]

The emergence of a visible gay male subculture in many large American cities at the turn of the century gave an even greater moral urgency to men's flight from being perceived a sissy. Here were real-live gender inverts, men acting like women, and therefore any manner of behavior or action that was reminiscent of these inverts might be a man's undoing. The increased fears of feminization eroded the casual coexistence between homosexual and heterosexual men that had characterized urban life in the 1870s and 1880s.[12]

By 1900 men would do whatever they could to appear manly. And, it appears, whatever they were told, no matter how contradictory. Take facial hair, for example. On the one hand, beards and moustaches experienced a cultural revival, as they had in the 1840s, as one of the easiest ways to sharpen the distinctions between the sexes. "There is nothing that so adds to native manliness as the full beard if carefully and neatly kept," counseled one advice book, *Decorum* in 1877. "The person who invented razors libeled nature."

At the same time, ads for shaving paraphernalia linked shaving to hard work and success. One Gillette advertisement proclaimed its product was

typical of the American spirit. It is used by capitalists, professional men, business men—
by men of action all over this country—three million of them.

Its use starts habits of energy—of initiative. And men who *do* for themselves are men
who *think* for themselves. Be master of your own time. Buy a Gillette and use it.

Perhaps more important than the rhetoric, the ad depicted five All-Star baseball players
(who were "clean of action and clean of face").[13]

Yet the very act of purchasing these toiletries created some uneasiness. Had not
consumption been branded as feminine, the new urban department store a female world
of abundance and delight? Several of the newly established department stores developed
separate entrances, separate elevators, and separate departments for male and female
shoppers, partly to ease the psychological threat to men entering such spheres there to
engage in such feminizing activities as shopping.[14]

This at the same time as men became increasingly concerned about the economic and
social impact of manly appearance. Talent and motivation may have become unreliable
predictors of success, but one could still make sure to look the part, to act as if one were
already successful, to, as we might say today, "dress for success." As Kenneth Wayne
advised his young male readers in 1912:

> A young man may have tons of virtue, talent, and ability, but he cannot get people to
> look for these things through a soiled, shabby dress, where there is no necessity for it to
> commend it. An indifferently groomed young man is at a disadvantage among a group of
> well-groomed young men applicants for a position.

Appearances also mattered in one's work. "Do work as if you meant it," Wayne advised.
"There is no substitute for enthusiasm." The inclusion of the words "as if" speaks volumes
about men's lives at the turn of the century. Work could no longer be relied upon to
express one's autonomy and success. But one had still to act as if it did![15]

Although fears of feminization were largely a preoccupation of middle-class men, the
problem could also be acute among the working class. These men also had to prove that
they were "men among men." The constancy of these efforts, the frequency with which
they reassured themselves of their "regular guy" status, indicates a preoccupation with the
obverse—"that men were in danger of being called something else: unmanly, a mollycoddle,
a sissy, even a pansy. Whereas manhood could be achieved, it could also be lost; it was
not simply a quality that resulted naturally and inevitably from one's sex."[16] Traditionally
working-class institutions, like the billiard hall, the saloon, or the street corner, occupied
an increasingly important place in working-class men's lives.

Take drinking, long a well-integrated part of such lives. In 1894 New York City had
one saloon for every 200 residents, while the working-class districts averaged one saloon
for every 129 residents. Chicago and Baltimore had similar figures: one saloon for every
212 in Chicago and one for every 229 in Baltimore, while their working-class neighborhoods offered one for every 127 and every 105 residents, respectively. Drinking together
cemented manly solidarity, even as the traditional artisanal conviviality was superseded in
impersonal factories. But more than that, drinking asserted "a glorious manhood unfettered
by the nagging demands of women who would, had they their way, ensconce men at home,

squander their wages, forbid them to drink—in short emasculate them." Drinking was a form of masculine resistance to feminization.[17]

This was as true in the rural South as it was in northern cities. In a revealing portrait of postbellum southern manhood, the historian Ted Ownby describes how drinking, brawling, hunting, swearing, and even a revival of dueling witnessed increased popularity as a tonic to restore lost manhood and provide manly solace and "respite from the constraints of female-centered evangelical life." The saloon, the street, the cockfighting and dogfighting rings were arenas of distinctly male vice, enjoyed lustily by men seeking to escape from the sweet virtue of the southern Christian home. It was the wife's Christian duty to convert and subdue these Rhett Butler wanna-bes, transforming them into dutiful Ashley Wilkeses. And it was men's duty to resist, lest Christian piety turn them into wimps.[18]

This world was attacked by the temperance movement, the Social Purity Movement, and other movements to clean up urban social problems; they all expressed a middle-class disdain for such working-class masculine sociability. "The Southern male who had once raised his hell, laughing at churchgoers while perhaps fearing occasionally for the state of his soul, now faced laws prohibiting much of his pursuit of pleasure." Campaigns against animal fighting and hunting further restrained a certain variety of masculine exuberance and problematized its homosocial bonding. Some reformers argued that these arenas expressed a psychologically unhealthy need for relations with other men. Perhaps homosociality was a breeding ground for homosexuality. Among the middle classes, of course, it was also feared that too *little* contact with other men and too much contact with women contributed to middle-class men's effeminacy and homosexuality.

Thus did psychologists and other reformers link the campaigns against vice, whether gaming, alcohol, or billiards, to sexual deviance. "The pool room diverts man power," wrote one representative of the Georgia Anti-Poolroom League. It encouraged moral and physical laxity—"idleness . . . dissipation . . . intoxicants . . . profanity . . . lascivious stories . . . [and] the love of chance"—particularly among young men. One psychological study of saloons frowned on any emotional expression of friendship between men as "abnormal" and likely due to the alcohol, since "to a healthy-minded man any kind of tender contact with other men is repugnant."[19] One psychologist suggested uneasily that alcohol also lowered men's guard around other men; that "when drinking, men fall on each other's necks and kiss one another; they feel that they are united by peculiarly intimate ties and this moves them to tears and intimate modes of address." And a psychoanalyst made the link between alcohol and homosexuality inescapable:

> Of recent years, there have been incidents which have led to a great deal of talk about "abnormal friendships between men." The expressions of feeling which in these cases were branded as morbid or immoral may be observed, by anyone who has eyes to see, wherever men are drinking heavily; and every drinking bout is tinged with homosexuality. The homosexual component-instincts, which education has taught us to repress and sublimate, reappear in no veiled form under the influence of alcohol.[20]

Fearing such a taint, many men—working- and middle-class, heterosexual or occasionally even homosexual—developed various strategies to ensure that others would continue to see them as manly. For example, one young Italian man remarked that he was always sexually active with men where he would "act as a woman," but he tried to protect his reputation by developing a conventionally masculine style in other arenas. He did not carry himself as a "fairy" and sought to establish his masculinity with other young men at a neighborhood gym by deliberately "talk[ing] about women." This participation in the "collective sexualization and objectification of women" was one of the "rituals by which he established himself as a man," writes historian George Chauncey.[21]

This young man points us to a new masculine hangout, a new institution where men could pump up those listless, lethargic, feminized bodies—the gym. At the turn of the century, thousands of American men trooped off to gyms and athletic fields as part of a national health craze, there to acquire manly physiques, shore up flagging energy, and develop masculine hardiness as ways of countering the perceived feminization of culture. The health craze was vital to the perpetuation of a virile nation; unlike the street corner or the pub, it was as morally purifying as it was physically imposing. A one contemporary observer claimed:

> Gymnasiums, athletic clubs, outdoor sports, and methods of exercise and other artificial means of contributing to and continuing the physical vigor and virility of the race take the place of the hard physical labor of the earlier periods, or the love of luxury and ease, when physical development is no longer a necessity, overcomes the promptings of intelligence and experience, and the moral illness of the civilization has begun its work of devastation and destruction.[22]

Or as G. Stanley Hall put it, "you can't have a firm will without firm muscles."[23] This preoccupation with physicality meant that men's bodies carried a different sort of weight than earlier. The body did not *contain* the man, expressing the man within; now, that body *was* the man.

Turn-of-the-century men flocked to healers who prescribed tonics and elixirs guaranteed to put hair on their chests and pep in their step. Men like Russell Trall, founder of the New York Hydropathic and Physiological School, who proclaimed the virtues of hydropathy—the famed "water cure," which involved steam-induced sweats or plunges in ice water. Or Robert Edis, who saw impurities hiding everywhere in the feminized household and railed against wallpaper, draperies, carpets and Europeanized furniture. Or Horace Fletcher, whose proposal that we masticate each bit of food one thousand times before swallowing was proclaimed as a way to recover health and challenge the "gobble, gulp, and go" table manners of the day. Or Bernarr Macfadden, the celebrated founder of Physical Culture, who promoted a new muscular manhood to be built from purified blood, deep breathing exercises, vigorous workouts with barbells, and large doses of his breakfast cereal, Strengthro. (Macfadden was also the proud inventor of a "peniscope," a cylindrical glass tube with a rubber hose at one end attached to a vacuum pump, designed to enlarge the male organ.)

And they consumed vast quantities of these manly concoctions. Like Sylvester Graham's crackers earlier in the century or C. W. Post's new Grape Nuts (1901), which was promoted as brain food for the burgeoning white-collar class because "brain workers must have different food than day laborers." Or J. H. Kellogg's rolled flakes of whole corn, which were but a part of his total health regimen. According to its promoters, such brain food also produced financial brawn. "What a man eats when he's twenty-five is more than likely to influence what he earns when he's fifty," noted one Post cereal advertisement. "If you hope for success, eat for success!" proclaimed another. An ad for Kellogg's All Bran warned about the other side, suggesting what might happen to those who failed to heed its advice. Underneath a pallid, drained man in a business suit was this caption:

> Lost . . . another big order . . . the fourth defeat of that day. All because he didn't have the energy to fight when his prospect said "No." Something had blunted his senses and stolen his strength. . . . That something was constipation, the world's most universal disease.[24]

And there was more. In 1900 one firm published a list of sixty-three imported and forty-two domestic bottled waters for sale, complete with the geographic source of each water and a brief note alerting potential purchasers to their specific medicinal properties and restorative powers. American men bought enormous numbers of advice manuals and guidebooks, such as William Haikie's *How to Get Strong and How to Stay So* (1879) and Macfadden's *The Virile Powers of Superb Manhood* (1900), both of which were best-sellers.[25]

As they had earlier in the century, many health reformers strove to control male sexuality, especially the body's fluids, as a way to gain control of the forces that were sapping men's energies. Self-making required self-control, and self-control required emotional control. So, for example, emotional outbursts of passion or jealousy, which had been associated with manhood in the eighteenth century, were now associated with lack of manhood; it was women, not men, who were now said to feel these emotions most acutely. Real men held their emotions in check, the better to channel them into workplace competition. A recurring economic metaphor marks many postbellum advice books as men were encouraged to "save," "conserve," and "invest" their seed, the fruits of their productive bodies, and to avoid unnecessary "expenditure" or profligate "waste." Masturbation would send a young man on an inevitable downward economic and social spiral. In his advice book, *The Crime of Silence* (1915), Orison Swett Marden told of a professor who was dragged slowly and inexorably down by self-abuse until at last he had no opinion on any topic whatever and ended up cleaning toilets in a large hotel. "The failure army is full of emasculated beings," he cautioned.[26]

Some books were concerned with preventing masturbation because of its association with enfeeblement and, hence, feminization. Joseph Conwell observed that muscles of masturbators become "flabby and weak" and the "enervated nervous system" loses its full virility. O. S. Fowler warned that masturbation "unsexes" the man, robbing boys of "future manliness" and leaving them "tame, discouraged, subdued, ungallant" drones. The quick discharge of semen leaves "its products extra nervous, yet minus the snap, vim, power, and condensed vigor they would otherwise have had." And Bernarr Macfadden observed that masturbation had "caused incomparably more sexual dilapidation, paralysis, and disease, as well as demoralization, than all the other sexual depravities combined," leaving men "maimed mentally, morally, and physically for life."[27]

Crusaders against masturbation were divided about the effects of the solitary vice. To some, it resulted in the immediate onset of sexual depravity—consorting with prostitutes, unbridled lusts that the young man could no longer contain, and ultimately, insanity and early death. Masturbation was a crime that "blanches the cheek, that shakes the nervous system into ruin, that clouds the intellect, that breaks down the integrity of the will, that launches emasculated ruin into asylums of hopeless insanity, collapsing in premature death," wrote G. Douglas in the *Official Report of the Twelfth International Christian Endeavor Convention* in 1900. To others, masturbation would so drain its practitioner that he would have no ardor left over for sexual activity. Winfield Hall's advice book, *From Youth to Manhood*, published by the YMCA in 1900, claimed that since masturbation is unnatural, it is "more depleting than is normal sexual intercourse." Thus, as if in compensation, nature would exact its revenge, "removing, step by step, his manhood."[28]

Specific physical and dietary regimens flourished to combat the scourge. Corn Flakes, for example, was designed by J. H. Kellogg as a massive anaphrodisiac to temper and eventually reduce sexual ardor in American men. Kellogg was perhaps the most successful and excessive of these health reformers. Like Sylvester Graham, Kellogg wrote books, like *Man the Masterpiece* (1886) and *Plain Facts for Young and Old* (1888), that were best-sellers of popular self-improvement via self-restraint, providing a guide for young men and their parents about clean living.

Kellogg was fanatical in his pursuit of masculine purity. His general health regime included:

1. Kneading and pounding on the abdomen each day to promote evacuation before sleep and thus avoiding "irritating" congestions.

2. Drinking hot water, six to eight glasses a day (same end in view).

3. Urinating several times each night (same end in view).

4. Avoiding alcohol, tobacco, and tea because they stimulated lecherous thoughts.

5. Taking cold enemas and hot sitz baths each day.

6. Wearing a wet girdle to bed each night.[29]

But Kellogg's chief concern was masturbation. In *Plain Facts for Old and Young*, he provided anxious parents with a frighteningly systematic list of thirty-nine signs of masturbation, including physical and behavioral changes.[30] Such a list could provoke anxiety in virtually all parents. What could they do about this plague? In a chapter called "Treatment for Self-Abuse and Its Effects," Kellogg listed a set of chilling home remedies. In addition to bandaging the genitals, covering the organs with cages, and tying the hands, Kellogg also recommended circumcision "without administering an anaesthetic, as the brief pain attending the operation will have a salutary effect upon the mind, especially if it be connected with the idea of punishment." Older boys may be forced to have silver sutures placed over the foreskin to prevent erection. "The prepuce, or foreskin, is drawn forward over the glans, and the needle to which the wire is attached is passed through from one side to the other. After drawing the wire through, the ends are twisted together, and cut off close. It is now impossible for an erection to occur, and the slight irritation thus produced acts as a most powerful means of overcoming the disposition to resort to the practice."[31] (Although the extent to which Kellogg's sadistic suggestions were followed by terrified parents is impossible to know, one can only cringe at the possibility that *any* of them did.)

Nor was Kellogg alone. Other reformers suggested bloodletting or applying leeches or heated pneumatic cups to the genitals to draw out "congestion" which led to arousal. One writer advised punching a hole through the foreskin and inserting a metal ring, while another suggested cutting the foreskin apart with a jagged-edge scissors. Red iron, tartar emetic ointment, and Spanish fly-blister could all be applied to make the genitals painful to the touch. "It is better . . . to endure any physical discomfort than to sacrifice one's chastity," wrote Henry Guernsey, M.D., in his *Plain Talks on Avoided Subjects* in 1882.[32]

By the middle of the second decade of the twentieth century, much of this explicitly sexual panic began to subside, in part because of the popularization of Freud's ideas. Freud was a fierce opponent of sexual puritanism and the ideology of the spermatic economy. To Freud the sexual instinct was just that, an instinct, inherited and normal. In "Sexual Morality and Modern Nervousness" (1908), Freud argued that the notion of physical depletion had it backward—it was continence or abstinence, not expenditure of semen, that was injurious to men. The only harm from masturbation was the guilt that traditionally attended it. "Masturbation as a rule does not much harm beyond that which we believe it to be wrong," was how one physician put it—as close as one can come to an iatrogenic, or even more accurately, a cultural etiology of disease as has ever been advanced.

Yet no sooner was the fear of depletion through masturbation ushered out as a problem for men than problems with male sexuality found another new, or rather, a very old, cause. Dr. William Robinson's *Sexual Impotence* (1912) was an enormously popular treatment of male sexual problems, going through thirteen editions. Robinson argued that "older doctors" had exaggerated the ills associated with masturbation; it certainly was *not* the cause of impotence. In fact, men were not to be blamed for impotence; women were, since it was women's lack of responsiveness to male sexual ardor which exacerbated and sometimes even caused impotence. The problem was, as he coined the term, "frigidity" in women, which "will not call out his virility." Once again, male sexuality was women's problem.[33]

The popularization of Freudian psychoanalytic theory echoed many earlier fears of masculine humiliation and also gave us some new ones. After all, the centerpiece of Freud's theory is that the rational, autonomous ego is the architect of the personality, which it creates by "appropriating" parts of the individual's instinctual drives and directing them to more socially appropriate outlets. To make the ego independent of the id, the master of its own fate, was a lifelong project, the triumph of mind and will over body and society. For the little boy it entailed the separation from mother, identification with father, and the subsequent assumption of the ability to stand alone. Failure to separate from mother led, Freud believed, to sexual "inversion" (homosexuality), while failure to develop independently from father led to a neurotic need for the authority of groups or organizations, such as the army or the church. The goal of psychoanalysis was to strengthen the ego, make it independent of those forces that threatened to overwhelm it. Just at the moment that autonomy and independence were disappearing in men's experience in the corporation, along came a theory that proclaimed the autonomous ego as the mark of maturity. If work prevented our self-making, psychology could facilitate it.

This created a new set of anxieties, especially because it linked the origins of homosexuality to the individual boy's experiences within his family. In brief, Freud argued that failure to break with his mother and identify with his father left the boy psychologically identified with mother (feminine gender identity) and therefore predisposed to feel like women; that is, he could only be completed sexually by the presence of a father figure— a strong powerful man. By linking gender behavior to sexual orientation and locating both within the family, Freudian theory sent many anxious parents scurrying to advice columns and child-rearing manuals to make sure that they wouldn't raise their children to grow up to be homosexual. This was even more pressing than, and more pressured by, the perceived feminization of the culture—as if American culture was conspiring to turn its men into a bunch of effeminate wimps barely a generation after the Civil War.

As the century progressed, psychiatrists and psychologists were blaming modern society for many of men's psychological problems.[34] Some reformers suggested that it was the pace of society that caused such problems—the rush of the modern, the clanking barrage of stimuli, the productive frenzy. Men simply wore themselves out mentally as well as physically. Dr. Edward Jarvis, speaking before the American Institutions for the Insane in 1851, pointed his finger at mobility and industrialization:

> No son is necessarily confined to the work . . . of his father . . . all fields are open . . . all are invited to join the strife. . . . They are struggling . . . at that which they cannot reach . . . their mental powers are strained to their utmost tension. . . . Their minds stagger . . . they are perplexed with the variety of insurmountable obstacles; and they are exhausted with the ineffectual labor.

And Dr. Peter Bryce, head of the Alabama Insane Hospital, observed in 1872 that mental illness was most common among men "at the most active time of life," ages thirty-five to forty. "Habitual intemperance, sexual excesses, overstrain in business, in fact, all those habits which tend to keep up too rapid cerebral action, are supposed to induce this form of disease. It is especially a disease of *fast life*, and fast business in large cities." Philip Hamerton's popular book *The Intellectual Life* (1873) laid the blame at the doorstep of the workplace and university when he wrote that "the excessive exercise of the mental powers are injurious to bodily health."[35]

Mental illness was gendered illness. In some cases the same symptoms would be diagnosed differently; in other cases the same diagnosis would result in different cures. Take, for example, the question of hysteria. Freud had treated female hysterics as women who were afraid to be fully women, who shrank into somatic illness when confronted with the constraints of femininity. Hysteria was the result of sexual wishes or desires that the women could not confront or accept. For men the new somatic illness of shell shock was defined as a similar inability to meet the demands of one's gender. During World War I a large number of men froze, could not return fire, or experienced psychic breaks with reality. For some, shell shock included "great weariness and profuse weeping, even in otherwise strong men." According to a 1916 article in the *Lancet*, a British medical journal, 40 percent of all British casualties in the war were attributable to shell shock. Another two hundred thousand on each side of the war deserted. S. Weir Mitchell explored dozens of cases of unexplained male paralysis, which he discussed in *Gunshot Wounds and Other Injuries of Nerves*.[36]

Most psychiatric treatments for shell shock involved treating the disease as the result of insufficient manliness. T. J. Calhoun, assistant surgeon with the Army of the Potomac, argued that if the soldier could not be "laughed out of it by his comrades" or by "appeals to his manhood," then a good dose of battle was the best "curative." Literary critic Elaine Showalter argues that both hysteria and shell shock were double-edged—failures to conform to gender demands that were so obvious and palpable that they also became expressions of resistance to traditional gender norms:

If the essence of manliness was not to complain, then shell shock was the body language of the masculine complaint, a disguised male protest not only against the war but against the concept of "manliness" itself. [It was] a protest against the politicians, generals, and psychiatrists. The heightened code of masculinity that dominated in wartime was intolerable to surprisingly large numbers of men.[37]

Just as contemporary critics understood hysteria to be a form of resistance to excessive standards of femininity, so too was shell shock a form of resistance to militarized manhood.

No one understood the psychological and somatic effects of modern civilization better than George Beard and Dr. S. Weir Mitchell. Beard's *American Nervousness* (1881) and *Sexual Neurasthenia* (1884; revised 1902) introduced a new psychological malady into American life: neurasthenia, or as it quickly became known in the popular press, "brain sprain." Neurasthenia, Beard claimed, was the result of "overcivilization"— changes such as steam power, the periodical press, the telegraph, and the sciences had so speeded up the pace of social life that people simply couldn't keep up despite their tireless efforts. The outcome was a host of symptoms, including insomnia, dyspepsia, hysteria, hypochondria, asthma, headache, skin rashes, hay fever, baldness, inebriety, hot flashes, cold flashes, nervous exhaustion, and brain collapse. "Modern nervousness is the cry of the system struggling with its environment."[38]

Beard argued that youthful masturbation and sexual excess contributed to neurasthenia and that, in this sense, "men could be considered responsible for their own insanity." To cure spermatorrhea, the collapse of male sexual vitality due to neurasthenic energy depletion, Beard prescribed cold baths, outdoor exercise, wearing a urethral ring, sleeping on a hair mattress with little covering of the genitals, and avoiding all erotic novels or dalliances with women of compromised virtue. Brain workers were to avoid intimate dinners, spiced foods, oysters, and alcohol.[39]

Never before had a cultural diagnosis resulted in a more gendered prescription and cure. Neurasthenia tended to invert gendered health, masculinizing women and feminizing men. So neurasthenic women were thus to be confined to their beds, idle and unstimulated, there to retrieve femininity. For example, Charlotte Perkins Gilman was diagnosed as neurasthenic in 1885, when she was 25, by Dr. Mitchell. "Live as domestic a life as possible," he counseled. "Have your child with you all the time. Lie down an hour after each meal. Have but two hours intellectual life a day. And never touch a pen, brush, or pencil as long as you live." Gilman was obedient; she "went home, followed those directions rigidly for months, and came perilously close to losing my mind," she wrote in her diary. (Her short story "The Yellow Wallpaper" [1892] offers a chilling description of her experience and what might have happened had she not had the strength to get out of bed.)

Men, by contrast, were pushed out to western dude ranches to take in the masculinizing freshness of the out-of-doors. Men, after all, had to rediscover masculinity. Riding the range, breathing the fresh country air, and exerting the body and resting the mind were curative for men, and in the last two decades of the century, large numbers of weak and puny eastern city men—like Theodore Roosevelt, Owen Wister, Frederic Remington, and Thomas Eakins—all came west to find a cure for their insufficient manhood. That each returned a dedicated convert, trumpeting the curative value of the strenuous life, is part of the story of how America was won over to the West.[40]

The rugged outdoors was consistently trumpeted as restorative of the flagging manhood of modern civilized men. The pages of the diaries of teenagers, college students, and young male clerks were filled with an endless list of their outdoor activities—from boxing to hiking, from ice skating to football and baseball. One physician proposed that a certain cure for hay fever was a "season of farm work," not because contact with the allergen would cure the malady, but because outdoor work would cure virtually anything. "Get your children into the country," one real estate advertisement for Wilmington, Delaware, urged potential buyers in 1905. "The cities murder children. The hot pavements, the dust, the noise, are fatal in many cases and harmful always. The history of successful men is nearly always the history of country boys." Naturalist John Muir added that thousands of "tired, nerve-shaken, over-civilized people are beginning to find out that going to the mountains is going home; that wilderness is a necessity." And George Evans advised that "[w]henever the light of civilization falls upon you with a blighting power, and work and pleasure become stale and flat, go to the wilderness. The wilderness will take hold on you. It will give you good red blood; it will turn you from a weakling into a man."[41]

In short, the turn of the century reinvented the frontier as simply the outdoors. Yet for many wilderness explorers or visitors to newly minted dude ranches—which were often nothing more than failed cattle ranches reopened as consumer health spas—the West had been transformed into a gigantic theme park, safely unthreatening, whose natural beauty was protected as in an art museum. The three men who so graphically memorialized the premodern West, who transformed nature into culture—novelist Owen Wister, painter Frederic Remington, and naturalist President Theodore Roosevelt—were all effete eastern intellectuals who spent time on these civilized western ranches and rediscovered their manhood.

Across the nation, hunting also experienced a renaissance at the turn of the century. Modern mathods of slaughtering beef made the hunt no longer a material necessity for survival. It returned as recreation and proving ground. Theodore Roosevelt organized the Boone and Crockett Club to encourage big-game hunting. "Hunting big game in the wilderness," he and cofounder George Bird Grinnell wrote in 1893, "is a sport for a vigorous and masterful people." William Kent, a California congressman concerned about the degeneration of the race since the disappearance of the caveman, rejoiced in the savagery of the hunt. After a kill, Hunt declared, "you are a barbarian, and you're glad of it. It's good to be a barbarian . . . and you know that if you are a barbarian, you are at any rate a man."[42] Some commentators didn't care how the meat was obtained as long as it was consumed. Many health reformers, including Graham, had shunned meat eating, believing it to excite the system and stimulate animal passions. But others proclaimed meat eating as a potent answer to feminized manhood; some claimed that a diet devoid of red meat would prevent the building of full manly power. George Beard described his encounter with a vegetarian in gendered terms; the hiker's "pale and feminine features, tinged with an unnatural flush" repelled Beard. Following a popular medical belief, Woods Hutchinson claimed that one needs blood to make blood, muscle to make muscle, and that the way to health was through consumption of large quantities of barely cooked beef. Hutchinson taunted vegetarians for being repelled by "Meat! R-r-red meat, dr-r-ripping with b-l-lood, r-r-reeking of the shambles." Eating red meat, men were literally consuming manhood.[43]

Perhaps the most important vehicle to re-create manhood was sports. In the late nineteenth century America went "sports crazy" as the nation witnessed a bicycle craze, a dramatic increase in tennis playing, golfing, weightlifting, and boxing, new excitement over football and racing, keen interest in basketball, and the spectacular rise of baseball. Sports were heralded as character building; health reformers promised athletic activity would make young men healthier and instill moral virtues. In short, sports made boys into men. Sports were necessary, according to D. A. Sargent, to "counteract the enervating tendency of the times and to improve the health, strength, and vigor of our youth" since they provided the best kind of "general exercise for the body, and develop courage, manliness, and self-control." Sports aided youth in "the struggle for manliness," wrote G. Walter Fiske in *Boy Life and Self-Government*. If masculinity required proof, one English newspaper championed athletics for substituting the "feats of man for the 'freak of the fop,' hardiness for effeminacy, and dexterity for luxurious indolence."[44]

Sports were celebrated for instilling moral as well as physical virtue. Sports developed "courage, steadiness of nerve . . . resourcefulness, self-knowledge, self-reliance . . . the ability to work with others . . . [and] readiness to subordinate selfish impulses, personal desires, and individual credit to a common end," claimed Frances Walker, president of M.I.T., in an address to the Phi Beta Kappa at Harvard in 1893. The *Wesleyan University Bulletin* observed in 1895 that the end of the century "is an era of rampant athleticism. But these contests play their part in making study citizens, and training men in the invaluable qualities of loyalty, self-sacrifice, obedience, and temperance." Sports could rescue American boys from the "haunts of dissipation" that seduced them in the cities—the taverns, gambling parlors, and brothels, according to the *Brooklyn Eagle*. Youth needs recreation, the *New York Herald* claimed, and "if they can't get it healthily and morally, they will seek it unhealthily and immorally at night, in drink saloons or at the gambling tables, and from these dissipations to those of a lower depth, the gradation is easy."[45]

Sports were also a way to resolve some class and racial tensions, offset others, and siphon off working-class or black discontent into other arenas. The playground movement put working-class children under the adult supervision of middle-class reformers to better control their behavior and socialization. "The free lands were used up. The cow country rose and fell. The safety valve was screwed down. But the explosion did not come," noted Frederic Paxson in 1917. How come? he wondered. "Because the safety valve of sport was designed, built and applied."[46]

It was through sports, not work, that self-making men could make themselves, at least physically, and demonstrate that "man was no longer fated to keep the body he was born with." Take Eugen Sandow, the German-born bodybuilder who gained an enormous following in the United States. "I know very well that I am not a perfect man as my manager frequently has for the purposes of advertising said, but I also know that by the application of certain broad principles I have acquired almost perfect control over myself."[47]

So off America went to the sporting green. The first tennis court was built in Boston in 1876, the first basketball court in 1891. The American Bowling Congress was founded in 1895, and the Amateur Athletic Union in 1890. "This vaunted age needs a saving touch of honest, old fashioned barbarism, so that when we come to die, we shall die leaving men behind us, and not a race of eminently respectable female saints," is what one boxing fan wrote in 1888.

Boxing was especially popular at the turn of the century. As were other sports, boxing was defended as a counter to the "mere womanishness" of modern, overcivilized society. But boxing was more than mere manhood; it heralded the triumphant return of the Heroic

Artisan as mythic hero. No sooner had he virtually disappeared into enormous, impersonal factories than he staged his triumphant return in the boxing ring. If the workaday world undermined working-class manhood—requiring obedience to rules and docility toward managers—then boxing celebrated his traditional virtues: toughness, prowess, ferocity. If men could not make things with the skill of their hands, they could at least destroy things, or others, with them.[48]

In his fascinating study of bare-knuckle prizefighting in America, *The Manly Art*, the historian Elliot Gorn describes the way that working-class bachelor subcultures in the late nineteenth-century city resurrected the language of skilled artisans in their descriptions of boxing matches. Just as industrialization had destroyed traditional skills and crushed artisanal autonomy, boxing revived it in a frenzied fantasy of violence. Boxing was a "profession," and boxers were "trained" in various "schools" of fighting. Newspapers reported that the combatants "went to work" or one "made good work" of his opponent. Admirers spoke of the way that particular fighters "plied their trades" or understood the "arts and mysteries" of the pugilistic métier. Words like "art," "science," and "craft" were tossed about as often as in universities. Boxers controlled their own labor like individual proprietors. Here was a "manly art," an act of violence which required craftsmanlike skill and deftness.[49]

No one symbolized this cult of "elemental virility" better than John L. Sullivan, perhaps the "greatest American hero of the late nineteenth century." With his manly swagger and well-waxed moustache, this Irish fighter recalled a lost era of artisanal heroism and symbolized "the growing desire to smash through the fluff of bourgeois gentility and the tangle of corporate ensnarements to the throbbing heart of life." And at the other end of the spectrum, no one could better symbolize the demise of artisanal manhood than Jack Johnson, the first black heavyweight boxing champion. Flamboyant and powerful, Johnson was the black specter that had haunted white workingmen since antebellum days—the fear that unskilled free blacks would triumph over skilled white workers in the workplace, the bedroom, and now, in the sporting world.[50]

Baseball, too, would have its darker moments, at least rhetorically, with the infamous Chicago Black Sox scandal, which rocked the sporting world in 1919 at the close of the era. But before that, baseball offered a rich palette of manly athletic expression for all of its players and fans. Theodore Roosevelt included baseball in his list of "the true sports for a manly race."[51] Just as horse racing had resulted in better horse breeding, Edward Marshall claimed in 1910, so baseball "resulted in improvement in man breeding." "No boy can grow to a perfectly normal manhood today without the benefits of at least a small amount of baseball experience and practice," wrote William McKeever in his popular advice manual, *Training the Boy* (1913). Perhaps novelist Zane Grey said it best. "All boys love baseball," he wrote. "If they don't they're not real boys."[52]

Baseball replaced the desiccating immorality of a dissolute life, providing a "remedy for the many evils resulting from the immoral associations boys and young men of our cities are apt to become connected with" and therefore deserving "the endorsement of every clergyman in the country." Baseball was good for men's bodies and souls, imperative for the health and moral fiber of the body social. From pulpits and advice manuals the virtues of baseball were sounded.[53]

Those virtues stressed, on the surface, autonomy and aggressive independence—but the game also required obedience, self-sacrifice, discipline, and hierarchy. Baseball's version of masculinity thus cut with a contradictory edge: If the masculinity expressed on the baseball field was exuberant, fiercely competitive, and wildly aggressive, it was so only in a controlled and orderly arena, closely supervised by powerful adults. Psychologically, baseball would always be a boy's game.

Like boxing, baseball recalled a bygone era of independent farmers and small shopkeepers. The first baseball parks were just that—parks or fields or grounds, all terms that referred to their bucolic rural origins (like Philadelphia's Shibe Park [1909], Chicago's Comiskey Park [1910] and Wrigley Field [1914], Boston's Fenway Park [1912], Pittsburgh's Forbes Field [1909], and New York's Polo Grounds [1911]; only Detroit's Tiger Stadium, built in 1912, broke this pattern until Yankee Stadium was built for the 1922 season). Here the pain and alienation of urban industrial work life were soothed, and the routine dull grayness of the urban landscape was broken up by these manicured patches of green.[54]

Baseball was fantasy; it was diversion, a safety valve, allowing the release of potential aggression in a healthy, socially acceptable way. In 1912 President William Howard Taft proclaimed himself a baseball fan, especially because it had salubrious moral effects on young people:

> Baseball takes people into the open air—it draws out millions of factory hands, of tradesmen and interior laborers of all kinds, who spend their afternoons whenever possible in a healthful, genuinely inspiring contest in the warm sunshine and fresh air, when many other sports, and in fact all natural tendencies conspire to keep them indoors engaged in various kinds of unwholesome and unhealthful pastimes.[55]

By the end of the second decade of the century, some of this innocence was lost as baseball became mired in several of those "unwholesome and unhealthful pastimes," especially drinking, gambling, and sexual promiscuity. With the 1919 World Series scandal, involving the infamous Chicago "Black Sox," commercialism had "come to dominate the sporting quality of sports"; heroes were venal, and the pristine pastoral was exposed as corrupt, part of the emergent corporate order and not the alternative to it that people had imagined.[56] But by then it was too late: Baseball had facilitated a casual accommodation to the new industrial economic order. The geographic frontier was replaced by the outfield fence, workplace autonomy by watching a solitary pitcher and batter square off against one another.

Useful Fictions

Men could also retrieve the heroic masculine virtues without ever leaving their living rooms or, at least, their dens. The frontier might be too elusive, the world of sports too corrupt, but literature could help promote savagery in even the most timid man's breast. Boys' literature found avid young male readers. Popular biographies of self-made successes were enormously popular. Some celebrated the self-made power and wealth of the robber barons; others were more interested in the manly virtues of the robber barons' nemesis, the outlaw. Jesse James, for example, developed armed robbery into a craftsman's skill. "Highway robbery as a fine art has been cultivated only in a way that has tended to bring it into disrepute," observed a writer in the *Republic* in 1874, until the James gang "burst upon us, and revealed a new field of worthy labor." The mythic figure of George

Armstrong Custer was also seen as "the incarnation of the heroic, virile, self-restrained and tough minded American." Dashing, debonair, and dutiful, Custer was also ruthless and monomaniacal in his pursuit of his manhood through the conquest of Indians. His carefully constructed persona was part flamboyant aristocrat, part cold sober professional, and part wild savage hunter.[57]

Tall tales and legends also reveal these masculine themes. Casey Jones (1900), John Henry (ca. 1873), and Paul Bunyan (collected 1912–1914) were mythic representations of the heroic triumphs in the same arenas and against the same forces that had defeated the older Heroic Artisan in reality. Jones's track skills are necessary to keep the Illinois Central trains running; John Henry outperforms a steam drill in a masterpiece of suicidal craftsmanship, dying "with the hammer in his hand"; and the giant logger Paul Bunyan outcuts the most technically developed chainsaws with his mighty ax. They were "heroes of an industrial world" projected back to the moment of the artisan's demise.[58]

In boys' fiction, heroes like Frank Merriwell embodied the strenuous ideal found in sports, excelling at every sport, always winning the big game for Yale when the chips were down—he could even throw a curve ball that curved twice!—without any compromise of his manly and moral virtues. Like Gilbert Patten (who wrote the Merriwell stories under the name Burt Standish), Horatio Alger offered his young readers fictional accounts of upward mobility gained through hard work, dedication, and a small dose of "luck and pluck." Alger's stories illustrate a distinctly American take on the making of the self-made man. Unlike nineteenth-century European novels, which often spend a good deal of time locating the young protagonist in a social landscape, these American novels begin with a dislocated individual, off to seek his fortune away from home. Horatio Alger's heroes are almost always orphans or at least living with and supporting their mothers. Henry Fleming (*The Red Badge of Courage*) and a host of soldier heroes are at the battlefield, aboard ship, or running away. And even after his transformation into a civilized man, Tarzan still is fatherless. "My mother was an Ape, and of course she couldn't tell me much about it. I never knew who my father was" is the last line of the novel. (Playwright Peter Schaffer noted also that "all cowboys are orphans.")

American novels often include a search for father—for legitimacy, perhaps, but also for the warmth and tenderness that readers felt lacking since their real fathers were preoccupied with their careers. This is particularly evident in Alger's stories. Richard Hunter, the hero of Alger's first book, *Ragged Dick* (1868), is an orphan whose honesty, hard work, and virtue earn him the respect of older men, who actually become his benefactors when Hunter rescues them from swindlers or their daughters from distress. What happy consolation to young male readers that in the world of work they may experience the love and largesse of the fathers whose absence they so painfully feel at home. These works obviously struck a nerve; Alger wrote at least 103 short novels, and their popularity made him perhaps history's most widely read novelist.[59]

Many of Alger's stories—such as *Risen from the Ranks, Strive and Succeed, Forging Ahead, Struggling Upward*, and *Slow and Sure*—describe the gradual ascent to respectability possible for the hardworking and dedicated young boy; others, like *Snares of New York*, document the "ominous geography" of the "urban juvenile underworld," warning young men of the "tricks, traps and pitfalls of city life" as the subtitle to another novel put it.[60] Alger constantly used descriptions of other young boys as the foils against which the hero undertakes his quest, his struggle "upward from a boyhood of privation and self-denial into a youth and manhood of prosperity and honor."[61] There's the lesser hero, a slightly younger and less vigorous boy who becomes our hero's apprentice; the snob, the son of a gentleman, who is "lazy, ignorant, arrogant, and unwilling to work because he considers it beneath his station" and who is both overtly contemptuous and secretly envious of the hero's success; and the poor boy, who lacks the intelligence or ability of the hero and is often susceptible to the corruption of his environment.

Some writers posed masculinist strategies for coming of age as men, offering vicarious accounts of young men being tested and proving themselves. Stephen Crane's *The Red Badge of Courage* (1895) is perhaps the most famous of these.[62] When Henry Fleming first sees the enemy, he is "not a man, but a member" of the army because he "felt the subtle battle-brotherhood more potent even than the cause for which they were fighting." His experience is less about virtue than about the fear of shame, humiliation, and disgrace. His initiation involves the substitution of one form of fear—the fear of social humiliation in front of other men—for an earlier, childlike fear, the fear of death. Fleming tries to "measure himself by his comrades" and falls short. Following his shameful inability to prove his manhood in battle, he was "amid wounds," feeling that his shame "could be viewed." He "wished that he, too, had a wound." But eventually, he rediscovers what contemporary masculinists might call his "inner warrior," and his shame and humiliation lead him to fight like a "barbarian, a beast," a "pagan who defends his religion," so that, ultimately, he was a "hero" like other "proved men." As we leave Henry Fleming, we see him now in the possession of

a quiet manhood, nonassertive, but a sturdy and strong blood. He knew that he would no more quail before his guides wherever they should point. He had been to touch the great death, and found that, after all, it was but the great death. He was a man.

Being seen as a man was important for adult men, too. And turn-of-the-century fiction offered a wide variety of masculine themes. Literary critics like W. Churchill Williams and Bliss Carman had fumed against "emasculated" literature; American writers "have become so over-nice in our feelings, so restrained and formal, so bound by habit and use in our devotion to the effeminate realists, that one side of our nature was starved. We must have a revolt at any cost."[63]

Frank Norris was among the chief rebels. He believed in a new masculinist fiction with less attention to style and more to action and adventure. "Who cares for fine style! Tell your yarn and let your style go to the devil. We don't want literature, we want life," Norris bellowed. The impulse for manly fiction must come "far from the studios of the aesthetes, the velvet jackets and the uncut hair, far from the sexless creatures who cultivate their little art of writing as the fancier cultivates his orchids" and lead one into "a world of Working Men, crude of speech, swift of action, strong of passion, straight to the heart of a new life, on the borders of a new time, and there only will you learn to know the stuff of which must come the American fiction of the future."[64]

In several of his novels, among them *Moran, Blix, A Man's Woman, Vandover and the Brute*, and *McTeague*, Norris fused two themes—the descent into animality and the civilizing influences of women—and claimed that manhood rests between both poles. In *McTeague*, perhaps his most famous work, Norris explores the seamy side of Self-Made Manhood and reveals the terrible consequences of greed on family and home life as well as in the society at large. McTeague is a modestly successful dentist, who is, as Norris describes him, a massive, powerful man, "immensely strong, stupid, docile, and obedient." His mantra is "you can't make small of me." McTeague is possessed by undercurrents of deep, dark, brooding animal brutality, which he struggles against but is unable to contain in the face of greed. Greed makes virtually everyone in McTeague's world psychotic—from Zerkow the pawnbroker, who listens to Maria, the maid's incessant chattering about fantasy gold-plated china, to Trina, his wife, who wins $5,000 in the lottery and becomes a cruel miser, salting away whatever pennies she can rather than use them to help herself and her husband. McTeague is double-edged tragedy: His own tragic flaw—his animality that he cannot completely contain—becomes enmeshed with the tragic flaw of social life at the turn of the century, an unbridled greed which destroys all human relationships and ultimately claims his life.[65]

In *Vandover and the Brute* (written in 1896, published posthumously in 1914), Norris explored this split personality between the civilized man and his primal, deep manhood in a style reminiscent of Robert Louis Stevenson's *Dr. Jekyll and Mr. Hyde*. First "there was himself, the real Vandover of every day, the same familiar Vandover that looked back at him from his mirror." But then there was also "the wolf, the beast, whatever the creature that lived in his flesh, and that struggled within him now, striving to gain ascendancy, to absorb the real Vandover into his own hideous identity."[66]

In *A Man's Woman* (1900) Norris explored this split in two figures, counterposing Ward Bennett, a brutish Arctic explorer, to Lloyd Searight, a strong-willed nurse with a masculine name, whose creed was "to *do* things." Bennett possesses a coarse but elemental masculinity. "The world wants men," he exclaims, "great, strong, harsh, brutish men—men with purposes who let nothing, nothing, stand in their way." Through the course of the novel, Lloyd discovers that it is the natural role of women to submit to men, while Ward learns that masculinity can consist of more than animal brutality.[67]

William Dean Howells agreed with Norris about cultural feminization, arguing that Americans had become a "weak and sniveling race," but he explored the cultural clash between the rising middle class and the traditional aristocracy in terms that found him labeled an "effeminate realist" himself. In his ironically titled *The Rise of Silas Lapham* (1885), the clash between these two classes, represented by two families, the Laphams and the Coreys, is also a clash between two forms of manhood, those of the genteel Bromfield Corey and the uncouth, brashly arrogant Lapham, whose demise is all the more pitiful because the Coreys have become effete and unable to help him when he falls. Silas Lapham is one of the first completely Self-Made Men in American literature, and his story is really about his unmaking—the fall of the Self-Made Man is, in the end, far more significant than his rise.[68]

The most famous novelist of the day, Henry James, was also pessimistic about the possibilities of revitalizing American manhood from the inherited models of manhood. Sentimental, prosaic, and favoring "genderless minds usually devoid of desire," as one critic put it, James's male characters seemed to embody everything that real men were not. For example, the floridly named Hyacinth Robinson in *The Princess Casamassima* is "small," with a "narrow chest," "delicate" hands, a "childishly slight" frame, and a "pale complexion." But even James also delivered a tirade against feminization through Basil Ransome in *The Bostonians* and then fled to a vision of natural aristocracy (although he remained contemptuous of aristocrats).[69] Norris descended to naive innocence and animal

Two Archetypes of Masculinity at the Beginning of the Nineteenth Century: The Genteel Patriarch. Although George Washington was frequently depicted as a virtuous man of the people, the Father of the Country was also its *pater familias*, and represented the gentility of the landed gentry. (*The Washington Family* [1798] by Edward Savage; courtesy of General Research Division, The New York Public Library, Astor, Lenox and Tilden Foundations)

The Heroic Artisan is the mythical ideal of the honest hardworking man whose virtue stems from his commitment to industry. This myth has lasted many decades, only recently fading. (Illustration by Thomas Nast, published March 26, 1882; courtesy of The University of Chicago Press)

The Self-Made Man Appears on the Historical Stage: Although Thomas Cole intended his *Daniel Boone at his Cabin on the Great Osage Lake* (1826) to celebrate transcendental virtues, he also reveals the loneliness of the Self-Made Man's constant quest. (Courtesy of Mead Art Museum, Amherst College)

The Myth and the Reality of the Self-Made Man in Politics: "General Harrison, the true Friend of the People"—a Whig Party campaign poster from the Presidential campaign of 1840 portrays William Henry Harrison in front of his log cabin. (Lithograph from Dorothy Goebel, *William Henry Harrison*, Indianapolis, 1926; reproduced in Carl Fish, *The Rise of the Common Man* [New York: Macmillan, 1927])

The Reality: William Henry Harrison's estate at North Bend. Ohio. (From an engraving in *The Ladies Repository* 4, 193 [July 1841]; reproduced in Carl Fish, *The Rise of the Common Man* [New York: Macmillan, 1927])

Manly Nurture and Effeminacy at the End of the Civil War: After his assassination, Abraham Lincoln is received in the heavenly arms of George Washington, while Jefferson Davis tries to escape Union capture by dressing as a woman. *Top: Lincoln and Washington Apotheosis* (1865). *Bottom*: "Jefferson Davis as an Unprotected Female!" (*Harper's Weekly*, 27 May 1865). (Courtesy of General Research Division, The New York Public Library, Astor, Lenox and Tilden Foundations)

A COUNTER-PART

Negative Images of Turn-of-the-Century Masculinity: At the turn of the century, Americans were presented with several negative images of manhood, from the dissolute and disheveled egghead intellectual and the brutish pinhead of this cartoon, to the effeminate clerk in a dry goods store who fixes his hair while his customers go unattended. *Left*: "A Counter-Part" (postcard, published ca. 1910, from the personal collection of Jonathan Ned Katz; reprinted by permission). *Bottom*: "Education: Is There No Middle Course?" (Illustration by Thomas Nast, *Harper's Weekly*, 30 November 1879; courtesy of General Research Division, The New York Public Library, Astor, Lenox and Tilden Foundations)

Manly Nurture and Homosocial Solace in Fraternal Orders: Middle-class men found both hearty camaraderie and masculinist protest against feminization in turn-of-the-century fraternal orders. By 1897, one in five American men had joined. With rituals heavily laden with religious symbolism and myth, fraternalists were devoted to a form of manly nurture. Lodges were the only place where men would wear aprons or dresses. *Left*: Daguerreotype of early fraternalists, 1850. *Bottom*: Rocky Hill Lodge Knights of Pythias Degree Team, Portland, Maine, early twentieth century. (Both courtesy of Scottish Rite Masonic Museum of Our National Heritage [80.45 and 84.6]; photographs by John Miller)

Muscular Christianity Remasculinizes Jesus: Railing against cultural feminization, Muscular Christians recast Jesus as a hypermasculine savior, "no lick spittle proposition," but the "greatest scrapper who ever lived," according to evangelist preacher Billy Sunday. Others retrieved the image of the Heroic Artisan to transform Jesus into a working-class socialist hero. *Top*: Billy Sunday preaches at a meeting for men in Atlanta, Georgia, 1917. (Courtesy of The Archives of the Billy Graham Center, Wheaton, Illinois). *Right*: "The Carpenter of Nazareth was 'a workman that needeth not to be ashamed.'" (Frontispiece illustration from *The Call of the Carpenter* by Bouck White [1913]; illustration by Balfour Ker)

Remaking Masculinity Through Western Fantasies:
No sooner was the frontier "closed" in reality than it
was reopened through fantasies of manly confrontation
with the wild and untamed. Theodore Roosevelt recast
himself from an asthmatic weakling into a more heroic
mold in the Dakotas, while Ernest Thompson Seton
invoked Native American rituals in the founding of
the Boy Scouts of America in 1910. Each of these
photographs was posed in a photographer's studio. For
over a century, American boys have heartily embraced
the myth. *Top*: Theodore Roosevelt as frontiersman.
(Courtesy of Theodore Roosevelt Birthplace National
Monument). *Right*: Ernest Thompson Seton in Indian
costume, 1917. (Courtesy Julia M. Seton Trust and
Ernest Thompson Seton Institute)

No writer was more convinced of the regenerative masculinizing capacities of western adventure than Owen Wister. Son of a wealthy Philadelphia merchant, Wister studied acting at Harvard before heading west. His 1902 novel, *The Virginian*, celebrated the cowboy and heralded the literary form of the Western. *Left*: Owen Wister in costume for a play at Harvard, 1880. *Bottom*: Wister at Yellowstone Park, 1887. (Both photographs courtesy of American Heritage Center, University of Wyoming)

brutality but could not offer it as hope in a world corrupted by greed. And Howells implied that both models of successful manhood—nouveaux riches businessmen and aristocrats of inherited wealth—were impotent for the twentieth century.

Other cultural media echoed the preoccupations of masculinist fiction. For example, painters such as Frederic Remington, Thomas Hart Benton, Thomas Eakins, and Ashcan School members like George Bellows, Robert Henri, and John Sloan challenged European painterly conventions of beauty with their stark evocations of the brutal reality of urban life, as in Bellows's painting of boxing matches or Remington's romanticized visions of western Indian slaughter and cowboy life. Whether painting the hurly-burly of the city streets or the rugged coast of Maine, Bellows's energetic style and rough-hewn subject matter brought appreciation from male viewers who felt excluded by dandified aesthetes. And Eakins finessed a homoerotic adoration of the male body into muscular shoulders and straining backs of scullers along the Schuylkill River, the studied determination of baseball players (*Baseball Players Practicing* [1875]), or the youthful sinewy male bonding (*The Swimming Hole* [1883–1885]). His paintings, one reviewer noted in 1875, were full of "pure natural force and virility."[70]

In music Charles Ives rejected what he heard as the "sweet" or "feminine" music of the impressionists—"easy music for the sissies, for the lilypad ears." Instead, Ives derived a masculine musical idiom, incorporating the manly dissonance of strong sounds and a virile patriotism. At the end of one composition he wrote, "To strengthen and give more muscle to the ear, brain, heart, limbs and FEAT! Atta boy!" Elsewhere he provides occasional marginal notation to "keep up the fight!" or "don't quit because the ladybirds don't like it."[71] And pioneer architect Louis Sullivan was also dissatisfied with the baroque forms of the late Victorian building and sought to create a distinctly masculine type of building, the skyscraper. A man who moved in an entirely homosocial world, Sullivan sought to recapture manly power in corporeal form. He claimed that he learned from Michelangelo "the power and possibility of being male, of being super male." Upon observing a warehouse of the Marshall Field Company, Sullivan wrote, "Here is a man for you to look at. A man that walks on two legs instead of four, has active muscles . . . lives and breathes . . . in a world of barren pettiness, a male," while at another retail store for the same company, he praised the building as a "virile force," a building with "red blood, a real man, a manly man . . . an entire male." Sullivan's skyscrapers were symbolic attempts to create a real man, and his disciple Frank Lloyd Wright brought the ideal of space as masculine into the vernacular design of his prairie houses, challenging the home as a feminine preserve.[72]

But nowhere could American men find a better exemplar of rugged outdoor masculinity than out west with the cowboy, that noble denizen of the untamed frontier. The cowboy occupies an important place in American cultural history: He is America's contribution to the world's stock of mythic heroes. But the cowboy was not always a hero. In the 1860s and 1870s the cowboy was called a "herder," and he appeared in public prints and writing as a rough, uncouth, shaggy, and dirty man, whose behavior was violent, barbarous, and rowdy. He was the brutal outlaw, not the good guy. Writing in 1875, Laura Winthrop Johnson saw no glamour in these "rough men with shaggy hair and wild staring eyes, in butternut trousers stuffed into great rough boots." But around 1882 a cowboy named Buck Taylor at the First Wild West Show captured the attention of a writer, Prentiss Ingraham. The Wild West Show was a re-creation of the West in the form of a traveling circus. Organized by Buffalo Bill Cody, the show depicted the conquest and taming of the

Wild West. When Ingraham wrote a fictional biography of Taylor in 1887, later expanded into a series of dime novels, the new cowboy was invented.[73]

By 1887 the great cattle drives that were his home had ended, and the "big die-up" of the winter of 1886–1887 had bankrupted many cattle outfits and so altered ranch life that the cowboy was "less a knight errant and more a hired man on horseback." In fiction the cowboy was all guts and glory. The cowboy thus emerged in literature at the exact moment of his disappearance as an independent craftsman and his transformation into a wage worker in a new industry of cattle ranching.[74]

The end of the century also witnessed the creation of the rodeo, a "celebration of the unique and daring sports indulged in and enjoyed by all the virile characters of the western frontier," as a promotional handbill for Cheyenne's Frontier Days put it. The first rodeo was held in 1883 in Pecos, Texas; five years later, folks in Prescott, Arizona, paid admission to see cowboys strut their cowpunching stuff in arenas. By the 1890s rodeos had defined formats and rules that governed the major competitions—steer wrestling, bareback riding, and bronco busting. Cheyenne's Frontier Days were inaugurated in 1897 as a self-conscious "annual resurrection of the west as it was, for the edification of the west as it is." One magazine writer explained the significance of Frontier Days in 1909:

> Civilization is pushing everything before it: thriving cities and well kept farms are taking the place of the cattle upon a thousand hills. But the pioneer still clings with a pathetic tenacity to the old customs . . . a pathetic but vigorous desire . . . to prove that strong arms and courageous hearts still existed on the range.[75]

Organizers had no doubts that it was rugged western manliness that was also being resurrected. Individual acts were extolled for their "peril to life and limb"; commentators were awed by the "sheer nerve" of the bareback rider, and one waxed poetic about broncos—"murderers that plunge with homicidal fury beneath the cinches of leather of a bucking saddle." For the participants the rodeo gave the "feeling of being part of the frontier that still lives in the professional rodeo arena. A cowboy on a bronco symbolizes the rugged individuality of the Western man and beast." For the spectators the rodeo was a "true taste of the wild and woolly."[76] The rodeo pen preserved the frontier as gladiatorial arena and its competitors as participants in a blood sport.

As a mythic creation the cowboy was fierce and brave, willing to venture into unknown territory, a "negligent, irrepressible wilderness," and tame it for women, children, and emasculated civilized men. As soon as the environment has been subdued, he must move on, unconstrained by the demands of civilized life, unhampered by clinging women and whining children and uncaring bosses and managers.[77] His is a freedom which cannot be "bounded by the fences of a too weak and timid conventionalism," as Harold Wright put it in his western novel *When a Man's a Man* (1916).[78] He is a man of impeccable ethics, whose faith in natural law and natural right is eclipsed only by the astonishing fury with which he demands rigid adherence to them. He is a man of action—"grim [and] lean, . . . of few topics, and not many words concerning these." He moves in a world of men, in which daring, bravery, and skill are his constant companions. He lives by physical strength and rational calculation; his compassion is social and generalized, but he forms no lasting emotional bonds with any single person. He lives alone, a "hermited horseman" out on the range, settling the West.[79]

But, of course, he doesn't really exist, except in the pages of the western, the literary genre heralded by the publication of Owen Wister's novel *The Virginian* in 1902.[80] Wister is not only the creator of the genre but one of its biggest boosters and celebrators. Born into an aristocratic Philadelphia family, Wister's first love was music, and he went to Harvard to study composition. When it became clear that he would never become a truly great composer, his father insisted that he return home to a position at Boston's largest brokerage house. Within a few months Wister had a nervous breakdown and developed Bell's palsy (a paralysis of the face). He consulted S. Weir Mitchell, who diagnosed Wister's problem as neurasthenia and prescribed a trip to a Wyoming dude ranch for a cure. At the ranch Wister slept outdoors in a tent, bathed in an icy creek each morning, spent hours in the saddle, hunted, fished, worked in the roundup, and helped to brand calves, castrate bulls, and deliver foals. "I am beginning to be able to feel I'm something of an animal and not a stinking brain alone," he wrote from the ranch in 1885. In three weeks Wister believed himself to be completely cured.[81]

And completely converted to western life, which he was now devoted to celebrating. The western was his creation, a vehicle for "an upper class composer–short-story-writer with doubts about his independence to claim a robust masculinity," according to literary critic Jane Tompkins.[82] As a genre the western represented the apotheosis of masculinist fantasy, a revolt not against women but against feminization. The vast prairie is the domain of male liberation from workplace humiliation, cultural feminization, and domestic emasculation. The saloon replaces the church, the campfire replaces the Victorian parlor, the range replaces the factory floor. The western is a purified, pristine male domain.

What are the traits of such a mythic figure as a cowboy? Of course, he is manly. He is a natural aristocrat—a "natural nobleman, formed not by civilization and its institutions but the spontaneous influence of the land working on an innate goodness." Like Natty Bumppo or Davy Crockett before him, the Virginian, as the narrator first meets him, is a "handsome, ungrammatical son of the soil"; "here in flesh and blood was a truth which I had long believed in words, but never met before. The creature we call a *gentleman* lies deep in the hearts of thousands that are born without a chance to master the outward graces of the type."[83] Having served his apprenticeship, he is now a master of his craft of riding, roping, and killing. His values are the old artisanal virtues: "self-discipline, unswerving purpose; the exercise of knowledge, skill, ingenuity, and excellent judgement; and a capacity to continue in the face of total exhaustion and overwhelming odds." He is free in a free country, embodying republican virtue and autonomy.

And he is white. To Wister, the West was "manly, egalitarian, self-reliant, and Aryan." A 1902 review of *The Virginian* in the *World's Work* saw this deeper theme in the western at the moment of its origins:

> To catch the deeper meaning of our life, one's path must be toward that Western verge of the continent where all white men are American born, because there only are the culture and conservatism of the East, the chivalrism and the fire-eating spirit of the South, and the broad, unhampered gambler's view of life native to raw Western soil, all transmuted into a democracy of no distinctions.

Frederic Remington echoed such sentiments. He was, like Wister, an elite easterner whose first trip west was designed to cure neurasthenia. He rejected effete conceptions of beauty, of the "cards and custards" of the eastern establishment, and he hated Europe with its "collars, cuffs and foreign languages."[84] And like Wister, Remington's masculinist revival was an all-white affair. He loathed immigrants: "Jews, Injuns, Chinamen, Italians, Huns—the rubbish of the earth I hate," he wrote. "I've got some Winchesters and when the massacring begins, I can get my share of 'em, and what's more, I will." And he detested blacks; writing to Wister, he commented on the tragedy of the Civil War, when "so many Americans [had] to be killed to free a lot of damn niggers who are better off under the yoke. There is something fateful in our destiny that way." He closed his letter with some relief that in the Spanish-American war, at least, "we will kill a few Spaniards instead of Anglo-Saxons," a change that "will be proper and nice."[85]

The cowboy hero of the western novel was an anachronism, obsolete at the moment of his creation. Wister knew full well that this new genre was in fantasy mode, as he wrote in an editorial preface to *The Virginian*:

> What has become of the horseman, the cow-puncher, the last romantic figure upon our soil? For he was romantic. Whatever he did, he did with his might. The bread that he earned was earned hard, the wages that he squandered were squandered hard. . . . Well, he will be among us always, invisible, waiting his chance to live and play as he would like. His wild kind has been among us always, since the beginning, a young man with his temptations, a hero without wings.

To Remington, the cowboy was the last cavalier; his illustrations for Wister's essay, "Evolution of the Cowpuncher" (1895), portrayed the cowboy as "the noble descendent of chivalric knights and crusaders." It was an image that resonated for generations of American men. *The Virginian* went through fourteen editions and sold over three hundred thousand copies between its initial publication in 1902 and 1904. Just as he had disappeared in real life, the cowboy had arrived in myth.[86]

No western writer of the era managed to cover all these themes as powerfully as Wister, but several writers plied a similar trade with powerful and popular results. For Jack London or Edgar Rice Burroughs the frontier could simply be transported elsewhere—for example, the African jungle or the Alaskan Klondike. Here men might reunite with their Darwinian ancestors and retrieve their pure masculinity by shedding all the trappings of modernity. Wrenched from effete, civilized life or born into the life of the primitive, Buck and Tarzan, two of the most popular male characters in American fiction, hear the call of their primitive instincts and return to become wolves and apes.

When we first meet Buck, in London's *Call of the Wild* (1903), he is a relatively tame house pet in California, dognapped by an impoverished gardener and sold to a Klondike expedition. There, in the wild, he learns quickly the "law of club and fang" and becomes the strongest and most successful and ferocious sled dog. He has a multitude of adventures, including a deep love for the man who saves him from a savage beating and then treats him kindly—a deep, manly love, not the love of a tame animal. But even that love could not "civilize" the "strain of the primitive":

> Deep in the forest a call was sounding, and as often as he heard this call, mysteriously thrilling and luring, he felt compelled to turn his back upon the fire and the beaten earth around it, and to plunge into the forest.[87]

To which he eventually succumbs, in a masterful regression that is at once evolutionary and developmental. London revels in Buck's muscular power and brute ferocity and provides a potent antidote to overcivilization. Here's London at his most eloquent:

> There is an ecstasy that marks the summit of life, and beyond which life cannot rise. And such is the paradox of living, this ecstasy comes when one is most alive, and it comes as a complete forgetfulness of living, comes to the artist, caught up and out of himself in a sheet of flame; it comes to the soldier, war-mad on a stricken field and refusing quarter; and it came to Buck, leading the pack, sounding the old wolf-cry, straining after the food that was alive and that fled swiftly before him through the moonlight. He was sounding the deeps of his nature, and of the parts of his nature that were deeper than he, going back into the womb of Time. He was mastered by the sheer surging of life, the tidal wave of being, the perfect joy of each separate muscle, joint, and sinew and that it was everything that was not death, that it was aglow and rampant, expressing itself in movement, flying exultantly under the stars and over the face of dead matter that did not move.

Another of London's novels, *The Sea Wolf* (1904), applied similar themes to the interaction among men. Humphrey Van Weyden, the effeminate, overcivilized narrator, receives his own initiation aboard the ship of the aptly-named Wolf Larsen, a working-class brute who possesses "a strength savage, ferocious, alive in itself, the essence of life . . . the potency of motion."[88] The narrator rejects his mentor's animal brutality as a way to shed his older, sissified identity and finally achieves a sense of himself as a man.

This contrast of civilization and animality is the bedrock of Burroughs's *Tarzan of the Apes* (1912) and the subsequent series of books that saw Tarzan have every manly adventure known to Burroughs including returning to the Old West and rocketing off to outer space. Tarzan is the personification, Burroughs writes, "of the primitive man, the hunter, the warrior," the Rousseauian innocent, the "naked savage" who is also, it turns out, a blue-blooded English nobleman. In his dramatic (and steamy) encounters with Jane, we fully understand the power of the primitive.[89] Tarzan embodies the "avenging hero, half animal and half human, fusing beast and patrician, [who] descend[s] into an evil under-class to save a helpless bourgeois civilization." Tarzan "has a man's figure and a man's brain, but he was an ape by training and environment." At the climax of this Darwinian nightmare, in which descending the evolutionary ladder is the only mechanism to retrieve manhood, Tarzan tells Jane that he has "come across the ages out of the dim and distant past from the lair of the primeval man to claim you—for your sake I have become a civilized man—for your sake I have crossed oceans and continents—for your sake I will be whatever you will me to be." Tarzan's triumph is that he will be civilized by a woman.[90]

This kind of civilization seemed perfectly reasonable to Burroughs and, in a sense, expressed the American ambivalence with the nobility. Genteel Patriarchs had been largely discredited as masculine role models, precisely because they were *already* tame. But what of Tarzan's aristocratic birth, the natural aristocracy of the cowboy avenger, or the primitive nobility of the reborn animal in Buck? The American middle-class man's fascination with natural aristocracy, a nobility of bearing, temperament, and demeanor that such a freeborn aristocrat possesses prior to his contact with the civilized world—this was a nobility worth retrieving. At times it appeared that any trait that was natural was virtuous, any trait gained through civilization was unmanly.

London and Burroughs transported the western to other, more exotic locales, but they did not transform it. The western remains the core cultural contribution of masculinist escapism, a vein mined no better than by Zane Grey. Like Wister, Remington, and other purveyors of the western motif, Grey came from a wealthy Philadelphia family but abandoned his career as a dentist to write westerns. In his first and most famous work, *Riders of the Purple Sage* (1912), the hero, Bern Venters, represents the nineteenth-century men who "have been enfeebled by the doctrines of a feminized Christianity," embodied by Jane Witherspoon, who has symbolically emasculated him in the opening pages by taking away his guns. Through his transformation "American men are taking their manhood back from the Christian women who have been holding it in thrall." "Harness the cave man—yes!" wrote Grey in 1924, "but do not kill him. Something of the wild and primitive should remain instinctive in the human race."[91]

Fantasies of western adventure, testing and proving manhood on the battlefield; the reclamation of the workplace for heroic artisans and the critiques of marketplace manhood and aristocratic snobbery; celebrating the manly in literature, music, and art and even going native in a Darwinian devolution to pure animality—these were the dominant themes of masculinist literature at the turn of the century. Like bodybuilding, becoming a sports or fitness fanatic, or perfecting the body as a way of perfecting the self, these were vigorous, desperate efforts to provide for men the possibility of imagining their manhood in its traditional settings, consuming their manhood in idealized versions of those settings —even as the real men who were its consumers had to find new ways to adjust to the changing circumstances that transformed their lives.

CHAPTER 5

A Room of His Own

Socializing the New Man

Manliness can only be taught by men, and not by those who are half men, half old women.
—R. S. S. Baden-Powell (founder of the Boy Scouts)

The purpose of our institutions is to manufacture manhood.
—Sen. Albert J. Beveridge *The Young Man and the World* (1905)

By the beginning of the twentieth century, testing manhood had become increasingly difficult. The public arena was crowded and competitive, and heading west to start over was more the stuff of fiction than possibility. What was worse, many believed, a new generation of young boys was being raised entirely by women, who would turn America's future men into whiny little mama's boys. Men sought to rescue their sons from the feminizing clutches of mothers and teachers and create new ways to "manufacture manhood."

Their efforts were also somewhat self-serving. The separation of spheres, it has been argued, had left women domestic prisoners, locked into the home by an ideology of feminine domesticity and Christian piety and virtue. By the end of the century, I've suggested, men began to experience the separate spheres as painful to them as well. Men were excluded from domestic life, unable to experience the love, nurture, and repose that the home supposedly represented. How could a man return to the home without feeling like a wimp?

One solution, as we've seen, was to colonize the home, to find a small corner that could be unmistakably "his," like the den or the study in the nineteenth century, or the basement, the workshop, the garage, or even the backyard barbecue pit today. But fears of feminization gave a new urgency to men's desires. Women were entirely in charge of socialization of young boys. The three principal institutions that dominate early childhood socialization—family, religion, and education—were completely staffed and run by women. Many men felt that they needed to wrest control over socialization and get more actively involved themselves. To that end, men decided to inculcate manhood into the next generation and create some parallel institutions for themselves as well.

But first, American men needed to come home. Earlier in the century reformers had promoted the separation of spheres, in part to maintain the public arena as a masculine testing ground. This had been so successful that by century's end the family looked very different from its early nineteenth-century antecedent. Now husbands and wives spent their days in separate worlds—he, away all day at work, at increasing distances from home, and she, at home all day, looking after the house and children. Both arenas were increasingly industrialized and mechanized—his, by the assembly line, mass production, and growth of white-collar clerical positions, and hers, by innovations in household technology that made the home look like a little factory. Fathers' roles diminished in proportion to the distance and time they spent at work away from the home.[1] An increasing number of industrial products and services designed for the home turned the housewife into a "household engineer," as domestic reformer Christine Frederick termed her in her treatise *Household Engineering* (1910).[2]

At the moment of perhaps their greatest separation, husbands and wives were told they should establish what critics called companionate marriage. Husband and wife should be more devoted, more emotionally *connected*, than before. On the one hand, it meant fewer children—from nearly five children per wife (4.94) between 1800 and 1849 to less than three (2.77) between 1870 and 1900 and less than two (1.92) by 1915. The percentage of women who had only one child jumped from 4 percent in 1800–1849 to 8.1 percent by 1870–1900 and to 20 percent by 1915. On the other hand, it meant increasing sexual activity. Ironically, however, it also meant an increasing number of divorces, foreshadowing the second wave of feminism and companionate marriage in the 1970s and 1980s. Husbands and wives were more likely to part if the companionship faltered. In 1916 one in four marriages ended in divorce in San Francisco; in Los Angeles it was one in five and in Chicago one in seven. Psychologist John B. Watson predicted that "in fifty years there will be no such thing as marriage."[3]

Along with companionate marriage came a fatherhood movement. "It is far more needful for children that a father should attend to the formation of their character and habits, and end in developing their social, intellectual and moral nature, than it is that he should earn money to furnish them with handsome clothes and a variety of tempting food," wrote Catharine Beecher and her sister Harriet Beecher Stowe in *The American Woman's Home* (1869). "The home is man's affair as much as woman's," wrote Martha and Robert Brueres in 1912. "When God made homemakers, male and female created He them!" "The responsibility of the home is not [the wife's] alone, but equally the husband's," announced the editor of *American Homes and Gardens* in 1905. "There is no reason at all why men should not sweep and dust, make beds, clean windows, fix the fire, clean the grate, arrange the furniture and cook."

Some men, it seems, heeded the advice. A large number of men participated in childbirth, often at the request of their wives, and despite much counsel against it.[4] In a new ideology of "masculine domesticity," men found

> a model of behavior in which fathers would agree to take on increased responsibility for some of the day-to-day tasks of bringing up children and spending their time away from work in playing with their sons and daughters, teaching them, taking them on trips. A domestic man would also make his wife, rather than his male cronies, his regular companion on evenings out. And while he might not dust the mantel or make the bed except in special circumstances, he would take a significantly greater interest in the details of running the household and caring for the children that [*sic*] his father was expected to do.[5]

Even at home, however, men were still men. They focused on their wives, but they felt on surer ground with their sons. Domesticity "was incorporated in to the concept of manliness, as men became convinced that in order to have their sons grow up to be 'manly,' they should involve themselves more substantially in their children's upbringing." These men were perhaps not the sensitive "new men" feminist women keep hoping for; their domestic participation was an "alternative to feminism, a way to deflect and even sabotage women's advances."[6] For young boys, though, the effort ushered in a period of dramatic transformation.

Boys' and girls' spheres of play were, for the first time, completely separated. Fathers sought father-son togetherness and feared a young boy's identification with his mother and sissification by playing with his sisters. Part of the change was in the ways baby boys and girls were dressed. Prior to the 1880s little boys and little girls were dressed identically. Both wore what looked like white christening gowns during infancy and short, loose-fitting dresses in early childhood—that is, boys and girls looked like little girls. But that changed in the late 1880s as parents dressed their toddlers in gender-appropriate clothing, and knickerbockers and trousers made their first appearance for little boys.

In the first decades of the twentieth century, clothing became color coded. The only problem was choosing the right color scheme. A 1918 editorial entitled "Pink or Blue?" in the magazine *The Infants' Department* explained:

> there has been a great diversity of opinion on the subject, but the generally accepted rule is pink for the boy and blue for the girl. The reason is that pink being a more decided and stronger color is more suitable for the boy; while blue, which is more delicate and dainty, is prettier for the girl.

It is unclear exactly why these colors were subsequently reversed. At the time, boys wore pink or red because they were manly colors, indicating strength and determination, and girls wore light blue, an airier color, like the sky, because girls were so flighty. Parents debated the question in the letters column of the Sears, Roebuck catalog and eventually flipped over to the present color arrangement. But as late as 1939 the debate continued, as "What Color for Your Baby?" an article in *Parents Magazine*, suggested that "red symbolizes zeal and courage, while blue is symbolic of faith and constancy."[7]

By the first decades of the new century, boys and girls were not only wearing different clothes but playing with different toys. Toys were increasingly marketed as appropriate only for boys or for girls.[8] One writer advised parents about boys' fighting:

> There are times when every boy must defend his own rights if he is not to become a coward, and lose the road to independence and true manhood. . . . The strong-willed boy needs no inspiration to combat, but often a good deal of guidance and restraint. If he fights more than, let us say, a half-dozen times a week,—except of course, during his first week at a new school—he is probably over-quarrelsome and needs to curb. The sensitive, retiring boy, on the other hand, needs encouragement to stand his ground and fight.[9]

So boys were to average a fight a day—except during the first week at a new school, during which, presumably, they would have to fight more often than that! By contrast, a boy with no interest in fighting was unnatural, a "nonentity," argued G. Stanley Hall in his celebrated work *Adolescence* (1904). It was "better even an occasional nose dented by a fist . . . than stagnation, general cynicism and censoriousness, bodily and psychic cowardice."[10]

For boys growing older, advice books returned to the same advice as that given earlier in the century, counseling parents to maintain the separation of spheres for boys and girls. Boys were to avoid dancing, sleeping on feather beds, warm rooms, and reading books—these last because they were "artificial," providing only "second hand information" compared with "completely natural experience," the real instructor of manhood. "The tendency of novel reading is most pernicious," Mrs. S. B. Dana had written. "It enervates the mental powers, and unfits them for close study and serious contemplation. It promotes sickly sensibility, and renders its votaries unfit for the pursuits of real life"—just as it had done in the early nineteenth century.[11]

Schooling for Manhood

There were two worries for men with young sons in school. As discussed in the previous chapter, teaching was dominated by women. The era also witnessed new pseudoscientific theories claiming to demonstrate that women and men were essentially different species and that the education of the two together would destroy both manhood and womanhood. Opponents believed that "constant intimacy between maturing boys and girls fosters an undesirable precocity and introduces unnecessarily perplexing problems." Namely, one presumes, sex.[12]

Most opponents believed that attending school together would harm girls "by assimilating them to boys' ways and work, robbing them of their sense of feminine character," and make boys "effeminate and unfit for the serious business of life in a man's world," as G. Stanley Hall put it. Hall's massive, two-volume, fourteen-hundred-page treatise *Adolescence* (1904) made him the instant expert on the topic and provided an important justification for opposing coeducation.[13] Hall based his arguments on the theory of recapitulation, a still-popular view that the lifelong development of each individual recapitulates the entire history of the species as a whole. Each child passed through all the evolutionary stages of human history, from savagery to civilization, through the course of development. "Ontogeny recapitulates phylogeny" is the theory's epigrammatic formulation. In this model, adolescence was pivotal, the moment of transition from the barbarian state of childhood to the civilized stage of mature adulthood. But according to Hall, women and men represented different stages of this evolutionary development. Women were evolutionarily older, more primitive, and conservative, while men were more modern, adaptive, and variable. In a sense, women were perpetual adolescents, representing "childhood and youth in the full meridian of its glory in all her dimensions and nature."[14]

Boys and girls thus had different educational needs and experiences, though most schools forced them to be similar. The effect was disastrous: Boys protected their sexuality by channeling it into schoolwork, while girls destroyed their sexuality by sublimation. Studying too hard robbed them of their maternal capacities. Contemporary education had it entirely backward. Rather than being separated, young boys were being forced to absorb girl culture and young girls were being forced to absorb boy culture, processes that would "virify women and feminize men." Actually, Hall believed the consequences had been more severe for boys because they were forced to "sink to a standard purposely set low for girls." Children's literature was "flabby, nerveless, inactive" or "light and chatty" with "too many illustrations" or "goody Sunday school books"—exactly what young boys did not need. "All that rot they teach to children about the little raindrop fairies with their buckets washing down the window panes must go," he said in a speech to Chicago teachers in 1899. "We need less sentimentality and more spanking." Hall's mission was the restructuring of education to make "man more manly and woman more womanly."[15]

Adolescent boys should be recognized as being in a "hoodlum stage" of development, "young barbarians" to be relinquished by mother into the care of the father. "Never has the American boy been quite so wild as now, and never in the world have so many young cubs been so half-orphaned and left to female guidance in school, home, and church." Boys needed different forms of understanding and different forms of punishment—flogging was a good idea for boys, "coddling" for girls. Adolescent male rebellion is necessary and vital, the "natural revolution of the young male just beginning to sense his virility against the prim pedagogue propriety of petticoat control to which he has been too much committed," Hall wrote, with a flair for alliteration.[16] In college, Hall advised, boys should endure fraternity hazing and practical joking as ways of asserting manly independence. "The practical joke is war, cruelty, torture reduced to the level and intensity of play," he wrote. "A good course of rough and roistering treatment" by one's peers has made "many a callow youth" develop a more "flexible" nature and prevented "inspissation of the soul."

Other observers took up the celebration of male adolescent marauding. J. Adams Puffer's *The Boy and His Gang* (1912), written under Hall's guidance, suggested that gang membership was healthy for young boys, "the result of a group of instincts inherited from a distant past," a "natural and a necessary stage in normal development." When some critics urged restraints on rowdy forms of male bonding, like gangs and fraternity hazing, Senator Albert Beveridge retorted that we "cannot change our sex, or the nature and habits of it. A young man is like a male animal after all, and those who object to his rioting like a young bull are in a perpetual quarrel with Nature."[17]

Hall went further than most educators in his evocation of contra-Darwinian "devolution." If children represented the earlier stages of social development, then it was the innate primitive savagery of young boys that could point the way to the resolution of the crisis of masculinity—we should learn to be more like boys and less like overcivilized men. Perhaps the savage child could be father to the man and reinstill manly behavior. Toward that end, Hall became increasingly enamored of boxing and violence in general, claiming that men enjoy "a quite unparalleled tingling of fibre and a peculiar mental inebriation" from violence.[18]

The coeducation debate was hotly argued in the 1890s and 1900s.[19] Some antifeminists had earlier argued that women's admission to formerly men's colleges would unsex women. As one Wesleyan College student put it as that college began a short-lived experiment with coeducation:

And thus she makes a farce of this fair life
By stepping out of Nature's goodly plan
Into the dusty tumult and the strife
Absurdly trying to become a man.[20]

New arguments stressed the effects on the college and upon men—that, for example, educating women and men together would weaken the curriculum with subjects better omitted or by slowing down the pace to allow women to keep up. Or that coeducation would distract men from the discipline of their studies or that contact between the sexes would "dilute" the mysteries of heterosexual attraction and thus promote homosexuality among men. Or that the entry of women would sap the virility of the male students and thus the ranking of the school would fall. "Where coeducation exists, there is invariably a noticeable weakness in the calibre of the large majority of men attending such institutions and a corresponding loss of rank of such institutions among the colleges in the country," observed the editor of Wesleyan University's college newspaper, the *Argus*, in 1898. Still others were concerned that if men's institutions were to admit women, men would no longer want to come. "The average young man will not go to a coeducational institution if other things are anywhere near equal. . . . He is not comfortable with the women in the classroom," warned F. W. Hamilton, president of Tufts College, in 1907.[21]

It was also feared that alumni would stop giving funds. The *Hartford Courant* quoted a "prominent athlete" on the consequences. "Only last year," he said, "we lost a star pitcher for the baseball team, and this year four crack-a-jack football men, three of whom eventually entered Princeton, owing to their feeling on the matter of coeducation." Here's one Wesleyan graduate's fantasy, as he wrote it to the administration in 1890:

> Banish football . . . Banish baseball! I expect you fellows, excuse me, you girls, will soon be sending little pink envelopes to the alumni soliciting subscriptions to the Wesleyan Croquet Club, Wesleyan Sewing Circles, and similar organizations. Say, girls, please take my name off the list, won't you?

The pink slips never came. Rather than risk it, Wesleyan's trustees abandoned their flirtation with coeducation (begun in 1872) in 1912.[22]

Other colleges and universities were similarly ambivalent, although some went through these wrenching debates earlier than others. Women had first entered the University of Wisconsin in 1863 but had been abruptly banned in 1867, when the university formed a female college, and then readmitted to segregated classes in 1873. When the University of Chicago opened in 1892, two-fifths of its entering class was women. By 1900, the enrollment of women was greater than that of men, and women earned more than half the Phi Beta Kappa awards, prompting fears that Chicago would soon turn into a women's college. In 1902, over the objections of women students and faculty, President William Harper instituted "segregation" to, as he put it, "solve the problem of effeminization," separating women into a separate junior college, separate sections of upper division courses, and separate chapels and laboratories.[23] Harvard President Charles Eliot believed that "girls and boys are better taught separately than together, especially after the age of puberty."[24] And Columbia's trustees thwarted President Barnard's plans to admit women to Columbia in 1882; they founded the college that bears his name seven years later. At the University of California, the student newspaper, the *Daily Californian*, which was edited by the fraternities, argued that since the "minds of men and women are radically different," they should be taught separately. And the yearbook, *The Blue and Gold*, added that "familiarity breeds contempt. The intimate associations which go with co-education prohibit forming the idealism about feminine charms which makes them charming." Therefore, "coeducation might destroy the dissimilarity between the sexes."[25]

Hall's theories informed several generations of educators, psychologists, and parents, and his legacy is still with us in recurring ideas of separation of the sexes. In 1899 Theodore Roosevelt was effusive in his praise of Hall's ideas:

> I must write to thank you for your sound common sense, decency, and manliness in what you advocate for the education of children. Over-sentimentality, over-softness, in fact washiness and mushiness are the great dangers of this age and of this people. Unless we keep the barbarian virtue, gaining the civilized ones will be of little avail. I am particularly glad that you emphasize the probable selfishness of a milksop. . . . I feel we cannot too strongly insist upon the need for the rough, manly virtues. A nation that cannot fight is not worth its salt, no matter how cultivated and refined it may be. . . . It is just so with a boy.[26]

Others were not so sanguine about Hall or his opposition to coeducation. M. Carey Thomas, president of Bryn Mawr, for example, claimed she had "never chanced again upon a book that seemed to me so to degrade me in my womanhood as . . . President Stanley Hall's *Adolescence*." John Dewey, the noted philosopher and educator, argued that coeducation was beneficial to both girls and boys. "Boys learn gentleness, unselfishness, courtesy; their natural vigor finds helpful channels of expression instead of wasting itself in lawless boisterousness." Girls, on the other hand, become less manipulative; they "acquire greater self-reliance and a desire to win approval by deserving it instead of by 'working' others. Their narrowness of judgment, depending on the enforced narrowness of outlook, is overcome; their ultra-feminine weaknesses are toned up." He found the argument that women teachers feminize boys to be "nonsense," "utterly absurd."[27]

Other advocates of collegiate coeducation, like John Van Vleck and William North Rice at Wesleyan, James Fairchild at Oberlin, Robert Maynard Hutchins at Chicago, and Andrew D. White at Cornell, confronted Hall's and others' fears of emasculation. If men were uneasy about educational equality or opposed to women's education, Dewey had a simple response. "The kind of man that will be kept from the University simply because he will have to associate upon equal terms with his equals is not the kind the University wants or needs."[28]

Play

The possibilities of feminization lurked also outside the classroom. In 1886 a striking change swept through the Young Men's Christian Association, one that illustrates these fears. Founded in Boston in 1851, the YMCA had originally been a sedentary place that spurned the gymnasium and sporting field. In its early decades that attitude modified only slightly. After the first gym was built in the New York City branch, for example, the organization began to promote "Athletic Sundays," during which boys would gather for morning Bible study and afternoon lectures by famous sports figures like Amos Alonzo Stagg, the legendary Yale football coach, or members of the Princeton football team, or Billy Sunday, the fleet right fielder of the Pittsburgh baseball club. But when Luther Gulick took over the directorship of the organization, the promotion of physical culture suddenly became a major part of the YMCA program. Gulick wanted to create a "manly boy," a potent combination of physical hardiness with Christian morality and duty. "Activities calling for cooperation and self-sacrifice form the natural basis upon which a life of service can be built," he wrote. "This life for others is far more probable, natural and tangible, when it comes as the natural unfolding or development of that instinct which has its first great impulse of growth in the games of adolescence."[29]

The turn of the century also witnessed the birth of a handful of "boys' lib" organizations. The Boys Brigades, the Boone and Crockett Club, Knights of King Arthur, and the Men of Tomorrow all foreshadowed that major American institution of boyhood, the Boy Scouts of America. The Boone and Crockett Club was founded originally in 1888 for adult men, to "promote manly sport with the rifle" and "to promote travel and exploration in wild and unknown or partially known lands." Membership in the club required shooting "at least one adult male . . . of each of three of the various species of American large game," including bears, cougars, buffalo, mountain sheep, elk, or moose. Theodore Roosevelt soon transformed it into a training club for boys.[30]

The Knights of King Arthur and the Men of Tomorrow were both founded by Rev. William Forbush, author of *The Boy Problem* (1901) and promoter of the single-sex summer camp for boys—"a place where the boy will develop those savage virtues which are the admiration of boyhood." The Men of Tomorrow promoted a general fellowship of men who worked with boys to study boys and their needs, and it provided a clearinghouse for information on adolescent male development. The Knights, also for boys alone, was an order of Christian knighthood designed to "bring back to the world, and especially to its youth, the spirit of chivalry, courtesy, deference to womanhood, recognition of noblesse oblige, and Christian daring." Modeled after collegiate Greek-letter fraternities, the Knights reveled in "ritual, mystery, and parade" in an effort to bring fraternalism to high-school and noncollege-bound boys.[31]

By far the most important organization developed to rescue boys from their mothers and reunite them with a virile ideal was the Boy Scouts. Originally founded in England by Lord Baden-Powell, the Scout vision stressed a kind of obedient and patriotic masculinism, seeking to create strong men who were also reliable workers. "God made men to be men," he wrote. "We badly need some training for our lads if we are to keep up manliness in our race instead of lapsing into a nation of soft, sloppy, cigarette suckers."[32] In the United States, scouting achieved its greatest success—over sixty-six million members since its founding in 1910 by Ernest Thompson Seton.[33] The Boy Scouts of America (BSA) yoked the development of manhood to a nostalgic re-creation of the frontier, partly through an evocation of Indian legend and lore and partly through the celebration of the white man's conquest. The Scouts were thus "laying the foundation for a self-disciplined and virile generation worthy to follow the trail of the backwoodsman," wrote Frederick Jackson Turner in 1918. "It is an inspiring prophecy of the revival of the old pioneer conception of the obligations and opportunities of neighborliness." As Daniel Beard put it in the Boy Scout manual, *Scouting* (1914):

> Wilderness is gone, the Buckskin man is gone, the painted Indian has hit the trail over the Great Divide, the hardships and privations of pioneer life which did so much to develop sterling manhood are now but a legend in history, and we must depend upon the Boy Scout Movement to produce the MEN of the future.

This was well beyond Seton's intentions. In his mind the frontiersmen were "almost without exception, treacherous, murderous, worthless, without the shadow of a claim on our respect but this: at best, a measure of dull brute grit." Seton celebrated the other "real man" of the West, the noble savage, the Indian. From its origins the BSA minted several "traditional" Indian rituals. Headdress feathers became merit badges, symbolizing exemplary activity; Indian names or animal totems became symbolic representations of the troop.[34]

Seton's antimilitarism and his devotion to Native American symbols and rituals, combined with personal awkwardness, eventually clashed with other scouting leaders, who embraced both the idealized frontiersman and Baden-Powell's efforts to turn the Boy Scouts into a patriotic youth brigade. Beard claimed that Seton's love of the Indian was unpatriotic, and most other Scout leaders agreed. One critic told Seton that there were simply "too many Americans who think of Indians as dirty and loafing degenerates or as savages" for them to remain symbols of manly heroism to young boys. By 1915 Seton was forced to resign.[35]

What the Boy Scouts did take from Seton, however, was his critique of urban industrial society. "Not one boy in a thousand is born bad," he wrote. Boys have their badness thrust upon them. They are made bad by evil surroundings during the formative periods between school and manhood—evil surroundings that included "money grubbing machine politics, degrading sports, cigarettes, false ideals, moral laxity and lessening Church power—in a word 'City rot.' "[36] The urban, civilized life was unmanly: "I do not know that I ever met a boy that would not rather be John L. Sullivan than Darwin or Tolstoi," he wrote in *Boy Scouts of America: A Handbook of Woodcraft, Scouting, and Life-Craft* (1910), the first Boy Scout handbook and manual. The natural, gender-based division of labor had been compromised; in a chapter of his memoirs, "Primitive Home Life," he wrote:

> the home life of those frontier days was nearly ideal; and so sanely adjusted that it may have valuable lessons for those who are wrestling with modern problems of living. . . . Those who cooked and sewed did so in an atmosphere of fun and frolic. The men no more thought of serving food than the women did of cutting the firewood. When a woman was seen chopping or carrying in firewood it was understood to mean that she had failed as a man-charmer. When a man was seen washing the dishes it was understood . . . that he had absolutely surrendered, and become the service thrall of some female enchanter.

Modern society had instead given us the sissy—"more effeminate than his sister, and his flabby muscles are less flabby than his character."[37]

Seton loved play, but the city promoted indolence. A chief culprit, he believed, was spectator sports, which sapped virility; "spectatoritis," he wrote, was turning "robust, manly, self-reliant boyhood into a lot of flat chested cigarette smokers with shaky nerves and doubtful vitality." Like school and church, spectator sports created a "society for sitting still." The Scouts were thus a kind of "boys' liberation movement" to free young men from mothers, teachers, and the more generally enervating experiences of the soft city life.[38]

For the college man, collegiate fraternities promoted male bonding through rough play and Christian service. Although fraternities had existed at elite universities since the turn of the nineteenth century, they received their greatest push at large midwestern campuses in its last decades. In part, this growth was an effort to retain a homosocial white world in a rapidly diversifying collegiate environment, shielding "traditional" students from women, blacks, and non-Protestants (especially Jews) who now sought admission. Land-grant institutions, universities like Michigan, Wisconsin, and Illinois, were required to admit all state residents—and thus were ripe for fraternities. Harvard's Hasty Pudding Club, founded in 1795 as a literary society, was transformed into a social club in 1875 in order to keep out the newcomers. "The great glory of the American college fraternity is that throughout a chaotic era of educational experimentation, and throughout its own groping for its proper place and function, it has remained the one last stronghold where youth did for itself and by itself" was the way fraternity historian and booster Francis Shepardson put it.[39] By the end of the century, fraternities had become an important part of collegiate life, with over 140,000 members by 1898.[40]

Men's Rites

But what would become of these boys when they grew up to be men, away from their college fraternity, their Scout troop, the other Knights? What would become of the men trapped in cities and towns across the country, locked into work lives and lifestyles that left them sedentary, soft, without vigor? G. Stanley Hall might have suggested that adult men were supposed to be more civilized, but few wanted to lose the hardy camaraderie, the rough-edged naturalism, the tried and tested brotherhood of their youth. Today, they might sign up for a "Wildman" weekend retreat. At the turn of the century, they developed a variety of organizations that together provided a kind of masculinist alternative to the female-controlled home and church, places where men could experience the succor of domestic life and Christian fellowship and still feel like men.

For one thing, American men joined fraternal organizations. The turn of the century was "the Golden Age of Fraternity," according to W. S. Harwood in 1897. By his count, over three hundred different fraternal orders boasted a total membership of 5.5 million American men out of a total adult male population of about nineteen million. This included 810,000 Odd Fellows, 750,000 Freemasons, 475,000 Knights of Pythias, 165,000 Red Men, as well as members of the dozens of smaller orders that gathered weekly at the more than 70,000 fraternal lodges nationwide.[41] At a time of economic stagnation and thwarted economic mobility, fraternal orders provided a symbolic arena in which men were moving up the ladder. At virtually every meeting, someone was being initiated into the next, highest level of the order. (If they couldn't make it in the economic sphere, here, in the comfort of the lodge, American men experienced the mobility the nation had promised but had not delivered.) But more than that, fraternal orders allowed men to reinvent themselves as men, to experience the pleasures and comforts of each other's company and of cultural and domestic life without feeling feminized. The lodge was alternately the artisanal guild, the church, or the home—or all three simultaneously.

Most fraternal orders provided an innocuous brew of bogus medieval mysticism, symbolic frontier naturalism, and ritualistic birth and rebirth, providing middle-class men with the fellowship, friendship, and solace that they no doubt otherwise missed. Work in the Gilded Age, before Progressive social reforms, demanded cutthroat competition and aggression, while the family home made men feel enervated and feminized in the wife's domain, and the combination left them lonely for each other's company. Fraternal orders filled that gap, re-creating the artisanal brotherhood, the masculine parish, and the patriarchal family that had virtually disappeared from men's lives. But mostly they provided male friendship. As one member of the Knights of Pythias put it in a speech in Fall River, Massachusetts, in 1885:

A man may be in a crowd and have no society. He stands within himself alone. He feels tremendously this loneliness, and is impelled to make friends, even if it be among the worst of mankind. Here appears one of the reasons why so many of our sons and daughters are rushed to their ruin on entering our large towns and cities . . . lack of socialness and the rarity of neighborhood society . . . is very marked in our large cities and towns. It is a growing evil of our times. . . .

The world at large, cold in self-aggrandizement, eager in pursuit of wealth, careless of the comforts or even the lives of others, feels, perhaps, no sympathy with our symbolic rites and ceremonies; laughs to scorn our friendship. . . . The wealth and pleasure of the outside world are but tinsel when compared with the pure gold of brotherly love.[42]

Some fraternal organizations that catered especially to working-class men provided death and sickness benefits and paid funeral costs in this era before life insurance, thus reinventing the craft guild's economic as well as social ties. If the ideals of craft brotherhood "could no longer be realized at work, they could instead be transferred to a purely social setting, the fraternal order."[43]

Fraternal orders attempted to create a domestic sanctuary outside the home—a place where men might experience fellowship and intimacy without the feminizing influence of women. The fraternal order was the motherless, wifeless, womanless family, the band of brothers. The lodge was also the unfeminized church, devoid of clucking mother hens and effete ministers. Victorian men felt deprived of a "religious experience with which they could identify" and a "family environment in which they could freely express nurturing and paternal emotions," writes the historian Mark Carnes. Fraternal orders filled both needs. They offered a "theology" that contrasted sharply with the milquetoast moralism of feminized Protestant doctrine and a "mass secret society" where men could express "feminine" emotions like compassion, nurturance, and charity.

Male bonding promoted "the innate principles of man's nature," wrote Reverend Mr. Beharrell about the Order of Odd Fellows. Here was a vehicle for men to reclaim emotion without feeling feminized in the process. Men needed "banding together to stimulate their better affections," noted Reverend A. B. Grosh of the Odd Fellows in 1871. But one could only experience these emotions in the company of other men; the man who was emotional with women was despised as effeminate. Men could publicly shun feminization and privately act like women.[44]

The centerpiece of fraternalism was the initiation ritual. Nearly all initiation rituals were modeled on baptism, the symbolic death of the old profane (workaday) man and his symbolic rebirth into the community of believers. The initiate is not yet a man as he undertakes an arduous journey to prove his worthiness and "grow up" into a new family of brethren and patriarchs. Such ceremony rested on secrecy and inversion and the appropriation of symbols of those very groups against whom fraternal members were framing their identities. Thus did middle-class, white-collar men proclaim their artisanal brotherhood (Modern Woodmen, Mechanics of the World), complete with symbols of the Heroic Artisan, like hammers and compasses. And thus did white men call themselves Red Men, imitating warrior initiations of the very tribes their fathers had "pacified." And thus did men don aprons and dresses to symbolically give birth to other men.

Across the Atlantic, Sigmund Freud was theorizing that women grow up envying men. In the lodges, however, men seemed to be the envious ones. They "played Indian," they pretended to be artisans, and they pretended to be women. But they refused to let women join, and they certainly acted manly at home—a place from which they could now, with justification, remain distant. The real purpose of fraternal orders, wrote suffragist Matilda Joslyn Gage, was "to set one sex against another."[45]

Some of them, unfortunately, also set one race against another. Several fraternal orders, such as the Order of United American Mechanics, the Red Men, Modern Woodmen, the Loyal Order of the Moose, and the Patriotic Order of the Sons of America, admitted only whites by charter. (The OUAM also had a paramilitary arm, the Loyal Legion, which marched in parades and was used as a racist and nativist goon squad.) In the first two decades of the century, a resurgent Ku Klux Klan deliberately linked fraternal brotherhood to a violent vision of American manhood dedicated to expunging "aliens" and destroying "commodity madness" as well as excessive taxation, religious infidelity, and political corruption. Klan rhetoric was soaked with masculine imagery.[46]

In addition to fraternal orders, there was at this time an explosion of men's organizations and clubs. Some, like the Elks (1868), Eagles (1898), and the Sons of the American Revolution (1889), were middle-class service organizations that doubled as homosocial retreats for white, native-born men. These groups' "backslapping camaraderie helped meliorate the personal and community disturbances associated with modernization" and "countered the impersonality associated with an increasingly bureaucratic society."[47]

Others were exclusively patrician enclaves, like Boston's Somerset Club, New York's Knickerbocker Club, Philadelphia's Rittenhouse Club, San Francisco's Bohemian Club, and the Union Club in both Boston and New York. These clubs were conceived of as islands of "homogeneity in an ever-diversifying urban ocean," places where, according to one genteel member, a gentleman found "his peculiar asylum from the pandemonium of commerce and the bumptiousness of democracy." And they were alternative families, where each member could "seek the comforts of a home," according to one magazine article in 1876.[48] Some held weekend retreats, where the men could escape urban riffraff and experience the tonic freshness of the outdoors and the good fellowship of their upper-class comrades at the same time.[49]

Despite its continued popularity among some American men today, fraternalism had lost much of its luster by 1925. Membership declined precipitously, and many organizations folded. It wasn't that young men born after 1900 were any less "afflicted with the fathers' and grandfathers' gender anxieties"; those anxieties were as palpable as ever. But the institutional solutions that men used to ground their manhood and to dispel those gender anxieties moved from separate clubs outside the world of work to the corporation itself and to male bonding within the work world as well as in the world of leisure—from spectator sports to the local golf course.[50] By the 1950s Ralph Cramden and Ed Norton's weekly sojourns to the Loyal Order of the Raccoons had become a joke, a couple of pathetic men searching for something they could never find—that homosocial Eden away from their wives that would revirilize them to take command in the very homes that were supposed to have been their castles.

The Manly Church

Just as men sought to reenter their homes and to create islands of manly nurture outside the home, they also moved to reclaim religion and create an alternative institution for manly religious expression and the socialization of their sons. Religion had been women's domain, and the sentimental piety and obsessive moralism were experienced by men as a brake on manly exuberance and a constraining critique of marketplace competition. A typical Protestant minister catered to an increasingly female clientele; he "moved in a world of women," writes cultural historian Ann Douglas. And as religion became more feminized, men's attendance at church dropped precipitously. As early as 1832 Francis Trollope had commented that he'd never seen a country "where religion had so strong a hold upon the women or a slighter hold upon the men" than the United States, and Joel Hawes claimed that "the sword of the spirit" is "muffled up and decked out with flowers and ribbons." No one listened to ministers any longer "except women and superstitious men," as one critic put it. "Religion in the old virile sense has disappeared," lamented Henry James, Sr., at mid-century, "and been replaced by a feeble Unitarian sentimentality."[51]

Feminized religion was graphically illustrated by late nineteenth-century Protestant iconography. Jesus was commonly depicted as a thin, reedy man with long, bony fingers and a lean face with soft, doelike eyes and a beatific countenance—a man who could advise his congregations to love their enemies or turn the other cheek, while gazing dreamily heavenward. Ministers emulated this pacific angel; one was favorably described by contemporaries as having an "almost feminine sensibility," an expression as "bland and gentle as a woman's," with "a most amiable spirit, with much of the ethereal in his countenance," while another had "poetry in his countenance and manners as well as in his mind and heart."[52] Was this a model for turn-of-the-century manhood? One Methodist minister described a man's transformation upon accepting Jesus into his life:

> It is wonderful to see a great burly man, mostly animal, who has lived under the dominion of his lower nature and given rein to his natural tendencies, when he is born of God and begins to grow in an upward and better direction. His affections begin to lap over his passion. . . . The strong man becomes patient as a lamb, gentle as the mother, artless as the little child.

No wonder men had developed their clubs and fraternal orders as alternative religious institutions and used the saloon or the Grange Hall as their secular temples. "Have we a Religion for Men?" asked Howard Alan Bridgeman in 1890.[53]

Enter Muscular Christianity—a religious movement designed "to bring manliness in its various manifestations to church and to keep it awake when it got there." In its first incarnation Muscular Christianity was imported from England through the novels of Charles Kingsley and Thomas Hughes, which fused a hardy physical manliness with ideals of Christian service.[54] Thomas Wentworth Higginson picked up the call in a series of articles in the *Atlantic Monthly* from 1858 to 1861. "The professional or business man, what muscles has he at all?" Higginson inquired in "Saints and Their Bodies" (1858), an essay that promoted athleticism as a way to build manly and moral character. Higginson warned Protestants that Roman Catholics were far more hardy and had greater stamina and admonished parents who said of their "pallid, puny, sedentary, lifeless, joyless, little offspring, 'He is born for a minister,' " while the "ruddy, the brave and the strong are as promptly consigned to a secular career!"[55]

The goal of the Muscular Christians was to revirilize the image of Jesus and thus remasculinize the Church. Jesus was "no doughfaced, lick-spittle proposition," proclaimed evangelist Billy Sunday, but "the greatest scrapper who ever lived." Look to Jesus, counseled Luther Gulick of the YMCA, for an example of "magnificent manliness." Books such as *The Harvest Within* (1909), *Building the Young Man* (1912), *The Call of the Carpenter* (1913), *The Manhood of the Master* (1913), *The Manliness of Christ* (1900), *The Manly Christ* (1904), and *The Masculine Power of Christ* (1912) portrayed Jesus as a brawny carpenter, whose manly resolve challenged the idolaters, kicked the money changers out of the temple, and confronted the most powerful imperium ever assembled. This was no "Prince of peace at any price."[56]

One common strategy was to recast Jesus as the first Heroic Artisan, a "working man," whose "bench work gave him experimental knowledge of life" where he "toiled but never whimpered."[57] Pictures and drawings of Jesus at his carpenter's bench, with sleeves rolled up, leather apron around his torso, and his strong set eyes gazing heavenward, fused the sacred and the muscular. Bouck White's *The Call of the Carpenter* (1913) went further, retelling Jesus's story as a socialist allegory. According to White, Rome was "a world wide confederation of aristocracies for the perpetuation of human servitude," composed of effeminate parasites. Jesus was the working-class hero, "a skilled artisan," a "master of his craft . . . who took pride in his work." Roman oppression made it impossible for him to earn his living by the sweat of his brow, and so he became a "working class agitator," whose mission it was to "awaken the proletariat."[58]

Jesus was not, however, simply some testosterone-juiced, muscle-bound lout. "The Carpenter did not make his impress upon history through any advantages of physique, but through a master intellect, coupled with a master heart and will." And those who followed him were not passive little sheep. They burned Rome, didn't they? So today, White claims, as civilization is "threatened with the sleeping sickness," the working class, led by a masculine Jesus, will be the nation's savior. "Stiffened by manly fibre, refusing doles of charity, the working class shall be the saviors of a civilization threatened with dry rot."[59]

This revirilized Jesus was remarkably adaptable to other political agendas. Some Muscular Christians sounded a more militaristic tone, recasting Jesus as a kind of religious Rambo, always ready to fight. The Ku Klux Klan signed on to its own version of Muscular Christianity, invoking the manly Christ who was "a robust, toil-marked young man" who "purged the temple with a whip," according to Hiram Wesley Evans, a Georgia Imperial Wizard. The Church of Christ in America would be tempered by "the red blooded and virile" into a "thing of rugged steel . . . forged in the terrific stress . . . of wresting a continent from savages and from the wilderness."[60] Others retained the emphasis on Christian service and social reform but toward decidedly different purposes, including ministering to the poor and to unemployed black men.

In the Muscular Christian iconography, Jesus had dark hair, calloused hands, and a well-developed physique. Gone was the sad, sweet man with flowing robes and pacific gaze. And gone was the image of the religious life as sedentary and feminizing. Muscular Christians looked for the "exacting masculine pages of their Bible," the study of which was "worthy of the best time and mightiest effort of the manliest man," writes the historian Gail Bederman. Bible study "produces a virility, a ruggedness of character, an altruistic spirit, a hopeful temper, a power of patience and endurance, a fearlessness, a stability of manhood that nothing else gives," gushed Rev. Luther Peacock in 1915. Sunday schools must offer a "ruddy religious reality" to students. Prayer was "a manly duty"; faith was "mountain moving, galvanic," according to Rev. Billy Sunday.[61]

Sunday was the most famous of all Muscular Christians—that former professional baseball player who became America's foremost itinerant evangelical preacher. The fleet, former right fielder for the Chicago and, later, Pittsburgh baseball teams left his lucrative athletic career for the ministry, not because baseball was immoral but because it was amoral—because "morality was not an essential to success; one may be a consummate rogue and a first class ball player," as he explained in 1893. Triumphing over childhood physical frailty—he was sickly and scarcely able to walk as a child and had to be carried around on a specially made pillow—Sunday transformed himself into a strong, sinewy physical specimen whose boundless energy was injected into his rousing tent sermons. Sunday "brought bleacher-crazy, frenzied aggression to religion"; one journalist effusively described a Billy Sunday sermon thus:

> He stands up like a man in the pulpit and out of it. He speaks like a man. He works like a man. . . . He is manly with God and with everyone who comes to hear him. No matter how much you disagree with him, he treats you after a manly fashion. He is not an imitation, but a manly man giving all a square deal.[62]

Sunday's mission was the complete transformation of feminized religion, to "strike the death blow at the idea that being a Christian takes a man out of the busy whirl of the world's life and activity and makes him a spineless effeminate proposition," he claimed. A Christian cannot be "some sort of dishrag proposition, a wishy-washy, sissified sort of galoot, that lets everybody make a doormat out of him. Let me tell you, the manliest man is the man who will acknowledge Jesus Christ." Sunday offered his followers a "hard muscled, pick-axed religion, a religion from the gut, tough and resilient," not some "dainty, sissified, lily-livered piety."[63]

Sunday took on the church establishment in colorful rhetoric, from biblical scholars (those "anemic rank skeptics" who would "dissolve the atoning blood of Jesus into mist and vapor") to their cronies, intellectuals ("fudge-eating mollycoddles" who would rather eat "fried oysters and tea" than red meat). Protestant ministers had become "pretentious, pliable mental perverts" who worked hand in glove with the idle rich, those lazy slackers —"big, fat, hog-jowled, weasel-eyed, pussy-lobsters." "Lord save us from off-handed, flabby cheeked, brittle boned, weak-kneed, thin-skinned, pliable, plastic, spineless, effeminate, ossified, three karat Christianity," Sunday thundered.[64]

One sermon, "The Fighting Saint," brought these themes together, as Sunday attacked both industrial capitalism and liberal Protestantism as enervating conspirators. "Men are feeding their muscle and bone and sinew into the commercial mill that grinds out the dividends . . . and the men who get the dividends sit by and watch it," he roared. The only solution was not the moral equivalent of war, but "moral warfare" itself. "Moral warfare makes a man hard. Superficial peace makes a man mushy," he argued. "The Prophets all carried the Big Stick." Don't tell me about the peaceful, gentle Jesus, Sunday admonished. "Jesus Christ could go like a six cylinder engine," he claimed. "I'd like to put my fist on the nose of the man who hasn't got grit enough to be a Christian."[65]

Here was a religion rippling with hard muscles, manly grit coupled with moral resolve, a faith that could move mountains. Like other masculinist efforts to counter feminization, Sunday's brawny theology did not extend to blacks or non-native-born Americans. "If they don't like it here, let 'em go back to the land where they were kennelled," he snarled.[66] And it was a potent mix: In a 1914 *American Magazine* poll of "the Greatest Men in the United States," Sunday tied for eighth place with Andrew Carnegie and Judge Ben Lindsey.[67]

Sunday was so successful that others quickly imitated his method. The Men and Religion Forward Movement of 1911–1912 was a church-based spinoff that sought to bring into Protestant denominations the virile ardor that Sunday inspired in his rural tent sermons and sought especially to bring men back into established churches. "The manly gospel of Christ should be presented to men by men," argued M&RF leader Henry Rood in "Men and Religion." Women "have had charge of the Church work long enough," agreed movement founder Fred Smith.[68] The movement "swept the country like a spiritual storm," according to one observer, increasing by up to 800 percent the number of men coming to church. The M&RF movement was most noted for organizing weeklong community-based revivals for young men and boys to help these revirilized Christians act ethically and manfully in their communities, "closing brothels, passing dance hall regulations, working for adequate garbage collection, or better housing regulations, or an open dialogue between business leaders and the city's unions."[69] For the men of the Men and Religion Forward Movement, manly religion implied strength and social concern.

TR, the Strenuous Life, and Bully Manhood

The fin de siècle mission to thwart feminization and revirilize boyhood—and by extension, manhood—reached its symbolic apotheosis in Theodore Roosevelt. TR "epitomized manly zest for the new imperial nation in part because of his jaunty energy, but also because his image brought together both aspects of the new myth: the top rung of the ladder of social aspiration and the gladiatorial animal arena sensed at the bottom." America's self-proclaimed and self-constructed "real man," Roosevelt was, as he proclaimed, a completely Self-Made Man.[70]

Roosevelt's story of self-creation begins, as all such stories do, with his triumph over the body. He was, he recalled in his autobiography, "a sickly and delicate boy, [who] suffered much from asthma, and frequently had to be taken away on trips to find a place where I could breathe." On one of those trips, to Europe, he was seasick most of the time and rarely came on deck. Here was a "shy and timid boy, frail in body . . . thin, pale, asthmatic, outwardly the typical 'city feller,'" as the *Boy's Life of Theodore Roosevelt* put it. "Teedie," as his family affectionately called him, was a childhood wimp; his father constantly exhorted him to "make your body."[71]

Making his body was also a strategy for making his political image. Entering politics in the early 1880s, TR was called "Young Squirt" and "Jane Dandy" by the local press, and the *New York Star* threw in a little gay-baiting by calling him "our own Oscar Wilde." Roosevelt needed "to attain a state of manliness, and attempt to exorcise through exercise his effeminizing sickness, and at the same time . . . attempt to masculinize and thereby strengthen his political position."[72] And where would a wimpy upper-class sissy go to make his body and thereby remake his political image?

Out west, of course. Roosevelt arrived in the Dakota territory in April 1885, determined to try his hand at ranching in the rapidly disappearing Old West. Like Owen Wister, Frederic Remington, and other eastern boys, Roosevelt had journeyed west to stake a claim on his manhood. On his arrival a reporter from the *Pittsburgh Dispatch* observed "a

pale, slim young man with a thin piping voice and a general look of dyspepsia about him
. . . boyish looking . . . with a slight lisp, short red moustache and eye glasses"—in short,
the "typical New York dude." A local railroad man recalled "a slim, anemic-looking
young fellow dressed in the exaggerated style which newcomers on the frontier affected,
and which was considered indisputable evidence of the rank tenderfoot." Locals found him
initially a laughingstock, calling him "Roosenfelder" and "Four Eyes" and "the Eastern
punkin-lily." When he first mounted his horse, he tapped it and said meekly, "Hasten
forward quickly there," which made local cowboys double over with laughter; the phrase
soon became part of Badlands lore.[73]

But TR persevered and eventually triumphed over his effete dudeism, becoming the
embodiment of "strength, self-reliance, determination," the three terms which defined his
vision of manhood. He became a booster of the western cure, claiming that he owed "more
than I could ever express to the west" because the frontier brings out manly virtues—
mutuality, honor, self-respect—not the "emasculated milk-and-water moralities" of the
eastern elite.[74] This personal credo for his self-making became the basis for a moral and
political philosophy.

Using himself as the example, Roosevelt expressed fears that "overcivilization was
sapping the strength of the civilized few, who therefore needed remedial training in
barbarism, violence, and appropriation."[75] In two speeches, "The Strenuous Life" (1899)
and "The Pioneer Spirit and American Problems" (1900), Roosevelt railed against "the
cloistered life which saps the hardy virtues," the "flabbiness" and "slothful ease," and
trumpeted the call for the "strenuous life." In G. Stanley Hall's terms, overcivilized adult
men needed to recall more of their barbarous, prehistoric youthfulness. Roosevelt used his
fears of feminization—of men with "small feet and receding chins"—to great political
effect, equating individual manliness with national strength and international power:

> We cannot avoid the responsibilities that confront us in Hawaii, Cuba, Porto Rico, and the
> Philippines. All we can decide is whether we shall meet them in a way that will redound
> to the national credit, or whether we shall make of our dealings with these new problems
> a dark and shameful page in our history. . . . The timid man, the lazy man, the man who
> distrusts his country, the over-civilized man, who has lost the great fighting masterful
> virtues, the ignorant man, and the man of dull mind, whose soul is incapable of feeling the
> mighty lift that thrills "stern men with empires in their brains"—all these, of course, shrink
> from seeing the nation undertake its new duties; shrink from seeing us build a navy and an
> army adequate to our needs; shrink from seeing us do our share of the world's work, by
> bringing order out of chaos in the great, fair, tropic islands from which the valor of our
> soldiers and sailors has driven the Spanish flag. . . .
>
> I preach to you, then, my countrymen, that our country calls not for the life of ease,
> but for the life of strenuous endeavor. The twentieth century looms before us big with the
> fate of many nations. If we stand idly by, if we seek merely swollen, slothful ease and
> ignoble peace, if we shrink from the hard contests where men must win at hazard of their
> lives and at the risk of all they hold dear, then the bolder and stronger peoples will pass us
> by, and will win for themselves the domination of the world.[76]

Of course, not everyone was so taken with Roosevelt's strenuous manhood. Thorstein
Veblen, John Dewey, and William James, for example, demurred from the national frenzy

about bodybuilding and the sporting life that Roosevelt heralded. Dewey cringed at the "hunting psychosis" he saw, while Veblen saw sports as a case of "arrested spiritual development," and James cast Roosevelt's vision as adolescent ranting. In a letter to the *Boston Evening Transcript*, he wrote:

> Although in middle life, and in a situation of responsibility concrete enough, he is still mentally in the Sturm and Drang period of early adolescence, [he] treats human affairs . . . from the sole point of the organic excitement and difficulty they may bring, gushes over war as the ideal condition of human society, for the manly strenuousness which it involves, and treats peace as a condition of blubberlike and swollen ignobility, fit only for huckstering weaklings, duelling in gray twilight and heedless of the higher life.[77]

A few singled out military heroics as a particularly disingenuous method for retrieving manhood. Joseph Dana Miller's "Militarism or Manhood?" (1900) posed the choice most starkly. To Miller, Teddy Roosevelt was a "splendid savage," whose "Rough Rider government is conspicuously lacking in those higher qualities which single out the man from among men." In fact, the battlefield was ill suited for demonstrations of manly valor:

> The anesthetics of battle smoke and battle music induce a sort of somnambulistic state in which prodigies of valor may be performed. . . . Most of the heroism exhibited on the battlefield is of the passive sort, disguised somewhat by the activity of maneuver, the noise of cannon, and the onslaught of cavalry. There is but a small individual initiative to the great fighting mass.

Instead of celebrating military manhood, Miller advocated a revision of the word *courage* to include being "true to conscience."[78]

Such throwbacks to barbarian forms of manhood were understood by some feminist women to bode ill for the advancement of equality. "I think a whole community of men in perfect physical condition would be very interesting, but extremely dangerous," wrote a woman in a letter to the editor of *Physical Culture* in 1901. And Charlotte Perkins Gilman worried, in her impassioned treatise *Women and Economics* (1899), about "the brutal ferocity of excessive male energy in the marketplace as in a battlefield" and the "destructive action of male energy in its blind competition," whether in sports, war, or business.[79] But few were persuaded by these critics, many of whom could be dismissed as whining women or their emasculated male sycophants.

The formation of the Rough Riders catapulted TR into the hallowed halls of American myth even during his lifetime. The symbolic capstone in TR's manly edifice, the Rough Riders consisted of twelve troops, all but one of which came from the western territories. This last, K troop, came from the East and was widely believed to be a collection of "swells" who had left their upper-class men's clubs, dress suits in their hands, to follow Roosevelt up San Juan Hill. And yet, though some may have worn "the broad brim hat and had the bronze cheek of the plains" while others "bore the unmistakable stamp of the student and club man," as one reporter wrote, all "mingled with easy good fellowship." The *Denver Post* reported (21 May 1898) in verse the western men's perspective:

We was somewhat disappointed, I'll acknowledge, fur to see
Such a husky lot o' fellers as the dandies proved to be,
An' the free an' easy manner in their bearin' that they had
Sort o' started the impression that they mightn't be so bad.
There was absence of eye-glasses, an' of center parted hair,
An' in social conversation they was expert on the swear,
An' the way they hit the grub pile sort o' led us to reflect
That our previous impressions mightn't prove so damn correct.

To which the *Chicago Tribune* (12 July 1898) responded two months later with the easterners' perspective:

They scoffed when we lined up with Teddy,
They said we were dudes and all that;
They imagined that "Cholly" and "Fweddie"
Would faint at the drop of a hat.
But let them look there in the ditches,
Blood-stained by the swells in the van,
And know that a chap may have riches,
And still be a man![80]

From TR's bully pulpit he promoted the strenuous life for individuals for their sake and as a grounding for the American Empire. He opposed policies as "half-and-half, boneless," and railed against opponents he called spineless sissies. Westward continental expansion had been "the central and all-important feature of our history," he wrote, and imperialist annexation completed the project. He promoted work as heroic, moralizing, and masculinizing and saw big capital and finance as emasculating effeminacy—he chastised the "moneyed and semi-cultivated classes" for "producing a flabby, timid type of character which eats away at the great fighting qualities of our race." He prescribed sports to develop a hardy masculinity—but only "the true sports for a manly race," like running, rowing, playing football and baseball, boxing and wrestling, shooting, riding, and mountain climbing. No president before or since has been a bigger promoter of exercise and sporting life, and no number of photos of Bill Clinton jogging, George Bush sailing or fishing, or (in another vein) Michael Dukakis driving a tank could make the point as emphatically as one photograph of TR in full hunting gear. In a 1900 essay, "The American Boy," TR echoed the same sentiments as Muscular Christians and bodybuilders:

Forty or fifty years ago the writer on American morals was sure to deplore the effeminacy and luxury of young Americans who were born of rich parents. The boy who was well off then . . . lived too luxuriously, took to billiards as his chief innocent recreation, and felt shame in his inability to take part in rough pastimes and field sports. Nowadays, whatever other faults the son of rich parents may tend to develop, he is at least forced . . . to bear himself well in manly exercises and to develop his body—and therefore, to a certain extent, his character—in the rough sports which call for pluck, endurance, and physical address.[81]

Roosevelt celebrated the outdoors as an "arena for manly exertion," creating five national parks, sixteen national monuments, and fifty-one wildlife refuges in America's wilderness and organizing the Boone and Crockett Club to promote the strenuous life for young boys.[82] He sought personal refuge in the wilderness. As late as 1912, after the failure of the Bull Moose crusade, a fifty-three-year-old Roosevelt joined an expedition to probe the unknown regions of the Amazon. Encountering a river never before seen by a white man, Roosevelt was ecstatic—though the expedition cost the life of one of the explorers in an accident that nearly killed all of them. The river was named Rio Roosevelt by the Brazilian government. Asked why he risked his life for such a venture, he replied that he "had to go. It was my last chance to be a boy."[83]

TR consistently opposed coeducation and praised G. Stanley Hall's efforts to stem the tide of feminization. Although he supported woman suffrage "tepidly," he was more fervent in his support of women as mothers and furious at college-educated women who delayed childbearing or did not bear children at all. Accusing them of race suicide, TR suggested that women who did not bear at least four children be tried as traitors to America, much the same way as soldiers who refused to fight. A woman who "shirks her duty as wife and mother is . . . heartily to be condemned," he commented in an address to the Congress of Mothers in 1908. "We despise her as we despise and condemn the soldier who flinches in battle." Soldiers and mothers—this was the way TR saw the fulfillment of patriotic duty.

As G. Stanley Hall had identified adolescence as a fragile stage requiring special attention to a rite of passage, so too did Roosevelt offer an adolescent nation the initiation rites to a new manhood. TR was the perfect embodiment of American-as-adolescent boy-man. His definition of manhood was reactive, defensive, an effort to repudiate a sickly childhood and his overdependence on his mother. To accomplish this end, Roosevelt engaged in a frenzied effort to appear a man in every possible guise; "changing frenetically from cowboy costume to safari suit to Rough Rider garb, Roosevelt shot more animals, rode more dusty trails, and risked his neck in combat" more than any American before John Wayne.[84] TR wore every conceivable hat—warrior, statesman, pioneer, cowboy, Rough Rider, president, father, historian, hunter, husband, naturalist, diplomat, and preacher—a well-rounded yet hardened manly presentation. For TR, manhood was a relentless test to be proved constantly and in every arena in which men find themselves. And it was enormously "attractive to men who feared their own impotence in an increasingly complex world."[85]

As for TR, so too for the typical American man, although on a far less grandiose scale. As turn-of-the-century American men had confronted social and economic limits to their ceaseless struggles to prove themselves, they had sought to preserve their workplaces as sites of self-making, shaped their bodies as disciplined instruments of their will to succeed, worked to rescue their sons from feminization, created parallel institutions of nurture and solace for themselves, and occasionally escaped to a more pristine earlier world where men were men and women virtually nonexistent. Yet all these heroic efforts could not bring the relief that American men so desperately sought. As the nation faced a new century filled with new opportunities and new obstacles, the Self-Made Man would again return to these themes, as well as invent some new ones.

PART THREE

The New Man in a New Century, 1920–1950

CHAPTER 6

Muscles, Money, and the M–F Test
Measuring Masculinity Between the Wars

Want to call it Men Without Women [because] in all of these [stories], almost, the softening feminine influence through training, discipline, death or other causes [is] absent.
—Ernest Hemingway letter to Maxwell Perkins (1927)[1]

Under ideal circumstances, the father should be an understanding, tolerant but virile and decisive male. The mother should have the gentleness, patience, and passivity usually associated with womanhood. Any mixture, such as an effeminate father and an aggressive masculine mother is likely to be disconcerting to the child and accentuate homosexual tendencies.
—Dr. George W. Henry (1937)[2]

In William Wellman's powerful film *Heroes for Sale* (1934), a World War I veteran returns home and tries to rebuild his life. Unable to find a job, he stoops to a terrible humiliation: He enters a pawnshop to hock his Congressional Medal of Honor. The pawnbroker is sympathetic but unwilling to offer any money. As the camera pulls away from their faces over the counter, we see that the entire display case is full of pawned medals. Heroism had lost its currency in the postwar world.

The end of the war was supposed to usher in a "return to normalcy," as President Warren G. Harding promised in 1920, a time not for "heroism but healing." And for American men, the postwar era was to be a period not of "agitation but adjustment." The turn-of-the-century crisis had been resolved—or at least temporarily muted. Wartime victories had allowed a generation of men to rescue a threatened sense of manhood, and the expanding peacetime economy augured well for economic success. In their work and in their families, middle-class men entered the decade optimistically convinced that they could be successful breadwinners.

But such reassurances soon gave way to a new restiveness. For one thing, as we've seen, military glory had proven elusive to the typical G. I. Joe, and cases of "paralysis, convulsions, paraplegias, tics and tremors of the battle-weary (and battle-shy) soldiers" flooded the psychiatric literature after the war.[3] For another thing, the workplace was anything but stable and reliable. The optimism ushered in by the Roaring Twenties was ushered out by the Great Depression and widespread unemployment in the 1930s. Never before had American men experienced such a massive and system-wide shock to their ability to prove manhood by providing for their families.

Even before the economic collapse of 1929, though, men's work was an increasingly unreliable proving ground, more the domain of the dull and the routine of George Babbitt than the arena of vaulting ambition and adventure of TR. Robert and Helen Lynd's masterful portrait of middle America, *Middletown* (1929), and its sequel, *Middletown in Transition* (1937), showed a people barely making do, clinging to traditional forms and unable to move beyond them, with high rates of unemployment, poverty, and divorce. Other social scientists saw a dramatic attenuation of social mobility during the decade and the rise of technicians and managers at the expense of ordinary workers.[4] Even the traditional image of the heroic toiler had become tainted by associations with bolshevism.

That's not to say that men weren't counseled to aim high. But frequently the targets were different. One sales manual urged readers to develop "the faculty of combativeness" by exercising each morning before going out to sell. "Combativeness functions through the shoulder and arm muscles as shown by the soldier, prize fighter, athlete, etc., and, well developed, it imparts a feeling of enthusiasm, physical vigor, and power of decision that no other faculty can give," wrote Clarence Darrow in a 1925 review of these manuals.[5] And rapid upward mobility brought no peace from anxiety; just different ones from lack of mobility. As Frederick Millard put it in his popular self-help book *What a Man Goes Through* (1925):

> Men are made nervous not so much, as a rule, by their business cares, as by various things they are doing that may become uncovered to a certain extent, or are liable to be uncovered at some particular time when they are just reaching a height where they want everything to run smoothly. It is when the express train is speeding along at the highest rate of speed that there is the most danger.[6]

Men certainly had it tough. One woman called for "a movement for the emancipation of men" in a letter to the editor of the *Nation*, while another writer asserted that "from a masculine standpoint life is not necessarily that unending round of Sunday dinners without dishwashing, that ever verdant series of love affairs without responsibility, that continuing vaudeville of adventure and daring which literary ladies imply it to be." There was, he concluded sadly, "no salvation in being born a man."[7]

Especially not once the Great Depression took hold. Wages plummeted and relief rolls swelled. The unemployment level rose from about 16 percent in 1930 to just under 25 percent barely three years later and remained almost as high for the rest of the decade.[8] With nearly one in four American men out of work, the workplace could no longer be considered a reliable arena for the demonstration and proof of one's manhood. And many men simply lost faith in a system that prevented them from proving their masculinity in the only ways they knew.

Even those men who still had jobs had a more difficult time proving their manhood in the 1930s. The competition was increasingly fierce, and the complexion of the American workforce seemed to many to grow increasingly dark. Racial exclusion and anti-immigrant nativism were again a recourse for some who searched for a foundation for secure manhood. Successive waves of immigrants were depicted as less mentally capable and less manly—either as feminized and effete or wildly savage hypermasculine beasts—and thus likely to dilute the stock of "pure" American blood. Henry Goddard's series of bogus mental tests, published in 1917, in which immigrants were given a battery of tests in English, led him to conclude that 79 percent of Italians, 80 percent of Hungarians, 83 percent of Jews, and 87 percent of Russians were "feeble minded." In 1923 Carl Bingham concluded definitively that there had been a "gradual deterioration in each class of immigrants" who had come to the United States in each succeeding five-year period since 1902. This deterioration was easily measured, he discerned, by the decreasing percentage of "nordic blood" in each group. (Bingham, incidentally, was no racist hack writer, nor did he toil at the margins of academic respectability. A psychology professor at Princeton, he was later secretary of the College Entrance Examination Board and the designer of the Scholastic Aptitude Test.)[9] Followers of Lathrop Stoddard, author of the best-seller *The Rising Tide of Color* (1920), envisioned a global struggle to the death between white and dark races.

Such themes echoed through the debates about the Immigration Act of 1924, which passed after bitter controversy and significantly reduced the number of immigrants allowed into the nation. Both the American Legion and the American Federation of Labor urged increasingly restrictive immigration policies, especially regarding Asians. A particularly virulent campaign targeted Filipinos. Since the United States had acquired the Philippines during the Spanish-American War, Filipinos were classified as "American nationals" and therefore entitled to unrestricted immigration. And their number grew quickly, from only 406 Filipinos in the United States in 1910 to 5,603 in 1920 and 45,208 in 1930. Racist impulses were suffused with gender imagery, and this new immigrant group was tainted with the same gender slanders that earlier groups had been. "He is not our 'little brown brother,'" thundered the secretary of an agricultural association in California. "He is no brother at all! He is not our social equal." And as before, exclusion from brotherly equality rested on twin gender images; the Filipino was both too much and too little of a real man.

Racism and nativism bore the mark of gender, as if depicting "them" as less manly would make "us" feel more manly. So on the one hand, Filipinos were cast as effete and effeminate; small with delicate features, great dancers who possessed an obsessive concern with clothing and appearances. On the other hand, Filipinos were hypermasculine "jungle folk," "scarcely more than savages," with "primitive moral codes." Filipino sexuality was demonized. "The love making of the Filipino is primitive, even heathenish," and certainly "more elaborate," noted a deputy labor commissioner in 1930, while a businessman called them "hot little rabbits." In 1934 Congress passed the Tydings-McDuffie Act, giving the Philippines independence, in part so that Filipinos would no longer enjoy their status as American nationals, and thus their immigration could be restricted.[10]

Black men remained a most potent screen against which middle-class white men played out their masculinity. The widespread migration of blacks to northern cities (and within the South, from rural to urban areas) spurred recharged efforts to exclude blacks from public office and residential neighborhoods. Fewer than 10 percent of southern blacks lived in urban areas in 1890; by 1910 that percentage had more than doubled, reaching 25 percent in 1920 and 31.7 percent in 1930. A resurgent Ku Klux Klan flourished in the 1920s, especially in midwestern border states like Indiana. Lynchings and other forms of racist violence increased dramatically during the decade.

A special issue of *The World Tomorrow* in 1924 examined the re-emergence of the Klan with alarm. While one theologian criticized the Klan's "small boy buffoonery," anthropologist Alexander Goldenweiser's insightful cultural critique located the rise of the Klan in the "vacuity and dullness of our lives," the "insufferable boredom" that accompanied industrial society. The Klan, he argued, is "the back parlor of Main Street. It is the conventional, the mediocre, those whose outlook is narrow and whose imagination is deadened by routine, who seek stimulation in the activities of the secret brotherhood."[11]

Like the Klan, fraternal orders experienced a brief rise in popularity in the 1920s, but they also came in for increased criticism. Though these roughly eight hundred secret societies met "a hunger which lies near the heart of gregarious mankind," as Devere Allen wrote, their rituals were obviously hokey:

> Once in so often you march around your lodgeroom in the wake of the Grand Exalter of the Holy Mackerel and absorb a certain luster from his glittering insignia. . . . You get the same thrill from the secret grip and password that you got from the gang which met after school in the Enchanted Haymow of the Sacred Neighborhood Barn.

and their politics were dangerous:

> Is it a healthy thing when so many Americans have to satisfy the normal craving for brotherhood by banding together on a basis which ineradicably mingles loyalty to one's own group with superiority and sometimes hostility to one's next door neighbor of another color, creed, or nationality?[12]

The Klan and other fraternal orders appropriated many of the iconographic images of Jesus first used by the Muscular Christians, declaring their campaign a "holy crusade" and depicting Jesus as "the unflinching, accomplishing, achieving Christ, because he was the purposeful, steadfast, determined Christ," as their national newspaper, *Searchlight*, put it in 1924.[13] But the Jesus who really caught the public's attention in the 1920s was a businessman. Bruce Barton's best-selling *The Man Nobody Knows* (1924) fused Muscular Christian images of Jesus with the persona of the modern corporate leader.

Typically, Jesus had been portrayed as "a frail man, under-muscled, with a soft face—a woman's face covered by a beard" and wearing a "benign but baffled look, as though the problems of living were so grievous that death would be a welcome release." Nonsense, railed Barton.

> A physical weakling! Where did they get that idea? Jesus pushed a plane and swung an adze; he was a successful carpenter. He slept outdoors and spent his days walking around his favorite lake. His muscles were so strong that when he drove the money changers out, nobody dared to oppose him!

With muscles "hard as iron" and nerves of steel, Jesus was extremely attractive to women and "the most popular dinner guest in Jerusalem." Most important, Jesus was the founder of a modern capitalist enterprise, harnessing his immense talents, organizational skills, and business acumen to create the first multinational corporation. "He picked up twelve men from the bottom ranks of business and forged them into an organization that conquered the world." Jesus, it turns out, was the epitome of the Self-Made Man, a successful entrepreneur who showed none of the anxieties and insecurities that so plagued his followers. He was the businessman's role model.[14]

At the same time that business was appropriating religious imagery, it also seized on the male-only retreats that had formerly been an escape from corporate culture. General Electric, for example, sponsored camps for lighting engineers and managers and brought in potential managerial recruits whose "behavior in sporting events, casual discussions, and the ceremonies of camp life gave officers of the company more insight into their strengths and weaknesses." Homosocial retreats had been harnessed to serve the corporation rather than provide solace away from corporate life or even, as in some earlier cases, serve as a form of resistance to corporate domination.[15]

These efforts to remasculinize the workplace through bonding and to exclude others from it echoed similar strategies in earlier decades, but they fell short of providing men with the security they seemed to promise. The chief problem seemed to be women, both at work and at home, as coworker, as mother, and as symbol. Everywhere men looked, there were women. Work itself was seen as increasingly feminized, with more women employed in increasingly feminine offices—hardly the world of real men at all. The enactment of woman suffrage in 1920 accelerated women's entry into the public sphere. By 1920 about one-half of all college students and one-third of all employed Americans were women.[16] The New Woman of the 1920s was that fast-talking, cigarette-smoking libertine known as the Flapper—an exciting and passionate sexual and gender nonconformist.

But many men did not find her especially enchanting. The public sphere has been "invaded" by the "gentler sex," warned Frederick Millard in *What a Man Goes Through.* "It may take a century or more for men to realize the situation and be sufficiently good sports to tolerate such changes," he conjectured, somewhat more presciently than he might have imagined. Architect Charles Loring recalled that the "offices of our grandfathers were without steel frames and files, without elevators and radiators, without telephones—and without skirts." One writer in *Fortune* magazine was disgusted with "this callipygian nation of silk knees, slender necks, narrow fingers, and ironic mouths which has established itself upon our boundaries," while another surveyed the modern office and found "an ocean of permanent waves." "Feminism really spells Masculinism," wrote Anthony Ludovici in 1927, since "exposure to the vicissitudes and asperities of the struggle for existence brings out the combative, predatory, and latent male side of female nature, and represses and impoverishes its dependent, peace loving and sequacious side."[17]

The acerbic journalist H. L. Mencken's *In Defense of Women* (1918) offhandedly praised women in the abstract while chastising feminists and suffragists as unhappy women incapable of getting a man to the matrimonial altar. Mencken portrayed American men as egoistic boobs—"complete masculinity and stupidity are often indistinguishable" —manipulated into marriage by conniving women. He saved his bitterest invective for men who supported feminism and would even stoop so low as to marry a woman's rights advocate.

> The iron-faced suffragist propagandist, if she gets a man at all, must get one wholly without sentimental experience. If he has any, her crude manoeuvers make him laugh and he is repelled by her lack of pulchritude and amiability. All such suffragists (save a few miraculous beauties) marry ninth-rate men when they marry at all. They have to put up with the sort of cast-offs who are almost ready to fall in love with lady physicists, embryologists, and embalmers.[18]

The acclaimed novelist Sherwood Anderson's astonishing little tract *Perhaps Women* (1931) echoes many of these same themes, but he drew a very different conclusion. Modern man is lost, Anderson wrote, "impotent" before the machine, which dominates industrial production. "The machines make me feel too small. They are too complex and beautiful for me. My manhood cannot stand up against them yet. They do things too well. They do too much." As a result, Anderson wrote, in words reminiscent of Tocqueville a century earlier, man was a member of a lost sex with

> no definite connection with the things with which he is surrounded, no relations with the clothes he wears, the house he lives in. He lives in a house but he did not build it. He sits in a chair but he did not make it. He drives a car but he did not build it. He sleeps in a bed but he does not know where it came from.

But instead of urging women's exclusion, Anderson welcomed them, because he found "something still alive in the women that seems to be going dead in the men." Women, he believed, were "not enervated spiritually by the machines. They have not accepted the vicarious feelings of power, got from machines, as their own power." And so women, grounded still in the world of humanity, were men's only salvation.[19]

Few others agreed. For most men the Depression was emasculating both at work and at home. Unemployed men lost status with their wives and children and saw themselves as impotent patriarchs. And the consequences for men were significant. One New Jersey man spoke of his intense guilt as a father: "I haven't had a steady job in more than two years. Sometimes I feel like a murderer. What's wrong with me that I can't protect my children?"[20] And a young boy wrote to President and Mrs. Roosevelt about his father's plight. Concerned that his family would not get relief, the boy asked for help directly from the president. "My father, he's staying home. All the time he's crying because he can't find work. I told him why are you crying daddy, and daddy said why shouldn't I cry when there is nothing in the house. I feel sorry for him. That night I couldn't sleep. The next morning I wrote this letter to you."[21]

Who was to blame? And what were men to do about it? The author Norman Cousins provided rather simpleminded answers. After noting that the unemployed ranks numbered about ten million, roughly the same number of women who were working, he suggested that we "[s]imply fire the women, who shouldn't be working anyway, and hire the men. Presto! No unemployment. No relief rolls. No Depression."[22] Other theories and solutions were not much more clearheaded. One idea was to try and pin the blame on the wives for re-victimizing their depressed nonbreadwinning husbands. As one psychiatrist explained it to journalist Studs Terkel, the men

> hung around street corners and in groups. They gave each other solace. They were loath to go home because they were indicted, as if it were their fault for being unemployed. A jobless man was a lazy good-for-nothing. The women punished the men . . . by withholding themselves sexually. By belittling and emasculating the men, undermining their paternal authority, turning to the eldest son. These men suffered from depression. They felt despised, they were ashamed of themselves.[23]

Even if contemporary readers would not go as far as to blame the women for reemasculating their husbands in some twisted incestuous plot, we cannot but feel compassion for men whose twin identities as worker and father/husband, a dual identity expressed in the term "breadwinner," was suddenly eroded, seemingly beyond repair.

No wonder Dale Carnegie's *How to Win Friends and Influence People* (1936) was so instantly popular. Carnegie counseled readers away from traditional measures of achievement like status, wealth, and power—a wise move if one was going to be one of the era's few success stories. One's worth was not to be measured by standing out from the crowd but rather by fitting in. Carnegie's self-help scheme seemed to shift attention away from external trappings of success to more internal forces, one's personality. But twentieth-century "personality" meant something very different from nineteenth-century "character"—it meant a malleable instrument that could be applied in social situations to elicit from others approval and advancement. "You have a product and that product is yourself," Carnegie counseled his would-be salesmen readers. Men, Carnegie argued, could shape their personalities to shape the forces around them and get what they wanted.

But the picture of men that emerges in the 1930s is far more poignant than Carnegie's best-selling boosterism. In her pathbreaking study *The Unemployed Man and his Family* (1940), the sociologist Mirra Komarovsky provided a poignant description of the impact of this dual erosion of the identities of father and worker. The unemployed man "suffers from deep humiliation" since he fails in his core role as family provider. He appears bewildered, "as if the ground has gone out from under his feet."[24] Many of the men Komarovsky interviewed described the "humiliation within the family" as the "hardest part" of being unemployed. With their economic power eliminated, their status as head of the household is eroded and with it their sense of manhood. "When a man is at home all day he cannot possibly command as much respect as when he returns to the family for a few hours of concentrated conversation," noted one man, who felt himself to be a "fallen idol" without a job. "Before the Depression," says another, "I wore the pants in this family and rightly so. During the Depression I lost something. Maybe you call it self-respect, but in losing it I also lost the respect of my children, and I am afraid I am losing my wife."[25]

In the face of this humiliation, men turned increasingly to their sons. "The boy is building from infancy his conception of manhood, making little models in his thoughts of how he must behave to be a man," wrote one parental adviser, with words that must have reassured the unemployed fathers who were reading her words. "How false models in his thoughts must be when they are based on brief, superficial glimpses of his father."[26] By the 1930s three-fourths of American fathers said they regularly read magazine articles about child care, and nearly as many men as women were members of the PTA. "In the highest animal of all, man, we should expect to find the fullest development of a father's concern for his offspring," began one passage in a popular advice book from 1933. "A man would be lower than some beasts if he did not protect and aid his wife while she was bearing his child and if he did not do everything he could for it through all the years in which it needed his care."[27]

The workplace was too unreliable to enable men to prove their manhood; in fact, it eroded their authority at home. Many men returned to the home, as fathers and modest breadwinners (instead of as economic success stories), in the hope that by raising their sons to be successful men they could themselves achieve some masculine redemption. The popularization of psychology in the 1920s gave their efforts at domestic participation a real boost. Freudian ideas had made parental participation in child rearing a requirement of healthy gender development and appropriate sexual development. If a boy's behavior was feminine or a young girl's behavior was masculine, it was a sure sign that something had gone wrong in the child's psychosexual development, and it was feared that homosexuality might be the result. If women abandoned their traditional role as homemakers or if men abandoned their traditional role as breadwinners, it could easily send the wrong message to young children. Psychology thus weighed in with a new imperative in the re-separation of spheres, providing ammunition against women's efforts to enter the public sphere and ensuring, as Sinclair Lewis wrote in *Babbitt*, that "the realms of offices and of kitchens had no alliances."[28]

In the 1920s and 1930s many writers attempted to resolve parental anxieties by discouraging women from working outside the home and encouraging men to participate in domestic life. For example, some states passed laws that required that women teachers be fired when they married so they would be unable to attempt motherhood and career. Popular magazines and advice manuals promoted both a "child care" movement and a "domestic science" movement meant to reassure women that motherhood and housework were deeply satisfying vocations whose importance could not be overestimated. Mother's Day, originally established to celebrate women's work *outside* the home (in civic projects such as public sanitation and as volunteers in hospitals during the Civil War), was transformed, via a mass-marketing campaign that delighted the nation's florists, into a celebration of traditional homemaking. Meanwhile, in 1924 the National Congress of Mothers' Clubs changed its name to the Parent-Teacher Association (PTA) in an effort to encourage fathers to join without fear of feminization.[29]

Some of the era's most popular psychological writers gave parents an increasing role to play in their children's development. J. B. Watson's enormously influential *Psychological Care of Infant and Child* (1928), a precursor to Dr. Benjamin Spock's post–World War II best-seller, implored parents to be actively involved with their children. "Children are made, not born," he wrote, but to Watson, the makers of children were women; one searches in vain through his work for specific references to fathers. "Parents" really meant "mothers," and the work's preoccupation was with the outcomes for the children, not for any intrinsic pleasures or important experience of the parents themselves. So while Watson promised mothers directly that they, too, could raise bankers, artists, merchants, if they set their minds to it, his interest was in the children's appropriate adjustment. And mothers must be especially attentive to the threat of overdoing maternal affection. In a chapter called "The Dangers of Too Much Mother Love," Watson cautioned readers against becoming the mother whose "heart is full of love which she must express in some way. She expresses it by showering love and kisses" upon her hapless children, threatening their independence and mental health, and transforming healthy little boys into whining, dependent mama's boys. "Mother love is a dangerous instrument," he declared. Mothers must guard against their own impulses in shaping the lives of their offspring, which could be accomplished by separating boys from girls and treating them differently. "Never hug [boys] and kiss them, never let them sit on your lap," Watson advised.[30]

Pushing women out did not assuage the pressure on young fathers: They were required, on the one hand, to be successful or at least competent and employed; on the other, to be active parents to their sons at home so that their sons would not remain overly attached to their mothers. Half a century before women claimed that they wanted to "have it all"—successful careers and warm, intimate family lives—men experienced having it all as an enormous headache.

Homosexuality hovered like a specter over anxious parents, who were convinced that effeminacy in young boys was a certain predictor of adult male homosexuality. About a third of Joseph Collins's *The Doctor Looks at Love and Life* (1926), one of the decade's best-selling advice books to parents, was devoted to male homosexuality. In general, he argued, the homosexual was effeminate and unmanly—a "man of broad hips and mincing gait, who vocalizes like a lady and articulates like a chatterbox, who likes to sew and knit, to ornament his clothing and decorate his face." Clement Wood's advice book *Manhood* (1924) tried to reassure anxious young men that homosexuality was a stage of development out of which they would soon, thankfully, pass. Wood maintained that a twelve-year-old boy's proclivities were 40 percent autosexual, 50 percent homosexual, and 10 percent heterosexual; by puberty the percentages shifted to 20, 30, and 50 percent, respectively.[31]

One popular song, "Masculine Women! Feminine Men!" (1926), ridiculed the entire reversal of sex roles to a catchy ragtime beat. While "Sister is busy learning to shave, / Brother just loves his permanent wave"; while "Auntie is smoking, rolling her own, / Uncle is always buying cologne"—no wonder the singer laments that "it's hard to tell 'em apart today." And the consequences are dangerous: "You go in to give your girl a kiss in the hall / But instead you find you're kissing her brother Paul."[32]

These anxieties about homosexuality and effeminacy quickly and decisively eroded the casual acceptance of the gay male subculture in major American cities. The late 1920s and 1930s witnessed a "pansy craze," as new fears of gay men were raised. Once, a gay man had been seen as "an effeminate fairy whom one might ridicule but had no reason to fear"; now, though, tabloid newspapers terrified and titillated their readers with stories of degenerate child molesters who committed acts of unspeakable depravity. Gender arrangements were now so fragile, it seems, that "even a glimpse of an alternative might endanger them." The closet was hastily built, and gay men immediately pushed into it.[33]

The inseparable pair of parental fears—feminized boys and homosexuality—led many educators and popular writers to counsel continued separation of boys and girls. The YMCA suggested in a 1926 project booklet that "former efforts in Boys' Work centered upon keeping boys busy at almost any activity in order to keep them away from evil associations and bad environments, What boys learned in these substituted activities was not a matter of great concern." Contact with girls could dilute boyhood purity, and idleness would breed evil thoughts and deeds. Strenuous exercise was thus even more vital to healthy boyhood, as William Allen White wrote in 1926:

> The boy of today, whose work is done by machinery, who lives in a house heated by oil, or gas, or who lives in an apartment where the janitor does the work, would grow flabby and weak if he had to depend upon the work that he could not do about the home. But he comes home from the gymnasium and the ball field, renewed in body, and takes up his task of mastering the intricate problems of the radio and the motor-car, a young giant refreshed.[34]

Paternal involvement was seen as a central element in a healthy boy's development. The new fatherhood confirmed the new role of the psychologist as expert and the idea that the perilous project of shaping manhood began in the family, not in the workplace.

These new demands on parents were accompanied by increased marital tensions. In 1920 the nation recorded 7.7 divorces per one thousand marriages. Throughout the decade the number spiraled; between 1922 and 1926 there was one divorce for every seven marriages, and by 1927 there was one for every six—about sixteen times the rate for 1870.[35] One source of strain was men's efforts to juggle their roles as fathers and breadwinners, especially when many fathers weren't very good at child rearing and had been so poorly trained for it. Men were groomed for their work outside the home and had spent little time or energy developing the skills necessary for successful nurturing of children—patience, compassion, tenderness, attention to process.

Mocking fatherly incompetence became something of a boom industry in the popular press of the 1920s and 1930s, as in new comic strips like *Blondie* and plays like Clarence Day's *Life with Father* (1936). Dagwood Bumstead, Blondie's bumbling, incompetent, antihero husband, is the epitome of the breadwinner as boob:

> an untidy office worker who has to run every morning to catch the bus from his suburb; he is generally incompetent, inefficient, greedy (he is always sneaking into the kitchen to make the most incongruous sandwiches), sensuously lazy (outside the office and the kitchen he spends much of his time trying to take a nap on the sofa or laze in a hot bath), generally good tempered and easygoing but given to sudden and completely ineffective rages.

Dagwood isn't a *bad* man—he's "kind, dutiful, diligent, well meaning within his limits" —but he is a bad *man*, a model of the impotent patriarch, whose life would disintegrate without the quiet efficiency of his wife. He's so ineffectual that he doesn't even have the comic strip named after him![36] And Clarence Day, who said he saw more of his own father as an adult than as a child, portrayed Father as a blustering tyrant but one whose bark was decidedly worse than his bite.

If fatherhood was precarious, motherhood was out of the question. In one of their first films, *Their First Mistake* (directed by Hal Roach), Laurel and Hardy set up housekeeping together, and then decide to adopt a child without first consulting Ollie's wife. When she walks out, the two determine to raise the child alone. Before long, they are sleeping together, with the baby, in Hardy's marriage bed. In one scene Laurel sucks the bottle that Hardy holds. In another scene Hardy holds the bottle in his lap and strokes it so hard that the milk spurts out of it. Such hilariously homoerotic domesticity is soon shattered when the couple receive notice that Hardy's wife is suing for divorce and that Laurel is named as corespondent.[37]

These examples point to the difficulty men seemed to have grounding a sense of manly accomplishment in their performance as parents. The Depression had forced many men to abandon their faith in the marketplace as certain to confirm their manhood. Masculinity had to be reconceived so that any man could achieve it and pass it on reliably to his sons. Here, again, psychology offered some solace. Masculinity could be redefined away from achievement in the public sphere and reconceived as the exterior manifestation of a certain inner sense of oneself. Masculinity could be observed in specific traits and attitudes, specific behaviors and perspectives. If men expressed these attitudes, traits, and behaviors, they could be certain that they were "real" men, regardless of their performance in the workplace. If a man failed to express these attitudes, traits, and behaviors, he was in danger of becoming a homosexual. A key psychological question for the 1930s, then, was whether homosexuality could be "cured" by a healthy dose of manhood.

Enter Lewis Terman, a Stanford psychologist best known as the creator of the Stanford-Binet intelligence test, the famous IQ test that measured supposedly innate intelligence. In a 1936 volume *Sex and Personality*, Terman and his associate, Catherine Cox Miles, reported on the development of an "M-F" scale that measured gendered behaviors, attitudes, and information by which parents could plot their child's "mental masculinity and femininity"—the successful acquisition of gender identity.[38] "If holding a job to support a family could no longer be counted on to define manhood," writes the contemporary psychologist Joseph Pleck, "a masculinity-femininity test could."[39] Terman and Miles were not the first behavioral scientists to attempt to measure masculinity and femininity and apply those measures to sexual orientation, but they were the most thorough. Their M-F scales included an inventory of 456 items and utilized state-of-the-art psychological personality tests—including Rorschach ink blots, projective tests that asked children to imagine themselves in various situations, and standard attitude and knowledge inventories—to position each test taker along a continuum from Masculinity at one pole to Femininity at the other. An individual's answers to these tests, administered primarily to adolescents, both boys and girls, in junior high schools across the country, spelled success or failure in acquiring gender-appropriate identity. For those who failed, their gender-inappropriate personality could be seen as a kind of "early warning system" for future homosexuality. Parent-teacher conferences would be scheduled, and a variety of therapeutic interventions might be proposed, including encouraging him to engage in more manly activities like sports and outdoor work, and prohibiting him from continuing what pleasure he might have taken from reading, painting, cooking, or listening to classical music.[40]

Never before had masculinity undergone such rigorous scrutiny and elaboration; never before had it seemed so urgent that it do so. Terman and Miles had recodified masculinity and femininity so that they could be measured and charted, thus encoding into science what had been historical and social arrangements. For example, some sentence completions made it clear that there were some things that men should—and should not—know:

1. Things cooked in grease are boiled (+), broiled (I), fried (−), roasted (+).
2. Most of our anthracite coal comes from: Alabama (−), Colorado (−), Ohio (−), Pennsylvania (+).
3. The "Rough Riders" were led by: Funston (−), Pershing (−), Roosevelt (+), Sheridan (−).
4. The proportion of the globe covered by water is about: 1/8 (−), 1/4 (−), 1/2 (−), 3/4 (+).

(To keep score in the way that Terman and Miles suggested, score a "+" for a masculine response and a "−" for a feminine one. I don't think they intended their own biases to be so transparent.)

A large set of items elaborated what men should and shouldn't feel; respondents were to quantify their emotional responses (a lot, some, a little, none) to explore the following emotions:

- Anger: being called lazy, seeing boys make fun of old people, seeing someone cheat on an exam.
- Fear: being lost, deep water, graveyards at night, Negroes.
- Pity: a fly caught on sticky fly paper, a man who is cowardly and can't help it, a wounded deer.
- Wickedness: boys teasing girls, indulging in "petting," not brushing your teeth, being a Bolshevik.[41]

The M-F test also included possible careers and their obvious sex typing, such as librarian, auto racer, forest ranger, florist, soldier, music teacher. There were also lists of character traits (loud voices, men with beards, tall women) that testees were asked to either like or dislike and a list of children's books (*Robinson Crusoe, Rebecca of Sunnybrook Farm, Little Women, Biography of a Grizzly*) that they either liked, disliked, or had not read. Another set of questions included a list of famous people one could either like or dislike (Bismarck, Florence Nightingale, Lenin, Jane Addams). Not having read a book or knowing about a famous person was seen as gender-conforming or nonconforming for both girls and boys. Other questions included what one might like to draw if one were an artist (ships or flowers); what one might like to write about if one were a newspaper reporter (accidents, theater); and where you might like to go if you had plenty of money (hunt lions in Africa or study social customs, learn about various religions or see how criminals are treated).

Finally, the test included some self-reporting about the respondent's own behaviors and attitudes. *Yes* or *no* items (here listed with the scoring of a *yes* answer) included:

- Do you rather dislike to take your bath? (+)
- Are you extremely careful about your manner of dress? (−)
- Do people ever say you talk too much? (+)
- Have you ever kept a diary? (−)

The M-F test was perhaps the single most widely used inventory to determine the successful acquisition of gender identity in history and was still being used in some school districts into the 1960s. The test also formed the basis for virtually all studies of gender-role acquisition ever since, including some of the most widely used psychological tests in our nation's history: the Strong Vocational Interest Blank (1943), the Guilford Temperament Survey (1936), and the Minnesota Multiphasic Personality Inventory (1972), still the most widely used complete personality inventory.[42]

Despite their comprehensiveness, Terman and Miles came up with results that were counterintuitive to the prevailing norms of the day. For example, they found that boys brought up "chiefly or only" by their mothers were somewhat more masculine than boys brought up by only their fathers or by both parents. It was equally true that girls raised "chiefly or only" by their fathers were slightly more feminine than those raised by only their mothers or by both parents. "So much for the necessity of a same-sex role model for learning cultural sex role norms!" writes one historian of psychology.[43]

Terman and Miles—and Terman's student, E. Lowell Kelly—also compared the scores of heterosexuals with those of "active" and "passive" homosexuals and found that male heterosexuals and active male homosexuals had very similar gender-role identities and that passive male homosexuals manifested a feminine gender-role identity. (The "normality" of the active homosexuals was theoretically finessed by the authors, whose theories required that all homosexuals be pathologized.) The authors argued that the etiology of homosexuality was always to be sought in the sinews of gender-role acquisition:

> too demonstrative affection from an excessively emotional mother, especially in the case of a first, last, or only child; a father who is unsympathetic, autocratic, brutal, much away from the home, or deceased; treatment of the child as a girl, coupled with lack of encouragement or opportunity to associate with boys and to take part in the rougher masculine activities; overemphasis on neatness, niceness, and spirituality; lack of vigilance against the danger of seduction by older homosexual males.[44]

Here was one of the origins of the infamous "strong mother = gay son" theory, which held sway for many decades, well into the 1970s. Contemporaneous research by the psychiatrist George W. Henry came to similar conclusions, as have several significant subsequent studies.[45] Masculinity was now understood to be learned through the successful mastery of a variety of props. Freudian assumptions grounded the male sex role—a static, ahistorical container of attitudes, behaviors, and values that are appropriate to men and define masculine behavior.[46] A century after Henry Clay first declared us a nation of self-made men, American men were no closer to experiencing a secure, confident sense of themselves as men.

Of course, that didn't keep men from trying. And if acquiring all the traits and attitudes and behaviors that Terman and Miles had identified seemed too overwhelming, one could at least appear to have acquired them. As at the turn of the century, a masculine physique could signify success, physical strength could stand in for strength of character. Arms could make the man—or at any rate biceps and triceps could. At least that was true according to Charles Atlas, who stressed transformation of the body instead of the personality and taught successive generations of American men how to pump themselves up. Atlas provided an answer to the M-F test, a course of study the end of which was certain manliness.

Born in Italy in 1893, Angelo Siciliano came in 1910 to the United States, where he lived in a poor section of New York City with his mother. He was a scrawny young man, "a 97 pound runt . . . skinny, pale, nervous, and weak."[47] One summer day Angelo had the experience that changed his life: "One day I went to Coney Island and I had a very pretty girl with me. We were sitting in the sand. A big, husky, lifeguard . . . kicked sand in my face. *I couldn't do anything* and the girl felt funny. I told her that someday, if I met this guy, I would lick him." The girl quickly moved elsewhere on the beach, and Angelo, walking home, dejected, passed a large poster of the mythic Atlas lifting the weight of the world. He resolved at that moment to transform his body into one capable of heroic feats, and he adopted the name of his mythic hero.

After personally transforming himself into "the world's most perfectly developed man,"—the nation's "ranking collection of muscles," according to one reporter—the newly renamed Charles Atlas developed his technique of "dynamic tension," a muscle-making and -building technique designed to turn other "ninety-seven-pound weaklings" into real he-men.[48] His advertisements in boys' magazines and later in comic books asked, "Are

You a Redblooded Man?" and "Do You Want to be a Tiger?" One text from his 1925 ads linked physical success to economic success. "It's the Tiger Men who grab everything they want these days. The new race of Tiger Men win the battles . . . in the mad, dizzy, jazzy marathon for personal success! They whiz by you in stunning limousines. They have fine homes and bulging bank accounts." Atlas built his first gymnasium in 1927, and during the Depression, business for this man-making machine was never better. By 1942 he was running the most successful mail-order business in the nation's history, and this "muscle maestro" boasted that he had added no less than six million pounds of solid rippling flesh to the American body.[49]

Atlas saw his mission as building "a perfect race, a country of perfect human master-pieces," a statement with dangerous overtones in 1942. Concerned with racial degener-ation that derived from sedentary urban life, Atlas saw muscles and exercise as the route to national salvation. As one typical consumer of the Dynamic Tension system wrote: "Some time ago, I enrolled as one of your students. I was very skinny, with small bones. Enclosed you will find my picture taken after faithfully following your instructions. Today I feel that no man can rule or oppress me."[50]

This transformation of wimpy weaklings to "muscular mastodons" was soon echoed in one of the most famous fantasy heroes in history. In 1938 Clark Kent first magically transformed himself into the most courageous, heroic, manly man who had ever lived. Superman was so powerful that he wasn't really from this planet; his transformation was actually the Atlas program in reverse—a superhuman extraterrestrial who transforms himself into a wimpy bespectacled newspaper reporter in order to fit unnoticed into the emasculating metropolis. Yet as fantasy image, Superman gave a promise to every other obsequious American office worker: Behind those glasses and that mild-mannered demeanor beat the heart of the hero. As cartoonist Jules Feiffer writes, Clark Kent was

> Superman's opinion of the rest of us, a pointed caricature of what we were really like. Superman's fake identity was our real one . . . [if] the glasses and cheap suits, when removed, revealed all of us in our true identities [as supermen]—what a hell of an improved world it would have been![51]

Atlas's advertisements for his physical fitness regimen graced that first issue of *Superman* and virtually every issue since.

Superman and Clark Kent sanitized the gendered schizophrenia that had been the stuff of masculine fantasy for some time, making this version of Mr. Hyde every bit as respectable as Dr. Jekyll. And even more sexually chaste. As Clark constantly pursued Lois Lane, seeking the comforts of marital stability, Lois had eyes only for his more manly alter ego, who could not, and would never be, tied down into a life of domestic drudgery. What Clark craved, Superman avoided. Like Natty Bumppo and Huck Finn before him, Superman was also born to run—or rather, to fly.

Heroism was a masculine dream possible only in mythic fantasy or in daytime reverie. James Thurber's biting short story "The Secret Life of Walter Mitty," published in the *New Yorker* in 1939, opened a lens into the psyche of the henpecked husband as an emasculated daydreamer, whose wife has to remind him to wear his overshoes. In his fantasies, though, Mitty is so heroic that he even disdains a handkerchief as he stoically faces a firing squad.[52]

Another fantasy hero was the cynically crusty detective of novels and films. He first made his appearance in the late 1920s in the work of Dashiell Hammett and, in subsequent decades, in the stories by Raymond Chandler and Mickey Spillane. The detective thus joined Tarzan and myriad cowboy heroes as a vehicle for male escapist fantasy. Here, adventurous and cold men stalked the urban jungle, a world where women were either seductive vixens enticing men to their doom or angelic innocents needing their help (but never their marital commitment). The detective was the urban pioneer, making the world safe for women and children. He was, as Hammett wrote, a "little man going forward . . . through mud and blood and death and deceit—as callous and brutal as necessary."

This new hard-boiled tough guy repackaged rugged artisanal manhood for modern urban audiences. Chandler's detective novels celebrated the autonomy of the private eye as Heroic Artisan; his essay "The Simple Art of Murder" provides a most eloquent description.

> Down these mean streets a man must go who is not himself mean, who is neither tarnished nor afraid. . . . He must be a complete man and a common man, yet an unusual man. He must be, to use a rather weathered phrase, a man of honor. He is neither a eunuch nor a satyr. I think he might seduce a duchess, and I am quite sure he would not spoil a virgin. If he is a man of honor in one thing, he's that in all things. He is a relatively poor man, or he would not be a detective at all. He is a common man or he could not go among common people. He has a sense of character or he would not know his job. He will take no man's money dishonestly, and no man's insolence without due and dispassionate revenge. He is a lonely man, and his pride is that you will treat him as a proud man or be very sorry you ever saw him.[53]

And Dashiell Hammett's private eye hero, Sam Spade, was more coldly cynical than his peers, a "defensive loner who is suspicious of all relationships, romantic and otherwise," which made him all the more manly. "After the high minded detective heroes, their artistic leanings and their elaborate deductions," one ecstatic reviewer cooed when *The Maltese Falcon* was published in 1930, Sam Spade "is as startling as a real man in a shop window full of dummies. His actions and his language will shock old ladies."[54]

Less shocking, perhaps, were many of the era's most celebrated novels and films. But they were equally concerned with helping men cope with increased pressures, scale back their expectations, or at least provide momentary escape. There were rumblings of discontent among American men between the wars, and the fiction of the era expressed it eloquently. Some suggested that the traditional methods for self-making were unreliable in a modern world. For example, Ernest Hemingway's novels suggest the brittleness and vulnerability of male bonding, even as his impulse is to trust homosocial intimacy, especially when compared with relations with the opposite sex. Personally, Hemingway eschewed the upper-class gentility into which he had been born and embraced a rough-hewn artisanal manhood demonstrated and tested in the most highly ritualized ways—boxing matches, bullfighting, hunting, soldiering. His novels are also always about men's relationships with one another—fathers and sons, battle companions, friends on a fishing trip, fellow patients in a hospital, a couple of waiters preparing to close up shop, a bullfighter and his manager, a boy and a gangster. Only these "move him to simplicity and truth," writes Leslie Fiedler, although these men are almost always "maimed, unmanned, victimized." In a review of *In Our Time*, D. H. Lawrence said that Nick Adams,

Hemingway's long-term protagonist, may have been "a type one meets in the more wild and woolly regions of the United States" but that he was only really "the remains of the lone trapper and cowboy."[55]

In *Men without Women* (1927), a short story collection, Hemingway's battle-scarred, weary warriors reveal a biting cynicism and emptiness at the core of modern American masculinity. In a hard-boiled, lean, and muscular prose Hemingway searches among the shards of European culture for a lost American manhood. The men are bullfighters, boxers, soldiers, hired gunmen, and the women are unwelcome—they're pregnant ("White Elephants"), prostitutes, deceivers, or fools. In one story, "Soldier's Home," Harold Krebs returns from the front only to feel suffocated in civilian life and tries to disengage from the world, to "live alone without consequences."

In *The Sun Also Rises* (1926), his first full-length novel, Jake Barnes and his comrades wander across the European continent searching for something to believe in. Like many of Hemingway's male characters, their scars leave them either incapable or uninterested in sexual passion with women, interested only in the most chaste bonds among men. Jake's shell-shocked impotence animates his rage at homosexuals and women and his sneering tone toward Lady Brett Ashley. "Somehow they [gay men] always made me angry," Jake says. "I know they are supposed to be amusing, and you should be tolerant, but I wanted to swing on one, any one, anything to shatter that superior, simpering composure"—a composure that was at once, he thought, daintily ineffective and haughtily arrogant. But he reserves some of his bitterest invective for himself. "It is awfully easy to be hard-boiled about everything in the daytime," he admits, "but at night it is another thing."[56]

Other novelists turned their attention to characters who were captives of their own illusions, captives of the American Dream and the vision of the Self-Made Man. Sinclair Lewis's character George Babbitt is a classic self-deceiver; this flabby, would-be-tough midwestern realtor is constantly pumping himself up with phrases like "gotta hustle" and "real he-stuff." (He names his son Theodore Roosevelt Babbitt to ensure a hypermasculine lineage.) Babbitt's gushing about manhood, in a moment of "hysteric patriotism," at a realtors' convention reveals Lewis's critique of this small-town, small-minded masculine booster:

> The ideal of American manhood and culture isn't a lot of cranks sitting around chewing the rag about their Rights and their Wrongs, but a God-fearing, hustling, successful, two-fisted Regular guy, who belongs to some church with pep and piety to it, who belongs to the Boosters or the Rotarians or the Kiwanis, to the Elks or Moose or Red Men or Knights of Columbus or any one of a score of organizations of good, jolly, kidding, laughing, sweating, upstanding, lend-a-handing Royal Good Fellows, who plays hard and works hard, and whose answer to his critics is a square-toed boot that'll teach the grouches and smart alecks to respect the He-man and get out and root for Uncle Samuel, U.S.A.[57]

When Babbitt does rebel against this "duty of being manly," Lewis allows us to see through those illusions, thus giving to American literature a synonym for disaffected suburban manhood.

Much of the era's fiction depicts men attempting to cope with forces that are far beyond their control. Jay Gatsby, in F. Scott Fitzgerald's *The Great Gatsby*, was a Self-Made Man who rose "rapidly from poverty and obscurity to the highest pinnacles of wealth and power." Gatsby's fall is destined by his own illusions about self-making; he is ultimately "destroyed by an agency which he himself has brought into being."[58] Gatsby is, perhaps, the era's ultimate Self-Made Man, a compassionate fraud, a hero whose tragic flaw is that he actually believes his own myth of self-creation as the way to realize the American Dream. Gatsby, as Nick puts it, "sprang from a Platonic conception of himself"; shedding his former identity as Jay Gatz, he "invented just the sort of Jay Gatsby that a seventeen-year-old boy would be likely to invent, and to this conception he was faithful to the end."

After his death, Gatsby's father, Mr. Gatz, shows Nick the young Gatsby's copy of *Hopalong Cassidy*. Inside the back cover Jay had neatly printed the word "Schedule," dated September 12, 1906. In that brief passage, so reminiscent of Benjamin Franklin's prescriptions for self-making over a century earlier, Fitzgerald reveals the tragedy of the myth of the Self-Made Man and also its allure:

Rise from bed . . . . .6.00 A.M.
Dumbbell exercise and wall scaling . . . . .6.15–6.30 "
Study electricity, etc . . . . .7.15–8.15 "
Work . . . . .8.30–4.30 P.M.
Baseball and sports . . . . .4.30–5.00 "
Practice elocution, poise and how to attain it . . . . .5.00–6.00 "
Study needed inventions . . . . .7.00–9.00 "
GENERAL RESOLVES
No wasting time at Shafters or [a name, indecipherable]
No more smokeing or chewing
Bath every other day
Read one improving book or magazine per week
Save $5.00 [crossed out] $3.00 per week
Be better to parents

Here was a prescription for self-creation—perfecting body, mind, and presentability. The realization of the Self-Made Man had become a set of instructions for moral uplift.[59]

Gatsby's self-making took him from the humble Midwest to the stately Long Island mansions of an aristocratic elite. By contrast, John Steinbeck conferred a heroic dignity on the pained efforts of the working class to make themselves. No novelist captured the 1930s better than Steinbeck, whose powerful and poignant depictions of Americans' struggle to survive the Depression found him a wide audience. Many of Steinbeck's novels center around men made marginal by economic hardship. "The roads became crowded with men *ravenous* for work, *murderous* for work," Steinbeck wrote in *The Grapes of Wrath* (1939). "What's it coming to?" asks Tom Joad. "Fella can't make a livin' no more. Folks can't make a livin' farmin'. I ask you what's it coming to?" And yet each offers temporary solace in human connections, so that the deep love between George and Lennie in *Of Mice and Men* (1937) or the resilience of the family bond, especially Ma Joad, in *The Grapes of Wrath*, offers the only hedge against the pain and isolation of economic marginality: "Guys like us got no fambly," says George to the simpleminded behemoth Lennie in the beginning of a story that is repeated throughout the novel. "They make a little stake and they blow it in. They ain't got nobody in the world that gives a hoot in hell about 'em—"

"But not us," Lennie cried happily. "Tell about us now."

George was quiet for a moment. "But not us," he said.

"Because—"

"Because I got you an'—"

"An' I got you. We got each other, that's what, that gives a hoot in hell about us," Lennie cried in triumph.[60]

Such sentiments may seem "austerely mawkish" to contemporary readers, but Lennie's death is the highest expression of George's sacrifice and love.[61] Given how Steinbeck "traffics in the humble dreams of the lowliest workers in an age before social security and unemployment insurance," it is fitting that Aaron Copland was commissioned for the score of the 1939 film of the novel. In most of Steinbeck's novels, we also find a fanfare for the common man.

A fanfare is also offered in the plays of Clifford Odets, who offered a sobering look at men's plight. In *Awake and Sing* (1935) and *Waiting for Lefty* (1935), Odets painted sympathetic portraits of men's search for their souls, for a reason to live, amidst the pain and humiliation of the economic crisis. Calling the American obsession with success a "peritonitis of the soul," Odets wrote against the myth of abundance and described instead the "unmanning fiscal panic" and the "demoralized resignation" that came with the fact of scarcity. In *Awake and Sing* the playwright creates a climate of humiliation and frustration that settles around the Berger household like "a thick fog," according to theater critic John Lahr.[62] Each of the male characters tries to figure out ways to hedge against that creeping humiliation. Morty's success becomes a weapon to humiliate others, while Sam craves the invisibility of the shamed; stage directions describe Sam as "conditioned by the humiliation of not making his way alone."[63]

While Odets drew on the image of the Heroic Artisan as a model for the new proletarian man, other leftist polemicists used him as a weapon in cultural critique. Socialist critic Michael Gold, for example, called writers like Thornton Wilder a "typical American art pansy" who wrote "Chambermaid literature" with a "homosexual bouquet." "Send us a giant who can shame our writers back to their task of civilizing America," he wrote in *New Masses*. "Send a soldier who has studied history. Send a strong poet who loves the masses and their future. . . . Send an artist. Send a Bolshevik. Send a Man."[64] The Left, claimed these socialists, was more manly than the suburban middle class.

They seemed to get everything—artist, Bolshevik, and man—in the figure of Charles Chaplin, whose films captivated audiences in the 1930s just as his politics and romantic intrigues disillusioned many of them. Chaplin's films, especially *Modern Times* (1936), portray the assembly line as a site of humiliation and alienation, in which the worker is turned into a machine to serve omnivorous cannibalistic machines. Yet the individual working man is not the object of ridicule or even pity but rather, through humor, is rendered with both respect and pathos.

Chaplin was only one of a host of new American celebrities who emerged in the new film era of the 1920s and 1930s. Many early films promised fantasy escape from quotidian routine, and several also served as meditations on manhood. Cecil B. DeMille's *Male and Female* (1919), for example, was an adaptation of J. M. Barrie's play *The Admirable Crichton*. In this film Crichton, a handsome, virtuous butler, possesses admirable manly qualities but is, by immutable circumstances of his birth, destined to serve his moral inferiors—rich courtiers who are languid and idle. The women's suitors are all portrayed as effete fops, while the liveries, butlers, and servants are given a kind of Lawrencian virility and rugged handsomeness. When the entire crew is stranded on a remote desert island, only Crichton is capable of teaching the others to survive, and he becomes the veritable "King of Babylon" as he carries Mary, the daughter of his master, onto the island, limp and lifeless. When the party is eventually rescued, it is not without some remorse and regret on Mary's part, now that she has experienced true virility. In the final scene Crichton serves Mary drinks on a tray. Order is restored, De Mille suggests, but at an enormous cost—the reemasculation of the Heroic Artisan.

Other films fueled fantasies of upward mobility in the midst of economic crisis. Busby Berkeley extravaganzas offered the glittering surfaces of being "in the money," while *It Happened One Night* (1934) and *Mr. Deeds Goes to Town* (1936) invited Americans on a breathless tour of the life of the newly wealthy elite. In the latter film Gary Cooper portrays a tuba-playing Clark Kent-type called Longfellow Deeds, who, by no virtue of his own, inherits millions and spends the largest part of the movie giving his money away, gaining his manhood as a paternalistic savior. Deeds thus reassured Americans that help was on the way, that upward mobility was just an inheritance away, and that the wealthy were really rather noble characters, capable of enormous generosity to those in need.

The enormously popular gangster movies presented the other side of the coin, a Depression-era countermyth of Self-Made masculinity. The gangster was depicted as a successful capitalist, a genuine Self-Made Man; the Mafia, we learned in these and later films, calls its members "made men" when they've passed an initiation ritual test—a contract killing. But the gangster serves up the Self-Made Man in a negative cast. Only occasionally, as in *Angels with Dirty Faces* (1938), does the gangster become a positive role model, and then only when James Cagney feigns cowardice at his impending execution in order to dissuade a gang of young ruffians from following in his footsteps.

In 1939 American men got a choice of heroes in one of the most popular films of all time, *Gone With the Wind*—a choice that has persisted in Americans' minds, both male and female, for the ensuing decades. On the one hand, there was the chivalrous aesthete Ashley Wilkes, whose loyalty and dedication are both noble and effete, and on the other hand, there was Rhett Butler, a rogue and scoundrel, a man who thinks of no one but himself, a model of a Self-Made Man whose individualism prevents any connection with lofty noble contrivances such as country or honor. Guess whom Americans chose?

Gone With the Wind presented a crowning moment for both women and men. For women, it was the fulfillment of the Victorian feminine fantasy—that a woman's love could transform an implacably self-centered scoundrel and turn him into a dutiful, though no-less sexy, husband. For men, the contrast between Rhett and Ashley represented the fantasy triumph of the Self-Made Man as hero—competitive individualism and callous indifference both to other people and to political causes win out easily and are guaranteed to seduce even the most gorgeous and impetuous of women and transform them into loving and dutiful wives. Chivalry and the masculine devotion of the Genteel Patriarch were gone with the wind.

American men tried to come home, both literally and symbolically. And yet try as they might, they couldn't seem to ground their manhood on firm footing. King Vidor's *The Crowd* (1928) offered a particularly poignant and bleak picture of the possibilities for this generation of Self-Made Men. The film's hero, Johnny Sims, is the "new man" for a new century. "There's a little man the world is going to hear from all right," his father exclaims when Johnny is born in 1900, at the dawning of the era. But Johnny does not do "something big" at all but rather takes a job as a faceless bureaucrat in a large insurance company, "a cog in an impersonal machine, undifferentiated from other men." He is part of the crowd.

Yet he longs for heroism, for success, to stand out from that crowd as a rugged individualist, a mythic American hero. He marries the lovely Mary, but even their romance cannot survive the absence of heroic opportunities for men. The couple lives in a shabby tenement, where daily annoyances slowly erode their love. When their youngest child dies in an automobile accident, Johnny falls apart and, bereft, quits his job. He ends up as a juggler, luring passersby into a local restaurant—a clown of a man who tries to hold many balls in the air at once. He is too cowardly to kill himself.

The film's final scene seems to offer Johnny a moment of surcease. As the camera pulls away from the close-up on his beaming face, though, we see a large audience at a theater, watching a show. Johnny is again, whether at work or at play, just another face in the crowd. Rarely has the cinema offered as bleak or as powerful an image of the dilemmas of twentieth-century American men.[65]

CHAPTER 7

"Temporary About Myself"

White-Collar Conformists and Suburban Playboys, 1945–1960

WILLY (*longingly*): Can't you stay a few days? You're just what I need, Ben, because I—I have a fine position here, but I—well, Dad left when I was such a baby and I never had a chance to talk to him and I still feel—kind of temporary about myself.

—Arthur Miller *Death of a Salesman* (1949)

"When it's all over . . . just think . . . being able to settle down . . . and never be in doubt about anything." So said one aviator to his buddies in the 1944 film *Thirty Seconds over Tokyo*. And by most calculations he should have been right. Employment had risen dramatically during the war mobilization. Men had been able to prove on the battlefield what they had found difficult to prove at the workplace and in their homes—that they were dedicated providers and protectors. Reports of battlefield heroism provided some sorely needed manly templates. When the war took on the tone of a moral crusade, saving the world from Nazi genocide and terror, the virtuous tenor of military manhood was enhanced.

But war proved again to be only a temporary respite, and reentry proved more difficult than many men had anticipated. The sanitized versions offered up by Hollywood movies little prepared their families for the lingering effects of the war. Many films had muted both racial and ethnic tension and soldiers' longing for home and family by reconstituting the infantry squad as a kind of surrogate multicultural family, as men named Goldstein, O'Reilly, Vanelli, and Kowalski shared the same foxhole. But when men returned to their real families, life was not so simple.

One film that bucked the trend of postwar patriotic amnesia was William Wyler's *The Best Years of Our Lives* (1946). This poignant film chronicles the fitful reentry of three veterans: Al (Frederic March), a banker, who tries to reconcile his wartime experiences with his postwar life of relative ease and privilege; Fred (Dana Andrews), a glamorous flyer and war hero, who is haunted by nightmares and cannot find a decent job and whose hasty prewar marriage cannot survive the trials of separation and reentry; and Homer (Harold Russell), former star quarterback of his high school football team, who lost both his hands in the war and struggles to reveal his dependency to his steadfast fiancée. (One of the more innovative elements of the film was that Russell was actually a veteran who had lost both his hands, not an actor playing such a role.) Reentry was painful, and

147

adjustments necessary. "Last year it was 'Kill Japs!' This year it's 'Make money!'" says Al on his first morning back from the war. But reintegration was possible, especially through the heroic compassion and generosity of the moral women who waited patiently and preserved the home front. Only through their support and understanding, it was suggested, was masculine recovery and repatriation possible for those returning vets.[1]

Advice columnists picked up these sentiments. Wives were urged to return to a docile domesticity to placate their wounded men. "He's head man again," reminded *House Beautiful*. "Your part in the remaking of this man is to fit his home to him, understanding why he wants it this way, forgetting your own preferences." If successful, *Good Housekeeping* predicted, their husbands should stop their "oppressive remembering" in about two to three weeks.[2] Sadly, such memories often lasted a very long time, and in some cases they never went away. War shock, difficulty reintegrating, unexplained lethargy, emotional mood swings, and nightmares were common.

After the war, psychiatrists probed past the military veneer to reveal a trembling terror underneath the soldier's bravado. Many soldiers in the Second World War, it turned out, could not fire their rifles and return enemy fire, and about 75 percent of all infantrymen rarely fired their weapons at all. A large number became incontinent in battle, and many men would "feign emotional disorder" in order to get out of the line of fire. The breakdown rate among the troops was higher than anyone predicted, as the "loss of personal freedom, sexual deprivation, physical misery, chronic exhaustion, and immersion in a chamber of horrors coalesced to produce strain beyond endurance."[3] In a startling volume of psychiatric reports on battle stress and emotional disorders published by the U.S. Army Medical Department in 1949, psychiatrists attempted to normalize men's battlefield anxieties. As one clinician put it, "in combat, most men have anxiety."[4] Indeed they did, but such claims set up the "Catch-22" that novelist Joseph Heller would later capture so brilliantly in his novel. Since stress and anxiety were normal, soldiers should not be excused from the front for displaying these symptoms but rather returned immediately. As one psychiatrist put it:

> The soldier is saying in effect that he feels he cannot subject himself further to this reaction. Management consists in pointing out to the soldier that these sensations represent a normal response to combat, not differing greatly from that experienced by men who have remained in the lines. The physiologic mechanisms may perhaps be explained in simple terms. Then the soldier must return to duty, either immediately, or after a few hours' rest at the aid station. Neither he nor the physician should expect that he will be relieved of the symptoms, since they are merely the normal autonomic response to fear in this soldier. It is as irrational to expect psycho-therapy to relieve or remove such symptoms as to expect it to prevent dampness and chilling during combat in inclement weather. The soldier must "learn to live with it."[5]

"Learning to live with it" became one of the dominant ways to maintain American manhood through the next decade.

The difficulties in coping with the aftermath of the war were perhaps best expressed by the character Joseph Samuels, an insightful Jewish man, in Edward Dmytryk's film *Crossfire* (1947) just before he is murdered by Montgomery (Robert Ryan), a psychopathic anti-Semitic soldier. Describing postwar anomie, Samuels observes:

I think maybe it's suddenly not having a lot of enemies to hate anymore. Maybe it's because for four years now we've been focusing our minds on . . . on one little peanut. [*Samuels holds up a peanut.*] The "win the war" peanut, that was all. Get it over, eat that peanut. [*Samuels eats peanut.*] All at once, no peanut. Now we start looking at each other again. We don't know what we're supposed to do. We don't know what's supposed to happen. We're too used to fightin'. But we don't know what to fight. You can feel the tension in the air. A whole lot of fight and hate that doesn't know where to go. A guy like you maybe starts hatin' himself. One of these days maybe we'll all learn to shift gears. Maybe we'll stop hatin' and start likin' things again.[6]

In this bleak film, however, most men are despondent and dissolute after the war, living in crowded hotel rooms, unable to return to their families or their previous lives. Only Mitchell (George Cooper), falsely accused of the murder, can go home again. "It'll be a bit rugged," says Robert Mitchum, as Mitchell is reunited with his wife, "but they'll be all right." All right, perhaps. But never the same.

One arena that provided the possibility of "likin' things again" was the family, and fatherhood loomed larger and larger as the war came to a close. It was often as fathers that men sought to anchor their identities as successes as men. First, the fathers who left their homes as soldiers were honored as heroes; those left behind found jobs in wartime production. Fathers were indispensable to the adequate development of their sons, to the provision for the family, and for the health of the nation. Fathers provided "masculine companionship and influence" to boys who "need a man who will take them to do 'men's things' in a 'man's way,'" as one columnist put it.[7] What's more, fathers need do nothing more than *be* fathers in order to serve this vital function. They didn't need to prove anything; they had already done so. Such ideas were particularly comforting to men who had come to manhood in the era of the Great Depression and the war because they faced a postwar world of limited opportunities and shrinking possibilities.

During the war the absence of so many fathers had been seen as a contributor to growing juvenile delinquency and other social problems. In 1943 the Memphis Tennessee Youth Service Council sponsored a drive to enlist men in the fight against delinquency. Several thousand men signed a promissory note pledging to spend a certain number of hours each week with their sons.[8] That same year congressional hearings over a proposed draft exemption for fathers centered around whether the manpower needs of the military could offset the need for social stability and fatherhood on the domestic front. The sponsor, Senator Burton Wheeler, and his supporters predicted dire consequences if the bill failed, including rising rates of juvenile delinquency and the "complete breaking down of the morale and the morals of the boys and girls" of the nation. To avoid this catastrophe, the social order required both a breadwinning father and a homemaking mother.

Opponents claimed that exemption would deplete the armed forces of necessary manpower and, they suggested, deprive these fathers of the opportunities to demonstrate their manhood. "There is, I know, a sufficient number of men in the father pool, who, if they were properly employed and were not working in department stores and other places, would be sufficient to fulfill the immediate manpower needs of the entire United States," argued Gen. Joseph McNarney against the amendment. However, he claimed, if fathers were exempted that "particular class then is not required to furnish any effort for the successful completion of the war. If they see fit, they can still dress women's hair." Exemption from military service would emasculate fathers. The exemption amendment failed.[9]

In the increasingly suburban postwar world, fathers embodied masculinity—an idea confirmed by academic social science and psychology. "The process of transferring from the mother to the father is essential for emotional development, since the girl has to love and respect some man early in life if she is to grow up to marry one and the boy needs to have some male ideal if he is to wish to grow up to be a high type of man," wrote one social scientist.[10] Identification with father was central to the theories of Harvard sociologist Talcott Parsons, perhaps the most important social scientist of the postwar era, who attempted to develop a unified social science theory called structural functionalism. In a celebrated essay, "Certain Primary Sources and Patterns of Aggression in the Social Structure of the Western World" (1947), Parsons built on his earlier arguments for the emotional normality of the nuclear family, as father and mother embodied instrumental and expressive functions, both of which are necessary for social order and stability. Here, Parsons focused on the ways that the structure of the contemporary nuclear family produced specific problems, particularly the problem of adolescent male rebellion. The psychological requirement that the boy repudiate maternal nurture as the method of achieving healthy masculine identity means that his revolt against mother becomes a revolt against all he associates with femininity, including goodness. Becoming a "bad boy" becomes a positive goal, with important social consequences:

> Western men are peculiarly susceptible to the appeal of an adolescent type of assertively masculine behavior which may take various forms. They have in common a tendency to revolt against the routine aspects of the primarily institutionalized masculine role of sober responsibility, meticulous respect for the rights of others, and tender affection toward women. Assertion through physical prowess, with an endemic tendency toward violence and hence the military ideal, is inherent in the complex and the most dangerous potentiality.[11]

But the boy needs a father toward whom he can reorient his rebellion and grasp a positive identity. Father absence, caused by the occupational structure, makes this transition perilous; when the "boy does not have his father immediately available," he can develop a "large reservoir of repressed aggression," which can lead to a kind of "cult of 'compulsive masculinity.'" Parsons was loathe to locate masculine aggression in biological predisposition; he suggested that its cause was father absence and overdominant mothers. Now strong mothers could be blamed for both gay sons and delinquent sons. Only by reestablishing the coherence of the traditional nuclear family could such problems be averted. These preoccupations became the standard fare of studies of delinquency in the 1950s, one of the growth areas of American social science.[12]

Pundits, too, went after mom—and with a vengeance. Philip Wylie's *Generation of Vipers* (1942) set the tone for a decade of mom-bashing and was followed in short order by David Levy's *Maternal Overprotection* (1943) and Edward Strecker's *Their Mothers' Sons* (1946).[13] Strecker, a consultant to the Surgeon General of the U.S. Army, attributed the unmanliness of those rejected by the military to their mothers' overprotectiveness. Wylie, a disillusioned federal bureaucrat, went further, blaming mothers for virtually every characterological flaw among American men. Mom was a "destroying" angel, who rules her man by wiles and manipulation, and a cultural disease, "megaloid Momworship," ruled the land with narcissistic glee:

> Our land, subjectively mapped, would have more silver cords and apron strings criss-crossing it than railroads and telephone wires. Mom is everywhere and everything and damned near everybody, and from her depends all the rest of the U.S. Disguised as good old mom, dear old mom, sweet old mom, your loving mom, and so on, she is the bride at every funeral and the corpse at every wedding. Men live for her and die for her, dote upon her and whisper her name as they pass away, and I believe she has now achieved, in the hierarchy of miscellaneous articles, a spot next to the Bible and the Flag, being reckoned part of both in a way.[14]

Anthropologist Margaret Mead would have none of it. She painted a far less rosy portrait than Parsons did, given his expectation that a return to the nuclear family could ameliorate American men's restlessness. Nor did Mead buy Wylie's contention that the destruction of mother spelled the resurrection of manhood. In her brilliant dissection of the American character, *And Keep Your Powder Dry* (1942), a cultural critique that painted American masculinity as a retaliatory and vindictive hedge against fears and threatened humiliation, Mead worried about the consequences of continuing to pin gender identity on such outmoded ideals:

> Has the American scene shifted so that we still demand of every child a measure of success which is actually less and less possible for him to attain? . . . Have we made it a condition of success that a man should reach a position higher than his father's when such an achievement (for the many) is dependent upon the existence of a frontier and an expanding economy?[15]

If American men were chronically restless and anxious, she argued, it was because of the contradictory cultural messages that form the backbone of male socialization. "We teach them to be tough and to stand up for themselves, and, at the same time, teach them that aggression is wrong and should be suppressed, and, if possible repressed." As a result, American men are remarkable for a capacity to fight best only "when other people start pushing us around." Only in America do boys wear the proverbial chip on their shoulder, so that by waiting for someone to knock it off, he can "epitomize all the contradictory orders which have been given." Here is the typically American form of aggression—"aggressiveness which can never be shown except when the other fellow starts it; aggressiveness which is so unsure of itself that it has to be proved." Even our capacity for violence leaves us anxious and restless.[16]

Many of the chief sources of the decade's contradictory messages were cultural —from films to comic books. *Archie* comics, for example, begun in 1941, traded on masculine stereotypes in presenting Archie as the all-American high school kid. Archie plays off two negative archetypal poles familiar from previous decades of American history. Reggie Mantle and Dilton Doily, for example, represent two versions of the discredited Genteel Patriarch, imagined as either an unctuous upper-class fop (Reggie) or nerdy, egghead intellectual (Dilton). By contrast, the wise guy and buffoon (Jughead) and the brawny, muscle-bound numskull (Moose), provide two examples of the discredited

Heroic Artisan, depicted as wiseacre or Neanderthal. Archie steers down the middle of the road with just a hint of the impetuous smart aleck, the all-American guy who stands out by fitting in. And only he gets both Betty and Veronica (the blond, freshly scrubbed cheerleader and the somewhat darker, menacingly sexual brunette) to swoon over him. Archie is the Self-Made Man as Riverdale High School senior, even if he never manages to graduate.

The 1940s also resounded with voices of rage and pain, the voices of those groups of men who had historically been marginalized and emasculated by such self-made middle-class white men. The decade began with a violent scream from novelist Richard Wright, who, in *Native Son* (1940), and the more directly autobiographical *Black Boy* (1945), foretold a building black rage. As *Native Son* opens, Bigger Thomas's mother berates him for not being able to provide for a family: "We wouldn't have to live in this garbage dump if you had any manhood in you," she scolds. "You the most no-countenest man I ever seen in my life." Filled with shame, self-loathing, and rage, this encounter sets in motion the novel's violence and tragedy. When Bigger is finally captured—there have been eight thousand white men searching for him—the prosecutor calls for the death sentence as a reassertion of white manhood:

> the law is strong and gracious enough to allow all of us to sit here . . . and not tremble with fear at this very moment some half-human black ape may be climbing through the windows of our homes to rape, murder, and burn our daughters! . . . Every decent white man in America ought to swoon with joy for the opportunity to crush with his heel the woolly head of this black lizard.

When, at the novel's end, Bigger's mother visits him in prison and begs on her knees to Mrs. Dalton for Bigger's life, he is again "paralysed with shame" and feels "violated." In the coming decades black men turned that shame into anger and transformed white fears of black violence and sexuality into an attempt to reclaim their manhood. As Wright put it in his short story "The Man Who Was Almost a Man":

> The first movement he made the following morning was to reach under his pillow for the gun. In the gray light of dawn he held it loosely, feeling a sense of power. Could kill a man with a gun like this. Kill anybody, black or white. And if he were holding his gun, nobody could run over him; they would have to respect him.[17]

If rage was the new threat from the world of black men, anomie was its white counterpart. And anomie and masculinity were hard to reconcile. The cowboy or detective hero of the 1930s returned from the war with a darker, more sinister, and more sexual undertone in the film noir of the postwar era. Noir films utilized the conventions of true-crime and gangster dramas but offered virtually no avenues of masculine redemption. The heroes of noir films were grittier, tougher, colder, and far more cynical. Typically, the noir hero was a returning soldier who was alienated from the life he had left. "A guy like me after the war hates himself because he's scared to get going again," says the troubled veteran in *Crossfire* (1947). They were still less corruptible than the society they moved through but only because virtually everything in that world was already corrupt. Violence did not cathartically purge evil, nor did it even necessarily resolve the problems created by the plot. And forget about getting the girl and riding off into the sunset: The hero is nearly as likely to shoot her as marry her. Women are seductive temptresses—"alluring but ambitious *femmes fatales*"—who are as capable of the double cross and murder as men; not exactly the kind of equality that working women had in mind.[18]

Noir films had dark, viscous undercurrents of male sexual paranoia, of lugubrious forces out of control, of failure everywhere. Billy Wilder's films, especially *Double Indemnity* (1944) and *Sunset Boulevard* (1950), offer gloomy evocations of family disintegration, vacuous heroism, and the inability of the veteran to reintegrate into society. Raoul Walsh's *White Heat* (1949) suggests that the gangster can no longer pretend to be a heroic model of the Self-Made Man, a kind of alter ego to corporate conformists. *Dead Reckoning* (1947) suggests that the wartime leveling of class tension could not survive the peace. The bonds of friendship forged between two discharged paratroopers, Rip (Humphrey Bogart), a taxi driver, and Johnny (William Prince), a Yale-educated college professor, unravel as they travel together to receive medals for bravery in the war. The film turns into an anguished drama of the loss of those bonds in postwar America. Unstable and confused, and with the interjection of a woman, their abiding love forged in battle cannot survive.

Other works also took on the corrupting qualities of American society. Orson Welles's monumental film *Citizen Kane* (1940) provided a portrait of a man (loosely based on the life of newspaper magnate William Randolph Hearst) consumed by a cancerous greed and lust for power. Yet his downfall is caused, as was Jay Gatsby's, more by Kane's believing in the American Dream and in the American myth of self-made manhood than by his own moral failings. He believes his self-creation can transcend moral limits, turning him into an object of pity rather than veneration. What Kane (Welles) discovers is that even the creation of vast empires of wealth and power cannot compensate for the loss of childhood innocence and the intact, loving, nuclear family.

Perhaps the decade's most celebrated film star was Humphrey Bogart, a short, rather unattractive man who expressed the kind of reluctant heroism that both women and men found palpably masculine. As Clark Gable had done with Rhett Butler, Bogart often played a self-interested and selfish man who, during the course of the film, finds himself putting aside his self-centeredness and taking a moral and political stand for good. Bogart thus repudiates the Self-Made Man's dogged egoism; his characters become exemplary when they leave self-interest behind and act ethically. In this sense Bogart strikes a balance between self-made wealth and power and aristocratic virtue (without its class basis)—a tenuous balance that American men have found difficult to strike. In *Casablanca* (1942), for example, Bogart's character Rick retains his autonomy by not getting involved in other people's dramas, his detached demeanor mirroring American isolationism. In *To Have and Have Not* (1944), he plays a freewheeling adventurer who leases his boat out to tourists. Later, in *The African Queen* (1951), Bogart's Charlie Allnut doesn't particularly care about Germans and doesn't seem to know what the war is even about.

Yet in each film the transformative moment comes when he decides to act ethically: to facilitate the escape of a freedom fighter hunted by the Gestapo, or to blow up a German freighter, the *Louisa*. And in each case it is his love for a woman—Ingrid Bergman, Lauren Bacall, Katharine Hepburn—that provides the impetus for ethical manhood. None of these women sits atop a pedestal, passively adored; each is a leading actress, a powerful presence, and in Hepburn's case, his ally, accomplice, and mentor. Bogart's triumph is not through the conquest of these women—he doesn't even end up with two of them. Sacrifice of sexual desire, a most pivotal expression of self-interest, is necessary for the self-transcendence that is required of every real man as hero.

Partnerships between women and men also were the axis around which the Spencer Tracy-Katharine Hepburn dramatic comedies revolved. Yet in most cases the tension between the couples was resolved by the woman's compromise and the reinscription of the nuclear family in which a wife subordinated her ambitions to her husband's. In *Woman of the Year* (1942), Hepburn's Tess Harding is a sort of superwoman—the efficient, smart, businesslike star reporter for a major New York City newspaper, whose feud with a crusty sports reporter, Tracy's Sam Craig, provides the comedic fuel for this renegotiation of the war between the sexes. Their marriage is the constant power struggle of the dual career couple, resolved in Hollywood fashion by Tess's capitulation and her return to Sam, recipe book in hand, ready to make domestic amends. She even takes his last name.

In *Adam's Rib* (1949), Tracy and Hepburn play married lawyers who find themselves arguing opposite sides of the same case. Hepburn wins in the courtroom by resorting to her "feminine wiles," but Tracy's revenge is exacted in their own relationship, as he bursts into tears as their relationship begins to unravel and she comforts him. To comfort the audience that Tracy wasn't *really* emasculating himself by crying, he later bursts into tears on cue to show Hepburn that men can be as manipulative as women, using feminine affect as well as women do to get their way. Thus can men outwoman women as an act of defiant manhood.

Arthur Miller's *Death of a Salesman* (1949) may be the most compelling portrait in literary history of the pathos of middle-class manhood and its consequences. Willy Loman, a tired, used-up salesman—a genuine "low-man"—is afraid to even take to the road. With his wife, Linda, he is alternately bullying and boastful, feeble and frightened. "I just couldn't make it, Linda," he tells her of his inability to get on the road as the play opens. "You know the trouble is, Linda, people don't seem to take to me," he confesses. When she reassures him, he say, "I know it when I walk in. They seem to laugh at me." When she asks why, he says mournfully, "I'm not noticed."[19]

Willy's relationship to his absent brother Ben provides another axis around which the elegy for failed manhood is organized. Ben represents the road not taken for the Willy Lomans of the world, those stolid, middle-class American men, frightened into conformity and saddled with familial responsibilities. Ben went off for adventure, to be a hero on the frontier (Alaska). In Willy's soliloquies, rendered as conversations with Ben, Willy meditates on his own manhood and finds himself still feeling "temporary about myself." "Once in my life I would like to own something outright before its broken!" he exclaims. "I'm always in a race with the junkyard! I just finished paying for the car and it's on its last legs. The refrigerator consumes belts like a goddam maniac."[20]

Perhaps most tragic is the way in which Willy's failure becomes the mantle that he leaves to his sons, Biff and Happy. In their presence Willy sounds like a page out of Dale Carnegie boosterism. "It's not what you say it's how you say it—because personality always wins the day," he tells them. And so both of them avoid traditional expressions of manhood, alternately subscribing to Willy's idealized vision and hating him for their own failures. Biff rejects the life of the salesman as a "measly manner of existence," while confessing to his mother that he "just can't seem to take hold . . . of some kind of a life." Happy is equally restless and unhappy, seeking solace with women and believing himself better than anyone else. Happy's fantasy of upward mobility ends in isolation and recalls

Tocqueville's statement in 1832 about American men building houses in which to pass their old age and then selling them before the roof is on:

> All I can do now is wait for the merchandise manager to die. And suppose I get to be the merchandise manager? He's a good friend of mine, and he just built a terrific estate on Long Island. And he lived there about two months and sold it, and now he's building another one. He can't enjoy it once it's finished. And I know that's just what I would do. I don't know what the hell I'm working for. Sometimes I sit in my apartment—all alone. And I think of the rent I'm paying. And it's crazy. But then, it's what I always wanted. My own apartment, a car, and plenty of women. And still, goddammit, I'm lonely.[21]

Biff's only response is an ineffectual invitation to go out west together. But even they know the frontier is closed.

It is Biff who in the end lashes out the hardest on Willy in what may be his only chance to break free of his father's illusions:

> Pop! I'm a dime a dozen and so are you! . . . I am not a leader of men, Willy, and neither are you. You were never anything but a hard-working drummer who landed in the ash can like all the rest of them!

And at Willy's funeral Biff's comment provides an epitaph for the new man of the postwar era. "He never knew who he was."[22]

Such a powerful indictment rolled across the lawns and rattled the windows of suburban housing developments for the entire decade of the 1950s. If the suburban bread-winner father didn't exactly know who he was, he could at least figure out who he wasn't. In the 1950s American men strained against two negative poles—the overconformist, a faceless, self-less nonentity, and the unpredictable, unreliable nonconformist. American middle-class men faced what I think of as the "Goldilocks dilemma," from that fairy-tale heroine's search for commodities (chairs, beds, porridge) that were not too something yet not too much the other side. Men had to achieve identities that weren't too conforming to the march of the empty gray flannel suits lest they lose their souls; but they couldn't be too nonconforming lest they leave family and workplace responsibilities behind in a frantic restless search for some elusive moment of ecstasy.

And they had to do it in surburban housing developments in which their homes were distinctive only in how uniform they were in design and decor. The suburbs had become a central fact of postwar America and the new arena for proving one's manhood. Over the first half of the century, suburban housing developments had gradually risen from a tiny slice of American dwelling to its majority form of housing. Thus, while men sought to define a normal masculinity, they situated themselves in a vast sprawl of "normalcy."

In our stereotypic image, the 1950s was an era of quiet, order, and security. What we like to remember as a simple time, "happy days," was also an era of anxiety and fear, during which ideas of normality were enforced with a desperate passion. "The effort to reinforce traditional norms seemed almost frantic," writes the historian William Chafe.[23] The 1950s was a decade of containment.

No wonder Senator Joseph McCarthy so easily linked homosexuality and communism —both represented gender failure. McCarthy raged against both as "egg sucking phony liberals," effete eastern intellectuals, emasculated half men who, with their "pitiful squealing," had sold the country down the river and lost China and Eastern Europe through indecision and fear. "You can't hardly separate homosexuals from subversives," argued Senator Kenneth Wherry. "A man of low morality is a menace in the government, whatever he is, and they are all tied together." McCarthy's witch-hunt for "pinks, punks and perverts" uncovered a State Department that was "a veritable nest of Communists, fellow travelers, homosexuals, effete Ivy League intellectuals and traitors," according to one of the senator's aides.[24]

This link between intellectualism and effeminacy also contributed to the defeat of Adlai Stevenson in 1952 and 1956. Not only was Stevenson labeled "soft" on communism, but he was the classic "egghead." The candidate whom the *New York Daily News* called "Adelaide" used "tea cup words," which he "trilled" with his "fruity" voice, and was supported by "Harvard lace cuff liberals" and "lace panty diplomats." It's amazing that Stevenson—vilified as effeminate and weak, as was no other candidate since Martin Van Buren—got any support at all in his campaign against America's most recent warrior president.

The trappings of gender failure were all around us in the 1950s, and American men discovered what happened to men who failed, especially the sons of men who failed as breadwinners and fathers. They became homosexual, they became juvenile delinquents, they became Communists—soft, spineless dupes of a foreign power who were incapable of standing up for themselves. Few experts really knew what a real man was; most were content to tell us what he was not. In part, as social scientists understood, the definition of masculinity had become so fuzzy because of the "conflicting nature of multiple role demands, lack of clear positive definitions . . . and the rigidity of role demands."[25] In J. D. Salinger's novel *The Catcher in the Rye* (1951), the decade's first antihero, Holden Caulfield, captured the increasing malaise of adolescent boys as they faced uncertain manhood. Confused about what it meant to be a man, about girls, about sex, Caulfield dreams a typically American male dream of escape:

> Finally, what I decided to do, I decided to go away. I decided I'd never go home again and I'd never go to another school again. I decided I'd . . . start hitchhiking my way out West. . . . [I]n a few days I'd be somewhere out West where it was very pretty and sunny and where nobody'd know me and I'd get a job. . . . I didn't care what kind of job it was, though. Just so people didn't know me and I didn't know anybody.

Holden finds that those old masculine themes are more difficult these days. "You can never find a place that's nice and peaceful, because there isn't any. You may *think* there is, but once you get there, when you're not looking, somebody'll sneak up and write 'Fuck you' right under your nose."[26]

The adult man's version of Archie's pals proffered the corporate clone and the outlaw rebel to represent the two negative poles of American manhood against which men attempted to carve out meaningful lives. For Holden Caulfield, one was the terrifying future of most of his preppy classmates, the other the unrealizable goal of rebellion. These poles appeared in pop psychological advice books, academic social science, and virtually every cultural medium that men faced. How could men remain responsible breadwinners and not turn into docile drudges? How could men become active and devoted fathers—to make sure that their sons did not become sissies—and not turn into wimps themselves? How could men let their hearts run free with a wife and kids to support?

On these questions, both sides of the political spectrum seemed to converge. Several jeremiads argued that we were in danger of becoming—or that we had become—a nation of sheep. Ayn Rand's objectivist philosophy celebrated a cult of supreme egoism, as the only force capable of combatting the combination of big capital and the bureaucratic state that lulled the masses into a condition of soporific stupefaction. Real men, in her enormously popular books, like *Anthem* (1961), *Atlas Shrugged* (1957), and *The Fountainhead* (1943) (which were more thinly fictionalized political tracts than novels), battled heroically to live their own lives against the pressures of conformity. King Vidor's film of Rand's most famous work, *The Fountainhead* (1949), cast western- and war-movie hero Gary Cooper as the unrepentantly modernist architect Howard Roark, who struggles to realize his individual vision of form following function. Roark stands at the pinnacle of two triangulated relationships. The apparently central triangle involves Roark with his true love, Dominique Francon (Patricia Neal), and self-made newspaper magnate Gale Wynand (Raymond Massey). Here, Wynand's waffling support reveals to both Roark and Dominique his ultimate failure as a man, and Roark eventually replaces Wynand as Dominique's husband, just as Wynand could not replace Roark as the object of her deepest love.

The purely homosocial triangle among Roark, Wynand, and the newspaper's pompous architectural critic, Ellsworth Tooey (Robert Douglas), reveals Rand's vision of manhood. Wynand, who escapes from Hell's Kitchen to become one of the wealthiest men in the city, is undone by the necessity of pandering to mass tastes and is ultimately ruined not by Roark but by Tooey, the effete intellectual. "You left to impractical intellectuals like me the whole field of ideas to corrupt as we please while you were making money," Tooey states in triumph. "You thought money was power. Is it, Mr. Wynand?" Here is the clash between the discredited Genteel Patriarch, now reduced to pretentious intellectual snobbery and clever manipulation, and Self-Made Masculinity, which has been so busy making money that it lost all semblance of heroic virtue.

Only Roark can rescue American society and, thus, American manhood as the resurgent Heroic Artisan, though in this right-wing incarnation he is an independent professional and decidedly non–working class. "Greatness comes from the independent work of independent minds," Roark claims in his defense, and it is his ideas which are his property. He rails against the "soulless collectivism" of mass society—whether capitalist or communist—which can only build "great big marble bromides" to the crassness of mass taste. (As if to make the contrast more potent, when Dominique first sees Roark he is a laborer in a granite quarry, holding erect a large drill in his sweaty, muscular forearms.) Only the professionalized artisan can stand against all the forces arrayed against him and redeem his manhood—and get the icily stunning woman to swoon with desire.

To critics on the left, the impersonal forces of mass society worked best for scions of big capital, who both manipulated potentially virtuous working people into blindly consuming things they neither needed nor wanted and kept middle-class men isolated and afraid. The psychologist Erich Fromm, for example, a wartime refugee from Germany's most celebrated intellectual hotbed, the Frankfurt School, criticized middle-class conformity in *Escape from Freedom* (1941) and *Man for Himself* (1947). Fromm wrote of the "market orientation" of American men, through which the sense of self becomes anchored in activities and accomplishments and measuring up to social norms and standards. As a result, emphasis rests not on who the person is but on what the person has: It is what other people think of us that counts most. To Fromm, the contemporary alienated man was an individual who "has opinions and prejudices but no convictions, has likes and dislikes, but no will," and the new man was one who "escapes the burdens of freedom in group conformity."[27]

To other liberal critics, the demands of corporate life had transformed potential marketplace men into frightened "little men," as the sociologist C. Wright Mills called them in *White Collar* (1953). Mills offered a relentless critique of this new middle-class manhood. In his view, the middle-class man was more pathetic than protean; he did "not threaten anyone" and did "not practice an independent way of life." He'd been "stood up by life,"

> living out in slow misery his yearning for the quick American climb. He is pushed by forces beyond his control, pulled into movements he does not understand; he gets into situations in which his is the most helpless position. The white collar man is the hero as victim, the small creature who is acted upon but who does not act, who works along unnoticed in somebody's office or store, never talking loud, never talking back, never taking a stand."[28]

Modern corporate capitalism had transformed a nation of small entrepreneurs—Self-Made Men—into a nation of hired employees. "Just as the working man no longer owns the machine but is controlled by it, so the middle class man no longer owns the enterprise but is controlled by it," Mills wrote. "The men are cogs in a business machinery that has routinized greed and made aggression an impersonal principle of organization."[29] Depersonalized cogs in the corporate machine also lost their sense of themselves as men. Their feelings were "deadened," and they felt "dwarfed and helpless," worried and distrust-ful," "bored at work and restless at play," a "chorus, too afraid to grumble, too hysterical in their applause."[30]

Sociologist David Riesman's portrait of the social psychology of conformity, *The Lonely Crowd* (1950), revealed a diffuse anxiety among American men. The nineteenth-century American man was "inner-directed," animated by conviction and principle, Riesman argued; now, men had become "other-directed," concerned more with fitting in than standing out, "at home everywhere and nowhere." Modern man was animated by "anxiety rather than pride" an engaged in "veiled competition rather than openly rivalrous display."[31] Like Riesman, the historian Frank Tannenbaum argued in *A Philosophy of Labor* (1951) that the Industrial Revolution had "destroyed the solid moorings of an older way of life and cast the helpless workers adrift in a strange and difficult world."[32]

That world was made all the more strange by the changes in the workplace itself. Men faced more than emasculating demands and humiliating hierarchies; it was also getting quite crowded in there. Urban and suburban housewives alike ached to get back into the workplace from which they had been pushed after the war. Black men's anguished cry for full recognition of their manhood would not subside, as readers learned from Ralph Ellison's *The Invisible Man* (1952). And the winds of change began to erode the walls of white resistance in cases like *Brown v. Board of Education of Topeka* (1954), beginning, at least, the juridical integration of blacks into the American mainstream. And gay men were, it seemed, everywhere—in every florist shop or beauty salon and invading the suburban home to help wives decorate it.

Popular writers of all political stripes picked up these themes and translated them for mass-marked readers. Vance Packard's books, such as *The Status Seekers* (1959) and *The Hidden Persuaders* (1957), frightened readers about the threats to their individualism from soft-voiced manipulators.[33] Business writer William H. Whyte's *The Organization Man* (1956) gave popular expression to these analyses, recognizing the irony of Dale Carnegie's method of winning friends and influencing people or Norman Vincent Peale's power of positive thinking.[34] Gone, Whyte argued, is the rugged individualist and in his place is a conception of "individualism *within* corporate life." Motivated more by a "passive ambition," urgently trying to belong, "obtrusive in no particular, excessive in no zeal," the future of these organization men is "a life in which they will all be moved hither and yon and subject to so many forces outside their control."[35]

Fiction writers, too, picked up the terrors of conformity. In Richard Matheson's *The Incredible Shrinking Man* (1953), an allegory of the disappearance of real manhood, it is financial failure that squeezes the hero, even before he gets hit with the chemicals that shrink him. The title of Sloan Wilson's novel *The Man in the Gray Flannel Suit* (1955) gave the era its most enduring rhetorical reference point, although the novel chronicles Tom and Betsy Rath's growing awareness that Self-Made Manhood is a trap, keeping men locked into soul-shattering routines of vicious competition and frenzied consumption.[36]

In a strange essay, "The White Negro" (1957), novelist Norman Mailer chafed at the fate of American men, who faced "a slow death by conformity with every creative and rebellious instinct stifled." In its stead Mailer offered a romanticized appropriation of the Negro as hipster-outsider—the delinquent, the hipster, the black man, the "male urban outlaw, living on the edge, searching out sex, using marijuana, appreciating jazz, finding momentary truth in the body":

> If the fate of twentieth century man is to live with death from adolescence to premature
> senescence, why then the only life-giving answer is to accept the terms of death, to live
> with death as immediate danger, to divorce oneself from society, to exist without roots, to
> set out on that uncharted journey into the rebellious imperatives of the self.[37]

Failure to undertake such a journey had significant political implications: These cookie-cutter men were raised for sameness, raised never to question authority, raised, some feared, to be unable to resist communism. Fears of brainwashing, especially after the Korean War, were also fears of loss of masculine control, of loss of will. That specter of hollow zombies incapable of individualistic resistance haunted America through the 1950s, as in *Invasion of the Body Snatchers* (1954), a transparent allegory of potential Communist takeover, and later *The Manchurian Candidate* (1962), in which the brainwashed emasculated soldiers take orders from a woman.

On the other side of the tracks from respectable middle-class conformity lurked the dangerous men, the rebellious nonconformists, who threatened social stability, domestic harmony, and corporate responsibility. The decade's preoccupation with juvenile delinquency and the disheveled rebelliousness of the beatniks, or the new fears of effeminate homosexual men, provided several negative stereotypes against which American men played out their yearnings. In black leather on his motorcycle, the delinquent represented sexual and interpersonal power, control over himself and his environment. In a sense he was the era's Heroic Artisan, but this time cast entirely in negative terms. No wonder Beat poet Allen Ginsberg claimed that "the social organization most true to itself and to the artist is the boy gang"—here was the closest institution to the artisanal crafts shop of the eighteenth century, re-created with menacing, homoerotic overtones. The motorcycle gang of the 1950s was a descendant of the Arts and Crafts Movement's re-creation of the medieval guild—control over the machinery, individual autonomy, and mastery within a context of blood brotherhood. As Heroic Artisans themselves, the Beats had to create something, and what they created was the rhetoric of rebellion. They knew more what they were against railing against the drone of self-made masculinity, the relentless pursuit of happiness through material possession—than what they were for. In his electrifying poem *Howl* (1956), Allen Ginsberg screamed at a Moloch "whose mind is pure machinery! Moloch whose blood is running money!"

Casting the nonconformist as negative role model, however tempting, also gave middle-class men a way to restore manhood, a manhood threatened by corporate and suburban sameness. As fathers, they could prevent their sons from becoming delinquent, gay, Communist, or irresponsible beatniks. Their return home was not the retreat of world-weary would-be warriors but a daring rescue mission, a campaign to save their sons.

That American boyhood was becoming a collection of sissies was "the overriding fear of every American parent," wrote anthropologist Geoffrey Gorer. "Are we staking our future on a crop of sissies?" asked a writer in *Better Homes and Gardens*. "You have a horror of seeing your son a pantywaist, but he won't get red blood and self-reliance if you leave the whole job of making a he-man of him to his mother."[38] Psychologists, child-development experts, sociologists, and educators all chimed in in a growing chorus of anxiety about the gender development of boys. Men had to be dedicated fathers to offset overdominant motherhood and to help their sons resist the temptations of gender nonconformity. On the other end of the feminized, potentially homosexual son lurked the other danger besetting American boyhood: the juvenile delinquent. Studies of delinquency were a growth industry in social science and psychology in the 1950s. Ironically, such seeming opposites as hypermasculine juvenile delinquency and hypomasculine homosexuality were traced to the same familial roots: the absent father and overdominant mother.

Talcott Parsons argued that the middle-class boy, dominated by his mother and with a weak identification with his father (whose absence made identification even more difficult), would be driven to prove himself by delinquent hell-raising. Parsons's student Albert Cohen's study *The Culture of the Gang* (1955) linked the sources of delinquency to the "masculine protest." Without adequate assurance that he is "indubitably, in his own eyes and those of the world around him," a man, the boy turns to dangerous methods of proof; "engaging in bad behavior acquires the function of denying his femininity and therefore asserting his masculinity."[39]

For working-class boys, Cohen claimed, the delinquent subculture provided not only grounds to demonstrate manly aggression but also an alternative work environment where men might experience success in deviant behavior and the chance to retaliate against those norms that they believed had emasculated them. Walter Miller's oft-cited study "Lower Class Culture as a Generating Milieu of Gang Delinquency" (1958) echoed this theme and tied it once again to smothering motherhood; the working-class boy's preoccupation with toughness was related to the fact that a significant proportion of lower class males are reared in a predominantly female household and lack a consistently present male figure with whom to identify and from whom to learn essential components of a "male" role. Since women serve as a primary object of identification during pre-adolescent years, the almost obsessive lower class concern with "masculinity" probably resembles a type of compulsive reaction-formation.[40]

The masculinity of working-class adolescents was thus, almost by definition, deviant; collectively, they were always in rebellion, not against a class, but against the "feminine principle" in society.[41]

In such studies hypermasculinity was a hedge, an effort to offset feelings of masculine inadequacy. If someone acted excessively masculine, these theories held, he must be the least secure in his manhood. Countless young boys must have heard the same message I did from my parents—that the local schoolyard bully was the boy who was "least secure," and therefore he had to keep "proving it" against boys who were smaller and weaker than he was. Thus did countless studies of hypermasculinity explain masculine excess as a compensation for insecure and anxious gender identity. In the celebrated studies that were collected in *The Authoritarian Personality* (1950), for example, psychologists at Berkeley and Yale determined that the personality complex of authoritarianism—which included racism, anti-Semitism, and general bigotry—was actually a form of "pseudo-masculinity," an effort to mask such gender insecurity. In the end, lead author Theodor Adorno wrote a year later, "the tough guys are the truly effeminate ones, who need the weaklings as their victims."[42]

It was not only for their sons, however, that men were advised to stay put in their suburban homes. Being a breadwinner and family provider remained the centerpiece of middle-class masculinity. It may have required subordinating one's heroic vision to a dull routine, but it was exactly that sort of compromise that separated the mice from the men. As it had earlier, academic social science added a scientific gloss to middle-class respectability and responsibility. "Virtually the only way to be a real man in our society is to have an adequate job and earn a living," wrote sociologist Talcott Parsons in 1959. "It is perhaps not too much to say that only in very exceptional cases can an adult man be genuinely self-respecting and enjoy a respected status in the eyes of others if he does not 'earn a living' in an approved occupational role." Real men were breadwinning men.[43]

They were family men, too, actively involved in the raising of their children. *Life* magazine declared 1954 the year of "the domestication of the American man," the climax of a decade of dedicated fatherhood and husbandry.[44] The 1950s elevated family life to a level of sacredness never before witnessed in our history. Family was ideology, as cultural historian Warren Susman observed. We watched "family-oriented TV" in the "family room," with "family size" packages of snacks; we traveled in "family cars" on "family vacations" and ate in "family restaurants."

For men the celebration of the family was not supposed to be an emasculating retreat. "Being a father is not 'sissy' business," wrote a psychiatrist in *Parents* magazine in 1947. "It is an occupation," perhaps "the most important occupation in the world." When a man cooked, for example, in the family barbecue pit, he was achieving and expressing his masculinity. "When a barbecue goes into operation, it automatically becomes a masculine

Esquire magazine's *Handbook for Hosts*. "After all, outdoor cooking is a

. . . the new baby boom were told to get involved—but not *too* involved. "Of course I don't mean that the father has to give just as many bottles, or change just as many diapers as the mother," Dr. Benjamin Spock wrote in an early edition of his best-selling *Baby and Child Care*. "But it's fine for him to do these things occasionally. He might make the formula on Sunday." Social scientist Morris Zelditch agreed with this prescription for weekend nurturing, urging fathers to cross over only sparingly.

> Father helps mother with the dishes. He sets the table. He makes formula for the baby. Mother can supplement the income of the family by working outside. Nevertheless, the American male, by definition, *must* provide for his family. He is *responsible* for his support of his wife and children. His primary area of performance is the occupational role . . . and his *primary* function in the family is to supply an "income" to be the "breadwinner."

In fact, Zelditch concluded, there is "simply something wrong with the American adult male who doesn't have a 'job.'" The truly nurturing dad, emotionally expressive and available, Zelditch regarded as effeminate, with "too much fat on the inner side of his thigh."[46]

This conclusion presented an exceedingly thin line between feminization of the overdomesticated dad and the irresponsibility of the absentee father who was producing a generation of lost sons. One way to straddle that line was to pursue one of the myriad hobbies that suburban men were encouraged to develop. A hobby, like woodworking, or stamp and coin collecting, kept dad around the house, but not as a henpecked husband or domestic drudge—these were *his* hobbies after all. Some hobbies seemed designed simply to fill time and keep dad around, while others were trumpeted as lucrative sidelights to their breadwinner roles. But virtually all were celebrated because they could bring dad and son together in a project that was theirs alone. The 1950s hobbies boom was thus more than a consumerist cornucopia designed to mindlessly fill leisure time. Hobbies could both salvage fathers and save sons.

Men needed help in fulfilling their domesticating mission. Much of the child-development literature aimed its advice specifically at fathers, many of whom were "not fully grown up and self-reliant themselves" and therefore needed the help. *Parents* ran articles like "A Build-up for Dad," which began with basic Parenting 101 skills about how to interact with children and ran through attendance at PTA meetings, carpentry for tots, and sports. *Parents* also ran a column, ". . . Specially for Fathers," which gave monthly parenting tips. *Woman's Home Companion* reminded mothers that "fathers are parents too" and offered a pictorial collage of fathers in aprons feeding their children, helping them to make a boxcar, and teaching them about automobiles. Advertisements for a fourteen-volume *Childcraft* guide promised to inform anxious parents about everything they always wanted to know about childhood but didn't know how to ask. Four volumes were specifically devoted to expert advice on "every phase of child development," including "what is normal and what is not," and tips on how to "direct your child's growth and character."[47]

One article in *American Home*, "Are You a Dud as a Dad?" suggested that fatherhood gave men the opportunity for achievement they might not receive in the workplace. "Here is one area of your life which doesn't depend on 'breaks' or ability, on education or money. A man can be a success as a father, a real 'dad,' if he cares enough to try." Fathers were counseled to share hobbies, laugh at their sons' jokes, and listen to their problems—"the kinds of things a fellow wants to talk over with a man."[48]

Television, the newly created carrier of entertainment for the whole family, rushed in quickly to give dad a boost. In shows such as *Ozzie and Harriet, Father Knows Best, Leave It to Beaver*, and *The Donna Reed Show*, fathers were seen as nurturing, caring, and devoted to their children. They could always find the time to listen to their children's problems, to help with homework, or to ferry them around their suburban neighborhoods—partly because their jobs were so unimportant in the overall depiction of their lives. Who now remembers the occupations of Jim Anderson or Ward Cleaver? Critic Mark Crispin Miller hints that this shift in emphasis away from the workplace and toward the family spelled the return of American man as the Heroic Artisan of the Home Front. "Since we almost never saw him working, we had no sense that there was any class above his own, and he had no competition in the class below him." Or as Ozzie Nelson put it, "by not designating the kind of work I did, people were able to identify with me more readily." An unemployed former bandleader, Nelson mostly sat around the house reading the newspaper and, in so doing, helped American men laugh at their retreat from heroic masculinity. Shows like *Bachelor Father* and *My Three Sons* centered around men raising children alone and proving to be adequate mothers and fathers rolled into one.[49]

By contrast, films and television shows about working-class men or childless men offered consolation to middle-class breadwinners and their sons. A few television shows cast the working-class family as a dysfunctional site of emasculated men or adult delinquents. If middle-class fathers were depicted as comfortably nondescript and devoted, working-class men were seen as both marital and workplace failures. Few working-class families on television seemed to have children. In *The Honeymooners*, for example, it was Ralph Cramden (Jackie Gleason), the crass blowhard, who played a male version of Lucy, while his wife, Alice (Audrey Meadows), played the female Ricky Ricardo; it was Ralph, after all, who was always coming up with harebrained schemes that left him humiliated and requiring rescue. In the childless working-class couple, the man rants and raves, his emotions out of control, while his wife, cool and calm, rationally sets things right.

Without wives and children, working-class men were transformed into wisecracking grown-up delinquents, like the well-named Sgt. Ernie Bilko (Phil Silvers) on *You'll Never Get Rich* (later *The Phil Silvers Show*). Bilko and his little platoon of thieves and con artists showed viewers that the army, once the site of heroic military manhood, was really a gigantic con game, staffed by inept bureaucrats and pursuing a Cold War that was nothing but a joke. Two decades before "the Fonz," Bilko was a middle-class delinquent with a heart of gold.

Most of the continuing cult audience seems to have misread the film version of Robert Linder's warning *Rebel Without a Cause* (1955) as a celebration of rebellion against dull conformity. To be sure, the movie turns on Jim's confrontation with his ineffectual father (played by James Dean and Jim Backus, respectively), who wears an apron in the scene as if to underscore his inability to relate to his desperately needy son. But it's also a celebration of the nuclear family—not the ones that the three teenage waifs were given by nature but rather the alternative family that they are able to create for themselves. Jim and Judy (Natalie Wood) find each other and together provide a home for Plato (Sal Mineo), whose wealthy parents are too preoccupied with their own lives to care at all about him. Plato's death enables Jim to hear his father's promise that he will "try to be as strong as you want me to be."

Not all working-class men were objects of middle-class ridicule, but they had to redeem themselves by subscribing to middle-class values. Retrieving one's manhood was not about the color of one's collar but about the values one held and the willingness to stand up for them. Take, for example, the characters played by Marlon Brando. More than any other actor of the era, Brando captured the repressed rage of the caged animal—recall his primal scream in *A Streetcar Named Desire* (1951), the adolescent alienation of the delinquent (*The Wild Ones* [1953]), and the brooding confusion of the stand-up working-class guy (*On the Waterfront* [1954]).

Like Bogart's before him, Brando's characters follow a path of self-discovery that moves from dispassionate self-interest to ethical connection. In the beginning of *On the Waterfront*, which won the Academy Awards for Best Picture and Best Actor, Malloy is asked by the local priest where he stands, who he's with, "Me, I'm with me," Brando replies. He's a hero to the local neighborhood boys, but Brando himself is not taken in by his own hype. "I could have been a contender," the punch-drunk ex-fighter tells his brother Charley (Rod Steiger) in one of the film's most critical scenes. "I could have been somebody, instead of a bum, which is what I am."

From the ashes of his failed masculinity, Malloy finally acts ethically, manfully, confronting the corrupt union boss Johnny Friendly (Lee J. Cobb) and breaking the immoral code of masculine silence. And he takes the consequences—including the murder of his brother, the slaughter of his beloved pigeons, and one of the most savage beatings in film history—with a Christlike resignation. As Malloy rises from this terrible humiliation and walks fitfully toward the warehouse gates, he has reclaimed his manhood. He is no longer a bum. He can now go to work on the waterfront, another working-class stiff remade as a working-class hero, confident that he is a real man.

For middle-class men, though, the work world offered none of those possibilities for manly redemption. It was as fathers, not as employees nor even as soldiers, that they experienced the autonomy and control that had once marked artisanal manhood. In one episode of *Leave It to Beaver* I especially remember as painfully familiar, Beaver and his class are asked by the teacher to describe what their fathers did during the war. Beaver, who considers his father "the neatest dad in the whole world," describes Ward as a veritable Audie Murphy, capturing dozens of enemy soldiers and dragging home enormous quantities of war booty. When challenged to back up his story, he breaks into his father's old footlocker only to discover a bunch of T squares and surveying instruments. Ward comforts Beaver, who is crushed by this obvious lack of heroism, by explaining that his role was important, too. "There were thousands of us in the service who weren't heroes. They put a man where they thought he could do the best job," he says. Thus, the past was symbolically and safely put away; so that, as the cultural critic Gerard Jones writes, "the day of the manly hero had yielded to the day of the builder, the planner, the quiet team player." And the dad.[50]

These periodic forays into masculine domesticity have returned men to home and family at various times in our history and in various guises—to provide adequate role models to potentially homosexual or delinquent sons or to remain a steadfast mate to wives and thus thwart those wives' ambitions, for example—rarely, though, for the intrinsic pleasures of domestic life, which only the Genteel Patriarch probably enjoyed, and then only because his class position freed him from workplace obligations. Domestic retreat and caring fatherhood were little compensation for the restless anxiety that has continued to haunt American men; all that sober responsibility left a gaping void in the hearts of men, where once adventure, risk, and sexual passion had reigned. At least in their dreams.

By mid-century many of American men's traditional alternatives were gone. Of course, the frontier had all but disappeared. "No, no place to go," Carl says to Jody in John Steinbeck's story "The Red Pony" (1945). "Every place is taken. But that's not the worst—no, not the worst. Westering has died out of the people. Westering isn't a hunger any more. It's all done." Fraternal orders, once so popular, were now the objects of ridicule; men who joined, like Amos and Andy, or Ralph Cramden and Ed Norton, were seen as working-class oafs seeking a night out with the guys and away from the little woman (who was probably bigger than he was).

Of course, some of those methods retained some vitality. Fitness guru Jack LaLanne recapitulated the American success story of re-creating the body as a way of reinventing the man. Like Charles Atlas a couple of decades earlier and Bernarr Macfadden at the turn of the century, LaLanne transformed his own "puny and embarrassing" physique into a physical marvel. As a youth LaLanne had been "a pathetic little world-hating, heart-aching boy" with an "ungovernable hunger for candy and soft drinks," who had grown thin, weak eyed, and weak spined. When his father died of a heart attack in his early forties—caused, LaLanne believed, by chronic "pooped-out-itis"—young Jack started exercising and eating wisely. From his humble origins as a calisthenics instructor in San Francisco in 1951, LaLanne became the star of the most widely viewed daytime television show on the air by 1960 and filled forty thousand orders a month for the Glamour Stretcher, his "whole gym on a rubber cord," offered to both bored housewives on perpetual diets and to men on the go who needed quick pick-me-ups.

LaLanne may have offered worldly ectomorphic salvation through an oversized rubber band, but many men wanted escape without any effort at all. So in the 1950s, as for over a century, it was to fantasy that middle-class men turned. So long as they remained reliable breadwinners and devoted dads, they could become wild and adventurous consumers, savoring real men's "true" adventures or grabbing fantasy thrills with traditional heroes like cowboys or with those delinquents with hearts of gold that Hollywood was fond of creating. It appeared that the more boring and dull the routine of men's work became, the more exciting and glamorous were their fantasies of escape.

None were more glamorous than those rhetorical returns to those thrilling days of yesteryear offered by the western. Over 10 percent of all fictional works published in the 1950s were westerns, and eight of the top ten television shows—a total of thirty prime-time television shows in all—were "horse operas." Fifty-four western feature films were made in 1958 alone. Westerns provided the re-creation of the frontier, the "meeting point between civilization and savagery," where real men, men who were good with a horse and a gun, triumphed over unscrupulous bankers and other rogue versions of Self-Made Manhood. *The Lone Ranger* provided a new homosocial interracial couple in which the moral and innocent white Ranger, removed from society and left for dead, is then nursed back to health by the male mother and Native American spirit guide, Tonto. This deeply bonded couple, suspended in the liminal world between society and nature, allowed male viewers to experience an escape from the helplessness of childhood without having to succumb to adult responsibilities; the television show provided "a fantasy of the perpetuation of moral innocence and freedom from guilt into an adult world of power and aggression."[51]

Rodeos also experienced an unprecedented boom in popularity at the same time. Hailed as a "primitive, reckless and ruthless" sport that featured the "self-righteous virility" of its performers, the rodeo was part of a general cult of the cowboy. Families ran off to dude ranches to reestablish family togetherness through nature. Little boys thrilled to boy westerns like *Old Yeller* and television shows like *Lassie, My Friend Flicka*, and *Fury*—all love affairs between boys and their animals—while their fathers thrilled to grown-up shoot-outs and horseback chases.[52]

The cult of the cowboy's most celebrated hero, the man who best represented that "vanishing symbol of individualism in an age of togetherness and conformity," was an actor whose real name was Marion Michael Morrison.[53] But in this age of self-invention, Marion was urged by his agent and potential director to take a more manly name, preferably one composed of two first names, each with one syllable. So Marion Michael Morrison became John Wayne, the only American who fought in every war in American history, a two-fisted loner who would not get tied down by domestic responsibility but always kept moving toward the edges of society, toward the frontier. For much of the 1950s and for all of the 1960s and even into the 1970s, Wayne topped popularity polls as the American man that other American men most admired. And in films like *Fort Apache* (1948), *Red River* (1948), and *Rio Grande* (1950), Wayne embodied a frontier masculinity as had no one else in this century since Theodore Roosevelt. He, too, spoke softly and carried a big stick, and he, too, lived the strenuous life—even if his cinematic sets were constructed so that he would appear too large for the tables and chairs at which he sat and even if he was filmed from a slight upwards angle to make him appear taller than his 6'4" frame! Describing his directorial debut in *The Alamo* (1960), which he also produced and in which he starred as Davy Crockett, Wayne saw his mission as "to remind people . . . that there were once men and women who had the guts to stand up for the things they believed." The way Wayne saw it, the Alamo was a metaphor for America: Mexicans against us; black and white, simple. "They tell me everything isn't black and white," complained Wayne. "Well, I say why the hell not?"[54]

One of Wayne's films, *The Man Who Shot Liberty Valance* (1962), provides a fitting coda for this era of mass conformity, men's retreat to the home as frightened fathers preventing the next generation's sexual deviance or adolescent rebellion, and men's escapist fantasies of rugged individualism, luxurious sensuality, and outdoorsy adventure. The film turns on a case of mistaken identity as Ransom Stoddard (James Stewart) is credited with killing Valance, even though it was really Tom Doniphon (John Wayne) who had done it. Rather than a climactic revelation and reversal of fortune, Doniphon lives out his life in obscurity, while Stoddard gets all kinds of glory and accolades, including Doniphon's girlfriend, as rewards for his putative heroism. Only Stoddard and his wife come to Doniphon's funeral. "The values remain," film critic Joan Mellon writes sadly, "but the men who profess them are no longer worthy."[55]

Perhaps even more central than the western, however, were the flights of sexual fantasy that captivated suburban men. The bevy of men's magazines that started up in the 1950s—such as *Male* (1950), *Real: The Exciting Magazine for Men* (1950), *Impact: Bold True Action for Men* (1957), and *True* (1956)—glorified the testing of manhood, whether it was in hand-to-hand jungle combat or against the primal forces of nature, but always with the sexual conquest of a large-breasted woman as a kind of masculine payoff. These hairy-chested outdoorsmen were real men, who took no guff from women. The magazine "stimulates his masculine ego at a time when man wants to fight back against women's efforts to usurp his traditional role as head of the family," crowed *True*'s editorial director.[56]

What was perhaps the decade's most significant cultural contribution to the stock of masculine escape hatches dispensed with the heroic warrior or grisly outdoorsman altogether. In the *Playboy* philosophy, sexually alluring and available women were the reward for adventurous masculine consumerism, as they languidly draped themselves over the high-priced accoutrements of his bachelor pad. *Playboy* transformed the way men viewed women, separating them into distinct categories. Wives were the enemy, mothers were abstractions to be venerated, and other women were soft playthings to be seduced. The playboy "loved women," but he "hated wives" as Barbara Ehrenreich put it.[57] Wives were "an idle class, a spending class, a candy-craving class," according to Philip Wylie; they turned healthy, sexy, fun-loving guys into domesticated Caspar Milquetoasts, "tweedy, corpulent, hornrimmed dollar chasers," who, as sex-starved wimps, give money, homes, clothing, and stability in return for . . . what? "It is her man who worries about where to acquire the money while she worries only about how to spend it, so he has the ulcers and she has the guts of a bear."[58]

First published in December 1953, *Playboy* instantly became "the Bible for the beleaguered male" and one of the most popular magazines in American history—an indication that it had struck a nerve with American men and, perhaps, an indication of men's yearning for something different from the hands they felt they had been dealt.[59] *Playboy*, Ehrenreich argues, attacked "the bondage of breadwinning," offering instead "a coherent program for the male rebellion: a critique of marriage, a strategy for liberation (reclaiming the indoors as a realm for masculine pleasure) and a utopian vision."[60] The playboy was all sexual prowess without responsibility, blemish-free sex fantasies with blemish-free nubile women. As the magazine's title intimated, American men experienced their manhood most profoundly when they were boys at play, not men at work.

Playboy offered men "a little diversion from the anxieties of the Atomic Age," as editor Hugh Hefner announced in the magazine's inaugural issue. But the elements of diversion were strikingly different from the usual masculine magazine fare. Other men's magazines may spend all their time "thrashing through thorny thickets or splashing about in fast flowing streams," Hefner wrote, but playboys "spend most of our time inside. We like our apartment. We enjoy mixing up cocktails and an *hors d'oeuvre* or two, putting a little mood music on the phonograph, and inviting in a female acquaintance for a quiet discussion on Picasso, Nietzsche, jazz, sex." The playboy was a domesticated bachelor, closer to the dandified Billy Dimple in *The Contrast* than either of the other male roles, a stereotypic ladies' man now offered up as a new model for manliness.

It is therefore somewhat surprising that it was in the pages of *Playboy* that a midtwentieth-century debate about the feminization of American manhood was taking place. But it was a central tenet of the "Playboy philosophy" that women were not men's enemy; the magazine's editors and writers strove to carefully delineate the sources of masculine malaise, to celebrate some women even as it vilified wives and mothers. Philip Wylie, for example, announced the "womanization" of America in an article in 1958, followed four years later by a panel discussion on the topic.[61] Wylie cast a wide net in describing a "general male emasculation," carried out in large part by pushy protofeminists who sought "to invade everything masculine, emasculate it, cover it with dimity, occupy it forever —and police it." Bars now served "alcoholic substances with the hues and flavors of cake frosting" at "little Chinese tables you could tip over with a mere emphatic gesture." Through organized dances and Ladies Nights, women had even infiltrated men's clubs.[62]

Not only the public sphere but also the home had been completely feminized—"a boudoir-kitchen-nursery, dreamed up by women, for women, and as if males did not exist as males." In this colonization of domestic space, women had lots of help, first from male traitors, like interior decorators, who were of suspect sexuality, "usually males in form only—males emotionally so identified with the opposite sex they could rout reluctant husbands because their very travesty made men uncomfortable." And they'd also had help from husbands, who "defaulted" on their responsibilities and had turned into "flabby parodies of the physical male." Abandoning his role in imparting proper masculine social-ization, his sons "grew up without paternal guidance and adult male companionship" and became "she-pawns" by age twelve.[63]

Masculine collaboration with these forces of cultural feminization was a dominant theme in other *Playboy* articles. In a later panel, artist Alexander King found the American man "no longer willing or ready to accept complete responsibility for the family as he did in my father's and grandfather's days," so that now he has "resigned his prerogatives, and by default, woman has taken over." Anthropologist Ashley Montagu, whose book *The Natural Superiority of Women* (1952) had ruffled more than a few feathers, also blamed men for women's noisome trouble in prescient language that equated racial and gender conflict in terms that would become familiar in coming decades. "The male is in the pos-ition to do what the whites could have done to make the so-called inferior races feel that they were as good as anyone else and no longer inferior. They didn't and will probably pay the penalty for it in the long run. And, similarly, males."[64]

Writer Norman Mailer stated the case most baldly. For Mailer, "masculinity is not something one is born with, but something one gains. And one gains it by winning small battles with honor. I'm saying that because there is very little honor left in American life, there is a certain built-in tendency to destroy masculinity in American men." This emasculation is not women's fault alone, Mailer argues. Sure, they've become "more selfish, more greedy, less romantic, less warm, more lusty, and also more filled with hate," but men have collaborated with them. And the consequences are catastrophic—far more homosexuality in 1962 than fifty years earlier, which he attributes to "a loss of faith in the country, faith in the meaning of one's work, faith in the notion of one's self as a man."[65]

One crucial difference between turn-of-the-century critiques of cultural feminization and those of the late 1950s, then, concerned the role of men. In the late nineteenth century men had resisted feminization, and when they could not, it was because the demands of the workplace prevented them from expressing their deep, now repressed, manhood. But the men of the 1950s seemed willing participants in their own emasculation, loving little lambs being led sheepishly to she-devil slaughter.

Playboy's men were on a rescue mission. But amidst all the advertisements for high-end consumer products and the pinup photographs of lusciously large-breasted ladies, the magazine never offered a coherent political philosophy. On the one hand, work and family were the twin harnesses which constrained middle-class men from living out their playboy fantasies. *Playboy* encouraged men to search for a way to "break with the responsibilities of breadwinning, without, somehow, losing their manhood." For a while the male fled, as *Look* magazine had claimed in a 1958 feature series on the American male, "to the basement and busied himself sawing, painting, and sandpapering. But the women followed him, and today they are hammering right along with him. No place to hide there."[66] But on the other hand, below Wylie's clever conceits lay a lurking fear that overprotective mothers produced effeminate or delinquent sons. And underneath Mailer's masculine quest lay fears that men who abandoned meaningful work risked gender inversion. Men needed to rescue their sons and recommit themselves to their careers, that is, retrieve work and family as masculine preserves. Ultimately, it was fathers who might be able to resolve this tension. When men were bonding with their sons as dedicated fathers, they could legitimately claim homosocial freedom from their nagging wives. The stakes were high, the rewards potentially great.

As the 1950s drew to a close, American men still felt temporary about themselves, even more restless in the midst of even greater abundance than Tocqueville ever imagined. Responsible breadwinners and devoted fathers, they were still anxious about overconformity but unable and unwilling to break free of domestic responsibilities to become rebels on the run. Besides, they were *needed* at home to raise those sons to be real men. "I don't know what's the matter with us," says Betsy Rath to her husband, Tom, in Sloan Wilson's *The Man in the Gray Flannel Suit.* "Your job is plenty good enough. We've got three nice kids, and lots of people would be glad to have a house like this. We shouldn't be so *discontented* all the time."[67]

But discontented they were. Both husbands and wives yearned for something more, something neither could put a finger on exactly. Within a few years, though, Betty Friedan christened the discontent that women felt as the trap of "the feminine mystique" and began a movement that would bring to women the chance for a different life—fulfilling and equal. While the emerging feminist movement offered married suburban housewives hope for a life outside the domestic trap, their husbands also searched vainly for something, something they were unable to get from their work, from their relationships with their wives or their children, from their friends, and even, it turned out, from their fantasies. Men's efforts to hold fast to traditional manhood in the wake of the powerful currents of change in the 1960s and 1970s precipitated the contemporary masculine malaise.

PART FOUR

The Contemporary "Crisis" of Masculinity

CHAPTER 8

The Masculine Mystique

> How could we ever really know or love each other as long as we kept play-
> ing those roles that kept us from knowing or being ourselves? Weren't men
> as well as women still locked in lonely isolation, alienation, no matter how
> many sexual acrobatics they put their bodies through? Weren't men dying
> too young, suppressing fears and tears and their own tenderness? It seemed
> to me that men weren't really the enemy—they were fellow victims, suffering
> from an outmoded masculine mystique that made them feel unnecessarily
> inadequate when there were no bears to kill.
> —Betty Friedan *The Feminine Mystique* (1973)[1]

In 1963 Betty Friedan's *The Feminine Mystique* resounded like a tocsin across the country, heralding the birth of a new wave of feminism. In June of that same year, Rev. Martin Luther King, Jr. delivered perhaps his most impassioned plea for racial equality, inviting his audience to dream with him of a time when the "grandsons of slaves and the grandsons of slaveowners" would "sit down together at the table of brotherhood."

There were even a few rumblings of discontent among men, rumblings which grew louder and more insistent as the decade progressed. The historian Arthur Schlesinger, Jr. noticed it in an article in *Esquire* in November 1958:

> What has happened to the American male? For a long time he seemed utterly confident in his manhood, sure of his masculine role in society, easy and definite in his sense of sexual identity. Today men are more and more conscious of maleness not as a fact but as a prob-
> lem. The ways by which American men affirm their masculinity are uncertain and obscure.
> There are multiplying signs, indeed, that something has gone badly wrong with the
> American male's conception of himself.[2]

What had gone wrong? Actually very little was new, despite Schlesinger's anxious warning. Rather, the eminent historian had indulged in a bit of ahistorical nostalgia, as we often do during periods of uncertainty, suggesting that earlier times were happier, easier, and more stable times. As I've shown, this was a projection; those bygone days came weighted with their own gendered anxieties.

In the 1960s the "masculine mystique"—that impossible synthesis of sober, responsible breadwinner, imperviously stoic master of his fate, and swashbuckling hero— was finally exposed as a fraud. The constant search for some masculine terra firma upon which to ground a stable identity had never provided firm footing for Self-Made Men; by the 1960s gradual erosion and uneasy footing had become a landslide. All the marginalized groups whose suppression had been thought to be necessary for men to build secure identities began to rebel. Friedan had finally named the "problem that has no name"—the confusion, self-blame, and anguish of women who had been told "to seek fulfillment as wives and mothers." For the second time in our history, women began to find their voices. At first, Friedan noticed, women spoke with "a tone of quiet desperation" about their problems, the same quiet desperation that Thoreau had observed among American men a century earlier. But soon that muted tone gave way to righteous indignation, as women were finally answering that old saw about what they wanted that Freud and countless other men had asked in bemused resignation. "I want something more than my husband and my children and my home" was the answer Friedan exclaimed we could no longer ignore.[3]

The civil rights movement challenged the exclusion of black people from full citizenship and, thus, the exclusion of black men from claiming their stake in American manhood. Gender images saturated militant black rhetoric, equating the demands for civil rights with a demand for full recognition of blacks as men. The gay liberation movement challenged the facile and false equation of homosexuality with failed gender identity, the popular misperception that gay men were not real men. And the counterculture, populated largely by the sons and daughters of the white middle class, challenged the illusions of suburban comfort and security. In a sense, the hippies represented another revolt of the sons against the fathers. In their long hair and flowing, feminine clothes, hippies rejected the corporate clone as a model for manhood. "Are You a Boy or Are You a Girl?" was the title of one popular song and the plaint of many a suburban parent.[4]

Even our earlier attempts to extend the frontier beyond national boundaries could no longer be relied upon. Despite JFK's inaugural promise of a New Frontier, the world was getting smaller, closing in on men seeking military heroism as a way to demonstrate manhood. By the middle of the decade, as we sank deeper and deeper in that morally indefensible political quagmire in Vietnam, many Americans came to realize that extending the frontier had consequences: The empire was striking back. And one of the most reliable refuges for beleaguered masculinity, the soldier/protector, fell into such disrepute as the news about Vietnam filtered home that even today Vietnam veterans are seen by some as having acted out an excessive and false hypermasculinity. Once a paragon of manly virtue, the soldier was now also coming to be perceived as a failed man.

The sustained, insisted demands for inclusion by those who have historically been marginalized did not begin in the 1960s, but it then became a permanent fixture in the national social and political agenda. And whether one welcomes them today to full economic, social, and political equality as the fulfillment of democracy's promise or dreads them with all the self-righteous indignation of the traditionally privileged, these groups are here to stay. They trumpet neither reveille for the Age of Aquarius nor taps for American culture, but they have irreversibly transformed the landscape on which American men have sought to test and prove their manhood.

Just as they had for over a century, many American men didn't take these new challenges particularly well, retreating to tired formulae of exclusion or escape. By the mid-1970s there were calls for "men's liberation" to free men from the restrictive roles to which they had been assigned. Men, it turned out, needed liberating, too. If middle-class white men couldn't beat 'em, perhaps they could join blacks, gays, and women in the ranks of the oppressed.

Work

After all, the breadwinner role brought few of its anticipated rewards. By the 1960s American men felt increasingly alienated, stuck in a rut, unable to escape the dull monotony of a cookie-cutter corporate identity, a suit that was ready-made and waiting to be filled. These feelings resonated through all levels of American society, as successful businessmen, middle-class managers, and blue-collar workers all experienced alienation. The sociologist Robert Blauner's important study of factory workers, *Alienation and Freedom* (1964), identified several dimensions of alienation that were as pervasive for middle-class men as they were for blue-collar workers. Blauner argued that the experience of powerlessness (having no control over their actions on the job), meaninglessness (performing specialized tasks that they cannot relate to the whole), isolation (inability to identify with the firm or its goals), and self-estrangement (the lack of integration between their work and other aspects of life) led men to search for affirmation and identity outside the workplace, in the realm of consumption.[5]

It wasn't only industrial workers. A 1963 study of big business leaders asked:

What is the point at which these men can stop, look back, and announce to themselves and their world that they have completed this long journey, that they will rest now? There does not seem to be such a point, for an essential part of the system is the need for the constant demonstration of one's adequacy, for reiterated proof of one's independence.[6]

And a Connecticut therapist described a middle-level manager at IBM:

He's under constant fear and tension. He's constantly worried about whether he's going to get ahead or isn't he? He's not worried about being dropped, but he's very worried about what people are thinking about him. He's been with IBM for something like eight years, and he hasn't moved ahead. He's putting the pressure on himself. It's him in relation to the society of IBM. He's afraid of taking the risk of getting a promotion, afraid he might not be able to handle the new responsibilities. He's also afraid of the competition. His idea is that if he fails, he'll look worse than if he didn't try at all. So he doesn't try. The failure becomes much more difficult for him to handle.

The pressure to be a successful breadwinner was a source of strain and conflict, not pride and motivation.[7]

In the 1960s the relentless striving and competition that had defined the Self-Made Man and the fears and anxieties that accompanied him were cast as the problem, not the cure. Self-making was now characterized as a disease, the type A personality—that impatient, driven, hostile, and competitive workplace successmonger, who, according to cardiologists, was far more prone to heart attacks and other stress-related diseases than his more calmly cooperative and accommodating type B brother. Immediately seized upon by psychologists and magazine writers, the type A man was, according to a *Business Week* article in 1964, "aggressive, hard-driving, vigorously competitive, continuously subject to deadline, and [subject to] an exaggerated sense of time urgency," while another observer saw his "restlessness, hyperalertness, explosiveness of speech, tenseness of facial musculature" as early warning signs of type A.[8] A 1974 study of one thousand seven hundred people over age eighty, including 129 people who were one hundred years old or older, found absolutely no "intense, driving, highly competitive business executive types in the whole bunch."[9] Literally sick at heart, Self-Made American men were driving themselves to early death.

Such relentless striving in the competitive crowd left men feeling isolated and alone. Loneliness, emptiness—these became the dominant terms in the era's cultural analyses of masculinity. The breadwinner role left men feeling like cogs in the corporate machine, and conspicuous consumption in sprawling suburban shopping malls was hardly a compensation. The pursuit of happiness promised by our Founding Fathers had become, as Philip Slater's compact indictment was titled, a "pursuit of loneliness"; our growing into manhood was, as Paul Goodman's equally insightful work had been titled a decade earlier, "growing up absurd"; and the culture of abundance was now what Christopher Lasch called a "culture of narcissism."

Each of these works brilliantly dissected the cultural malaise that lay at the heart of American self-making, the empty anxiety that sprang directly from the blind pursuit of a marketplace masculinity. The rugged individualism of the nineteenth century had been replaced by the shallow sociability of the modern American personality. Eagerly dependent upon the approval of others, the contemporary narcissist was not a gentle neo-hippy but a competitive, insecure manipulator. We could no longer have it both ways, Goodman had warned, maintaining "a conformist and ignoble system *and . . .* skillful and spirited men to man that system with."[10]

Only Charles Reich, in *The Greening of America* (1970), waxed optimistic in the face of these changes. To Reich, a Yale Law School professor, the cultural crisis was the dawning of a new age, in part exemplified by the hippies, and the new age signaled the birth of a new man. Reich's truncated history of America rested on the transitions in forms of consciousness. In republican America (what Reich called Consciousness I) small businessmen and farmers, heirs to republicanism and frontier individualism, carved out the manhood of what I have called the Heroic Artisan, characterized by the Jeffersonian virtues of the yeoman and the autonomous shopkeeper. The turn of the century spelled the triumph of the organization man, the professional animated by hierarchy, marketplace rationality, and order (Consciousness II—roughly equivalent to what I have called Self-Made Masculinity.) But now (the late 1960s) Reich euphorically observed a new consciousness, Consciousness III, which replaced liberal marketplace individualism with a globally aware, environmentally sensitive, freely flowing androgynous cultural identity. Reich's breathless celebration of Consciousness III may have been premature, but his insight that hordes of American men were seeking to shed the burdens of preceding forms of consciousness suggested something significant in American culture.[11]

Politics

The emerging student movement also was uneasy about the possibilities for personal fulfillment promised by Self-Made Masculinity. The Port Huron Statement (1962), the founding document of the Students for a Democratic Society (SDS), is an anxious plea for a new definition of manhood. Contemporary society used men, treated them as "thing[s] to be manipulated . . . inherently incapable of directing [their] own affairs"; we had become docile and dependent. But the solution was not "egotistic individualism," which led only to "loneliness, estrangement, [and] isolation," but rather the exploration of our "unfulfilled capacities for reason, freedom and love" and our "unrealized potential for self-evaluation, self-direction, self-understanding, and creativity."[12]

For many young Americans, before personal fulfillment came a commitment to ending the war in Vietnam. The growing antiwar movement provided a new lens into the dynamics of American manhood in the 1960s and 1970s; the conflict between old and young, between hawks and doves, was also a test of wills; questions of loyalty became questions of standing up for what one believed. It was a central expression of the growing crisis of masculinity.

The struggle between the Vietnam policy makers and the antiwar protestors held the gendered psyches of Washington policy makers up to a new lens. No longer did we lionize presidents and their cabinets as they stood fast against aggression, totalitarianism, and imperial expansion. Kennedy was, perhaps, the last president cast in that heroic mold, even though recent revisionist historians have significantly tarnished his image. Like both Roosevelts, Kennedy overcame the perceived burdens of his aristocratic family lineage and youthful infirmity or injury—a World War II hero on PT-109, Kennedy presented a youthful vigor, a hardy manhood that, despite his chronic back injury, made him as comfortable sailing or playing touch football with his family on the lawns of their Hyannisport home as he was leading the nation into the New Frontier. The shock wave that jolted the American psyche when Kennedy was assassinated in 1963 was, in part, that a man in the prime of his life, so vital and active, had been cut down by a sniper's bullet (or snipers' bullets). If Kennedy could be shot down, then the manhood he embodied was itself vulnerable.

The re-creation of the frontier loomed large in JFK's imagery. In his speech accepting the Democratic presidential nomination in 1960 in Los Angeles, Kennedy evoked the search for the frontier as the source of renewal and hope:

> I stand tonight facing west on what was once the last frontier. From the lands that stretch 3,000 miles behind me, the pioneers of old gave up their safety, their comfort and sometimes their lives to build a new world here in the West. . . . [But] the problems are not all solved and the battles are not all won, and we stand today on the edge of a new frontier—the frontier of the 1960s, a frontier of unknown opportunities and paths, a frontier of unfulfilled hopes and threats.[13]

New frontier boundaries were drawn against communism and especially against the Russians—whether in the rice paddies of Vietnam, in building American bodies (through the President's Council on Physical Fitness), or in the space race. Exploring outer space offered the chance to win a war against the Russians without earthbound weapons and physical injury, and it also offered some new versions of American heroes. The astronaut was "the triumphant single-combat warrior," the "Cold Warrior of the Heavens," facing a challenge that was "ancient, primordial, irresistible," according to Tom Wolfe in his meditation on military masculinity couched as a portrait of aeronautical disillusionment, *The Right Stuff* (1979). Wolfe suggests that the astronauts, instead of being the triumphant reincarnation of the Heroic Artisan, were actually glamorized proletarians; each was little more than a passenger in his capsule—"a redundant component, a backup engineer, a boiler room attendant—in an automated system!"[14]

Kennedy's constant confrontations, both real and symbolic, with the Russians revealed a sense of manliness that was animated by a "keyed up, almost compulsive competitiveness," according to biographer Theodore Sorenson. Assembling around him the "best and the brightest," Kennedy saw many of his brief administration's tests as tests of manly resolve, from the Bay of Pigs crisis, to his own Vietnam policies, which began the rapid escalations of U.S. involvement. This foreign policy's aim, according to James McNaughton, assistant to Secretary of Defense Robert McNamara, was "70 percent—to avoid a humiliating U.S. defeat (to our reputation as guarantor) . . . 20 percent—to keep South Vietnam (and the adjacent territory) from Chinese hands . . . 10 percent to permit the people, of South Vietnam to enjoy a better, freer way of life."[15]

Kennedy managed to balance his compulsive competitiveness and aggression with a fresh-scrubbed handsome, energetic charisma—qualities that LBJ lacked in equal abundance. Johnson appears to have been so deeply insecure that his political rhetoric dripped with metaphors of aggressive masculinity; affairs of state seem to have been conducted as much with the genitals as with political genius. There was a lot at stake for LBJ, as David Halberstam noted in his monumental study, *The Best and the Brightest*:

> He has always been haunted by the idea that he would be judged as being insufficiently manly for the job, that he would lack courage at a crucial moment. More than a little insecure himself, he wanted very much to be seen as a man; it was a conscious thing. . . . [H]e wanted the respect of men who were tough, real men, and they would turn out to be hawks. He had unconsciously divided people around him between men and boys. Men were activists, doers, who conquered business empires, who acted instead of talked, who made it in the world of other men and had the respect of other men. Boys were the talkers and the writers and the intellectuals, who sat around thinking and criticizing and doubting instead of doing.[16]

Johnson's crisis of manliness contributed to, though of course it did not cause, the escalation of the war in Vietnam, his refusal to admit that the war was lost, or to see the error in the war in the first place. Bill Moyers, then President Johnson's press secretary, recalled that the president told him of his fear that if he withdrew from Vietnam, then McNamara and the other advisers would think him "less of a man" than Kennedy. When opposed by enemies real or imagined, Johnson questioned their manhood. "In decision making," Halberstam writes, "they proposed the manhood position, their opponents the softer, or sissy, positions." When informed that one member of his administration was becoming a dove on Vietnam, Johnson retorted, "Hell, he has to squat to piss." And as he celebrated the Christmas bombings of North Vietnam in 1966, Johnson declared proudly, "I didn't just screw Ho Chi Minh. I cut his pecker off." As Moyers noted, it was as if the war had become "a frontier test," with LBJ swearing, "by God I'm not going to let those puny brown people push me around."[17]

Nixon, too, was chronically afraid of appearing soft on communism—or on anything else. He was "afraid of being acted upon, of being inactive, of being soft, of being thought impotent, of being dependent on anyone else."[18] Nixon resolved to "overcome the weak-kneed, jelly backed attitude" of Congress and to press ahead with escalating the war in Vietnam, according to Barry Goldwater. When one Republican senator shifted his position on the war from hawk to dove, Vice President Agnew called him Christine Jorgensen, in reference to the most famous transsexual of the era. And in labeling antiwar protestors "effete intellectual snobs" and the press "nattering nabobs of negativism," speechwriter William Safire allowed Agnew to place into common currency the equation of manhood with support of the American war effort. Nixon's compulsive manhood formed an explosive amalgam with his political paranoia as he faced George McGovern, a soft-spoken ex-minister and college professor and the antiwar, Democratic presidential candidate in 1972. Nixon's desperate efforts to win, including the Watergate break-in and cover-up, eventually brought him down and, with him, the nation's failed Vietnam policy.

In a sense, the Carter presidency was McGovern's vindication—here was another soft-spoken, deeply religious man, who made compassion and concern the apparent cornerstone principles of his domestic and foreign policy. But the "new man" represented by Carter proved to be a case of too much too soon for an American psyche still traumatized by defeat in Vietnam, the women's movement, and the relentless grind of urban problems. As the president in the resurgently masculinist 1980s, former actor Ronald Reagan would promise one last swing in the saddle for the western cowboy hero as president—and most Americans went happily along for the ride.

The erosion of confidence in a masculinity based on martial virtues that attended our involvement in Vietnam was only part of the problem for American men in the 1960s and 1970s. Men were besieged at home; the social movements of those two decades—the women's movement, the civil rights movement, and the gay liberation movement—all offered scathing critiques of traditional masculinity and demanded inclusion and equality in the public arena. No longer could the marketplace and the political arena be the preserve of heterosexual white men. The very groups who had been so long excluded from American life were making their own claims for identity. And for manhood.

Black men, for example. James Baldwin's powerful essays and best-selling novels focused a tormented rage on white men's projections of their fears and longings on black men, a cultural psychosis that meant that the black man was "forced each day to snatch his manhood, his identity, out of the fire of human cruelty that rages to destroy it."[19]

As the civil rights movement of the mid-1960s enlarged to include movements for black power and black pride, so too did the rhetoric of gender. The Reverend Martin Luther King, Jr., asked America to live up to the promise of democracy by integrating and including black people into full humanity. In the 1968 sanitation workers' strike in Memphis, during which King was assassinated, workers carried signs that read, in bold block letters, "I *am* a man." Malcolm X developed a parallel political rhetoric that was equally gendered, as he spoke about reclaiming a manhood stolen from black men by white slavers and denied by two centuries of racist politics. "Malcolm was our manhood, our living black manhood!" exclaimed the actor and civil rights leader Ossie Davis, in the aftermath of Malcolm X's assassination. "This was his meaning to his people."

The Black Panther party, a militantly defiant organization, made black manhood a centerpiece of its appeal to young blacks. In the works of such Black Panther leaders as Huey Newton, Bobby Seale, and Eldridge Cleaver, there was a growing preoccupation with proving a manhood long suppressed and denied by racism. "We shall have our manhood. We shall have it or the earth will be leveled by our attempts to gain it," wrote Cleaver in *Soul on Ice* (1968), his incendiary manifesto of black liberation. The sight of hundreds of angry black men in military formations, carrying machine guns, preparing to fight for their rights, was a stirring sight to all who observed the Black Panthers—no doubt a terrifying sight to some but, also no doubt, an inspiring sight to many young black men facing the crippling realities of racism, unemployment, and inner-city poverty.[20]

For some militants black pride meant pride in themselves as men, which led them to fuse their own homophobia with claims for manhood. "Most American white men are trained to be fags," with "weak and blank" faces with a "red flush" and "silk blue faggot eyes," asserted Amiri Baraka in his essay "American sexual reference: black male."[21] More than any of the others, Cleaver was preoccupied with black power as the vehicle to reclaim sexual potency. In an essay, "To All Black Women from All Black Men," Cleaver wrote about his struggle to "heal my castration"—the deep wound inflicted on black men through slavery and cultural dispossession. "Across the naked abyss of negated masculinity, of four hundred years minus my Balls . . . I feel a deep terrifying hurt, the pain of humiliation of a vanquished warrior . . . and a compelling challenge to redeem my conquered manhood." One of Cleaver's ideas of revolution was the rape of white women by black men, since such a violation was the ultimate violation of white male power. By raping "his" women, black men would be striking the ultimate blow against the white man. Such suggestions did not sit well with either his black sisters or with white women, who were themselves demanding that they cease to be the chattel of men.[22]

Women had a movement of their own for that purpose. Feminism posed perhaps the greatest challenge to a masculinity based on exclusion and affected men both personally and politically. For one thing, women had burst into public realms in sufficient numbers to really challenge the workplace, the classroom, and the political arena as homosocial preserves. For example, between 1968 and 1975 all but a small number of colleges and universities were opened to women—only a handful of college-educated American men currently under thirty-five has attended a single-sex institution of higher learning. That's quite a change from the experiences of every other generation of men in U.S. history. Women were not only voting but voting for women candidates and supporting the ERA. In 1973 the Supreme Court ruled in *Roe v. Wade* that women have the right to choose to terminate a pregnancy, thus allowing women to maintain control over their bodies—a right that men had been assuming for themselves since the Founding Fathers guaranteed men a sense of property in their own person.

Feminism also insisted that the women who were the victims of abusive masculinity —the battered wives, the abandoned families, the sexually abused young girls, the rape victims—be protected from men's violence and that the government institute policies to protect women from rape, sexual harassment, battery. At the same time as feminism demanded protection for victims, it also empowered women to claim autonomy in their personal lives, especially in interpersonal relationships with men. Women not only had the right to work but the right to sexual agency, a right to desire itself—perhaps, even, a right to orgasm. (The invention of the birth control pill provided technical assistance to women and men who wanted to claim sexual pleasure independent of procreation.) Women had the right to choose the kinds of lives they wanted to lead. No longer to be consigned to housework and child care, women could *choose* to be mothers, to have careers, to work around the home. As the Statement of Purpose of the National Organization for Women put it in 1966:

> We reject the current assumptions that a man must carry the sole burden of supporting himself, his wife, and family, and that a woman is automatically entitled to lifelong

support by a man upon her marriage, or that marriage, home, and family are primarily woman's world and responsibility—hers to dominate—his to support.[23]

Of course, such sentiments had enormous implications for American men, because feminism demanded that men change—that men cease abusing, raping, and battering women, that men begin to share in the daily chores around the household, and that they accept that women were working right alongside them. For many men, women's liberation meant increased anxiety, particularly sexual anxiety. After all, if women could now be more fully sexual, then men might fear sexual activity as a constant test, a "trial of manliness" that would find men perpetually wanting, according to British observer Myron Brenton in *The American Male* (1967). Women now had the right not only to respond sexually but also to initiate sexual activity; Brenton saw American men running away, in a somewhat spiteful escape, from women's sexual desires and right into impotence, decreased desire, homosexual encounters, affairs with other women, and visits to call girls.[24]

Animated by these fears, by the antipathy for women's entry into the public sphere, and by a growing resentment of any demands that they change, many men resisted women's efforts to either open up the public sphere or to transform the private sphere. Norman Mailer's *The Prisoner of Sex* (1971), itself a response to a feminist critique of his work, turned from a defensive plea to a meandering spiteful tirade, full of bathos and bombast. Confessing to exhaustion and confusion, Mailer moved back and forth, from calling his sexual instrument "the Avenger" to wincing at the "desperate bravado" that men exhibit in their "passion to be masculine."[25]

Academic works, like sociologist Steven Goldberg's *The Inevitability of Patriarchy* (1973), marshaled a limited and selective sample of anthropological and biological evidence to claim that women's liberation ran counter to the forces of nature and cultural stability, that male domination was encoded in the superior strength of the male. Male domination was universal, Goldberg claimed, and was therefore natural.[26] Conservative political theorist George Gilder also used a putative biological argument to support antifeminist claims in his books *Sexual Suicide* (1973) and *Naked Nomads* (1974). Men, Gilder argued, were biologically driven toward aggression, competition, and violence, naturally "disposed" to crime, drugs, and violence, and naturally "susceptible" to disease, and if women followed feminist ideals, they would abandon their traditional role as moralistic constraints on men's antisocial natures, and all hell would break loose. Since men were untamable, except in their traditionally responsible roles as father, husband, and breadwinner—he cites statistics that indicate that most violent crimes are committed by young men—then women's liberation would result in an anarchistic uprising among men, who would run rampant in an orgy of violence and aggression. And sex. Male sexuality is insistent and incessant; if not harnessed by women, there will be "aimless copulation," "slaked by masturbation and pornography" or uncontrolled promiscuous homosexuality.[27]

Gilder's solution was to reestablish the pedestal and replace women firmly on top of it. Women need to leave the public sphere and return to the home where they belong and where men desperately needed them to be. Feminists are their own worst enemies; "[a] society of wealthy and independent women will be a society of sexually and economically predatory males," he predicts. While his antifeminism is obvious, more subtle is the vehement rage at men. Gilder believes that masculinity is "at bottom empty, a limp nullity. While the female body is full of internal potentiality, the male is internally barren."

Thus, men need women and society to help them define their place in the world because without women, men would be "destined to a Hobbesian life—solitary, poor, nasty, brutish and short."[28]

Popular magazines and books curried masculine resentment and resistance—not only in soft-core pornography, which boomed during the 1970s (*Playboy* and *Penthouse* became two of the five top-selling magazines in the country), but also in a host of new men's magazines promising deliverance from women. In a self-promotional advertisement a newly made-over *True* magazine recalled its earlier incarnation two decades before:

> one word describes the new TRUE magazine: MACHO. The honest-to-God American MAN deserves a magazine sans naked cuties, Dr. Spock philosophies, foppish, gutless "unisex" pap, and platform shoes. It's time for a refreshing change. . . . A hardy slice of adventure, challenge, action, competition, controversy. Including informative features that bring the American man and American values back from the shadows. Back from the sterile couches of pedantic psychiatrists. Back from behind the frivolous skirts of libbers.

The ad ended with as much a threat as a promise. "If you're a man, you'll like it."[29]

Gilder and other antifeminists prescribed traditional marriage and nuclear families, with one male breadwinner and one stay-at-home female homemaker, as the solution to the male malaise. Other cultural critics worried that such arrangements would again result in the feminization of American manhood. Echoing themes from the turn of the century, the sociologist Patricia Cayo Sexton observed a general "enervating trend" in American culture—a trend directly traceable to women's monopoly over child rearing and early education. In *The Feminized Male* (1969) Sexton argued that this "overexposure to feminine norms" at home and at school was turning American boys into a weak-willed bunch of sissies, "afflicted by excessive caution and a virtual incapacity to *do* anything in the real world."[30]

Sexton based her claims on her observations at several urban schools, where it seemed that the boys who were the most academically successful consistently scored the lowest on masculinity scales, especially the still-employed Terman and Miles M-F test. School "makes sissies out of many boys and feminizes many more by insisting that they act like girls" so that, in the end, "the more scholarly the men the lower their masculinity score tended to be."[31] Here again were all the fears of feminization from nearly a century earlier: that boys raised by women will be less manly than boys raised by men and that the configuration of the modern family turns boys into mushy little wimps.

Other writers followed suit. Hans Sebald's frantic and frightened tract *Momism: The Silent Disease of America* (1976) chronicled a generation of emotionally frustrated women whose career ambitions had been thwarted and who therefore sank despondently into professional motherhood, demanding of their children the career successes that they, the mothers, had never been able to achieve—and making "psychological wrecks" of their sons in the process. Echoing Philip Wylie's vituperative 1942 fusillade *Generation of Vipers*, Sebald exposed the "crippling peril" of Momism, the "hidden savagery" of "Mom's repressive transaction." His motto? "When Learning Masculinity, Don't Imitate the Teacher."[32]

Robert Ardrey, one of a host of popularizers of the new field of sociobiology, argued that the American mother is "the unhappiest female that the primate world has ever seen, and the most treasured objective in her heart of hearts is the psychological castration of husbands and sons."[33] A writer in *True* magazine called on his brethren to resist the civilizing pulls of feminization, which meant resisting the city as a source of domestication, hence enervation, since cities and their "suburban occlusions" are run by women and since "Gloria Whosits and whoever started the current thrombosis are city women."[34] Anthropologist Lionel Tiger was so concerned about gender blending that he advocated, in *Men in Groups* (1969), that urban planners place men's clubs in their plans for urban redevelopment to facilitate male bonding and provide men with a surcease from female invasion of the formerly homosocial workplace.[35]

In one of the decade's more humorous turns at cultural feminization and the relationship between gender identity and class, Tom Wolfe observed the ways in which the desire to appear masculine animated the activities of a bunch of preppy mama's boys. In the essay "Honks and Wonks" (1976), Wolfe drew a distinction between the street masculinity of the working class and that of preppy "honks" who "get hung up on the masculinity thing" because their manhood is always in question:

> It seems to me that when it comes to prep-school honks like Averell Harriman or Thomas Hoving—well, it doesn't matter how many worlds they have conquered or how old they are. As soon as they open their mouths, a bell goes off in the brains of most local-bred New York males: *sissy*. Here are a coupla kids who woulda got *mashed* in the street life.[36]

Preppies were feminized, Wolfe argues, by a class culture that shielded them from the harsher realities of masculine life. When they talked tough, they revealed their phony claims to masculine credentials.

Jewish men were also seen as feminized because they came from a religious culture that stressed morality and literacy; thus, they were seen as bookish and effete. I recall, for example, marching in a protest demonstration against the war in Vietnam as an adolescent, when a heckler screamed at me to "go back to Russia, you Commie Jew faggot!" Though I was startled at the time by the venom of his accusations, stung by his rage, what is most significant to me now is the way that communism, Judaism, and homosexuality were so easily linked in his mind. All three, I came to understand, were not "real men."

Jewish men inherited a legacy of gendered dismissal as gentle, intellectual, and moral And generations of writers had moaned with pain at being left outside the hallowed gates of masculinity. The decade's most anguished cry came from Alex Portnoy, the angst-ridden antihero of Philip Roth's *Portnoy's Complaint* (1967), who screams to his psychiatrist, "Doctor, I can't stand anymore being frightened like this over nothing! Bless me with manhood! Make me brave! Make me strong! Make me *whole!*"[37] With the stereotypes of Jewish mothers as castrating and all-consuming, Jewish men were among the archetypal feminized men.

Many Jews fought back, both rhetorically and politically. A generation of writers followed Norman Mailer into Jewish tough-guy poses. Some Jewish men began to articulate a vision of Jewish virility, a kind of "Muscular Judaism." In part, celebrating Zionist militarism in Israel was a vehicle by which American Jewry could come to terms with the Holocaust. If the Holocaust had feminized European Jewish men, who were castigated as incapable of protecting their families and were therefore led sheepishly to the slaughter, then supporting Israeli territorial expansion was a way to rescue one's manhood. And the discovery of Jewish resistance to Nazism gave Jewish men "Jewish Buffalo Bills" or "Jewish Tarzans," according to Arthur Koestler. Leon Uris's *Exodus* (1958) offered a new version of heroic Judaism. "We Jews are not what we have been portrayed to be," Uris told an interviewer immediately after the novel appeared. "In truth we have been fighters," as he wrote in a new preface to the paperback edition:

> [A]ll the cliché Jewish characters who have cluttered up our American fiction—the clever businessman, the brilliant doctor, the sneaky lawyer, the sulking artist—all the good folk who spend their chapters hating themselves, the world, and all their aunts and uncles . . . all those steeped in self-pity . . . all those golden riders of the psychoanalysis couch . . . all these have been left where they rightfully belong, on the cutting room floor.[38]

As I learned on that New York City street in 1965, the fears of feminization only partially cloaked a simmering homophobic fear, a fear that homosexuality was "spreading like a murky smog over the American scene," as Betty Friedan had put it in *The Feminine Mystique*. Hans Sebald claimed that the mother had "cast a spell" on young boys, "preventing them from developing normal heterosexual interest," so that the mother "bore the main responsibility" for sexual "deviance." Some parents worried that opening home economics courses to boys would "rob" boys of their masculinity and lead to "sexual deviance."[39]

Peter and Barbara Wyden's *Growing Up Straight: What Every Thoughtful Parent Should Know About Homosexuality* (1968) provided anxious parents with a set of early warning signs of homosexuality in their sons. "Pre-homosexual" boys were identified by their "unmasculine" behaviors, which were reinforced by overdominant mothers and absent fathers. For these vulnerable boys to become well-adjusted heterosexual men, fathers must become role models for their sons, and mothers must accept their husbands' place at the head of the family. Pre-homosexual boys grew up with inverted gender identities because they were taught the wrong things by parents who enacted reversals themselves. Only "sexually normal homes" could be certain to produce normal, heterosexual men.[40]

The gay liberation movement posited a strong riposte to the facile equation of homosexuality and masculine gender identity and made the counterclaim that gay men were as much "real" men as straight men.[41] Following the Stonewall riots of 1969, in which gay men fought back against a police raid on a Greenwich Village bar, and the subsequent birth of the gay liberation movement, a new gay masculinity emerged in gay enclaves of America's major cities. In these "gay ghettos," the "clone," as he was called, dressed in hypermasculine garb (flannel shirts, blue jeans, leather) and had short hair (not at all androgynous) and a mustache; he was athletic, highly muscular. In short, the clone looked more like a "real man" than most straight men.[42]

And the clones—who constituted roughly one-third of all gay men living in the major urban enclaves of the 1970s—enacted a hypermasculine sexuality in steamy back rooms, bars, and bathhouses where sex was plentiful, anonymous, and very hot. No unnecessary foreplay, romance, or postcoital awkwardness. Sex without attachment. One might even say that, given the norms of masculinity (that men are always seeking sex, ready for sex, wanting sex), gay men were just about the only men in America who were getting as much sex as they wanted. And gay men were certainly making it plain that the traditional equation of gay man as failed man was no longer tenable. Gay liberation signaled that gay men, too, could stake their claim for manhood.[43]

Together feminism, black liberation, and gay liberation provided a frontal assault on the traditional way that men had defined their manhood—against an other who was excluded from full humanity by being excluded from those places where men were real men. It was as if the screen against which American men had for generations projected their manhood had suddenly grown dark, and men were left to sort out the meaning of masculinity all by themselves.

Enter "men's liberation," a curious mixture of a social movement and psychological self-help manual that emerged in the mid-1970s. Media pundits often excoriated men's liberation as a bunch of middle-class white guys feeling left out of the fun of being oppressed and trying to jump on the liberation bandwagon. But men's liberation was more than merely a case of oppression envy. Its impulse, at least originally, came from the effort to take to heart the critiques of Self-Made Masculinity first voiced by the women's movement and later by the gay liberation movement. If men were supposed to be so powerful and oppressive, how come so many men were still living lives of quiet desperation—working in boring and unfulfilling jobs, trapped in unhappy marriages with little or no relationship with their children, with few, if any, close friends, isolated, lonely, and unaware of their feelings? "Male liberation calls for men to free themselves of the sex-role stereotypes that limit their ability to be human," announced Jack Sawyer in "On Male Liberation" (1970), a founding text of the new men's lib literature. Following his call, dozens of other works poured into the growing field, including Warren Farrell's *The Liberated Man* (1974), Marc Feigen Fasteau's *The Male Machine* (1975), Herb Goldberg's *The Hazards of Being Male* (1975) and *The New Male* (1979), Jack Nichols's *Men's Liberation* (1975), and two anthologies, Deborah David and Robert Brannon's *The Forty-Nine Percent Majority* (1976) and Joseph Pleck and Jack Sawyer's *Men and Masculinity* (1974).[44]

As women had sought liberation from restrictive stereotyped sex roles, so, too, did men begin to understand traditional masculinity as a burden, a form of oppression. "It's becoming clear to many of us that many of our most important inner needs cannot be met by acting in the ways we have been expected to act as men," noted the psychologist Pleck in an interview in 1973. The Berkeley Men's Center Manifesto counted the ways: "We no longer want to strain and compete to live up to an impossible oppressive masculine image—strong, silent, cool, handsome, unemotional, successful, master of women, leader of men, wealthy, brilliant, athletic, and 'heavy.' "[45]

At its core, men's liberation provided a coherent critique of the Self-Made Man; in its eyes *he* was the failure. As a collection of dos and don'ts, the male sex role was a recipe for despair; given what it took to be a real man, few, if any, men could live up to the image, and hence all men would feel like failures as men. What's worse, the psychological costs of trying to live up to the image would lead men into lives of isolation and despair, of repressed emotion and deferred dreams. The blueprint for masculinity

is a blueprint for self-destruction. . . . The masculine imperative, the pressure and compulsion to perform, to prove himself, to dominate, to live up to the "masculine ideal"—in short, to "be a man"—supersedes the instinct to survive. . . . Close examination of a man's behavior reveals a powerfully masochistic, self-hating, and often pathetically self-destructive style.

Our society is therefore full of "success-driven men at the end points of their success voyage, living in a nightmarish world of not knowing whom to trust, unable to find satisfaction in intimate contact, unaware of what they want and feel, and rigidly resistant to opening up in order to find out."[46]

Men's liberationists offered a systematic assault on what they called the male sex role, echoing many of the earlier critics of the workplace and family life that had attended the rise of Self-Made Manhood. For the first time in American history, outside of those small groups of Greenwich Village bohemians earlier in the century, men themselves were refusing to live up to the prescribed package of behaviors and traits that defined American manhood. They did not run off to the West, seeking to reclaim their manhood in the wilds of nature, nor did they escape into masculinist fantasies of adventure and heroic struggle. And they didn't seek to reclaim their manhood by the further exclusion of women, men of color, and gay men. (Some men's liberationists actually saw those movements as inspirational.) The very notion of Self-Made Masculinity was under siege—and from the very men who were supposed to live up to its ideals.

In the introduction to *The Forty-Nine Percent Majority*, the psychologist Robert Brannon brilliantly reduced the male sex role into four basic rules of manhood. The first and perhaps most important rule is "No Sissy Stuff": One can never do anything that even remotely hints of the feminine. The second rule, "Be a Big Wheel," indicates that masculinity is measured by power, wealth, success. The third rule reminds men to "Be a Sturdy Oak," since real men show no emotions, are emotionally reliable by being emotionally inexpressive. And finally, "Give 'em Hell" meant to exude an aura of manly daring and aggression. Always take risks, go for it. These four rules sum up the masculine predicament, and men "have been limited and diverted from whatever our real potential might have been by the prefabricated mold of the male sex role."[47]

How were men to free themselves from the prison of the male sex role? For one thing, men's liberationists wanted out of the corporate rat race, a "bland and boring" arena with little opportunity for self-expression or self-fulfillment. Being a big wheel was unsatisfying and deadening to real human experience. Work was "fraught with dehumanizing—i.e. unmanning—influences," wrote British critic Myron Brenton. As one thirty-six-year-old civil engineer told him, "I just don't get it. I've got everything. I really have. All the same, now and then, I get the feeling I'm in a prison or something. Happens when everything's on top of me, closing in, you know?" The rugged individualism of the Heroic Artisan was gone, as men sat "in lushly carpeted offices where the faint crackling of typewriters can barely be heard above Muzak," added Jack Nichols. As one corporate manager put it, "Every so often I feel like making it all disappear—start fresh. Hey, man, wouldn't you like to have been a pioneer?" one corporate manager confessed, while another added that he wanted to "chuck it all and take a raft down the Amazon!" In the absence of any sense of adventure, accomplishment, or fulfillment, men turn to accumulation of wealth. But as psychiatrist Robert Gould warned in a 1973 essay in *Ms.*, "Measuring Masculinity by the Size of a Paycheck," money was a "pretty insecure peg on which to hang a masculine image."[48]

Blue-collar workers suffered an even more dismally emasculating fate. One study found these men playing out "dramas of manliness in work settings" in everything they did—except their work. They wrote off white-collar workers as "desk jockeys" and "pencil pushers," who had sold out their manhood for the "dubious merits of a white shirt and a higher social status," while their reveling in off-color jokes, pornography, obscenities, and "adopting a stance of indifference as a form of self-protection" became demonstrations of working-class manliness. Men's liberationists rejected competition, aggression, and alienation and claimed that by changing men's roles, men's work would be an expression of their selves, not the repudiation of their humanity.[49]

At home, men's liberationists argued that men were equally disconnected and despairing. Being a sturdy oak meant denying or suppressing emotion and spontaneity. A "man isn't someone you'd want to have around in a crisis—like raising children or growing old together," wrote actor Alan Alda as he signed up for men's liberation. And male sexuality operated on the performance principle, not the pleasure principle; men turned sex into work, experiencing "performance anxiety" while they worked to "get the job done." Sex was a "dangerous encounter," the ultimate test of masculinity; our sex-role conditioning had destroyed "the potential for joyful, authentic, spontaneous, sexual responsiveness," according to Marc Feigen Fasteau. The male sex role reduces fatherhood to a "financial functionary" to children, forcing men to be not only absentee landlords in their homes but also absentee fathers with their children.[50]

If the traditional role models were unsatisfying, men needed to find new models for manhood. Theologians Thomas Hearn and Leonard Swidler returned to Jesus as masculine archetype but, this time, with exactly the opposite intentions of the Muscular Christians nearly a century earlier. To Swidler, Jesus was a "feminist," while to Hearn he was a "sissy" who

> was given to feeling and expressing a wide range of the "tender" emotions; he wept without shame; he freely touched other men and even—I tremble to say it—*kissed* them. He was intuitive; he strongly sensed dependency on the human community as well as on the Father. He responded to beauty; he was touched with compassionate tenderness at the sight of suffering. He loved little children, and with kindred affection he regarded the birds of the air and the lilies of the field.[51]

Others proposed a desexualized androgyny by which women could get in touch with their "masculine sides" and men their "feminine sides" and thus both become whole people. A few suggested that gay men had already achieved such contact with their feminine sides, which explained what they took to be gay men's relative ease with intimacy, sensitivity, and emotion. Perhaps homosexual manhood could be a model for heterosexual men, who were, they suggested, still stifled by homophobic fears of expressing emotion or the need for physical contact with other men.

What virtually all men's liberationists promised was that by rejecting traditional masculinity, men would live longer, happier, and healthier lives, lives characterized by close and caring relationships with children, with women, and with other men. Where they differed was over feminism. Some men's libbers, like Herb Goldberg, saw feminism as "unbalanced, unfair and psychologically invalid." Dismissing feminist leader Gloria Steinem, for example, Goldberg wrote that she concocted "a mixture of facts, half-truths, hyperbole, sweeping generalizations, and the fiery adjectives of an old-time preacher or charismatic crowd manipulator" in order to "castigate, in wholesale fashion, the *entire* male sex." Another feminist, he wrote, who "reacts with rage and fury at men for their alleged abuses" only "reveals her lack of perspective and empathy" for the ways in which—and this is a key insight for many men's libbers—"*men* have been trapped."[52]

Others saw feminism as providing half the answer: Just as women had to liberate themselves from their sex role, so too did men have to liberate themselves from their oppressive sex role. Warren Farrell, a self-proclaimed "liberated man" and convener of the National Organization for Women's Task Force on the Masculine Mystique, was masterful in providing role reversals that revealed to men what had been women's experience as sex objects. At the consciousness-raising groups he initiated, he organized male beauty contests to give men a sense of how traditional masculinity was experienced by those against whom it was deployed. Farrell believed that men could actually benefit from women's liberation; individually a man could be freed of the work pressure to be a woman's "security object" and thus be free to pursue his personal life with less stress and anxiety.[53]

But for some the personal was not merely psychological, and it did not involve the false equivalences between women's and men's experiences. The personal was political, and by confronting and challenging traditional masculinity, they believed they were simultaneously striking a blow for the liberation of women, black people, and gays and lesbians. Marc Feigen Fasteau believed that feminism implied both "women's and men's liberation," and Glenn Bucher's *Straight/White/Male* (1976) used gay liberation and black liberation as the starting points for a critique of traditional masculinity. According to Bucher and his colleagues, straight white men are dehumanized, but they are not oppressed; they are, rather, oppressors, and they must "restructure their identities and reroot themselves in a way of life that is not dependent upon the benefits of the status quo."[54]

Psychologist Joseph Pleck's work provided perhaps the most significant and sustained scholarly effort to expose the male sex role as a fraud. In his more polemical essays, "My Male Sex Role—and Ours" (1974) and "Men's Power with Women, Other Men, and Society" (1977), Pleck placed the psychological experience of men within a larger context of social and political oppression. In a style far more honestly self-revelatory than many of the other writers and with nary a hint of self-congratulation, Pleck argued that patriarchy has been a dual system of oppression, a system by which men have oppressed women and in which some men have oppressed other men, so that "to be a man with other men means to always fear being attacked, victimized, exploited, and in an ultimate sense, murdered by other men."[55]

Pleck's 1981 scholarly treatise *The Myth of Masculinity* provided the culmination of men's liberation theory as academic social psychology, challenging the basic explanation of gender development that academic psychology had been advancing since the mid-1930s. Rather than begin with the anxieties, stress, and pressures that men feel and from which therefore they need liberation, Pleck begins with a dissection of the male sex role itself. What he calls the Male Sex Role Identity (MSRI) model is itself the problem; the MSRI model creates role demands that are so internally contradictory that no one could possibly live up to them. Trying to fulfill the role demands is the real source of stress in men's lives. For example, remaining cool under pressure on the one hand and giving 'em hell on the other hand pull men in opposing directions. Pleck argued that the MSRI was a testable hypothesis, not an established scientific fact; for that matter, he argued, the correlation between the prescribed behaviors and the feelings of secure manhood was actually very weak empirically. Even those men who conformed to the stereotypic definition didn't seem any more confident in themselves as real men. "How people continue to believe so fervently in values and norms according to which they can only be failures is an awe-inspiring phenomenon," he wrote.[56]

Instead of the MSRI, Pleck posited a model of Male Sex-Role Strain, which placed tension, contradiction, and anxiety squarely in the center of men's efforts to demonstrate manhood. Psychology was thus not going to be the liberator of men but was instead cast as the conduit for those very contradictory and confusing messages that kept us all in constant turmoil. It wasn't men as much as it was the prescription for masculinity that caused the crisis of masculinity and contributed to the oppression of women and minorities.

Men's liberation drew some modest curiosity from cultural observers, some tentative and wary alliances with some feminist women, and a large amount of indifference from the majority of American men. But there were telling signs in popular culture that the times were changing. Traditional genres continued, but they were more popular when they offered twists on their own standard formulae. With hindsight we now see how these traditional genres were beginning to break down.

Take, for example, the grizzled tough-guy detective of classic film noir. *Marlowe* (1969), a resetting of Raymond Chandler's detective novel *The Little Sister* into hippie, drug-infested Los Angeles, uses the ironic sneer of James Garner to express the inability of the old genre to sustain men's hopes. Marlowe, a smoking, hard-drinking private detective, is enlisted to help a naive, innocent Kansas girl who is searching for her lost brother. During the course of the film, he suckers an Asian kung fu fighter (played by Bruce Lee), who had earlier trashed his office, into jumping to his death by calling him "just a little bit gay," thus simultaneously linking Asian immigrants and homosexuality and disposing of them both as threats to his manhood. Of course, it turns out that the naive little sister is also hopelessly corrupt, demonstrating once again that any faith in women—or even men's role as their protector—is faith misplaced and earnest effort manipulated.

The classic buddy film also tended to end in tragedy in the late 1960s and 1970s; what's more, the settings for these films became increasingly ironic in films like *Easy Rider* or *Midnight Cowboy*, both released in 1969. The male bonding celebrated in these films is a defensive reaction to traditional masculine failure; the men turn to each other because the world (and women) have failed them. In *Easy Rider* frontier escapism becomes a tamed delinquency, complete with an unsettling hallucinogenic drug experience; but the macho defiance is ultimately tragic, even as its misogynist core goes unchallenged. In *Midnight Cowboy* a de-eroticized homosexuality—an emotional, but not sexual connection—occurs in a highly ironic context: the failure of Joe Buck to establish himself as a stud. Instead, Joe finds love and success as a male mother, nursing the tubercular Ratso to his peaceful death.

Carnal Knowledge (1972) and *Deliverance* (1973) also recapitulated the buddy film, again with the bitter theme that masculine failure solidifies friendship. The bonding between Sandy (Art Garfunkel) and Jonathan (Jack Nicholson) is animated in "the mutuality of sharing and recounting sexual experiences," writes film critic Joan Mellers. In their characters the viewers got a sense of masculinity in transition. On the one hand, Sandy represents an effort, ultimately unsuccessful, to articulate a different, emotionally-based way of relating to women. By contrast, Nicholson's portrayal of Jonathan unflinchingly exposes the negative aspects of conventional success-oriented masculinity: He is unable to move beyond the "objectification-fixation-conquest" described by men's liberationists. This model proves so devastating that it becomes sexually deflating; Jonathan is impotent.[57]

Deliverance provided one of the era's signal films about both the dangers and redemptive possibilities of male bonding. Both novel and film begin as conventionally masculinist voyages of discovery for Ed as he floats down the river with the darker, more earthily primal Lewis, his spirit guide in the masculine quest:

> Why on earth am I here? I thought. But then I turned back to the car to see what Lewis was doing, I caught a glimpse of myself in the rear window. I was light green, a tall forest man, an explorer, guerilla, hunter. I liked the idea and the image, I must say. Even if this was just a game, a charade, I had let myself in for it, and I was here in the woods, where such people as I had got myself up were supposed to be. Something or other was being made good. I touched the knife hilt at my side, and remembered that all men were once boys, and that boys are always looking for ways to become men. Some of the ways are easy too; all you have to do is be satisfied that it has happened.[58]

And the book underlines that such camaraderie is only possible outside any sexual relationship between men, that such a relationship may undermine friendship. *Deliverance* simultaneously eroticizes and glamorizes the friendship among the men while it de-eroticizes the sexual scenes of homosexual rape. In a sense, the film graphically provided one of the cinema's first clearly articulated feminist understandings that rape is a crime of power and violence and not a crime of sexual desire—although the rape had to happen to a man for men to understand this. What *Deliverance* expresses is a cautionary tale: The male desire for escape from women is fraught with danger—danger from other men who are not so civilized that they can repress their desires and from a nature whose wildness is actually a threat to men's effort to prove themselves. In short, watch out, men: When you escape from the civilizing constraints of women, you will rape and murder each other.[59]

If men were made uneasy by these buddy films, though, and if the rise of the gay liberation movement seemed to put all male friendships under a new homophobic scrutiny, then they could always take refuge in the novels of Norman Mailer, who reassured his readers in *Why Are We in Vietnam?* (1967) to:

> fear not, gentle auditor, they is men, real Texas men, they don't ding ding ring a ling on no queer street with each other, shit, no, they just talk to each other that way to express Texas tenderness than which there is nothing more tender than a flattened pan-fried breaded paper-thin hard-ass Texas steak.[60]

When historian and playwright Martin Duberman, in his 1977 play *Visions of Kerouac*, dared to suggest any erotic possibilities in the male bonding between Dean Moriarty and Neil Cassady in Jack Kerouac's Beat novels, he was vilified by several critics as if he'd tainted one of the most redemptive, purest of masculine archetypes, buddy bonding on the road.

Three other films, all from 1971, offer eerily negative portraits of contemporary manhood. In *Straw Dogs* Dustin Hoffman plays an effete intellectual who with his wife rents a house in the English countryside. She holds him in contempt as unmanly. Later, she is raped by working-class thugs who doubt his ability to fight back. Yet when he finally does fight back, unaware of her rape, we know his manhood is not redeemed. In *Shaft*, a prototypical blaxploitation film of the era, Richard Roundtree plays a private detective

—"a private dick that's a sex machine with all the chicks," as the theme song had it—
who is always one step ahead of the rather nerdy white police officers on the case. Little
wonder, in those sexually unrepressed 1970s, that black hypersexuality should have been
so crassly depicted and equally dehumanized. And in *Play It Again Sam*, Woody Allen
presents us with the first in a series of films about the revenge of the nerds, as yet another
bespectacled wimp confesses that "most men are secretly tortured by not being Bogart."
So Bogart returns as fantasy construction and imparts a series of lessons in manhood for
Allen-as-nebbish-Everyman to follow. Men needed to reclaim their manhood; all they
needed was the right role model.

By the end of the 1970s, positive role models were increasingly hard to find. The end
of the decade revealed the impotence of the stalwart friend in *The Deer Hunter* (1978); the
saga of the Self-Made Man was retold as tragedy as in Geoffrey Wolff's *The Duke of
Deception* (1979). Wolff's father was literally "the author of his own circumstances," able
to "disassemble his history, begin at zero, and re-create himself"—but only because he
completely fabricated his autobiography to suit his circumstances. The Self-Made Man
turned out to be a con artist. Male bonding was equally bereft of meaning in Leonard
Michaels's *The Men's Club* (1978), in which a group of upper middle-class professionals
in Berkeley, California, imitate their wives' consciousness-raising group, only to find
themselves more lost than before.[61]

On television the domestic patriarch of the 1950s and early 1960s had virtually
disappeared, replaced by a working-class blowhard, Archie Bunker, or a bossy ignoramus,
Mel, on *Alice*, behind whose back the waitresses rolled their eyes at his foolishness. On
sitcoms like *Three's Company, Benson*, and *Night Court*, middle-class masculinity had
become the butt of humor, not the object of veneration.

Star Trek revealed, perhaps more clearly, if unintentionally, than any other TV show,
the growing crisis of masculinity. Here manhood was divided into two halves—the
rational, abstract, and emotionally invulnerable alien, embodied in Mr. Spock, and the
aggressive, erotic, and intuitive traditional version of manhood, expressed by Captain
Kirk. Here again was that most American of literary themes: cross-race (in this case cross-
species) male bonding, although this time the white and nonwhite men were depicted as
coequal. Neither was complete, and therefore neither could serve as a role model for the
future. Full manhood could not even be reclaimed in space, the "final frontier."

One modestly hopeful sign was the emergence of a new vision of fatherhood,
signaled, in part, by Dustin Hoffman's Academy Award–winning portrayal of Ted Kramer
in *Kramer vs. Kramer* (1979). Masculine redemption for a failed marriage and a blind-
alley career is found, as in the 1950s, in fatherhood, but this time with an ironic slap at
feminism. We were invited to cheer when his ex-wife (Meryl Streep) finally decides to
renounce her efforts to gain custody, since we have just witnessed the emergence of the
sensitive new father from the chrysalis of an indifferent careerist. If put to the test, men
turn out to actually be better "mothers" than women.

An old theme, perhaps, but it still didn't work. Masculinity could not be reclaimed in
an arena so feminized. Nor could it be retrieved in outer space aboard the *Enterprise*. The
main theme of men's liberation—that changing men's *roles* would somehow magically
transform the enormous economic and social structures that held those roles in place—
revealed a theoretical naïveté that would easily sour into the whine of a new voice of vic-
timhood. Men were still searching, but they still hadn't found what they were looking for.

The Unmaking of the Self-Made Man: In the first decades of the twentieth century, former Heroic Artisans found themselves increasingly proletarianized, mere appendages to the machine. The world of work was increasingly competitive and crowded. *Top*: Charlie Chaplin as dispossessed worker in *Modern Times* (1936). *Bottom*: Police exam, New York City, 1931. (Photo courtesy of Bettman Archives)

Restoring Masculinity by Remaking the Body: Turn-of-the-century America went "sports crazy," as thousands of men sought to combat the enervating effects of their urban white-collar working lives with manly physiques, health regimens, and participation in sports. Muscular development revealed a Self-Made Man. The first professional bodybuilder, Eugen Sandow, used his sculpted body to become one of the world's most famous and wealthy men. Bernarr Macfadden promoted it all in his magazine *Physical Culture*, from muscle building, to clean living and healthy diet, to a "peniscope," a vacuum pump designed to enlarge the male organ. *Right*: Eugen Sandow. *Bottom*: Bernarr Macfadden. (Frontispiece from *The Virile Powers of Superb Manhood* by Bernarr Macfadden [New York: Physical Culture Publishing Company, 1900])

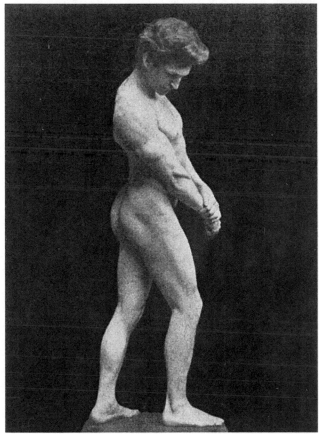

Restoring Twentieth-Century Manhood: Depicting a rogue, conniver, and self-interested scoundrel, Rhett Butler revived southern manhood, in contrast to Leslie Howard's aristocratic cavalier, who was now gone with the wind. In the 1950s, the self-made man returned as a bit of an aristocratic dandy in the image of the Playboy. With his smoking jacket, Danish modern furniture, and cigarette holder, the Playboy was neither a sexualized scamp nor working class hero, as the frontispiece illustration for the first issue of the magazine suggests. His idea was to invite a woman over to his well-appointed apartment for "a quiet discussion on Picasso, Nietzsche, jazz, and sex." *Top*: Studio still from *Gone With the Wind*, 1939. *Bottom*: Frontispiece, *Playboy*, December 1953; reprinted with permission of *Playboy* magazine.

Television Restores Domestic Patriarchy: As "family entertainment," watched in the "family room," early television shows reestablished the centrality of the father in the family, even as suburban men's working lives were increasingly distant from the home. That father was reinserted as the family's center of gravity held true whether they lived in a suburban development or in the jungle. *Top*: *Father Knows Best* replaces mom with dad. (Publicity photograph) *Bottom*: Tarzan and Jane recreate the nuclear family. (Publicity photograph)

Muscles Continue to Make the Man: Physical strength, once of significance in the real world, maintains profound symbolic importance in the making of Self-Made Men. Charles Atlas made a fortune promising to transform 97-pound weaklings into he-men, as have scores of his heirs to the muscle-building industry. At the Academy Awards presentation in 1992, Jack Palance showed that, despite his age, he was still man enough. *Right*: Charles Atlas advertisement. *Bottom*: Jack Palance does a set of one-armed push-ups after his acceptance speech for Best Supporting Actor at the Academy Awards presentation, 1992. (Courtesy of Reuters/Bettman)

Expanding the Definition of Contemporary Manhood: The contemporary era has witnessed a constant challenge to a definition of masculinity based on exclusion of the "other"—women, gay men, black men, ethnic immigrants. And some men have challenged the behavioral restrictions that label men as "sissy." *Top*: Civil rights workers proclaim their manhood, Memphis, 29 March 1968. (Courtesy of UPl/Bettman Newsphotos). *Bottom*: Bruce Springsteen and Clarence Clemons, 1990. (Photo by Ebet Roberts; reprinted with permission)

Boys and their Toys.
Contemporary self-making often requires dramatic re-invention. *Left:* A shy Midwesterner, Marion Michael Morrison, transformed himself into John Wayne, the most readily identifiable masculine icon of the decades following World War II. (Publicity photograph) *Bottom:* And President George W. Bush, son and grandson of aristocratic New England bluebloods, who prepped at Andover, graduated from Yale and Harvard, and "summered" in Kennebunkport, Maine, transformed himself into a "self-made" Texas businessman, a down-to-earth man of the people. The image of a back-country Heroic Artisan contrasts with his wife's description of him as a "windshield cowboy," meaning that he experiences the great western outdoors in his pickup truck, not riding the range. Neither he nor Wayne apparently liked horses very much. (Brooks Kraft/ Corbis)

Self-Making as Lifelong Project.
A small shy Austrian boy, Arnold Schwarzenegger followed the time-honored path of transforming his body in order to construct a masculine persona. *Left:* Having conquered the world of competitive body-building, he conquered Hollywood as a hypermasculine hero, whether as a primitive "barbarian" throwback, here as Conan the Barbarian, or as a futuristic muscle-bound cyborg in the "Terminator" series. (Dirck Halstead/Time Life Pictures/Getty Images) *Bottom:* Transformed again into a politician, Schwarzenegger was elected Governor of California, as someone who would be tough and firm. Once lampooned on *Saturday Night Live* as a muscle-brained oaf who disdained metrosexual "girly-men," Schwarzenegger, now as "Governator," appropriated the line and chastised his opponents in the same way. (David Paul Morris/Getty Images)

CHAPTER 9

Wimps, Whiners, and Weekend Warriors

The Contemporary Crisis of Masculinity and Beyond

> The male of the past twenty years has become more thoughtful, more gentle. But by this process he has not become more free. He's a nice boy who pleases not only his mother but also the young woman he is living with.
> —Robert Bly *Iron John* (1990)

Ronald Reagan's presidency heralded "morning in America." Perhaps now American men would awaken to a new, recharged manhood for a new, ambitious, and aggressive era. We've often thought of the 1980s as a decade of the reassertion of pride, the retrieval of political and metaphoric potency for America and, hence, for the American man. In a replay of the frontier cowboy myth, America was once again sitting tall in the saddle, willing to take on all comers, asserting its dominance in world affairs. "Americans are now standing tall and firm," Reagan commented after the invasion of Grenada; columnists praised him for "stiffening our foreign policy"—as if this masculine country had been suffering from a nationwide bout with impotence. Symbolically, we even returned to Vietnam in our movies, answering John Rambo's plaintive question about his own return, "Do we get to win this time?" Wall Street was imagined as a Social Darwinist corporate jungle in which only the fittest could survive the frenzy of mergers and acquisitions.

But the manhood regained under Presidents Reagan and Bush was the compulsive masculinity of the schoolyard bully, defeating weaker foes such as Grenada and Panama, a defensive and restive manhood, of men who needed to demonstrate their masculinity at every opportunity. Men who feel powerful in their lives do not need to wear "power ties" or eat "power breakfasts" or "power lunches" as did yuppie arbitrageurs in the 1980s. Power is not something to be applied like a fashion accessory; it is both an inner confidence and security, as well as referring to a real hierarchical position. This kind of power American men still did not feel.

By some evidence American men were more confused in the 1980s than ever before. Who were their role models? John Wayne, who had dominated surveys of the American men whom we most admired for over thirty years, was now absent from the list (and not merely because he had died). So were many politicians. Watergate and media revelations about other public figures so tarnished political life that our heroes would have to be drawn from elsewhere. Despite the writer Mark Gerzon's suggestion that in the 1980s we now could have *A Choice of Heroes* (1982), we had, in fact, a dearth of heroes.[1]

So instead, we sought out negative models to attack. The wimp, for example, emerged in the early 1980s. A virtual Great American Wimp Hunt repudiated the "new man" of the 1970s. Magazine articles and films had predicted that this new man—warm, sensitive, cuddly, and compassionate—would be the new hero of the 1980s. Betty Friedan, for one, was smitten; in a foreword to a new 1983 edition of *The Feminine Mystique*, she embraced Dustin Hoffman's *Tootsie* as the new man, whose experience masquerading as a woman "makes him a much better, stronger, more tender man." To Friedan this meant that America had "now clearly broken through and beyond the *masculine mystique* for man and woman to find such joyous adventure in being a woman." Not quite. As delightfully and playfully androgynous as they were, Hoffman's two new man films also had a darker side, implying that men could be not only better mothers than women (*Kramer vs. Kramer*) but also better *women* than women (*Tootsie*). The new man still emerged at the expense of women; he was not new enough for a truly egalitarian relationship with an equally strong woman.

But there he was anyway, the "sensitive New Age guy," poised as a masculine template for the decade, despite his receding hairline, flabby biceps, and enlarging waistline. In the film *Three Men and a Baby*, three swinging single men interrupt their routine sexual conquests to become surrogate "mothers" after a former lover drops off one's progeny—and they accomplish this feat without the slightest loss of a drop of androgen-laced manhood. In fact, they turn out to be even *more* attractive to women. Didn't Broadway Joe Namath model panty hose? And didn't Senator Paul Tsongas decide to resign from the Senate because, as he said, "[n]o man on his deathbed ever lamented that he spent too much time with his family"?[2]

Or what about John Lennon, ex-Beatle, pop superstar, Nixon "enemy." Lennon, who had earlier penned "Woman Is the Nigger of the World," one of the most feminist-inspired rock songs this side of Helen Reddy's "I Am Woman," opted out of pop superstardom to experience the simple joys of fatherhood and domestic bliss. "Isn't it time we destroyed the macho ethic?" he commented in an interview in 1980:

> Where has it gotten us all these thousands of years? Are we still going to have to be clubbing each other to death? Do I have to arm wrestle you to have a relationship with you as another male? Do I have to seduce her—just because she's a female? Can we not have a relationship on some other level?

Lennon concluded by confessing that he didn't "want to go through life pretending to be James Dean or Marlon Brando."[3]

But very few Americans bought the new man package. Alan Alda, Phil Donahue, Bob Newhart, and others could not fill the chasm left by cinematic machismo and political opportunism, despite the new man's vaunted decency, sensitivity, and liberal values.[4] Or, perhaps, because of them—as the new man was immediately on the defensive, afraid of being perceived as a sissy, a wimp. "Real men" hated wimps because they were so obeisant, as devoted as simpering puppies and just about as sexually compelling. The novelist George Stade, writing in the *New York Times Book Review* in 1984, bemoaned the current wimpiness of fictional male characters and lambasted novelists like Philip Roth, John Updike, and Leonard Michaels. "Their protagonists no longer venture forth; they retreat, admit defeat, take the heat, all with a sheepish grin," he brooded; they all have regressed "to the preadolescent condition of mama's boys, alternately bratty and eager to please." He yearned for a revival of manly literature, of sagas in which young boys sally forth to find and prove their manhood against the odds.[5]

Some women rejected the wimp as well. Wimps weren't interested in sharing power or equality, some women complained; they simply wanted to abdicate breadwinning responsibility. Equality, whether sexual or political, did not mean male passivity. A wimp lacks "a sense of purpose," including a sense of sexual purpose, one woman told an inquiring journalist. If a wimp were ever to sweep a woman off her feet, he'd probably help her up and make sure she was unhurt. "I appreciate a man wanting to please and all that," commented another woman, but wimps seemed to take it too far. "There's a lot of plaintive 'what do you like?' and 'what should I do?'" Far less common was a man with a "certain agenda," someone with "a sense of 'I like this and I know you're going to like it too.'" Some women openly regretted their demands that men become more emotionally expressive; it turned out they didn't like what the men wanted to express.[6]

Other women were a bit more sanguine. Film critic Janet Maslin, for example, found that the cinematic works of the wimp were "sweet"—a "celebration of the very sappiest good deeds and good intentions." In films such as 1988's Robert Redford's *Milagro Beanfield War*, Alan Alda's *A New Life*, and *Dominick and Eugene*, Maslin sensed something virtuous, even cinematically significant. Even in *A New Life*, Alda—"the pure embodiment of cloying, life-affirming hokum . . . the fullest flowering of wimp-mindedness"—had provided a film with "secret charms," which could provide pleasures even if one could barely admit to liking these films in mixed company.[7]

Some prominent men confessed their wimpiness—with a mea culpa of guilt-ridden angst that merely proved their critics' point. Television producer Mark Goodson confessed how his lifelong distaste for sports brought him humiliation and the terror of being found out that he was not a real man. Others were proud to be wimps. Novelist Paul Theroux called traditional manhood "pitiful, a little like having to wear an ill-fitting coat for one's entire life." The quest for manliness, he concluded, is "essentially right-wing, puritanical, cowardly, neurotic and fueled largely by a fear of women." Noel Perrin proclaimed himself an "androgynous man" and described his triumph over his dread of doing household repairs through using a manual called *Home Repairs Any Woman Can Do*. And the novelist Thomas Flanagan suggested that the "ways of the wimp" were the paths of integrity and virtue, not the marks of shame. After all, Flanagan argued, Hamlet is "literature's supreme example of the wimp"—he's "hesitant, indecisive, oppressed by an awareness of alternative possibilities . . . displays an unmanly love of language . . . [which is] sarcastic, sardonic, playful." And when Hamlet acted, he was decisive, littering Denmark with corpses, not least of them his own.[8]

But if all these men were wimps, who were the real men, the genuine articles? One index of the confusion engendered by this question was the popular reaction to a satiric little volume, *Real Men Don't Eat Quiche* (1982). Here, Bruce Feirstein jokingly enumerated the method in the madness of proving masculinity. All a man had to do in order to definitively demonstrate his masculinity was to follow the prescriptions of Flex

Crush, a 225-pound truck driver, who, between hauling loads of nuclear waste, paused to define the meaning of manhood. And as Terman and Miles wrote in 1936, everything a man did, said, touched, ate, wore, thought, or felt played a role in the definition. It was a joke, but a joke that resonated. Here's a guy whose breakfast consists of "steak, prime rib, six eggs and a loaf of toast," wolfed down with side orders of flapjacks, a pound of bacon, and a pound of roofing nails, all the while "idly cleaning his 12-gauge shotgun." Feirstein mocks masculinity as much as he mocks quiche-eating wimps. The real man's revenge is as much a send-up of Rambo as it is of Donahue.[9]

The 1984 presidential election again brought the fear of the wimp into the center of the political arena. Bumper stickers like "Mondale Eats Quiche" appeared on cars, and Republican Jeane Kirkpatrick accused the Democratic Party of being in the thrall of "San Francisco Democrats," a not-so-subtle reference to that city's substantial gay population. Although Mondale asked "Where's the beef?" voters believed he didn't have the meaty temerity to take the helm. In the *New Republic* "TRB" summed up the Reagan presidency as a massive injection of anabolic steroids, making us "economically and militarily virile." Unfortunately, "steroids, like sedatives, have side-effects, and already our national testicles are starting to shrink."

Then–Vice President George Bush's comment after his 1984 televised debate with Democratic candidate Geraldine Ferraro that he "kicked a little ass last night" was more than a good ol' boy cliché; it revealed Bush's fear of being seen as a wimp, a fear that haunted him throughout his own campaign. If Reagan represented the triumph of the new-moneyed, gas-guzzling, right-wing cowboys, Bush offered a return to the "kinder and gentler" policies of traditionally aristocratic noblesse oblige. But the "manhood thing" kept getting in the way.

Americans have believed since Andrew Jackson's time that blue-blooded aristocrats —the Genteel Patriarchs—were indolent wimps, incapable of manly resolve. This notion, what the media dubbed "the wimp factor," plagued Bush's presidential ambitions. His state of residence was an ill-defined, ever-shifting combination of dowdy and aristocratic Kennebunkport, Maine, where well-bred Yalies like Bush had traditionally "summered," with brashly swaggering Texas—Houston, no less—home of the most venturesome of venture capitalists. He worked ceaselessly to offset upper-crust mannerisms, to stage photo opportunities to counter the public image that he was a "listless, indecisive man" who lacked "the drive to turn things around," as an editorial in the British *Economist* put it.[10] Turning a widely viewed television interview with newscaster Dan Rather into a rhetorical shoving match also seemed designed to bolster his manliness quotient. But asking for "just a splash" of coffee at a trucker's diner on a campaign swing proved equally emasculating.

Fortunately for him, he had some help in seizing the more-manly-than-thou mantle. Short, nerdy Democratic candidate Michael Dukakis looked even more ridiculous riding around in a tank, complete with headgear, than Bush did in his hunting or fishing gear. One journalist found Dukakis's handshake "sort of wimpy," while another claimed that his predilection for dining at home with his family every evening while governor indicated that he was "Kitty whipped." Other pundits speculated about the candidates' food preferences—Bush's real-man pork rinds compared with Dukakis's fey fondness for coffee ice cream—and when Bush publicly banished broccoli from the White House menu, one got the feeling that Bush had to become the most powerful man in the world in order to get his way with a vegetable that, as a little boy, he had found yucky. Huck Finn triumphed over Aunt Sally after all.

Bush's years in office continued this preoccupation with demonstrating manhood. Immediately after his election journalists began to champion Bush as a "fighter, not a wimp"; "[t]he new George Bush looks rugged, even macho, standing chest deep in the Florida surf," noted *Newsweek*. "Something startling has happened to the man who was once marked as Ronald Reagan's lap dog. . . . George Bush walked into the polling booth as Clark Kent and emerged as the Beltway equivalent of Superman." Hyperbolic, yes— but also deliberate, calculated, and decisive. After the invasion of Panama, in which American forces deposed that nation's "strongman," Manuel Noriega, Bush celebrated that no one could call him "timid," that he was at last a "macho man." The press chimed in, hailing his "initiation rite," a demonstration of his "willingness to shed blood."[11]

The 1992 elections provided another dimension to Americans' fears of being seen as wimps. That year, though, it was something about tasseled loafers, as H. Ross Perot prohibited his male assistants from wearing them and Bush accused Bill Clinton of being in the pockets of "that tassel-loafered lawyer crowd." The Bush campaign focused on Clinton's indecisiveness as indicating insufficient manhood. "Clinton reminds you of Woody Allen," commented Bush press secretary Torie Clarke, "sitting there giving you fourteen different explanations of why he did something and what caused him to do something and how that affects what he's doing today."

But the effort to outmuscle, outmacho one's opponent failed for one of the few times in American history. In 1992, the nation elected a man closer to the median age rather than someone old enough to be the national father, a candidate whose warm camaraderie with his contemporaneous running mate gave friendship a political valence, and a husband whose partnership-marriage with a career-oriented, savvy lawyer withstood publicly expressed difficulties, marital therapy, and antifeminist critics who had already castigated her as a ball-busting bitch. Bill and Hillary Rodham Clinton thus became the first two-career couple to ever occupy the White House; in Bill Clinton we seemed to have elected our first new man as president.

The honeymoon didn't last long. Pundits quickly heckled Bill as the henpecked husband hiding behind his connivingly careerist wife's business suit. Clinton's "character problem"—his indecisiveness, his apparent infidelities as a husband, and the venomous opposition his liberal "softness" evoked—haunted him throughout his administration, and the erosion of support for his policies helped to make the crop of right-wing Republican leaders appear leaner and meaner than ever.

These competing images indicated just how confused we had become as men. Magazine articles and self-help books vied for men's attention, prescribing a wide variety of antidotes for gender troubles. Many offered quick-fix solutions, continuing to bait us with the fear of the wimp and then sending us right back into the fray. Indiana University basketball coach Bobby Knight, for example, put sanitary napkins in the lockers of his players to shame them as wusses and make them play more aggressively. (This is the same coach who, when asked by a television reporter how he handled stress, responded, "I think if rape is inevitable, relax and enjoy it.") Others sought to reclaim the proving ground from interlopers—like blacks, gays, and women. Many men sought to retrieve a lost manhood on a weekend retreat off in the woods where men beat drums and chant, initiate one another, and reclaim their "wild man" or "inner warrior." A few sought to overturn the traditional definitions of masculinity altogether, seeing in feminism or in gay liberation the possibilities of a new definition of manhood, a manhood based on compassion, trust, and nurturance.

If nothing else, though, the playing field had changed. The structural foundations of traditional manhood—economic independence, geographic mobility, domestic dominance—have all eroding. The transformation of the workplace—the decline of the skilled worker, global corporate relocations, the malaise of the middle-class manager, the entry of women into the assembly line and the corporate office—pressed men to confront their continued reliance on the marketplace as the way to demonstrate and prove their manhood. For some men the gender integration of the workplace made success a hollow victory anyway. What's more, global economic trends augured poorly for younger men's ability to demonstrate manhood in traditional ways. Downward mobility was more common than upward mobility for Americans in their twenties. Most Americans born in the suburbs in the 1950s and 1960s never earned enough to afford to buy the houses they grew up in.[12] It now took two incomes to provide the same standard of living that one income provided less than two generations ago. This generation would be the first in U.S. history that would leave its children poorer than itself. And despite the national exhilaration during the war in the Persian Gulf, the soldier represented a somewhat tarnished image of manhood, not just because of Vietnam—since those veterans have been partially rehabilitated as pawns in other men's games, pawns whose survival indicates a kind of everyday heroism—but also because of the Tailhook incident and debates about gays in the military or about women entering all-male military colleges.

American men felt themselves beleaguered and besieged, working harder and harder for fewer and fewer personal and social rewards. Women not only entered the workplace but demanded entry into men's social clubs. There were even women Boy Scout troop leaders and scoutmasters. The criminalization of sexual harassment and date rape left some men angry and frightened of demonstrating manhood through sexual conquest. Many men said they experience a "fear of flirting," lest it be misunderstood and provide the possibility of allegations against them.[13] AIDS compounded the fears of disease with a demand for responsibility (i.e., wearing condoms). And men were tired. Epstein-Barr syndrome, the "Yuppie flu," is a mysterious enervating ailment that leaves its victims listless and tired—a 1990s version of neurasthenia. What was a man to do?

Save the Males

If you ask a small but vocal group of men, we needed to return to the basics, revive the traditional version of Self-Made Manhood. The "old man," as opposed to the new man, was still around, not exactly enjoying a renaissance but far from slipping quietly into oblivion. The Reaganite retrieval of cowboy masculinity encouraged this crowd, even if the momentary reassertion of imperial dominance had more to do with the collapse of the opposing "evil empire" than it did with American virility and the feeding frenzy of corporate raiders, gobbling up smaller firms, and produced a few extremely fat cats but failed to trickle down to the lower 95 percent of Americans.

These traditionalists—the "angry white males" of headlines—felt besieged by frenzied "feminazis" and a culture of entitlements, affirmative action, and special interests. They said they were sick and tired of being oppressed by women and dominated by impersonal bureaucracies—and they were not going to take it anymore! They experienced feminism as an "emasculating force, for it exaggerates that familiar sense of unmanly guilt," and were fed up with efforts to make them feel guilty. It's *men* who are the victims, they said. Politically, this resentment and anger had fueled a new gender gap, the preponderance of middle-class, middle-aged, straight white males who were listing constantly to the right. Raised to feel "entitled" themselves, they resented any entitlement program that gave anything to anyone else. "If I can't have what I'm entitled to," they seemed to say, "then neither can you"—a new twist on the old exclusionary formula employed to retrieve a sense of manhood.[14] One writer fumed that he "will have none of the nonsense about oppressed and victimized women; no responsibility for the conditions of women, whatever that condition might be; none of the guilt or self-loathing that is traditionally used to keep men functioning in harness." And another wrote that women "have always dominated me, directed me, intimidated me, loaded me with guilt, sometimes inspired me, oftentimes exploited or shamed me."[15]

In a flurry of reversals characteristic of this "men's rights movement," these beleaguered men trotted out a set of empirical inversions that made the rational mind reel. It's men, they told us, who were the victims of sexual harassment by women, not the other way around. "The way young women dress in the spring constitutes a sexual assault upon every male within eyesight of them," wrote William Muehl, a retired professor at the Yale Divinity School.[16] Men, they claimed, were battered and abused by their wives far more frequently than the other way around; in fact, to hear them tell it, husband battery was one of the nation's most underreported crimes, and such men were in desperate need of shelters where they can feel safe from violent and abusive women. It's not that men abandoned their families after divorce, the basic tenet of laws about child-support payments and alimony, but rather that vengeful wives and conniving lawyers thwarted men's deep desires to maintain relationships with their children. Concern over sexual harassment and date rape made men so vulnerable at home, in the workplace, and on the town that they didn't know where to turn.[17]

Two groups of men lent their shrill voices to what the journalist Susan Faludi called the backlash. On the one hand, besieged traditionalists prescribed a biologically or theologically based separation of spheres as the cure-all for men's malaise. If only women would get out of the public sphere and go back into the private sphere where they belong, these crusaders told us, masculinity would be saved. Advocates of "men's rights," by contrast, used a somewhat different rhetoric, claiming that women have already achieved equality and that programs that favor women now served to discriminate against men.

Many of these conservative traditionalist tracks echoed the Social Darwinism of nineteenth-century antifeminists, as well as such 1970s conservatives as George Gilder. Journalist Nicholas Davidson's *The Failure of Feminism* (1987) claimed that feminism attempted to reverse the law of nature, which is the law of male dominance. Sexually, for example, feminism demands the "impossible," such as "trying not to feel aggressiveness or dominance toward a woman when making love to her"—a statement with which the most radical feminist would probably agree. "It will be a sad day when men no longer see women as the objects of their lust," Davidson concluded mournfully.[18]

While Gilder and Davidson relied on Social Darwinism for their political conservatism, philosopher Michael Levin's *Feminism and Freedom* (1987) used the rhetoric of radical libertarian individualism to argue that feminism was inimical to equality, in that it demanded special protections and special privileges for women. "Although feminism speaks the language of liberation, self-fulfillment, options, and the removal of barriers, these phrases invariably mean their opposites and disguise an agenda at variance with the ideals of a free society" because "equality of outcome entails inequality of opportunity," he wrote. But Levin, too, returned to the nuclear family as the foundation of the free society, since father absence was responsible for not only out-of-control masculinity but also feminism. "Nothing could have produced this degree of anger at men and hatred of self [i.e., feminism] but a childhood in which femaleness went unconfirmed by an ineffectual father, together perhaps with a dominant mother."[19]

Asa Baber, creator and writer of the "Men" column in *Playboy*, was probably the most widely read contemporary mouthpiece for the other version of male backlash, the "men's rights" movement. A column called "Men" in *Playboy*? you might ask. Isn't that just a little bit redundant? Not to Baber, who claimed to speak for legions of men struggling against the rising red tide of "politically correct" feminism. "Men have now had 25 years of sexists calling us sexists," he wrote about a feminism that was now "out of control" and which had become "an attack on masculinity itself." Baber celebrated manhood as if it had just come back into fashion. "It's fine to be male," he proclaimed, "a glorious, sexual, humorous thing to be male."

Baber's book, *Naked at Gender Gap* (1992), a collection of his columns, rehearsed the standard men's rights litany: Women should serve in the military to eliminate the sexism that forces only men to serve; men are the victims of discrimination in custody and divorce proceedings; men should have rights to determine whether or not a woman should have an abortion. Men have lost "power and control" while women reap all the benefits. They get out of military service—"there will never be equal rights for all in this country until that burden is shared by men and women"—and they also "perpetuate spousal violence almost as frequently as men."[20]

It's men, he whined, who were the real victims in America—victims of "antimale sexism," a veritable "sexual inquisition" making us "vulnerable in the extreme to false charges of sexual harassment." Feminists, he wrote, have us "walking on eggshells. . . . All it takes to lynch a man these days is the accusation of rape."[21]

Baber was passionate about his rights as a father—from conception onward. That fetus "is mine as much as yours," he encouraged men to proclaim. And after a divorce, Baber believed that men certainly should enjoy unimpeded visitation, equal custody, and the like—even if they were inactive as fathers *before* the divorce. Baber wrote as if he had just discovered parental nurture, a controversial issue with a long history. Who, after all, has been asking—indeed begging, demanding, and cajoling—men to take a larger part in child care and housework all these decades? Such inversions made the book a perfect illustration of men's rights rhetoric. Rather than express regret or take responsibility for the literal battery of women by men, Baber complained about rhetorical "male bashing" by feminists when they verbally rail against men's violence.

Davidson, Levin, Gilder, and Baber provided a theoretical foundation for the men's rights backlash; Warren Farrell and Herb Goldberg made that theory into therapy. Once heralded as the most visible "liberated man" in the nation, Farrell seemed to completely abandon his earlier support of feminism and suggested that we "embrace traditional masculinity." To him, too, men were the oppressed sex. "Men are just as powerless as women in relationships," he asserted. In fact, it's men who were at a "psychological disadvantage" because they must initiate sexual contact, complained one of Farrell's followers. "I just want my fair share of the options." Farrell thus bridged the time warp between mid-seventies men's liberation rhetoric and the more vitriolic antifeminist men's rights cant.[22]

Farrell offered a list of the most important myths of manhood and proposed in their place a kind of Bill of Men's Rights. Most central—men lacked power. "Power is not earning money that someone else can spend and dying earlier so they can get the benefits." To Farrell, men also: (1) were not threatened by equality; (2) wanted love as much as women; (3) were as much the victims of discrimination as women; (4) were good fathers; (5) wanted equal rights to children; (6) did not earn a dollar for a woman's fifty-nine cents; (7) were battered as often as wives; and (8) were not in short supply.[23]

What's more, workplace discrimination against women was a feminist falsehood. Take sexual harassment. "Consensual sex among employees," as he euphemistically called it, was "courtship" when it worked and "harassment" when it didn't. If there was a problem with employer-employee sex, it was because it "undermines the ability of the employer to establish boundaries because the employer often feels needy of the employee," he wrote in a characteristic reversal. The notion of sexual harassment was discrimination against men, and Farrell suggested that we need laws to protect men in the workplace.

Farrell expanded these dizzying counterfactuals to other arenas as well. In academic settings, for example, sexual contact between professor and student may confer on the young woman "potential academic advantages over other students." And he likened workplace incest to at-home incest, which reversed family authority dynamics, since "parental authority becomes undermined because the child senses it has leverage over the parent." What a novel theory—incest afforded undue power to the young girl over her father's actions! And I suppose that he might find some statistics that revealed that 50 percent of all participants in "family sex" reported it to have been a positive experience.[24]

Rape, Farrell argued, is not, as feminists have argued, simply a crime of violence. It's about sex. Younger, more attractive women are 8,400 percent more likely to be raped than older women. The general point that rape has a sexual component is, of course, not entirely wrong despite the hyperbolic statistics. But to suggest that rape is a crime of sexual frustration implies that if only women would put out a little more often, rape rates would go down. And pornography was, to Farrell, just another harmless way for men to cope with women's miniskirt power, cleavage power, and flirtation power. Pornography provides "access to a variety of attractive women without the fear of rejection at a price we can afford." Women's "pornography," on the other hand—books like *Smart Women, Foolish Choices*, or *Women Who Love Too Much*—is far more pernicious because it also objectifies the opposite sex.[25]

Compared to the chameleon-like Farrell, men's liberationist Herb Goldberg was a model of consistency. Just as his 1970s books sought to demolish the traditional definition of masculinity, so too do his later works, such as *The New Male Female Relationship* (1983), *The Inner Male* (1987), and *What Men Really Want* (1991). To Goldberg, traditional masculinity remained a disease of disconnection, a "silent cancer"; men were "intimacy mechanics" who had all the right tools but were trying to fix a heartless, contentless machine. "Masculinity is an addiction," he said, echoing trends in self-help.

Goldberg, however, blamed women for these problems; he remained wedded to abdicating responsibility in the guise of equality and sharing. Since he claimed that women supported, encouraged, and demanded that men act this way, Goldberg got to demolish traditional masculinity and blame women for its maintenance. "[M]ilitancy about women's rights is often a way of defensively avoiding recognition of one's own responsibility for helping to create the problem."[26]

The *real* victims in American society were men—so claimed the political organizers who built organizations around men's anxieties and anger at feminism, groups like the Coalition for Free Men, the National Congress for Men, Men's Rights, Inc. (MR, Inc.), and Men Achieving Liberation and Equality (MALE). These groups proclaimed their commitment to equality and to ending sexism—which was why they were compelled to fight against feminism. For while feminism actually gave women *more* freedom than men enjoyed, men were still responsible for initiating sexual relationships, for fighting in wars, and for paying alimony and child support. Feminism, they argued, was the most insidious and vexing form of sexism going. Feminist women were "would be castrators with a knee-jerk, obsessive aversion to anything male," wrote Richard Doyle, an administrator of the Men's Rights Association, in his book *The Rape of the Male* (1986). Fred Hayward, the founder of MR, Inc., claimed that men were the most common victims of violence, rape, abuse, and battery and that "women are *privileged* because they are more frequently *allowed* to raise children, while men are being *oppressed* by denial of access to children"—and it was women who controlled this situation. Another advised men who felt powerless in the face of divorce-court proceedings to "fight dirty and win" by exploiting their wives' vulnerabilities.[27]

Fathers' rights groups used a language of equality to take their revenge against women to court, to demand mandatory joint custody without demonstration of the father's prior involvement. Jon Conine's *Fathers' Rights* (1989) provided handy advice to the father facing the loss of his children and displaced responsibility onto women and onto society as a whole. "Society cannot take away a father's rights to his children and expect him to cheerfully pay child support. Society cannot expect a father to make enough money to support two separate households. Society cannot afford to support mothers who choose not to work."[28] Fathers must have equal rights: the right to custody and the right to freedom from any burdensome alimony and child support. And men also needed the right to choose—to choose whether a partner exercised her right to choose to terminate a pregnancy. Sidney Siller, divorce lawyer and *Penthouse* columnist, was so moved by feminist "inversions" that in 1983 he formed the National Organization for Men. NOM opposed affirmative action, forced collection of alimony and child support, and a single-sex military. "Men have been wimpified. They've been emasculated. We'd like to see them fight for their rights," said Siller.[29] Just not for their country—at least not alone.

Most advocates of men's and fathers' rights were disgruntled and divorced dads who blamed their wives and their wives' lawyers for their isolation and loneliness. Many felt punished for their attempts to live up to a traditional definition of masculinity that was unrealizable from the start. Such a definition demanded that they renounce the pleasures of home—family, fatherhood, and friendships with women and with other men—to make an adequate living to support their families. They thought this behavior was a form of nurture, but now the bottom seemed to have dropped out of their lives. Actually, though, men's participation with their children has steadily *declined* over time. Before World War I men spent several hours a day with their children; they spent about two hours a day between the wars and about twenty *minutes* a day since World War II—roughly the inverse of their increasingly heated rhetoric about how much they want to be involved.

Even if we were sympathetic with their feelings of despair and gaping loneliness, knowing that it always attends the blind pursuit of the elusive ideals of Self-Made Masculinity, the men's rights analysis was so misguided, its inversions so transparent, its anger so displaced onto those who have traditionally been excluded, that it hardly offered any man of reason a convincing picture of men's situation.

But who needed accurate pictures with the Hollywood dream machine around? Though traditional masculinity's foundations and definition were eroding, that definition was still the stuff of fantasy; books and films bolstered the masculine ego through fantasies of conquest and triumph against overwhelming odds. Though the western frontier was gone, it could be reconstituted on Wall Street. Capital, as one advertising jingle had it, "knows no boundaries." Popular biographies and autobiographies of Donald Trump and Lee Iacocca, movies like *Wall Street* and *Working Girl,* and novels like Tom Wolfe's *Bonfire of the Vanities* both celebrated and spoofed the primal glandular competition of male workplace rivalries. Donald Trump claimed that he had no interest in competing against women or weaker men; he saved all he had for competition with his peers. Manhood was still to be proved by a bulge—not the throbbing hypertrophied penis of pornographic fantasy but the bulging wallet.

Or bulging muscles. Hollywood regaled American moviegoers with a parade of testosterone-infused superheroes like Steven Seagal, Sylvester Stallone, Jean-Claude Van Damme, Bruce Willis, and, of course, Arnold Schwarzenegger, who all seemed to embody Stallone's admonition: "Screen characters seem more like young ladies than real men, and it's time to reestablish the balance." In adventure stories like *Die Hard, Terminator, Rocky, Rambo,* and all their sequels and prequels, one lone real man was pitted against a horde of pretenders to the masculine crown—criminals, Vietnamese soldiers, unctuously well-dressed Eurotrash mobsters, cutthroat Japanese capitalists, and futuristic aliens; sometimes, it seemed, all at once.

The films of actor Michael Douglas suggested the pitfalls of these efforts to reinvigorate masculinity. Leaving aside his earlier buddy-film television persona on *The Streets of San Francisco*—the young, less streetwise, and more ethical cop, the sidekick to Karl Malden's hardened judiciousness—Douglas emerged in the 1980s and 1990s as a kind of politically incorrect polymath, "the poster boy for male fear of aggressive female sexuality."[30] In *Wall Street* he played Gordon Gekko, an unscrupulous tycoon and financier whose cunning gamesmanship destroys other people's lives without remorse, only to be destroyed by his young protégé's late-developing scruples. In *The War Between the Roses,* Douglas reinvented his romantic team with Kathleen Turner, but this time as a couple locked in a lethal pas de deux that gave new meaning to the phrase "till death do us part." The film's false equivalence between his demand that she give up her ambitions and devote herself to him and her demand that he take her a little more seriously works itself out with deadly consequences for both.

In a later spate of films—*Fatal Attraction* (1990), *Basic Instinct* (1991), *Falling Down* (1993), and *Disclosure* (1994)—Douglas gave masculine vengeance full force, usually against independent women invading the male turf. In *Fatal Attraction* the married-with-family Douglas's fling with a hot, single Glenn Close transforms her into a menacing she-devil who hounds him with demands for commitment while he tries to "ethically" extricate himself. She takes revenge on his family, even boiling the family bunny, only to end up murdered by Douglas's mousey wife—to the cheers of the audience. Single women were seductive, literally femmes fatale, likely to explode at the least opportunity. In *Basic Instinct* Douglas again follows his lust into an encounter with a hot and potentially lethal single woman, while in *Disclosure* he is man enough to resist its consummation. Although his manhood was rescued in each case, it was only momentary. Women were never to be trusted—especially those who were single and sexually aware and active.

In *Falling Down* Douglas offered an allegory of the besieged middle-class white male in society. Having bought into the American promise even after his layoff from the aerospace industry—his vanity license plate reads "D-Fens"—Douglas becomes progressively unhinged as the traditional props of white male privilege are shed. His efforts to reestablish himself lead to angry confrontations with virtually every group that has been historically excluded by Self-Made Masculinity—upwardly mobile, hardworking immigrants; young Latino men; a beautiful policewoman—all of whom he blames for his failures to cling to his tenuous grasp on economic security and mental stability. His death is the death of the dream of exclusion: Traditional masculinity cannot be resurrected, and even the old tried-and-true strategies of sexism, homophobia, and racism cannot keep the edifice from falling down.

Escape Artists

So where did men go to feel like men? This was one of the questions that fueled the anger of the men's rights groups, who sought to prop up traditional definitions of masculinity in the ways that besieged men have always done: by clearing everyone else off the playing field. By reestablishing the early-nineteenth-century separation of spheres between women and men and by excluding from full manhood the "other" men—men of color, gay men, non-native-born men—these men clung to the belief that a secure and confident gender identity was possible through the fulfillment of Self-Made Masculinity. This question was also the dominant theme for a new generation of masculinists, who saw in contemporary arrangements a recipe for a new feminization of American culture parallel to the cultural feminization perceived at the turn of the twentieth century.

At that time, masculinists argued that changes in the nature of work, the closing of the frontier, and changes in family relations had produced a cultural degeneracy—American men and boys were becoming feminized. Men searched for homosocial preserves where they could be real men with other men (fraternal lodges, Muscular Christian revival meetings) and sought vigorous ways to demonstrate their hardy manhood (wilderness retreats, dude ranches and rodeos, health and exercise crazes, evocations of martial glory), while they also sought ways to ensure that the next generation of young boys would not grow up to be an effete elite (Boy Scouts, single-sex classrooms, a fatherhood movement). Virtually every one of those strategies had been retrieved as a way to alleviate a growing sense of cultural malaise with American manhood. Masculinists believed that men were still wimps; they needed to be rescued from the clutches of overprotective mothers, absent fathers, and an enervating workplace and needed to rediscover themselves through a manly quest against a pitiless environment.

For some that environment was the contemporary workplace. As they sallied forth into the urban jungle, middle-class men made themselves resemble their adventurous forbears through their fashionable clothes and masculinizing accessories. They were Timberland shoes or cowboy boots, denim shirts, and aviator sunglasses; they drove

Cherokees, Wranglers, Broncos, or Land Rovers; they splashed on a little Aspen, Stetson, Chaps, or Safari cologne. As at the turn of the twentieth century, so too now—if manhood does not come from within, perhaps it could be worn. "When I dress in my suit each morning I feel like a knight going forth to battle and I love to fight hard and win in a hard bargaining session with a publisher," commented a literary agent.[31] But for most the workplace was no longer the literal testing ground. Tom Wolfe's satiric novel *The Bonfire of the Vanities* sounded a hilariously near-hysterical elegy for the yuppie 1980s, an era of bond traders, "head hunters," and arbitrageurs who were, for a time, the "masters of the universe."

If masculinity could not be achieved at work, perhaps it could be achieved by working out. Men's bodies provided another masculine testing ground. Millions of American men participated in the health and fitness craze—dieting, jogging and bicycling, exercising, consuming health foods and various bottled waters, and purchasing high-end fitness equipment. "Iron man" triathalons pushed men beyond normal physical limits to explore the boundaries of the body. Of course, this craze was not limited to men; women remained a steady market for fitness, health, and diet fads. Women have been steady consumers over the years in an effort to remain "feminine"—to shed unwanted pounds and turn back the hands of time. But men's interest in health and diet has matched women's only twice in our history—at the turn of the century and today—and men's sporadic interest in the body was prompted, I believe, by the collapse of the workplace as an area in which to test and prove masculinity. When our real work failed to confirm manhood, we "worked out." Perhaps women's exclusion from the marketplace led them to turn first to the realm of consumption to achieve the perfect body, but men were soon standing—or rather aerobicizing—right alongside of them. Magazines like *Men's Health* and countless muscle magazines celebrated the new male cult of the body.

A subgenre of travel literature also re-created the frontier and, with it, the western novel of the turn of the twentieth century and the popularity of the male-bonding war movies of the 1950s and 1960s. This strain of male travel writers ventured to difficult, inhospitable territories, exploring the boundaries of civilization, crossing the frontier into uncharted territory. Works such as Charles Nicholl's *Borderlines*, P. J. O'Rourke's *Holidays in Hell*, Tim Cahill's *A Wolverine Is Eating My Leg*, Nick Danziger's *Danziger's Travels: Beyond Forbidden Frontiers*, and Stuart Stevens's *Malaria Dreams* all found the journeyman/writer/hero hurtling through some jungle at the edge of civilization, testing manhood in a Land Rover. The global frontier remained open to middle-class white men who sought a confrontation with the "primitive" at the boundaries of civilization. It was also an escape from the feminizing city and an anxious quest to test one's manliness.[32]

Other fantasies reinvigorated military masculinity. Theologian Michael Pakaluk argued that young boys should play with toy guns because "Christian life essentially contains a warlike aspect, [and] the military virtues are essential to it"—although he prescribed simple war toys to give the young boy ample room for imagination. Even without the theology, fantasy toys that dripped with militarism became the rage. Literary critic Susan Jeffords's fascinating studies of American war films and novels, *The Remasculinization of America* (1989) and *Hard Bodies* (1993), traced the cinematic and fictional efforts to return to the scene of defeat and retrieve lost manhood by rewinning lost wars.[33]

Some called for the literal remasculinization of America. For example, debates over the entry of women and gays into the military were fueled by the presumed relationships between masculinity and military values. Brian Mitchell's *Weak Link: The Feminization of the American Military* (1989) claimed that women's presence "inhibits male bonding, corrupts allegiance to the hierarchy, and diminishes the desire of men to compete for anything but the attentions of women." In his best-selling Vietnam memoir, Philip Caputo suggested that male intimacy was threatened by the integration of women:

> The communion between men is as profound as any between lovers. Actually it is more so. It does not demand for its sustenance the reciprocity, the pledges of affection, the endless reassurances required by the love of men and women. It is, unlike marriage, a bond that cannot be broken by a word, by boredom, or divorce, or by anything other than death. Sometimes that is not strong enough.

Lest anyone confuse the imperatives of homosociality for homosexuality, Caputo conflated the debate about women in the military with the debate about gays in the military, noting that "the emotion of camaraderie is, of its nature, chaste. It may be more intense than what happens between male and female lovers, but it has to be nonsexual. It's not just women. Warriors can't be homosexual lovers either."[34]

Of course they can—and have. Only a theory that casts male sexuality as a form of predatory domination, sexual attraction as lust for conquest, and emotional bonds as a form of property control could suggest that sexual bonds threaten emotional bonding among men. If sexual connection is about the possibility of deep emotional relationships, of love and commitment, then sexuality is no threat to military discipline—as long as everyone knows who everyone else is. Efforts to expel gays and lesbians from military service seemed to be so easily paired with efforts to keep women from military equality because if women only were excluded, the homosocial military might be mistaken for a homosexual military.

Some masculinists echoed the Muscular Christianity movement by recasting Jesus as a religious Rambo. The revival of evangelism, the journalist Carol Flake reported,

> brought with it a revival of muscular Christianity and a return to the social Darwinism of the athletic era. Jesus the teacher had become Christ the competitor. . . . From the pulpit, preachers prayed for winning seasons, sprinkling their sermons with so much athletic symbolism that they sometimes sounded like color commentators on TV sports broadcasts.[35]

One Jesuit priest claimed that contemporary Christianity makes Jesus out to be a "bearded lady," while another called him "Jesus, the Warm Fuzzy." "Christ wasn't effeminate," grumped televangelist Jerry Falwell. "The man who lived on this earth was a man with muscles. . . . Christ was a he-man!" Noting a "chronic absence" of men from church—only about one-third of American men attended church regularly, while nearly one-half of all American women did—one minister indicated that the long-term effects of cultural feminization of the church would be marginalization of the church, impoverishment of church life, and a coarsening of the tone of public society. What was a contemporary Muscular Christian to do?[36]

One minister suggested a program to bring men back to the church. This included ministers adopting masculine styles themselves—giving firmer handshakes, learning about hunting and car repair—since "pastors often seem sissified." Develop programs for men, he counseled. "Provide a place where they can feel safe—a home turf—and you may be surprised how many will show up and open up." Another suggested portraying the Christian life as a manly life, a heroic quest for spiritual manhood. After all, religion is a man's vision; the church is a man's sacred space. And going forth to battle against evil, to bear witness and convert nonbelievers, to make the world whole—this is a man's job. "Jesus battles all forms of evil," wrote one Jesuit priest, "but unlike other warriors his power does not kill." Other observers made no such distinction. "Sacred violence is the ultimate meaning of masculinity," wrote one. The religious life is a heroic quest. The battle for men's souls is of cosmic importance; spirituality is "not equated with prissiness," and "Jesus, the Bible, and the house of God are not just for sissies and girls."[37] The enormous response to the Christian men's organization called the Promise Keepers was a testimonial to the sustained drawing power of a Muscular Christian vision.

The book *Jesus CEO* repackaged the corporate Jesus of Bruce Barton's 1924 work, *The Man That Nobody Knows*, into a Wall Street middle manager. Jesus, we were told, was in "constant contact with his boss," "demonstrated a sense of ownership of all things," "had a plan," was "willing to do an end run" to put it into effect. Jesus, it turns out, was a "turnaround specialist" who motivated his workers to become "a lean, mean marketing machine."[38]

Among the most visible campaigners for Muscular Christianity were Christian athletes. "You think because I've accepted Christ into my life, I'm passive," laughed baseball player Brett Butler. "I play hard. If Christ played this game, he'd slide right into the second baseman, and then he'd help him up. Christ was no wimp." A former team-mate, pitcher Orel Hershiser, added that "[j]ust because I'm a Christian doesn't mean I'm a wimp." The Chicago Bears and New York Giants held a joint prayer circle at midfield after they had spent sixty minutes bashing in each other's heads in their 1991 playoff game. Mark Eaton, the towering center for the Utah Jazz, said Jesus would have been a great basketball player. "He would have been one of the most tenacious guys out there. I think he'd really get in your face—nothing dirty, but he'd play to win." Another basketball player wanted to prove that "Christians are not Casper Milquetoasts." Jocks for Jesus were visible in every sport, illustrating that the most manly of men could still experience salvation in religion and that the most religious of men need not appear unmanly.[39]

Some Christian athletes even made Muscular Christianity the basis for a second career. Bodybuilder John Jacobs, for example, founded "the Power Team," a group of massively muscular zealots who used a pumped-up theology as the basis for a kind of motivational preaching at revival-tent meetings around the country. "Jesus Christ was no skinny little man," Jacobs claimed. "Jesus was a man's man." He and the other men's men performed circus feats of masculine strength, like breaking stacks of bricks or large blocks of ice with their bare hands. By equating masculinity with spiritual and physical power, Jacobs and his Power Team sought to retrieve a model of "an idealized Christian patriarchy."[40]

Some masculinists insisted that the separation of the sexes was the only way to preserve what is different (and interesting) about either women or men. Writer Dotson Rader argued against coeducation because young boys were biologically *inferior* to young girls in both fine motor skills and innate intelligence; thus, he argued, boys were at a *physical* disadvantage in the coed classroom.[41] Some collegiate fraternities resisted coeducation, claiming the clubhouse preserves the best of manhood. In an "About Men" column in the

New York Times, William F. Buckley fondly recalled his club years at Yale through the "dreams" of a younger member:

> Someday, damn it, we'll have a treehouse of our own. We'll build it out in the woods where Mother can't find us. And we'll eat when we want, what we want. We'll bring our friends. Have a secret club. And no girls.[42]

He must have meant "gurls"—the boyhood misspelling that adorned many a cinematic boys' clubhouse, treehouse, or secret hideaway. The search for the "fraternity house that wouldn't end" led some grown-up men to promote the all-male club as a refuge. New Age masculinist writer Keith Thompson evoked early-twentieth-century fraternal orders when he claimed that "a man needs a lodge"—a "retreat from concerns about money and work, family pressures, and . . . responsibility to roles." That's why men fought so vigorously to protect single-sex men's clubs from integration, despite women's protests that these clubs reproduce men's power in society by providing informal arenas for networking and personal friendships to develop.[43]

But these homosocial preserves—single-sex colleges, fraternities, fraternal orders, men's clubs—were as much about the protection of men's privilege as they were arenas to facilitate closeness among men. At the Bohemian Grove, for example, America's elite men gathered for a two-week bonding binge, an extended drunken fraternity stag party. But unlike the Masons, the Red Men, or Sigma Chi, this "overgrown boy-scout camp," this "college fraternity system transplanted from the campus to the redwoods," as one former employee put it, consisted entirely of CEOs of *Fortune* 500 corporations, senators, congressmen, governors, and even presidents, vice presidents, and ex-presidents. Power brokers like George Shultz, Henry Kissinger, Ronald Reagan, and Richard Nixon mingled with corporate leaders like Thomas Watson and Lee Iacocca and celebrities like Walter Cronkite, all of whom were regular clubbers. This "refuge for the weary heart," this "balm for breasts that have been bruised," according to members, invited America's upper-class white-male ruling class to experience the depths of their cohesive bonding through ritual contact with nature and one another. These clubs were "a means by which these values are transferred to the business environment"—that is, a mechanism of reproduction of class power. The obsessive exclusion of women and the grudging admission of a few black men (like Vernon Jordan) suggested that these retreats also served a traditionalist agenda, regrounding masculinity on the exclusion of the various "others."[44]

The weekend retreat at Bohemian Grove began as the men danced in a circle, throwing their worldly cares into the roaring bonfire that rose through the redwood trees into the night sky. (From that moment until the end of the encampment, they did not talk about business.) They retreated to lodges with names like Cave Man Camp—that's the one where Richard Nixon stayed. They donned Native American war paint and masks, chanting and drumming, playing at rituals "full of schmaltz and nostalgia," reported sociologist G. William Domhoff. And they bonded, forging intimate, informal ties among the scions of business and government, cementing the allegiances of government and corporate power, and reassuring one another that they were all friends, all, really, on the same side.

Male bonding, Native American rituals, drumming, chanting, a virtual celebration of masculinity—it sounded like the media descriptions of the "men's movement," a motley collection of wounded men and their pop-psychological gurus, loosely led by poet and best-selling author Robert Bly. These men were conducting their own quest for their lost "deep" manhood in weekend retreats and workshops across the country. By donning totemic animal symbols and reclaiming ancient myths of male bonding, those weekend warriors hoped to tap into some primitive stream of essential masculinity, long buried by the feminizing worlds of work and home. This "mythopoetic" effort to retrieve deep manhood—the "inner warrior" or "wildman"—was by far the most interesting and seductive example of contemporary masculinism.

All across the country in the first few years of the 1990s, men were in full-scale retreat, heading off to the woods to rediscover their wild, hairy, deep manhood. What were they retreating from? And what were they hoping to find? Perhaps the most celebrated purveyors of the search for the deep masculine were Robert Bly and Sam Keen, whose *Iron John* and *Fire in the Belly*, respectively, topped the best-seller lists for much of 1991. In *Iron John*, Bly recounted a Grimm fairy tale as a timeless parable of male development. Here was a tale of separation from mother, frightening risk, a heroic quest, the scarring wound, and the recovery of manly virtue presented in a format to enable men to reclaim their "warrior" selves. And Keen provided a rough road map for a more individualistic psychospiritual quest for the grail of manhood. Contemporary mythopoetic masculinists spoke eloquently to men's spiritual hunger, a deep longing for lives of meaning and resonance. Their weekend retreats allowed men to break down the isolation and emotional repression that invariably attended efforts to demonstrate Self-Made Manhood; here, they gave voice, perhaps for the first time, to emotional needs for closeness and friendship with other men, to pain, confusion, and vulnerabilities that were long suppressed in the confused efforts to prove the unprovable.

Like their early-twentieth-century forbears, masculinists argued that men were listless, lifeless, enervated, feminized. Psychologically, they claimed that this was because men were not adequately separated from their mothers. The absence of the father at home and the disappearance of the apprenticeship system meant that men had to learn the meaning of manhood from women, especially from their mothers. Masculine authenticity was destroyed by the Industrial Revolution, Bly argued, because fathers abandoned their sons and went to work in factories. Mothers also retained an incestuous dedication to their sons, excluding the father and keeping the boy dependent on her long after he needed to break away. Thus, "mythopoets" argued, the problem for men was incomplete separation, and so off they ran to the woods, where they could escape the world of women—mothers, wives, and children—and workplace responsibility and drudgery. Here they could "bond" with each other, rediscover manly nurture, honor their ancestors as potential "mentors," and validate each other's, and hence their own, manhood.

Underneath all the trappings of mythopoetic manhood—the mythology, faux traditionalism, appropriated Native American and nonindustrial ritualism, bowdlerized Jungian archetypes, and evocations of non-Western initiation—lay a language that sounded more like the recovery movement than the strenuous life. Men, we heard, were also searching for their inner child, healing childhood wounds, and recognizing the addictive patterns characteristic of adult children. Men "suffered" in this society, argued Shepherd Bliss, partly because women maintained a monopoly on themes like oppression and powerlessness. "But women aren't victims," he insisted. "We all know the power of women."[45]

The mythopoetic call of the wild ran into the same problems that faced early-twentieth-century masculinists. For one thing, they displaced men's grown-up problems of economic contraction, political competition, social isolation, and interpersonal incompetence (the result of a definition of masculinity that was inseparably tied to performance in the marketplace, the bedroom, or the athletic field) onto overdominant motherhood and absent fatherhood. Our dilemmas had more to do with our adulthood than with a childhood struggle to wriggle free of clutching mothers or searching for absent fathers. As one critic argued:

> The massive contradiction between the public exhortation to aggressive individualism, and a social order in which most white-collar workers are embedded in massive organizations, is neatly resolved by transporting the scene of action into a mystic cult of masculinity. We can't all be Donald Trumps but, by God, we can be equally fierce in our hearts.[46]

As feminist psychoanalysts argued, the problem with men wasn't that they were not separated enough from mother, but that they were separated *too much*. The project of Self-Made Masculinity, of a manhood constantly tested and proved, became equated with a relentless effort to repudiate femininity, a frantic effort to dissociate from women. In daily life this translated into a devaluation of women, the psychological basis for sexism. Men had thus abandoned precisely those emotional skills that were most needed if women were to achieve equality: nurture, sensitivity, emotional responsiveness. But if mothers embodied responsibility, care, and nurture, why did men's movement leaders counsel that we should reject mother and run away, attempting to "heal the father wound"? Rather, we should heal the *mother* wound, close the gap between the mother who cared for us and the mother we've rejected. Reentering the domestic sphere through shared parenting, not flying in panic from it, would enable men to develop those emotional resources and allow their sons to experience nurturance and care as something that all adults did. Such reconnection was also about responsibility, at work and at home, such responsibilities as nurturance, compassion, and accountability—in short, responsibilities that were equated with the conditions for emasculation, not demonstration of manhood. Frankly, I'd prefer more Ironing Johns and fewer Iron Johns.

And what were we to make of the search through mythic literature and non-Western cultures for the rituals that could usher in manhood? Mythopoetic weekend warriors evoked a misty preindustrial past through which to view our dilemma. Keen, for example, believed that traditional life was harmonious and cooperative: Male and female, each in his or her sphere, living lives of meaning and coherence. Each gender was "half of a crippled whole." Men got the "feeling of power" and women got the "power of feeling"; men got the "privilege of public action" and women got the "privilege of private being," Keen quipped as if these were equivalent.[47]

Other men's movement leaders utilized Jungian archetypes in their efforts to retrieve deep conscious manhood. Robert Moore and Douglas Gillette, in *King, Warrior, Magician, Lover* (1990) and the four-volume series that dealt with each archetype separately, acted as spirit guides to our archetypal reclamation. Their version of the king was no wimp but "aggressive, masculine, potent, . . . a warrior who enforces order within his kingdom and who may take military action to extend his kingdom."[48]

The search for the wild warrior within led men's movement scions to wander through anthropological literature like postmodern tourists, as if the world's cultures were arrayed like so many ritual boutiques in a global shopping mall. Bly preferred nonindustrial primitivism, while Moore and Gillette searched for the king in a breathless world historical tour, extracting images of kingship from ancient Egypt, seventh-century Tibet, the Aztecs, Incas, and Sumerians. This was all slapped together in a ritual pastiche—part Asian, part African, part Native American. And all totally decontextualized. Rituals are deeply embedded in cultural life, and taking them out of that context was at least myopic, if not disingenuous.

Mythopoets celebrated cultures with elaborate rituals for men, all the while protesting that such rituals had nothing to do with women. Since the rituals excluded women, they must be only "about" men and manhood. But true traditional initiation ceremonies and sex-segregated mystical celebrations did not occur in a vacuum, and just as masculinist separation was not lost on feminists in the late nineteenth century, it was not lost on feminist women a century later. "The cry for revitalized initiation rites, for mentors, for sacred space, sounded ominously familiar—like a cry to reinforce the crumbling walls of those men's clubs whose primary interests were exclusion and self-perpetuation," wrote journalist Jill Baumgaertner.[49] In the real world, women and men occupied the same cosmic planes—and they worked desk to desk. Accessing an inner king that ignored or reduced woman's role—as wife, lover, friend, colleague, or mother—seemed more like a celebration of the usurper or, at best, a benevolent despotism.

Which was how I understood all these middle-class white men beating drums, chanting Native American chants, and dancing to Native American dances. How, exactly, was this "spiritual colonialism," as one writer put it, different from the Improved Order of the Red Men at the turn of the twentieth century, wearing war paint while whooping it up during fraternal initiation? Or for that matter, from the Tomahawk Chop? Perhaps the early-twentieth-century analogy was useful in another sense here. As I argued earlier, in nineteenth-century minstrel shows, white performers would don blackface in order to express racial anxieties as well as to gain access to emotions—longing for home and family (especially mother), urban loneliness from spatial displacement, confusions about modern life—that were denied expression by the rigidity of white manhood. Here were all these young Italian, Irish, and Jewish boys trying to make their way in a cold and unfriendly country, repressing their loneliness and voicing a nearly "universal lamentation for homeland and birthplace." Blackface gave them access to those repressed emotions, as they sang of "mammy," the Swanee River, "de ol' folks at home"—in short, the simple joys of home and hearth. Of course, such behaviors would be seen as transparently racist today. But the mythopoets adopted what we might call "Redface"—the appropriation of putatively Native American rituals to allow privileged white men access to that set of emotions—community, spirituality, communion with nature—that they felt themselves to have lost and therefore displaced onto Native American cultures.[50]

The search for the deep masculine is historically anachronistic, echoing late-nineteenth-century masculinist complaints against the forces of feminization. But it is also developmentally atavistic, a search for lost boyhood, an effort to turn back the clock to the moment before work and family responsibilities yanked men away from their buddies. Wildman retreats were grown-up versions of the clubhouse with the sign saying No Gurls Allowed.[51] Sure, one had to "wrestle with the wounds of childhood," but if one claimed to be an "adult child," one used the word "adult" only as an adjective—one remained the child. It is curious that these grown men, most of whom were between forty-five and sixty, identified more with the son in the Iron John fable. Identification with the son, the prince, revealed the traditional gender assumptions that lay at the heart of the masculinist project.

The prince, after all, was the rightful heir to power; he would be the king. He was entitled to it, but he was not yet ready for it. So, too, manhood. Weekend warriors seemed to believe themselves to be entitled to the power that was men's privilege. But they did not feel it yet. The mythopoetic retreats offered men a chance to reclaim their birthright, their right to power, and all the attendant privileges that derived from it. In that sense, it offered a subterranean, if inadvertent, political program that reproduced and reinforced the existing power imbalances between women and men.

One thing, though, was clear: Bly, Keen, and the other leaders of the mythopoetic men's movement tapped into a deep current of malaise among American men. The fears of feminization—that we have lost our ability to claim our manhood in a world without fathers, without frontiers, without manly creative work—have haunted men for a century. And nowhere have these fears been played out more fully for the past hundred years than in literature, film, and television. How else are we to understand the constant symbolic efforts to retrieve the lost father, to re-create the frontier testing ground, to experience romance and excitement in the workplace?

The deep bonds forged among soldiers have been celebrated in dozens of Vietnam films like *Platoon, Rambo, Full Metal Jacket*. Equally suggestive of the bonds forged in war were the films that evoked the life of the returning veteran. The warrior without a war is bereft, drowning in an anomic sea of meaningless routine. Films like *In Country* and *The Deer Hunter* provided the flip side to war movies, as men picked through the emotional rubble of a mundane postwar world in which deep meaning was no longer possible. Two films offered interesting contrasts. *Born on the Fourth of July* indicted not the mundane world for the collapse of meaning, but American foreign policy; Ron Kovic's heroic quest sets him against military masculinity, and he retrieves his manhood by becoming a tireless fighter against the very forms of manhood he had earlier proclaimed. And in *Casualties of War*, one young soldier challenges the bonding rituals of the others in his platoon, rituals that include the gang rape and murder of a young Vietnamese woman. Renouncing male bonding through violence and rape immediately brands him as less than a real man, his heterosexuality is questioned by the other soldiers, and later, his life is threatened, and he is nearly murdered by his brothers-in-arms. Male bonding, we are told, was certainly not a good thing for women—and it may not be a very good thing for men either, promoting excesses of violence and brutality, groupthink imperatives that obliterate individual responsibility, and an idealization of the warrior.

"Healing the father wound" as both the motivation for and the ultimate result of the masculine quest was the theme of some of the most popular films of the later decades of the twentieth century. Take, for example, five of those decades' most popular films—a pair of alien movies, *E.T.: The Extra-Terrestrial* and *Close Encounters of the Third Kind*, offered by Steven Spielberg, and the *Star Wars* trilogy of George Lucas. In *Close Encounters* Richard Dreyfuss's character abandons his family and job to retrieve his child-like wonder in a call to a spiritual reawakening. In *E.T.* the void left by Elliot's father's abandonment of the family is filled by a cherubic alien whose power to heal families is motivated by the simple desire to go home. And in *Star Wars* Luke Skywalker undertakes the most mythopoetic journey of all, a spiritual quest in which the young Jedi Knight is initiated into warriorhood by male mentors Obi Wan Kenobi and Yoda; he is motivated as well by his sister Leia's love. Skywalker defeats the evil emperor and redeems his arch-enemy, Darth Vader, who, it turns out, is Skywalker's long-lost father, transformed into a dark, menacing shadow warrior by addictions to power and wealth. The boy's quest literally heals the father wound and prepares him for adulthood as a heroic warrior.

In *Field of Dreams*, a search for boyhood innocence leads Kevin Costner's character to build a baseball field in his Iowa cornfield, an unconscious effort at reconciliation with the father who abandoned him long before. At the film's end the two are having a lazy catch on the mythic diamond. Baseball, that timeless masculine trope, has healed the father wound. In all these films, the boy's quest to find himself, his inner child, also heals the father and provides the grounding for their reconciliation. Talk about family values!

Costner's epic *Dances with Wolves* reminded us that the western frontier is still the quintessential mythic site for demonstrating manhood. Like Owen Wister and every generation of American men since, we come to the western to experience the initiation into manhood and the mythopoetic quest reinscribed into buckskin and revolvers. The search for authentic experience, for deep meaning, always led men back to the frontier, back to nature, even if it was inevitably the frontier of their imaginations. "I've always wanted to see the frontier," says Lieut. John Dunbar, "before it's gone."

Not only does Dunbar see the frontier, he is converted by it, like Roosevelt, Wister, and Remington before him. The slaughter of Pawnee attackers serves as Dunbar's ceremonial initiation. After the battle, where his introduction of high-level technology (repeating rifles) decimates the evil Indians, he writes in his journal that before that moment, he never really knew himself, but upon hearing his Sioux name, Dances with Wolves, "I knew for the first time who I really was." Unlike his real-life predecessors, Dunbar chooses not to return with his new vision to civilized life, here pictured as hopelessly venal and corrupt, but to go native, joining a tribe of Ogala Sioux on the trail of the vanishing buffalo and in full-scale retreat from the oncoming rush of white civilization. He finds his nonwhite spirit guides in Kicking Bird (Graham Greene), who brings him into the tribe, and Wind in His Hair (Rodney Grant), who finally accepts him and provides the coda of achieved equality for the film, shouting of their friendship. And of course, Dunbar gets the traditional reward for manhood regained: the beautiful woman, Stands with a Fist (Mary McDonnell), the white woman who had been raised by the Ogala (no miscegenation here!). Costner thus reinvents the heroic warrior as Rousseauian noble savage, inverts traditional cowboy and Indian mythologies (we cheer when the virtuous Indians kill the white soldiers), and retrieves lost manhood—a manhood that could never be achieved as long as our hero remained within the boundaries of eastern civilized life.

City Slickers transposed this mythic quest for manhood into the 1980s, as three yuppies —Mitch Robbins, Ed Furillo, and Phil Berquist, played, respectively, by Billy Crystal, Bruno Kirby, and Daniel Stern—resolve their midlife crises on a faux-western cattle drive that turns all too real as a test of manhood. Crystal's first foil is a seemingly ageless father figure/mentor (Jack Palance), who plays the genuine article, a real cowboy as ageless icon. His death releases Crystal and his friends to chase after the grail of manhood, which is pursued through the failure of several other characters. Crystal, Kirby, and Stern are successful in bringing in the herd of cattle; their initiatory moment is predicated on the failure of the others in their group—two rowdy ranch hands (traditional macho men), a father and son team of buppie dentists (black men), two effete and flabby Jewish ice-cream entrepreneurs (bespectacled Jewish wimps), and of course, a woman. The successful symbolic reclamation of manhood is possible for the white upper-middle-class man only via the failure of the traditional "others," the exclusion of the other from that same mythic quest.

One ironic postscript illustrated the disjunction between the fantasy retrievals of lost manhood and its anxious and relentless real-life quest. As Jack Palance accepted the 1992 Academy Award for Best Supporting Actor for his performance in *City Slickers*, he noted that at seventy-seven years old, many movie producers had thought him washed up, too old to play these arduous roles. They're wrong, of course, he snarled, as he dropped to the floor of the stage to do a set of one-armed push-ups. Regaining his feet, he also boasted that he could "still get it up." In fantasy the quest to prove manhood ends at the Hollywood climax; in real life, it seems, it never does.

In *Unforgiven* Clint Eastwood, the embodiment of remorseless manhood, wrote a countermyth, a story of manhood retrieved without redemption, without heroism. Eastwood plays William Munney, an aging widower, a failure as a father and domesticated farmer, who retrieves his manhood through cold, merciless, passionless murder. Like Crystal and his yuppie cronies, Eastwood reclaims his manhood via the failure of several others—English Bob (Richard Harris), a dandified British fop who stands in for the old aristocracy, revealed as just as brutal and vicious as the Self-Made Man (Bob made his living killing Chinese for the railroad); a cynical and sadistic sheriff, Little Bill Daggett (Gene Hackman), who reveals that the forces of law and order are as mercurial and law-less as those outside the law; Ned Logan (Morgan Freeman), a black comrade who has lost his ability to fight and whose death becomes the blood sacrifice Eastwood needs to complete his redemption; and the young Schofield Kid (Jaimz Woolvett), who wants to join the gang but who finds the reality of frontier virility so distasteful and horrifying that he returns home. When Eastwood reclaims his manhood, we realize that it is a manhood that no one in his right mind would want. The West is gone, we understand, and so too its supposed western heroes.

But the masculinist descent to the primitive resurfaced in another guise—the return of the monster as hypermasculine beast. How to explain films such as *Interview with the Vampire*, *Mary Shelley's Frankenstein*, *Bram Stoker's Dracula*, or *Wolf* except as later versions of Tarzan or Buck? And like their predecessors, the descent to a primal, natural, animal-like masculinity can cut either way. In *Wolf* Jack Nicholson's transformation reconnects his character, a somewhat stuffily effete book editor, with a fierce, heroic, and sensual nature that civilized discourse had all but completely sapped. (Even his vision gets sharper.) But for James Spader, his rival, that same descent brings out a deeper cruelty, less concealed by social convention. Nicholson uses his descent to elevate his manhood, while Spader uses his as an invitation to unchecked depravity. Nicholson becomes a passionate lover, Spader a rapist.

Many of these themes resounded in other cultural media. Popular music, for instance, for decades a form of masculine assertion—from teenage rebellion against work, family, and school to the wrenching passions of an awakening sexuality. A brief comparison between two popular rock performers can illustrate the different strategies and visions that men embraced. Guns N' Roses insisted angrily on exclusion, while Bruce Springsteen's career suggested a trajectory from rebellious rocker to responsible father.

Guns N' Roses had been among the nation's most successful hard rock bands; their *Use Your Illusion*, volumes 1 and 2 (Geffen Records), were the single fastest-selling records in history. Record stores scheduled extra hours to handle the demand as fans lined up to buy the record as if they were buying concert tickets. Yet to hear them tell it, we should feel sorry for them. Like the advocates of men's rights, Guns N' Roses claimed to be besieged on all fronts—as young working-class men by forces outside their control and as a rock band by demanding fans, tempting women, and rock critics who held them accountable for the racial and sexual rage they promoted. In one song, "One in a Million," lead singer Axl Rose sang about the newcomers to his neighborhood who were making life so difficult, who were potential harbingers of terrorism and disease:

> Immigrants and faggots
> They make no sense to me
> They come to our country
> And think they'll do as they please. . . .

At the end of the song, Rose warned both police and "niggers" to get out of his way. On later records it was no longer the invading hordes of immigrants, blacks, and gays streaming into white working-class neighborhoods. It was women, those seductive temptresses who really had all the power. "It's time for me to even the score," he screamed in revenge in another song, echoing the men who would fight dirty and win.

GN'R represented the worst tendencies of working- and middle-class white male politics, the politics of resentment and retaliation. Squeezed by a shrinking economy, ignored by politicians indifferent to their plight, they turned their rage on those just below them on the social ladder, those who were still hoping to land a piece of the American pie. Like David Duke's coded messages or Michael Douglas's *Falling Down*, GN'R tapped into homophobia, racism, and sexism and made them the bases for their hard-edged rock. (In an increasingly segmented musical marketplace the excluded others had their say as well, in "women's" music, gay and lesbian cabaret acts, and in gangsta rap, in which misogyny and homophobia often served as rhetorical counterpunches to racism. Predictably, it was only this last genre that found a mass-market audience.)

What a contrast with Bruce Springsteen, named by *Rolling Stone* as the rock artist of the 1980s. The changes in Springsteen's style and substance revealed a surprisingly compelling vision of a direction for men in the 1990s. From his first rebellious record in the early 1970s and his breakthrough *Born to Run* (1975), Springsteen joined a venerable American cast of characters in a line of "the last real man in America." And like Natty Bumppo, Huck Finn, or the Lone Ranger, he eluded domestic attachments while he set off in search of authenticity, freedom, and meaning—searching for manhood in an imagined America. "As a child, I felt the myth coming from everywhere, especially from television westerns with those big landscapes," he told one interviewer. "In rock music it was Chuck Berry, the cars, the guitars, the girls, the sense of endless highway and endless night and sexual power."[52]

And as it had done to every other "last real man," America let him down. Springsteen's lyrics painted a relentlessly bleak portrait of the downward spiral of the white working class. Rebuffed and rejected, he sought escape or solace in sex, cars, male camaraderie, adventure, and, finally, in rock and roll itself. "Let's get out while we're still young," he sang on "Born to Run" (1975). But it all turned out to be illusory; there was no escape from the pain and dejection of life at the bottom. There was no relief from the working life, only darkness at the edge of town.

By contrast, his sound was energized, upbeat, anthemic. As if to underline the contradiction, Springsteen sang about the dead-end lives of workers, but his nickname was

"The Boss." His hit song "Born in the U.S.A." embodied this contradiction. A desultory story of a returning Vietnam veteran, the song is also a jubilant celebration of hope in the American Dream—even as that hope is being dashed by unemployment and governmental bureaucratic indifference. The characters in his songs are classic American tragic figures, whose tragic flaw is that they believe in the Dream.

But Springsteen now seemed to understand that the pain at the dead-end of dull routine in the factory life of his working-class father led him on his own quest for manhood, a quest that celebrated the traditional escape hatches for American men even as he saw their limits. The answers were to be found, not by fleeing the home, family, and domestic responsibility or through a mournful resignation to the traps of domesticated manhood, but by embracing them. In *Human Touch* and *Lucky Town* (both 1992) and "Blood Brothers" from his *Greatest Hits* album (1995), Bruce Springsteen grew up. He made his peace with the real world, seeing in his new experiences as husband and father the quotidian compromises that are the stuff of everyday heroism.

CHAPTER 10

From Anxiety to Anger
Since the 1990s

The "Self-Made Man" Becomes "Angry White Men"

Just as in the past, the turn of the twenty-first century found American men increasingly anxious; men feel their ability to prove manhood threatened by industrialization and deindustrialization, immigration and a perceived invasion. Industrialization and deindustrialization made men's hold on the successful demonstration of masculinity increasingly tenuous; there are fewer and fewer self-made successes and far more self-blaming failures. The segment of the economy that has been hardest hit—small shopkeepers, independent farmers, highly skilled manufacturing workers—is exactly the segment that clings most tenaciously to the ideology of self-made masculinity. At the same time, native-born American white men faced increased competition for those scarce jobs from newly arrived immigrants, and women "invaded" even those last all-male bastions like sports, the military, and military schools.

And now, just as we saw at the turn of the last century, American men's recourse to self-control, exclusion, and escape has reached a fevered pitch, fueling everything from the Boy Scouts and a sports craze to nativist anti-immigrant politics and efforts to prevent woman suffrage and women's entry into the public arenas, lest their presence make it harder for men to prove their manhood. And, as we've seen, the past few decades have witnessed a reprise of these themes. We're pumping up and working out obsessively to make our bodies impervious masculine machines, carving and sculpting these bodily works-in-progress, while we adorn ourselves with signifiers of a bygone era of unchallenged masculinity, donning Stetson cologne, Chaps clothing, and Timberland boots as we drive in our Cherokees and Denalis to conquer the urban jungle. We sought to block women's entry into the military and kept them out of some of the nation's elite country clubs; men opposed the implementation of Title IX regulations on campus, on the premise that gender equality in sports would hurt young men. And we ran off to the woods with the mythopoetics, rallied at sports stadiums with Promise Keepers, and spent our leisure time in upscale topless bars and watching Spike TV and *The Man Show*.

And amidst the evangelical Christian revival, one notices a reiteration of Muscular Christianity along the lines of the turn of the twentieth century. While Promise Keepers reinfused Jesus with manly vigor, they also insisted that his manhood was best expressed

216

through service, responsibility and prayer. Not so the "JBC Men," who promise to deliver the "shock and awe" gospel to manly men. JBC stands for "Jesus—Beer—Chips"—and the organization provides the beer and chips! With film clips from *Gladiator*, *Braveheart* and *Matrix*, these religious Rambos expound a "manly gospel," saturated with images of redemptive violence. (Even their website links military masculinity, 9–11, and evangelical Christianity: it's www.letsrollmen.com).

But one also notices a shift in some of these contemporary manifestations of American masculinity. The turn of the twenty-first century also finds American men increasingly angry, not anxious. To be sure, American men's anxieties about demonstrating and proving masculinity remain unabated. But American men are also angry. And specifically, it is those American men—white, native-born, middle and lower-middle class—who were the rank and file of our historical march of self-made masculinity who have become the angriest.[1]

American Anger

You see them everywhere. They're the ones who cut you off on the freeway, screaming with road rage if you dare to slow them down. If their kid doesn't make that suburban soccer team or that heartland hockey team, they're the ones who rush out onto the field to hit the coach or strangle the referee. They seethe with rage at their ex-wives (and their ex-wives' lawyers) in family court. They hiss, sometimes silently, with venomous anger when their corporation or law firm hires a woman or a minority, exploding in "sensitivity" workshops about how "diversity" and affirmative action are really reverse discrimination and how they are now reduced to "walking on eggshells." And if a kid doesn't get into the college of his or her parents' choice, the parents sue the schools claiming reverse discrimination. They shout with glee when a woman drops out of their military training or their fire department. Some even take up arms against their own country, establishing semi-autonomous enclaves and blowing up federal buildings. And, of course, when threatened by external forces, they muster up their coldest steel-eyed Dirty Harry imitation and say "Bring it on."

The past decade has witnessed mainstream white American men exploding like never before in our history. They draw their ranks from the middle class—office workers, salaried salesmen—and from the lower middle class skilled workers, small farmers, shopkeepers. They're the "Pa" in the Ma and Pa store, Richard Nixon's "silent majority," and "Reagan Democrats." They feel they've borne the weight of the world on their back, and they can't hold it up any longer. And now, suddenly, these regular guys are organizing militias and joining survivalist cults, waging war on "feminazis," promoting protectionist and anti-immigrant policies. They're listening to angry white men like Rush Limbaugh, Mike Savage, and a host of other radio hosts who lash out at everyone else as the source of their woes. They're trying to roll back the gains made by women and minorities in corporate and professional life and resisting their entry into the working-class professional ranks of soldier, firefighter, and police officer. And their sons are busy destroying the galaxy in their video games, listening to rappers like Eminem, or actually opening fire on their classmates.

And when they're not exploding in seemingly inexplicable rage, they're just plain angry and defensive. They're laughing at clueless henpecked husbands on TV sitcoms, snoring derisively at clueless guys who say the wrong thing on beer ads, snickering at duded-up metrosexuals prancing around major metropolitan centers while they drink Cosmos or imported vodka. Unapologetically "politically incorrect" magazines, radio hosts, and television shows abound, filled with macho bluster and bikini-clad women bouncing on trampolines. These venues are the new "boys' clubs" —the clubhouse that once said "No Gurls Allowed."

How did the chronic restlessness of the nineteenth century self-made man, which became the general malaise and discontent of twentieth-century masculinity, morph into the explosive rage of the twenty-first century? For one thing, the very adherence to traditional ideals of masculinity now leaves so many of them feeling cheated, unhappy, and unfulfilled.

American white men bought the promise of self-made masculinity, but its foundation has all but eroded. Instead of questioning those ideals, they fall back upon those same traditional notions of manhood—physical strength, self-control, power—that defined their fathers' and their grandfathers' eras, as if the solution to their problem were simply "more" masculinity. Yet few, if any, are kings of the hill, Top Guns, the richest and most powerful. If they can't be Number One, they've decided to be Number Two—with a bullet.

At the same time as white American men cling ever more tenaciously to old ideals, women and minorities have entered those formerly all-male bastions of untrammeled masculinity. Gender and racial equality often feel like a loss to white men: If "they" gain, "we" lose. Even if white American men have lost exceptionally little—even if every corporate board; large law firm; university board of trustees; local, state, and national legislative bodies, and small or medium-sized business enterprise in the nation are still in men's hands—men seem to also believe that their control is eroding, their grip on power loosening. Despite the fact that only 18 percent of white men earn less than $30,000 a year and a third make $75,000 or more, men feel themselves besieged, their entitlement thwarted, their stature belittled. We employ what I call a "wind chill" psychology: It doesn't really matter what the actual temperature is; what matters is what it feels like.

Of course it's also true that many white American men *have* lost something. A large swath of American men has experienced a gradual, but increasingly rapid, economic slide. Between 1979 and 1999, real wages for male high-school graduates dropped 24 percent. Since March 1998, 3.1 million manufacturing jobs have been lost, 2.5 million since George W. Bush became president in 2000. As Ed Landry, a 62-year-old machinist interviewed on the *Lehrer News Hour* said, "We went to lunch and our jobs went to China."[2]

As Norman Mailer observed, "the good average white American male ha[s] had very little to nourish his morale since the job market had gone bad." If the promise of the American "self-made" masculinity was the possibility of unlimited upward mobility, its dark side was the nightmarish possibility of equally unstoppable downward mobility. American manhood—always more about the fear of falling than the excitement of rising, always more about the agony of defeat, as it were, than the thrill of victory—suddenly felt desperate, clinging to whatever it could find, just trying to hold on.[3]

In the new global America, the rich have become much richer and the poor much poorer, and far more American men are pushed down than elevated. Many of the economic trends of the 1990s—outsourcing of manufacturing jobs, plant closings, downsizing, layoffs, cutbacks, and the gradual erosion of the safety net (health insurance, medical benefits, Social Security) instituted by the New Deal—have ushered in a new era of "social *in*security." And that social insecurity is gendered: It confounds men's sense of entitlement, their ability to be family providers and breadwinners. The Self-Made Man was an ideology of an emerging middle class; in a nation now increasingly polarized between extremely rich and increasingly poor, that definition of masculinity may be anachronistic. Many middle-class men may feel that their place in the world has suddenly evaporated. (Even today, as the ranks of the unemployed and uninsured continue to spiral, manufacturers of luxury goods, such as Gucci and Louis Vuitton, are reporting huge increases in their profits.) Many middle-class American men simply don't feel much like real men anymore. No wonder a manufacturing trade magazine's headline declared "A Seething Political Anger Rises in America's Industrial Heartland."[4]

Everywhere around the world, globalization is a deeply gendered process. As some areas are incorporated into the global network, others become marginalized; as some are pulled into market economies, others are pushed out. Masses of formerly sedentary people who lived in small traditional villages are suddenly on the move: Millions of women from the developing world are now partially integrated into a shadow realm of service jobs as domestic workers, child care providers, informal wage workers, and millions of men now populate squatter camps, labor camps, and migrant camps. Across the United States, enclaves of young male immigrants have emerged almost overnight as they try to gain a foothold in an economy in which their native-born white male counterparts are only barely holding on.

The final years of the twentieth century and the first few years of the twenty-first were characterized more by stories of downward than upward mobility. And while some analysts, such as Barbara Ehrenreich in *Nickel and Dimed* (2000), focused more on the plight of working-class women who were working sixty to eighty hours a week and trying to raise families (while right-wing radio shows chastised them for laziness and lack of motivation), many analysts turned their spotlight on the declining fortunes of men. Their "ongoing malaise," Mailer wrote, is due to the "daily drubbing" they have been taking economically. A cover story in *The New York Times Magazine* chronicled the declining fortunes of several formerly well-paid white-collar men who had been reduced to clerical and sales jobs.[5] The popular film *The Full Monty* (eventually, without irony, turned into a Broadway musical) chronicled the efforts of a group of downwardly mobile blokes in Britain's deindustrializing midlands to regain their sense of worth. Other stories poured in from the nation's breadbasket and rust belt, as farmers and industrial workers became increasingly desperate. Journalist Dale Maharidge's books, like *Journey to Nowhere* and *Homeland*, offered an ongoing chronicle of increasing despair and anger among downsized, laid-off manufacturing workers in America's heartland.[6]

In *Stiffed*, the 1999 follow-up to her best-selling book *Backlash*, journalist Susan Faludi took readers on a cross-country tour of this American "male-aise." In the bars and union halls surrounding closing factories, among the football fans of relocating teams, among angry military school cadets and entitled teenage predators, she recorded this sense of loss among American men: "a useful role in public life, a way of earning a decent and reliable living, appreciation in the home, respectful treatment in the culture." And, she writes, as "the male role has diminished amid a sea of betrayed promises, many men have found themselves driven to more domineering and some even 'monstrous' displays in their frantic quest for a meaningful showdown." Many American men, she observes, are "clinging to a phantom status."[7]

The few structural mechanisms that buttressed the Self-Made Man's ability to be a successful breadwinner and provider—minimum wage, the GI bill, high wage employment, and unions—have eroded or disappeared. Unon membership has declined from about 40 percent after World War II to about 13 percent today, and if you remove federal employees, it's closer to 8 to 9 percent, which makes the tenacious clinging to traditional ideals of manhood that much more difficult. And the old moral contract between industrial employer and employee—the fierce mutual loyalty that employees felt toward the company and that the company seemed to feel for them—now elicits a quaintly nostalgic, if knowing, smile.

The combination of these twin forces—clinging to these old ideals in the face of such dramatic economic and social changes—has been explosive. Men are angry and restless because of what they experience as the erosion of their "rightful" privilege. Sometimes, men take that anger out on themselves. Psychotherapist Terrence Real chronicled a dramatic rise in depression among American men, a psychological malady that is often described as anger turned inward back on one's self (which is why it had long been understood as a "female" problem). In rural America, suicide is now the leading cause of fatalities among farmers; in the 1990s, men were five times more likely to die by suicide than by accident.[8]

Sometimes, this male malaise is expressed as a yearning for a deeper, more authentic version of masculinity than the one on offer from the consumer economy. Even among those who had weathered the storms of the roiling economic booms and busts, there was still a lingering malaise, hints that the old ideals of masculinity had left younger men feeling empty. While in the 1980s, this sense that the standard definitions of masculinity had left middle-aged men seeking more emotional resonance (and hence the popularity of Robert Bly and the mythopoetic men's movements), by the mid-1990s, this had trickled down to their sons who were just starting out in their footsteps. And things were not going so well. A gnawing sense that their fathers' world was hollow, meaningless, and inauthentic led these young men not to ponytails and red Miata convertibles but to "fight clubs." Theirs was not a mid-life crisis but what one journalist called a "quarter-life crisis," and Chuck Palahniuk's novel *Fight Club* and its dark nightmarish film rendition became a touchstone text for the young men of Generation X.

In that novel, and the film based on it, a young man's fretful masculine malaise, his sense that his modest office job offers little authenticity or integrity, leads him to a manic hallucination in which he creates a club where men, almost all white, fight one another in bare-knuckled competition. While defeating one's foe is important, equally important is the authenticity offered by the fight itself, as if the receiving of those brutal blows confers the authentic manhood missing from these guys' lives. In one scene, Tyler Durden, the movie's protagonist, proclaims that "[w]e are the middle children of history, man, with no purpose or place; we have no great war, no great depression; our great war is a spiritual war, our great depression is our lives."[9]

Sometimes, men just lash out at "them," the "others," who now occupy the positions that once belonged to native-born middle-class white men. Sociologist Arlie Hochschild noted that this anger stems from structural sources, but it is often misdirected downward, against "'welfare cheats,' women, gays, blacks and immigrants" and outward "at alien ememies." Bruce Springsteen captured the pain and the rage of these downwardly mobile guys in his song "The Promised Land":

I've done my best to live the right way
I get up every morning and go to work each day
But your eyes go blind and your blood runs cold
Sometimes I feel so weak I just want to explode
Explode and tear this whole town apart
Take a knife and cut this pain from my heart
Find somebody itching for something to start.[10]

Let me offer a more personal example. Recently I appeared on a television talk show opposite three "angry white males" who felt they had been the victims of workplace discrimination. They complained that affirmative action was really "reverse discrimination" and that it had ushered in a "new" ideology of unfairness in economic life. The title of this particular show, no doubt to entice a large potential audience, was "A Black Woman Stole My Job." In my comments, I asked the men to consider just one word in the title of the show: the word "my." What made them think the job was theirs? Why wasn't the show titled "A Black Woman Got *the* Job" or "A Black Woman Got *a* Job"? It's because these guys felt that those jobs were "theirs," that they were entitled to them, and that when some "other" person (black, female) got the job, that person was really taking "their" job.

Such sentiments about entitlement reveal a curious characteristic of these new legions of angry white men: Although they still have most of the power and control in the world, they feel like victims. These ideas also reflect a somewhat nostalgic longing for that past world when men believed they could take their places among the nation's elite simply by working hard and applying themselves. Alas, such a world never existed; economic elites have always managed to reproduce themselves despite the ideals of a meritocracy, but that hasn't stopped men from believing in it. It is the American Dream. And when men fail, they are humiliated, with nowhere to place their anger. Some are looking for answers; others want payback.

Masculinity on Display in the New Millennium

As the dawn of the millennium approached and then passed, American men still felt an urgent need to prove their masculinity. The ground may have been shifting under their feet and old structural buttresses eroding or disappearing, but men remained faithful to the traditional recipe for masculinity. And they searched again through the time-tested ways men had always searched: self-control, exclusion, and escape. A spate of new magazines and TV shows celebrated "men behaving badly"—without apology. *Maxim* and *FHM*, among others, sought to grab the ever-elusive younger men's attention with inviting hotties on every cover. (They boast of 2.5 million and 1 million subscribers, respectively.[11]) The most successful issue of a "sports" magazine is the one with the near-nude pinups. By the summer of 2003, TNN reinvented itself as "Spike TV—The First Network for Men" (just in case domination of virtually every television network but Lifetime, Oxygen, and WE weren't enough). It's filled with extreme sports, adult-themed cartoons such as *Striperella* (featuring the voice of Pamela Anderson), pro-wrestling, titillation, and movie reruns. *The Man Show*, originally hosted by Jimmy Kimmel (no relation), featured bikini-clad buxom babes jumping on trampolines, while guys offered up inane locker room humor. Here is *The Man's Show's* theme song, an unabashed and ironic invitation to masturbation:

Grab a beer and drop your pants
Send the wife and kids to France
It's the Man Show!!

Quit your job and light a fart
Yank your favorite private part
It's the Man Show!!

Such loutish resurgence, however unapologetic or ironic it appeared on the surface, revealed a desperate anxiety lurking just underneath. Men could no longer take their entitlement to ogle for granted; after four decades of feminist critique, it had to be reasserted loudly, angrily, with more than just a whiff of sadness.

After all, men were no longer the only ones looking. Feminism had empowered women to look at men's bodies, and those bodies—perfectly sculpted, hairless, tan, and muscular—were displayed everywhere. From the famous 1983 Calvin Klein underwear ad featuring a photograph of Olympic pole-vaulter Tom Hintinauss splayed languidly against a white phallic spire on the Greek Island of Santorini to Marky Mark and a host of perfectly sculpted and well-endowed models, men's eroticized bodies have been on parade. No wonder that most men actually believe their penises are underaverage in size![12]

It makes some sense that men's efforts to prove masculinity through bodily display would reach a fever pitch in the 1990s and into the new millennium. The relentless economic squeeze of working men was now coupled with an economic squeeze on middle- and even upper-middle-class men—the cutbacks, layoffs, outsourcing, and downsizing—meant that those bodies were of decreasing utility, replaced by what Susan Faludi decried as "the ornamental culture." And just as every other generation of American men sought to demonstrate their masculinity through bodily display, so too has this one.

One of the most successful new magazines in history was *Men's Health*, launched in 1988, which seemed to equate physical or psychological health with erections, abdominal muscles, and sexual performance. "Whether you're a lumberjack or a hard-driving CEO," its promotional flyer reads, "[T]oday's man really does care about his health, his good looks, his waistline, his emotional well-being, and his sexuality—just as much as the women in his life care about theirs—*if not more so*."[13]

Ministering to men's sexual anxieties also took on new meanings since 1998, when Viagra hit the market. The most successful new drug ever launched in the United States —over 35,000 prescriptions were filled in the first two weeks alone, and millions since —Viagra, and its recent competitors Cealis and Levitra, is designed to treat "erectile dysfunction" (the current term for what used to be called "impotence") by enabling men to achieve and sustain erections. Viagra is not an aphrodisiac, creating the desire in the first place, but is designed to work only when there is adequate sexual desire, that is, when the men want to have sex and are aroused. And what therapists call "inhibited sexual desire" or "low sexual interest" (once interestingly called frigidity in women) is now the leading sexual problem among men.[14]

No sooner did Viagra appear than it was misunderstood—or misrepresented. One Pfizer sales representative made it sound like the Fountain of Sexual Youth, a performance enhancer, not a medical treatment for a physiological problem. Although the medical treatment is "what it's intended to be used for," he told an interviewer, "I think the real use of Viagra is, say, for the guy who is probably forty-plus to age sixty-five that just isn't what he used to be and . . . Viagra is a real enhancer to, uh, I hate the word 'performance' but . . . it will make it like he was when he was twenty." And millions of men gobbled the pills up. Men were eager—indeed, desperate—to see these problems as physiological even though most also experience "morning erections," which suggests that their problems are more psychological in origin. Many men crowed that they had found the "magic bullet" that enabled them to reclaim something they had lost—their potency, their power, their manhood. "You just keep going all night," gushed one man. "The performance is unbelievable." America had created "a masculinity pill."[15]

The stakes seem higher and the lengths (literally) to which men will go seem to be more extreme, but this may be more a matter of quantity than quality. Excessive bodybuilding and the use of chemical enhancements are, after all, nothing new in men's quest to be the hardest, strongest, and most powerful—or at least to appear to be so. The tonics and elixirs men consumed, and the "peniscope" and other contraptions from a century ago, seem both familiar and tame when placed next to contemporary iterations. Standards of muscularity have now increased so that many men experience what some researchers have labeled "Muscle Dysmorphia," the belief that one is insufficiently muscular. Harrison Pope and his colleagues call it the "Adonis Complex": the belief that men must look like Greek gods, with perfect chins, thick hair, rippling muscles, and washboard abdominals.[16] As an example, in 1999, he took G. I. Joe's proportions and translated them into real-life statistics. In 1974, G. I. Joe was 5 feet 10 inches tall and had a 31-inch waist, a 44-inch chest, and 12-inch biceps. Strong and muscular, it's true, but at least within the realm of the possible. By 2002, he was quite different: He's still 5 feet 10 inches tall, but his waist has shrunk to 28 inches, his chest has expanded to 50 inches, and his biceps are now 22 inches (almost the size of this waist). Such proportions would make one a circus freak, not a role model.[17]

As role models, they make many men feel they don't measure up. Nearly half of all men in one survey reported significant body image disturbance. A 1997 study reported in *Psychology Today* found 43 percent of the men were dissatisfied with their appearance, compared with only 15 percent twenty-five years earlier. As one college student told a journalist:

> When I look in the mirror, I see two things: what I want to be and what I'm not. I hate my abs. My chest will never be huge. My legs are too thin. My nose is an odd shape. I want what *Men's Health* pushes. I want to be the guy in the Gillette commercials.[18]

And just as women have resorted to increasingly dangerous surgical and prosthetic procedures, such as having silicone-filled baggies placed in their breasts or being given mild localized doses of botulism to paralyze facial muscles and thereby "remove" wrinkles, so too are men resorting to increasingly dramatic efforts to get large. The use of anabolic steroids has mushroomed. While chemically enhanced athletes steal most of the nation's outraged headlines, it's college-aged men who have become the primary consumers of steroids. Legal prescriptions for steroids have doubled since 1997, to more than 1.5 million, and countless more illegal sources provide less regulated doses. Steroids enable men to increase muscle mass quickly and dramatically so that they look incredibly big. Prolonged use also leads to dramatic mood changes, increased uncontrolled rage, and a significant shrinkage in the testicles.[19]

In their efforts to appear strong and healthy, fit and trim, men have followed women under the cosmetic surgeon's scalpel. Male patients now make up about 20 percent of all procedures. "More men are viewing cosmetic surgery as a viable way of looking and feeling younger," observed ASPRS President Dennis Lynch, MD, "especially, to compete in the workplace." Such a comment underscores the homosociality of men's demonstration of manhood: It is performed before the evaluative eyes of other men. Nowhere is this more painfully revealed than in a more extreme example of cosmetic surgery: penile enhancement. This is a dramatic (and expensive) procedure—every year about 15,000 men pay about $6,000 to have it done—by which the penis can be lengthened by about two inches.[20]

While one might think that men undergo this painful procedure to become "better" lovers or to please women more, the primary motivation is that the men suffer from what one physician called "locker room syndrome"—the fear of being judged as inadequately masculine *by other men*. Take, for example, the testimonial letter from a satisfied customer:

> I was always afraid to get into situation where I would have to shower with other men or be seen by anyone. I can remember avoiding many of the sports and activities I loved dearly, all because I was afraid that I would be seen and made fun of . . . I even avoided wearing shorts and tight clothes because of my fear that others would notice me.

"The thing I missed most was the changing room camaraderie and male bonding associated with these sports, which was always something I enjoyed," writes another. "I felt ashamed to even go to the urinals in a public place and have made sure I never use these whilst other men are there too."[21]

Men's bodies have long been symbols of masculinity in America. They reveal (or at least they signify), manhood's power, strength, and self-control. As the functional economic utility of that strong, hard body has virtually disappeared, its association with masculinity remains as firm as ever. Maybe it's no longer through doing hard work but by working out, and maybe now it is chemically or surgically enhanced, but still men believe the title of that feminist health classic: Our bodies are ourselves.

Here, Queer and Ever so Trendy

The traditional big, buff, and brawny image of muscular masculinity has also come in for his share of criticism by women who found him an insensitive lout, boorish and boring. "Chick flicks" such as *My Best Friend's Wedding* and *The Object of My Affection* imagined straight guys as clueless clods, while in both films it was gay men who were suddenly the men whom women wanted to be around. All the gal pals of the hit HBO comedy *Sex and the City* had good gay male friends and hoped that their boyfriends could become "gay straight men" (heterosexuals who exhibited gay affect and style) as opposed to "straight gay men" (who were simply closeted gay men). "Why can't you be more like him?" whispered many a straight woman to her boyfriend, nudging him in the ribs and pointing to Rupert Everett or Eric MacCormack in the hit sitcom *Will and Grace*. The message was simple: Gay men know what straight women want. And if straight men could just be a "little bit gay," they'd do very well among women.

Enter the "metrosexual." He's manicured, pedicured, buffed, and shined. His clothes are tailored. He knows all the latest hair care and skin care products. He pumps up and shops 'til he drops. He cooks, cleans, and preens. Oh, and by the way, he's straight.

The term *metrosexual* was coined by British journalist Mark Simpson in 1994 to describe a decidedly urban, and urbane, new man who was emerging in the cosmopolitan centers of Europe and the United States (To Simpson, international soccer star David Beckham was the prototype metrosexual: An urban dandy, wearing nail polish, married to a former Spice Girl.) *New York Times* writer Warren St. John recognized a version of him in upscale eateries and boutiques in New York in the summer of 2003. According to Simpson, the "typical metrosexual is a young man with money to spend, living in or within easy reach of a metropolis—because that's where all the best shops, clubs, gyms and hairdressers are."

Fashionable, preoccupied with proper skin and hair care, he represented the return of a newly masculinized dandy or fop. As such, he expressed the acceptance of at least one expression of the urban gay male sensibility; the emergence of the metrosexual is predicated on the partial decline in homophobia among heterosexual men. But the metrosexual is just as much a meditation about class as he is a new embodiment of manhood. It's a particular type of manhood: trim and fit, to be sure, but hardly pumped, and far more urbane and stylish than those hulking steroid-enhanced ectomorphs. The metrosexual promised an alternate route to the achievement of masculinity through high-end consumerism. The metrosexual was promoted as an upwardly mobile aspiration—middle-class guys dressing and accessorizing for success.

But even these metrosexual pioneers were riffing off the "liberated" masculinity of the late 1950s and early 1960s, described by journalist Barbara Ehrenreich in her book *The Hearts of Men* (1987). Ehrenreich claimed that several cultural trends in the 1960s enabled a group of middle-class white men to reject the traditional definition of masculinity (the stable, suburban, married breadwinner) and express a cheerful narcissism as they pampered themselves with high-end stereo equipment, sports cars, and wine cellars.

As the older action heroes were increasingly laughed off as cartoons—Vin Diesel and The Rock are pale substitutes for Arnold Schwarzenegger and Bruce Willis—metrosexuals began turning up as a happy compromise: Still secure in his masculinity, he has little to prove to anyone, yet he is equally comfortable expressing emotions and dispensing advice about hair care products. In the popular TV show, *Will and Grace*, Will is a model, not for gay men but for straight men—exactly the men who really want to know what will captivate beautiful, sexy, and interesting women like Grace. (He's set off against Jack, the flaming queen, so that we're able to accept Will as a "good gay," maybe even a "straight gay," and laugh at Jack, the "fey gay," or maybe even the "gay gay.")

One startling example has been the surprising success of the television show *Queer Eye for the Straight Guy*, which debuted in 2003. In it, the "Fab 5" (five clever, campy, and culturally sophisticated gay men) target a forlorn, disheveled straight guy and give him (and his apartment) a total makeover. Each of the five has a specialty: food and wine, home décor, hair styles, clothing, and interpersonal manners. And each works his transformative magic with wit and flair. In the debut episode, they transformed an aspiring artist named Brian into someone who actually looked like his nickname "Butch." When he first appeared, Brian looked like he had just returned from the Altamont concerts—in 1970! Dirty brown overalls, long stringy hair, unkempt beard, and an apartment just one slight move up from cantaloupe crates for records and concrete blocks and boards for books. One half-hour later (in TV time, of course), he looks fabulous. His beard is now a goatee, his hair shaped and stylish, his clothing elegantly dressed-down chic, and his apartment the well-appointed home of a bachelor. That evening, women are so stunned by his transformation that their sexual interest oozes from every gaping stare. He's become a babe magnet—dashing, well mannered, utterly sexy.

Many critics argued that the metrosexual was hardly a progressive step toward a new masculinity but instead represented simply a narcissistic unapologetic consumer. And some felt *Queer Eye* only reinforced stereotypes of gay men as self-absorbed fashion plates. On the other hand, for once the stereotypes seem to work the other way: At the same time that gay men and lesbians are counseled that through "conversion therapy" they can become straight, in this "reality" show, the straight guy is transformed into an almost-gay guy. In that sense *Queer Eye* depends at least in part on the erosion of homophobia among straight men. Imagine such a show in 1993, not 2003. Most viewers would have thought a show with the title *A Queer Eye for the Straight Guy* was about gay men hitting on straight men in a bar. The second episode would have been called *A Black Eye for the Gay Guy*.

Yet a steady weekly parade of straight guys have invited the Fab Five into their homes and let them rifle through their closets while launching cutting campy barbs about their lifestyle. The men touch each other affectionately and make caustic remarks dripping with sexual innuendo. And by the end of the show, the straight guy . . . hugs them! He thanks them! He realizes he needs them! Ironically, it's the insecurity of heterosexuality that begins to erode homophobia. "We're here, we're queer, we're fabulous, and we know what women want" is the message of *Queer Eye*. And if you're going to make it with the *Sex and the City* type of sexy single modern woman, the show seems to say, you'll need us to show you how.

Of course, metrosexuality is not for every man, let alone Everyman. Many younger men remain insecure about their sexuality and are unwilling to be mistaken for gay. "I don't want to be associated with some pansy wearing Kenneth Cole," one young man explained. After all, "That's so gay" continues to be the single most common putdown in middle schools and high schools in the nation. Metrosexuals are also mostly white men. Some wealthier and older black men can and do represent themselves as metrosexuals, such as K-Street's Roger G. Smith. Others choose an urban aesthetic that is less demonstrably gay, less feminine, and much less white. A *New York Times Magazine* article examining black men's lives "on the down low" revealed that many black men having sex with other black men refused to call themselves gay, not just because of the stigma of gayness and the loss of masculinity they associate with it, but because of gayness' association with whiteness.

Metrosexuality expresses many of the tensions among contemporary American men. It's playful in its gender bending and sexual tolerance and in its depoliticized consumerism masquerading as freedom. At its best, metrosexuality may promote reconciliation between straight and gay men. "Gay guys and straight guys may do things a little differently in the bedroom," says *Queer Eye* creator David Collins, "but in the end, we're all just guys."[22] Since our culture has devalued "feminine" men for so long, metrosexuality offers a sense of vindication for some men. As one women exclaimed, "There have always been guys like these, but it wasn't the popular thing. . . . Guys who are acting this way today are considered attractive." It may be liberating to "bend it like Beckham"—gender, that is.

Nativism, Racism, and Downward Mobility

Metrosexual self-absorption represents the apex of bodily reinvention: Masculinity can be accessorized. But in the wake of the dramatic economic downturns of the post-dot.com market boom, such class aspirations may resound like a cruel joke. Other men remain wedded to exclusion as their way to stake a claim for manhood. In the wake of massive job displacement, the loss of entitlement, and increased competition in the public sphere and the erosion of unchallenged domestic power at home, many men have circled the wagons and defensively sought to demonstrate their manhood by keeping the "others" out. As in earlier generations, these men sought to restore their masculinity through renewed efforts to recalibrate the increasingly level playing field in their favor. Opposition to women's military service remained significant despite women's increased integration. (After women's admission, the number of male applicants to the Citadel and VMI increased; instead of women dragging standards down, they actually increased the schools' competitiveness.) Police and fire departments were increasingly gender battlegrounds.

Take, for example, the fire department of New York City, the whitest and most male firefighting force in any major city in the country. Less than one-quarter of 1 percent (0.245 percent) of the city's 12,000 firefighters is female. Statistically that's two out of every thousand firefighters. In reality, it's fewer than thirty women. Between 1982 and 1992, the NYFD hired no women at all. In addition, less than 3 percent of firefighters in New York City are black (2.87 percent) and 4.4 percent are Hispanic according to the Vulcan Society, an organization devoted to promoting the interests of black firefighters.

That's not the case everywhere. Nationwide, 5,600 women serve as full-time firefighters and another 40,000 in volunteer departments. Women account for greater than 15 percent of the total number of firefighters in Minneapolis, San Francisco, and Miami. Women account for about 3 percent of Los Angeles's firefighters and nearly 2 percent of Chicago's. In Los Angeles, 14 percent of firefighters are black and 30 percent are Hispanic. In Chicago, almost 19 percent are black. In Philadelphia, the only major city that comes close to New York in excluding women (with only 0.4 percent of firefighters being women), over 26 percent of firefighters are black and another 3.2 percent are Hispanic. Boston (29 percent), Baltimore (30 percent), Dallas (42 percent), Detroit (50 percent), Milwaukee (11 percent), San Francisco (40 percent), Cincinnati (35 percent), and Washington, D.C. (63 percent) all far surpass New York's paltry percentage.

The NYFD is both far whiter and more male than the NYPD. Nationwide, of the 176 largest departments, women hold about 14 percent of all sworn law enforcement positions. In New York, 15 percent of police officers are women, 14 percent are black, and 17 percent are Hispanic. Again, compare this to Chicago (where 22.16 percent of police officers are women, 26.1 percent are black, and another 14.4 percent are Hispanic) or Los Angeles (17 percent women, 14 percent black, 30 percent Hispanic) or Philadelphia (22 percent women, 33 percent black, 5 percent Hispanic). In Madison, Wisconsin, nearly 30 percent of police officers are women, the highest percentage in the country.

Why should there be such opposition to women and minorities in the city's firehouses? For one thing, New York's fire chiefs have remained indifferent and often hostile to women's entry. This attitude at the top only reinforces the fraternity house atmosphere of many firehouses. Unlike police officers, firefighters live and work together in twenty-four-hour shifts, cooking, cleaning, drilling, and sleeping in close quarters. The intimacy that arises from this same-sex living situation is superimposed on an older and more venerable fraternal tradition. Historically, fire departments grew out of the same impulses as mid-nineteenth-century fraternal orders, with their own rituals, symbols, hearty cama- raderie, and rites of initiation. Invading these homosocial preserves invariably produces resentment, and the first women in NYFD's firehouses were greeted by discrimination and harassment. They were subject to humiliating behaviors from male firefighters, who uri- nated in the women's boots and spied on their dressing rooms through secret peepholes.

Contrast this with the nation's military, another fighting force that requires close quar- ters, the activities sleeping and eating done together, trust, and intimacy. Women currently make up 15 percent of the U.S. armed forces, nearly double the percentage from 1980 and a one-third increase since the last Gulf War. The percentages of blacks (29 percent) and Hispanics (8.7 percent) in the military make the armed forces among the nation's most diverse institutions. The dramatic lack of diversity in New York City's fire department cannot be attributed to chance, inadequate recruitment, or lack of qualifications. Race and gender discrimination are a lingering stain on the magnificent heroism and courage shown by the city's firefighters on September 11, 2001. In their quest to prove their manhood, "New York's Bravest" seem to be afraid of gender and racial equality.

Downward mobility hit the lower middle classes hard. The skilled workers in America's manufacturing plants watched as their union-protected jobs were sent overseas. Highly trained, apprenticeship-based craft workers were displaced by ever-cheaper (and increasingly immigrant) laborers. Enormous numbers of small farmers lost their farms as American agriculture consolidated into gigantic agribusinesses today, less than 7 percent of all farms account for nearly 75 percent of all farm sales. And legions of small shop- keepers, owners of Ma and Pa stores, bore silent witness as Wal-Mart and other big-box emporia stores moved into nearby malls and drove them out of business. The Heroic Artisan, once the hardworking backbone of American labor, had all but disappeared. As Lillian Rubin writes:

> It's this confluence of forces—the racial and cultural diversity of our new immigrant population; the claims on the resources of the nation now being made by those minorities who, for generations, have called America their home; the failure of some of our basic institutions to serve the needs of our people; the contracting economy, which threatens the mobility aspirations of working class families—all these have come together to leave white workers feeling as if everyone else is getting a piece of the action while they get nothing.[23]

Especially hard hit were not the "Pas" of those Ma and Pa stores, but their sons. As their fathers' farms foreclosed, their shops closed, their jobs were shipped out, their sons were increasingly dispossessed of what they regarded as their birthright. And they grew increas- ingly angry—and politically mobilized. The Reagan Democrats of the 1980s had morphed into NASCAR dads, angry white male voters fed up with liberal handouts to the "unde- serving," eager to regain and restore their rightful inheritance.

The White Wing[24]

One of the most disturbing expressions of white male rage has been the increased visibility of the extreme right. The Southern Poverty Law Center cites 676 active hate groups in the United States, ranging from older organizations such as the Ku Klux Klan and American Nazi Party to Holocaust deniers, neo-Nazis, racist skinheads, White Power groups such as Posse Comitatus and the White Aryan Resistance (WAR), pagan and other religious extremists, and radical militia or other paramilitary groups.[25] Prior to 9-11, the single most lethal terrorist attack in U.S. history was the 1995 bombing of the federal building in Oklahoma City by Timothy McVeigh, a member of the Aryan Republican Army (ARA).

While the racism, homophobia, and nativism of these groups have long drawn comment and criticism, few analysts seem to have noticed the ways their ideologies and their paramilitary organizations are saturated with images of masculinity. In that respect, they remind the cultural historian of the Know Nothings of 1844, and other anti-immigrant groups in earlier eras of dramatic class dislocation, like the 1840s and the 1890s. The White Wing is composed almost entirely of downwardly mobile lower-middle-class young white men. They are the sons of small shopkeepers, skilled craft workers, and small farmers whose future, they feel, has been mortgaged by economic globalization, downsizing, the farm credit crisis, and the exporting of manufacturing jobs to the Third World. "The American Dream was a dead end for these men," writes journalist Mark Hamm, "and with the dream's demise came a profound sense of humiliation."[26] "For generations, white middle class men defined themselves by their careers, believing that loyalty to employers would be rewarded by job security and, therefore, the ability to provide for their families" is the way one issue of *Racial Loyalty* (a racist skinhead magazine) puts it. "But the past decade—marked by an epidemic of takeovers, mergers, downsizings and consolidations—has shattered that illusion."

The ideologies of White Aryan groups range widely.[27] Most celebrate a nostalgic vision of small-scale American villages populated by Heroic Artisans and Jeffersonian yeomen farmers. Politically, many fuse their critiques of international organizations such as the United Nations with protectionism and neo-isolationism, claiming that all international organizations are part of the great Zionist conspiracy to take control of the world. Some embrace a grand imperial vision of American (and other Aryan) domination of the rest of the world and the final subjugation of "inferior races." Theologically, they span the fringes from fundamentalist Christianity and Christian splinter groups, to neo-Pagans and "Odinists." They love America but hate its government. They are fiercely patriotic and pro-American but also see the government as captured by multiculturalism, feminism, and Zionism. And they love capitalism but hate corporations. Aryans support capitalist enterprise and entrepeneurship, especially the virtues of the small proprietor, but are vehemently antiurban, anticommunist, anticosmopolitan, and anticorporate. In their eyes Wall Street is ruled by Jewish-influenced corporate plutocrats who hate "real" Americans.

In many cases, their organization reflects their ideologies. Some live together in quasi-communal bands; others seek to establish white-only incorporated towns. Some integrate their movement participation with otherwise unremarkable suburban or small-town life; others live in isolated cabins in the woods, connected to the world by Internet. Many meet regularly at retreats, gun shows, or concerts by their "hate-core" rock bands (hard-core punk and metal music, laden with racist lyrics). A few of the more extreme groups operate as lone-wolf leaderless cells, securing their organizational structures from government infiltration and preventing arrest.

But the one thing that unites all these groups is their vision of masculinity. They see themselves as besieged white men, protecting white women and the traditional family from rapacious sexual predators and protecting a distinctly American vision of masculinity—the Self-Made Man. The rhetoric, recruitment strategies, mobilizing mentality, and organizational structures promise the restoration of masculinity and the reclamation of that entitlement.

Men on the extreme right feel they've been emasculated by the "Nanny State" through taxation, economic policies, and political initiatives that demand civil rights and legal protection for everyone. They feel deprived of their entitlement (their ability to make a living, freely and independently) by a government that now doles it out to everyone else —nonwhites, women, and immigrants. The emasculation of the native-born white man has turned a nation of warriors into a nation of lemmings; they call the unenlightened American people "sheeple." In *The Turner Diaries*, one of the movement's most celebrated texts, author William Pierce castigates his countrymen as having become "sissies and weaklings . . . flabby, limp-wristed, non-aggressive, non-physical, indecisive, slack-jawed, fearful."[28] As Day of the Sword, a popular racist skinhead band, puts it in "No Crime Being White":

> The birthplace is the death of our race.
> Our brothers being laid off is a truth we have to face.
> Take my job, it's equal opportunity
> The least I can do, you were so oppressed by me
> I've only put in twenty years now.
> Suddenly my country favors gooks and spicks and queers.[29]

As others before them, the extreme right also demeans the masculinity of "others," their perceived enemies. Consistently, the masculinity of native-born white Protestants is set off against the dehumanized masculinity of the others (blacks, Jews, gay men, other nonwhite immigrants) who are variously depicted as either too masculine (rapacious beasts, avariciously cunning, voracious) or not masculine enough (feminine, dependent, effeminate). The combined forces of their racism, anti-Semitism, nativism, and homophobia are all channeled into denunciations of the others' masculinity. Anti-Semitism unites these groups. They see Jews both as physically weak, unathletic, and unmanly and as omnivorously powerful, the creators of Zionist Occupied Government (ZOG) which controls the destiny of the entire world. In their eyes, Jews orchestrate immigration, distribute pornography, and foster homosexuality and decadent morality.

Finally, these groups use masculinity as a device for recruitment and mobilization, promising the restoration of manhood. "Real men" who join up will simultaneously protect white women from these marauding rapacious beasts, reestablish the patriarchal family, earn those women's admiration and love, and reclaim their Self-Made Manhood. Recruitment efforts often offer the promise of the newly virilized neo-Nazi warrior sailing off into the sunset with a buxom Aryan babe on each arm. This restoration can only be accomplished by violent direct action.

Musical Masculinities

If not through direct action, masculinity can at least be expressed through musical fantasy. Perhaps no cultural phenomenon expresses the new masculine anger better than popular music. Many attendees at hard rock and heavy metal concerts make barely a pretense of listening to the music, since the real action is in the mosh pits and slam dancing, stage jumping, and crowd surfing—all largely white middle-class hypermasculine domains. While it may be refreshing to express one's rage directly rather than rely on performers to express it for you, it's also significant that these white middle-class suburban guys have so much rage to express in the first place. "You gotta fight for your right to party," sang the Beastie Boys (white upper-middle-class prep-school sons of NYU professors who turned themselves into angry pseudo-rappers).

Since the early 1990s, two trends have dominated the pop music scene; not coincidentally, both are expressions of this new masculine anger: the increased popularity of a new amplified and "rockified" country and western sound that has become "the" vernacular music among NASCAR dads, and the spread of rap, and especially gangsta rap, into white middle-class suburbs. The mainstreaming of rap and country reflects the divergent musical and cultural sensibilities of rural and urban America (or red and blue zones). But both play so well in suburbia that it is not uncommon for young white males to collect CDs in both genres. These trends shouldn't come as too much of a surprise; after all, the two share some important qualities: compare country's preoccupation with lost love and rap's lyrics' attempt to mask that vulnerability by imagining women as meaningless playthings. Or compare the way they deal with economic hardships: country's celebration of simple pleasures like beer and cars and rap's celebration of vulgar wealth. And besides, they both grow out of a genre that's long been coded as "masculine," notwithstanding the plethora of female stars. Its twin themes of sexual urgency (love and longing) and teen rebellion against authority capture a developmental moment, a cultural sensibility, and a gender identity all at once. And the harder the rock, the more gender asymmetrical are its performers and fan bases.

Country music has long been the music of America's rural working class, farmers and small shopkeepers on Main Street, U.S.A. It's a somewhat forgiving music: Men and women both make foolish choices, but they are resilient and dust themselves off and get back in the saddle. And it's a deeply emotional music; indeed, while so many male rock and rap singers are boasting of their strength and sexual prowess, a long line of male country stars sing mournfully about grief, inadequacy, and confusion about what it means to be a man at all.

Garth Brooks was the paragon of this understanding and compassionate male; his fusion of emotional vulnerability and onstage bravado into a sort of "sensitive S.O.B." propelled him to crossover superstardom in the 1990s. Toby Keith, an emerging star, makes no such efforts to limit his sensitive side. Keith identifies with the hardworking Everyman, trying to be a father, a good husband, and proud solider—indeed, trying to be "Everything to everyone" because, simply, it's his responsibility. Unappreciated, unheralded, even scorned, he captures the political resentments of the white lower middle class and spits them back at those in power. Unabashedly politically right wing, Keith wouldn't want you to "take this job and shove it"; he'd just like to be left alone to do his job in the first place. But if you don't let him, watch out. He doesn't get mad; he gets even.[30]

Few cultural observers could fail to miss the increased rhetorical violence in American pop music, especially in the hypermasculine posing of heavy metal and hip-hop. And while there is little empirical evidence that this increased rhetorical violence mirrors any appreciable increase in real violence, there is also little doubt that the anger level has been ratcheted up several notches since even Axl Rose and his hard-rocking cronies of the mid-1980s. The denigration of women to, as Snoop Dogg sang, "bitches and ho's," the viciousness of the homophobic slurs, and the general full-throttle phallic posturing are evidence enough of an insecure masculinity in constant, incessant, even obsessive need of demonstration, determined to assert itself.[31]

Many of rap's defenders argue that these symbolic assertions of manhood are necessary for inner-city black youth, for whom racism and poverty are so emasculating. But who could have predicted rap's success among white suburban youth? Hardly confined to the idiom of the 'hood, rap has become the vernacular of adolescent American masculinity. Four of every five gangsta rap CDs are purchased by white suburban teenagers.

Perhaps the most successful purveyor of this crossover has been Eminem. Eminem burst onto the musical scene in 1999 with his *Slim Shady LP*. (Eminem alternates among three different personae: Shady, his rapper name, is his angry, vicious adolescent who imagines raping his male cousin and slashing his mother's throat; Marshall Mathers, his given name, reveals his "real" emotions, and Eminem, his "show name," allows him to become a show business spectacle.) Unlike previous white rappers, like Vanilla Ice, Eminem immediately established his street credibility based on class, not race. His impoverished downwardly mobile white working-class Detroit background matched that of so many other whites who had drifted to the far right; Eminem took himself into the urban ghetto rather than into the woods with the Michigan Militias. (In his autobiographical film *8 Mile*, his ultimate success comes as he defeats a middle-class black rapper who goes to prep school, thus asserting class solidarity over racial divisiveness.)

Since his earliest albums (all produced by the rap star and impresario Dr. Dre), Eminem managed to express the anger and malaise-driven angst of white suburban guys while maintaining his credibility among inner-city blacks, who are the arbitrators of the genre. Like other rappers, he drew from a deep well of class-based, gendered rage— a murderous rage directed largely at his mother and girlfriend—as well as adolescent declarations of manhood that were part protest and part phallic fluff. Poverty was emasculating; reclaiming manhood required confronting those who were his competitors. He tapped into the desire and thrill of revenge that animate much adolescent masculinity; his favorite targets for that revenge were women and gay people. "Eminem spoke of situations many of his fans shared," according to his biographer, "broken homes, dead-end jobs, drug overindulgence—while exploring taboo emotions many couldn't face—parental hate, gender hate, self-loathing."[32]

Several songs are explicitly violent. Some offer soliloquies of murderous revenge, like "Kim" from the *Slim Shady* LP in which he chokes his ex-girlfriend to death for leaving him:

> Grabbed her by the throat, it's murder she wrote,
> You barely heard a word as she choked,
> It wasn't nothing for her to be smoked

To most women, he has only this to say: "You ain't nothing but a slut to me." And he parades that he's been "put here to put fear in faggots" and then boasts of "rapin' lesbians while they screamin: 'let's just be friends!'"

Eminem's incessant homophobia and misogyny drew equally incessant criticism. Women's groups denounced his cavalier calls to murder the women who stand in your way; gay groups found his obsession with "faggots" threatening in an era when gay bashing is on the rise and young men like Mathew Shepard are murdered. But he's been neither contrite nor apologetic. He's self-righteous, angrier at liberal critics who demand that he hew to a confining politically correct line. "Now I'm catchin the flack from these activists, Why they raggin, Actin' like I'm the first rapper to smack a bitch and say faggot." In his defense, he blames everyone else: "parents who would rather blame entertainment than own up to their own shortcomings, the media who judged an artist by his words out of context, and everyone incapable of digesting a complex piece of entertainment no more violent than an R-rated film."[33]

His most recent albums, which stand as public pronouncements of this injured masculinity, still find Eminem posing as the besieged victim, "the hurt and angry misunderstood underdog," despite the millions of dollars he's earned as a rock superstar.[34] To his standard tormentors (his mother and women in general), he's added music critics and the general public, but his posture has lost its credibility and vitality; he's become a caricature of his earlier incarnation, a cartoon burlesque. Like Sylvester Stallone and The Rock and every other claw-his-way-to-the-top masculine icon before him, the luxuriant lifestyle of the rich and famous is equally enervating and soft; Eminem's assertion of hard-scrabble masculinity now puts him in danger of becoming a clown.

Defending the Caveman: The New Male Bashers

Traditional definitions of masculinity have their supporters. As has always been the case throughout American history, when masculinity is perceived as in crisis, there are those who defend a nostalgic traditional vision of gender relations that would return men to their "rightful" position of dominance. In the nineteenth century, this defense relied on theological arguments; by the turn of the twentieth century, biological arguments had supplanted religion as the dominant defensive discourse. Today it's both biology *and* theology—even if they do make rather strange bedfellows. In fact, defenders of traditional masculinity will use virtually any rhetorical means they can find. Many recapitulate backlash arguments from the 1970s and 1980s, blaming feminism for the gender "inversion" that has created men's plight. The sustained "assaults" by feminism and multiculturalism have made a biological imperative into a political liability. A few now go as far as to claim that in promoting girls and women, American society had swung the pendulum so far that we were making male biology a political "problem." Yet, in the guise of promoting and defending men and masculinity, these defenders actually celebrated a definition of masculinity that was far more insulting and "male bashing" than anything ever promulgated by feminists.

Take, for starters, the new academic field of "evolutionary psychology," which offers a pseudo-biological argument for male dominance. Taking up where sociobiology left off in the 1970s, evolutionary psychology sees men behaving badly as men behaving naturally, the way men are biologically programmed to behave. In the evolutionary psychological worldview, all human nature and all gender-based differences are encapsulated in the differences between males and females in the mating game. Males and females, we learn, have different reproductive "strategies" based on the size and number of their reproductive cells. From the cellular (sperm and egg), we get the psychological (namely, motivation, intention, perhaps even cognition). Male reproductive success comes from impregnating as many females as possible; females' success comes from enticing a male to provide and protect the vulnerable and dependent offspring. Sex is "something females have that males want," according to Donald Symons.[35] Thus males have a natural predisposition toward promiscuity, sex without love, and parental indifference; females have a natural propensity for monogamy, love as a precondition of sex, and parental involvement. "It is possible to interpret *all* other differences between the sexes as stemming from this one basic difference," writes Richard Dawkins in his celebrated work *The Selfish Gene*. "Female exploitation begins here."[36]

These arguments have been effectively exposed as ideology masquerading as science by primatologist Sarah Blaffer Hrdy, who has used the exact same empirical observations to construct an equally plausible case for females' natural propensity toward promiscuity (to seduce many males into believing the offspring is theirs and thus ensure survival by increasing food and protection from those males) and males' natural propensity toward monogamy (to avoid being run ragged providing for offspring that may—or may not—be their own). If I were a female at the mythic Darwinian moment of origin, Hrdy suggests, and if I knew that I had to invest a lot of time and energy in reproduction, I'd do the following: I'd "decide" to conceal ovulation so that any male I mate with would believe he is the father of my children and would then have to protect and provide for the reproduction of his genetic material. Then I'd promptly go out and have sex with as many males as possible so that each would believe the off spring to be his, and then each would run himself ragged feeding and protecting all the children who might—or might not—be his. Hoggamus higgamous, woman's polygamous! Female exploitation actually *ends* there; that is, it's a present day phenomenon read back into a mythic history, a faux-Darwinian "just-so" story.

In an effort to ensure successful reproduction, a reasonable man, by contrast, probably calculates the likelihood of any particular mating resulting in a healthy live offspring. Do the math, as journalist Natalie Angier does in her marvelous book *Woman, An Intimate Geography*. Let's say that I am able, somehow, to know when a woman is ovulating (unlike other mammals that go into heat, human females conceal ovulation, thus masking their periods of fertility) and therefore is likely to conceive. The odds are still nearly two to one against fertilization *on the day she is ovulating*. Even if conception occurs, the embryo still has nearly a one-third chance of miscarrying at some point. Thus, as Angier puts it, "[E]ach episode of fleeting sex has a remarkably small probability of yielding a baby—no more than 1 or 2 percent at best." But if a man were to invest a lot more time with one woman, mating with her often and preventing her from possible matings with others (what animal behaviorists call "mate guarding"), then his odds of successful reproduction would significantly increase. Higgamus hoggamus, it's man who's monogamous! And just to keep her in her place, he would surround his sexual control over her with an ideological veneer (let's call it "love") and by legally sanctioning it by church and state (let's call that "marriage"). What gender invented love anyway? And given that men control all other arenas of social, economic, and political life, why would they ever cede the single most important arena—successful reproduction, the raison d'etre of all life—to women?

While the feminist critique exposes evolutionary psychology's ideological view of women, its view of men is even more noxious. "Human males are by nature oppressive, possessive, flesh-obsessed pigs," writes Robert Wright. "Giving them advice on

successful marriage is like offering Vikings a free booklet titled 'How Not to Pillage,' "
he writes in his best-selling book *The Moral Animal.*[37] It would be hard to find a more
insulting view of masculinity than Randy Thornhill and Craig Palmer's *A Natural History
of Rape* (1999), which goes so far as to claim that rape is "a natural, biological
phenomenon that is a product of human evolutionary heritage."[38]

Since, they argue, each male's biological predisposition is to reproduce, and reproductive success comes from spreading his seed as far and wide as possible, women are
actually the ones with the power, since they get to choose which males will be successful.
"But getting chosen is not the only way to gain sexual access to females," they write.
"In rape, the male circumvents the females' choice."[39] Rape is the evolutionary mating
strategy of losers, males who cannot otherwise get a date. Rape is an alternative to
romance; if you can't always have what you want, you take what you need. As they write:

> [H]uman males in all societies so far examined in the ethnographic record possess genes
> that can lead, by way of ontogeny, to raping behavior when the necessary environmental
> factors are present, and that the necessary environmental factors are sometimes present in
> all societies studied to date.[40]

All men have the "motivation" to rape; all they need is social permission. Who says no one
in his or her right mind could possibly believe that all men are rapists? Since "selection
favored males who mated frequently," they argue, then "rape increased reproductive success."[41] But why should this be true? Might it not also be the case that being hardwired
to be good lovers and devoted fathers enabled us to be reproductively successful? One
might argue that selection did not favor males who mated frequently but those who mated
well, since successful mating is more than spreading of seed. Being an involved father may
ensure reproductive success far better than rape.

Thornhill and Palmer offer a far more "misandrous" account of rape than anything
offered by radical feminists. To them, men are driven by evolutionary imperatives to rape,
pillage, and destroy in order to ensure that they are still reproductively successful.
This view is echoed by several neo-conservative thinkers who, in their effort to discredit
feminism and gay liberation, actually end up insulting men.

The argument begins as a critique of feminism. By abandoning their natural roles as
wives and mothers in the home and seeking satisfaction in the workplace in some vain imitation of men, women (encouraged by feminism) have reversed nature's plan and wreaked
social havoc. Women's naturally demure sexual purity no longer tames men. Absentee
fathers, sexual promiscuity, gang rape, and homosexuality are the inevitable results. George
Gilder's 1986 *Men and Marriage* (the republication of his 1973 book *Sexual Suicide*)
offers a Hobbesian view of masculinity: "solitary, poor, nasty, brutish and short."[42]

Men are, by nature, violent, sexually predatory, and irresponsible:

> Men lust, but they know not what for; they wander, and lose track of the goal; they fight
> and compete, but they forget the prize; they spread seed, but spurn the seasons of growth;
> they chase power and glory, but miss the meaning of life.[43]

An "importunate, undifferentiated lust . . . infects almost all men." Male sexuality is hap-
hazard, irresponsible, non-procreative; intercourse is "the only male sex act."[44] Sexually

inferior, men compensate with sexual aggression and predation. Gilder reserves his fiercest animus for younger men and boys who are, in his eyes, untamed beasts:

> Every society, each generation, faces an invasion by barbarians. They storm into the streets and schools, businesses and households of the land, and, unless they are brought to heel, they rape and pillage, debauch and despoil the settlements of society.[45]

Who are they? "These barbarians are young men and boys," Gilder informs us, who are "entirely unsuited for civilized life." Without marriage, the single man is "poor and neurotic. He is disposed to criminality, drugs and violence. He is irresponsible about his debts, alcoholic, accident prone, and susceptible to disease."[46] These young men, single and unattached, must be brought into the civilizing project by women. It is women's job to "transform male lust into love; channel male wanderlust into jobs, homes, and families." It is women who "conceive the future that men tend to flee; . . . [and] feed the children that men ignore."[47]

Gilder suggests if men stay single, the sexual demons reign, leading to the worst scourge of all: homosexuality. In an interesting reversal of stereotypes, gay men are, in Gilder's view, untamed sexual beasts: "[W]ith their compulsive lust and promiscuous impulses [gay men] offer a kind of caricature of typical single male sexuality."[48] Gay men are real men after all; in fact they're more "real" than straight men.

Other conservative policy analysts continue to build on Gilder's shaky foundation. For example, Charles Murray, coauthor of *The Bell Curve*, holds that young males are "essentially barbarians for whom marriage . . . is an indispensible civilizing force." Christina Hoff Sommers, author of *Who Stole Feminism?* and *The War Against Boys*, told an audience that "masculinity without morality is dangerous and destructive." And sociologist David Popenoe warns that "[e]very society must be wary of the unattached male, for he is universally the cause of numerous social ills."[49]

Popenoe is one of the chief academic proponents of a position that holds that irresponsible men are the cause of a current crisis in the institution of marriage. Fathers must remain attached to their families. "Men are not biologically as attuned to being committed fathers as women are to being committed mothers. Left culturally unregulated, men's sexual behavior can be promiscuous, their paternity casual, their commitment to families weak," he writes.[50]

Pundit David Blankenhorn makes a similar case in his near-hysterical book *Fatherless America* (1995), a collection of specious correlations that together blame virtually every social pathology on absent fathers. Often the correlations simply have it backward: Fatherlessness is more often the *consequence* of poverty than it is the cause.[51] Instead of a clarion call for a new fatherhood, based on emotional receptivity and responsiveness, compassion and patience, care and nurture, though, Blankenhorn actually despises that model of a "nurturing" man who "expresses his emotions," is "a healer, a companion, a colleague," a "deeply involved parent." He has little use for a father who "changes diapers, gets up at 2:00 A.M. to feed the baby, goes beyond 'helping out' in order to share equally in the work, joys, and responsibilities of domestic life."[52]

In Blankenhorn's view, this sensitive New Age father does all this because he "reflects the puerile desire for human omnipotentiality in the form of genderless parenthood, a direct repudiation of fatherhood as a gendered social role for men."[53] So the *real* father is neither nurturing nor expressive; he is neither a partner nor a friend to his wife, and he sleeps through most of the young baby's infantile helplessness, oblivious to the needs of his wife and child. Men are fathers, but they are not parents; they don't actually have to do any child care at all. The father "protects his family, provides for its material needs, devotes himself to the education of his children, and represents his family's interests in the larger world"—all valuable behaviors, to be sure, but also behaviors that do not require that he ever set foot in his child's room.[54] The notion that men should be exempt from mundane housework and child care, which should be left to their wives, is, of course, insulting to women. But it's also insulting to men because it assumes that the caring and nurturing of life itself cannot be men's province; given how clumsy and aggressive men are, all that had better be done at a distance.

It's not men's fault, of course; it's women's. As at every turn in American history, some version of antifeminism has masqueraded as a defense of masculinity. This agenda is most simply made by Harvey Mansfield, Harvard political scientist, in a 1997 op-ed essay in the *Wall Street Journal*. "The protective element of manliness is endangered by women who have equal access to jobs outside the home," he writes. "Women who do not consider themselves feminist often seem unaware of what they are doing to manliness when they work to support themselves. They think only that people should be hired and promoted on merit, regardless of sex."[55] Lionel Tiger claims that "the principal victims of moving toward a merit-based society have been male." Imagine that: Feminists actually believe in meritocracy, while those who would support men want to keep that playing field as uneven as possible. Tiger's most recent book, *The Decline of Males* (1999), argues, topsy-turvy, that "the male and female sex in industrial societies are slowly but inexorably moving apart," just at the moment when all available evidence—epidemiological, economic, social, and psychological—suggests precisely the opposite.[56] Males are in decline because women now control sexuality. By gaining control over birth control, they claimed all the sexual power. Now that women are the captains of the social ship, men are listing badly.[57]

And that's where the pop psychologists come in. Both "Dr." Laura Schlessinger and "Dr." John Gray have become modest-sized industries that manufacture light equipment for successful relationships, building multimillion-dollar psychological empires by scolding women into scaling back their expectations and accepting men just as they are—the lunks.[58] Schlessinger, the nationally syndicated talk show host, has made her mark by dispensing pop psychological bromides like bitter little pills. She confronts her listeners, yells at them, and makes fun of their foibles. And they love it! Her advice book for women, *The Stupid Things Women Do to Mess Up Their Lives* (1995), was a best-seller, another on an already sagging shelf of volumes that blame women for the inconstancies, infidelities, and inadequacies of the men in their lives. Its companion volume, *Ten Stupid Things Men Do to Mess Up Their Lives* (1998), also spends a good amount of time chastising seemingly smart women for their foolish choices, as does the final volume in the trilogy, *Ten Stupid Things Couples Do to Mess Up Their Relationships* (2001).

Basically, she argues, men are total losers, but they can't help it, the lovable oafs. They're biologically driven toward violence, aggression, and dumb choices in love.[59] In one of the most brilliant rhetorical strategies this side of Jonathan Swift, she dispenses classically feminist advice to men in the guise of bashing those awful feminist harpies who are so bitter and angry all the time. She goes out of her way to bash "overgeneralizing, incredibly negative, hysterical, man-loathing" feminist ideas held by "insanely radical contemporary feminists."[60] Dr. Laura offers exactly the same critique of men that radical feminists have given for the past thirty years: Men are not caring, nurturing, loving, attentive, and emotional enough with their wives, their children, and their friends. She urges men to end rape, to stop beating up their wives, and to be more present in the home. But whose fault is that really? "Men would not do half of what they do if women didn't let them," she told an interviewer for *Modern Maturity* magazine recently. "That a man is going to do bad things is a fact. That you keep a man who does bad things in your life is your fault."[61]

John Gray may be the most successful self-help author of all time. His eight self-help books have sold tens of millions of copies worldwide; the flagship book, *Men Are from Mars, Women Are from Venus*, has sold more than 10 million copies in the United States alone. His central conceit is that men and women are completely different. To read *Men Are from Mars* or its identical cousins, you'd think we were different species, like, say, lobsters and giraffes are. Gray believes that not only do women and men communicate differently, but they also "think, feel, perceive, react, respond, love, need, and appreciate differently [and are] from different planets, speaking different languages, and needing different nourishment."[62]

The interplanetary differences in Gray's astronomy are hardwired into maleness and femaleness, the result, he says, of "DNA programming."[63] To demonstrate this, Gray recites a list of physical differences, aside from the rather obvious ones. Among other things, men have thicker skin, longer vocal cords, and heavier blood with more oxygen (to enable them to breathe more deeply). His books are liberally sprinkled with statements about how men "automatically" do some things and women "instinctively" do something else and how our "natural cycles" make communication difficult.

These biological differences are the origin of the fundamentally different personalities that men and women everywhere have. For example, men value power, competency, efficiency, and achievement; women value love, communication, beauty, and relationships. Women are "more intuitive, are more interested in love and relationships, and experience different reactions to stress," while men have a "greater interest in producing results, achieving goals, power, competition, work, logic, and efficiency."[64] In relationships, a man is like a rubber band: He pulls away, stretching only so far and then springing back; he "automatically alternates between needing intimacy and autonomy." A woman is like a wave, her self-esteem rising and falling depending upon whether she feels loved.[65] Women are afraid of receiving; men are afraid of giving. "Women have an incredible capacity to give without getting back"; men, on the other hand, "are not instinctively motivated to offer their support; they need to be asked."[66]

Communication problems are inevitable. Men "silently 'mull over' or think about what they have heard or experienced"; women gab about it with everyone in sight. Or, from a Venusian perspective, she knows to sensibly talk things through while he becomes an uncommunicative rock.[67] Perhaps the best one can hope for is a sort of interplanetary détente in which women simply accept that Martians are impatient, inexpressive slobs who hog the remote control. At the seminars and lectures I've attended, I've noticed that the men were significantly older than the women, old enough, perhaps, to be their fathers. Gray's message seems to appeal to younger women, between ages 20 and 35, trying to initiate and sustain romantic relationships with men as they're pulled between family and career. His message also appeals to somewhat older men, in their late 40s and early 50s trying to make their second marriage work better than the first. There "post-feminist" women and "pre-feminist" men get the same basic message: Women must abandon any idea of changing him. "The secret of empowering a man is never to try to change or improve him."[68]

That message has become staple fodder of women's magazines and reaches its apotheosis in *The Rules*,[69] a guide that promises to help women land a husband through a step-by-step retreat through the 1950s and back to the 1840s, when Catherine Ward Beecher, Sarah Hale, and others articulated the need for separate spheres and for women to be "the angel of the house," in Virginia Woolf's memorable phrase. Women's problem is that they can't find husbands, and the reason for that is that women have been too busy being men's equal to connive to trap men in the time-tested ways that our grandmothers did, by holding out through manipulative coquettery. The most successful rule: "[T]reat the men we *wanted* like the men we *didn't* want."[70]

If our man is a couch potato, here's what *The Rules* would counsel:

> When he watches the ballgame on TV all afternoon instead of helping you clean the house, don't zap the tube off in a moment of anger. Nicely tell him you need his help. If he still insists on watching the game, leave him alone. Tell yourself "No big deal."[71]

Though the book is intended to be read by women, it's an important book for men to read as well, especially because it tells men what conniving, manipulative women those *Rules* gals are being counseled to be! But also consider what such behavior by women actually says about men. Men are "born to respond to challenge," biologically "the aggressor" who must pursue the women. Men love to be treated badly—treated as though they were not wanted—because that will only prime that testostcrone to pump up their competitive hunting urges and really go after their prey. Men are overgrown babies who want everything their own way, who want "constant attention and companionship" as well as someone to clean up after them. Peter Pan is the icon for an entire gender: They won't grow up! And if you treat men like adults, they will run away and hide in their cave with John Gray.[72]

So the message here is simple: Women, your unhappiness is your own fault. For men, the message is far more insidious: You're fine just as you are; you don't have to change at all. "Don't try to change him because men never really change," write Fein and Schneider.[73] They're incapable of real change, and so fragile that they must be constantly coddled with kid gloves. But they're also destined to be unemotional grunters, at home nowhere in the world except their individually constructed caves. The best women can hope for is to come home, play by the rules, land a man of her very own, and hope he treats her well. Now *that's* insulting to men.

What about the Boys?[74]

One of the primary arenas of rhetorical struggle has been in the classroom. At the turn of the last century, you will recall, cultural observers worried that the dominance of female teachers, female Sunday School teachers, and especially mothers was emasculating young boys, turning hardy, robust boyhood into "a lot of flat-chested cigarette smokers with shaky nerves and doubtful vitality," as you'll recall Boy Scout founder Ernest Thompson Seton put it. Just as American men were now leaving home and heading off to work, becoming virtual absentee landlords in their own homes, critics found a way to blame women for their sons' enervation and emasculation.

Today, the argument is slightly different in origin but has a remarkably similar tone. The dramatic successes of feminist-inspired educational policy reforms initiated since the 1980s—policies to reduce the "chilly classroom climate," the dominance of boys and the prevalence of sexual harassment of girls—have now rebounded to the detriment of boys, we are told. Boys, we hear, are the new victims of gender discrimination in schools. After all, what happens to boys in schools? They have to sit quietly, take naps, raise their hands, be obedient—all of which do extraordinary violence to their "natural" testosterone-inspired rambunctious playfulness. "Schools for the most part are run by women for girls. To take a high spirited second or third grade boy and expect him to behave like a girl in school is asking too much," comments Christina Hoff Sommers, author of *The War Against Boys*. The effect of education is "pathologizing boyhood." While we've been paying all this attention to girls' experiences—raising their self-esteem, enabling them to take science and math, deploring and preventing harassment and bullying—we've ignored the boys.[75]

On college campuses, the gender disparities also seem to indicate a reversal of fortunes between women and men. Women now constitute the majority of students on college campuses (passing men in 1982), so by 2010 women will earn 58 percent of bachelor's degrees in U.S. colleges, and there are three women for every two men at the nation's community colleges. One reporter, obviously a terrible statistics student, tells us that if present trends continue, "[T]he graduation line in 2068 will be all females." (That's like saying that if the enrollment of black students at Ol' Miss was 1 in 1964, 24 in 1968, and 400 in 1988, by 1994 there would have been no white students there.) Women now outnumber men in the social and behavioral sciences by about three to one, and they've invaded such traditionally male bastions as engineering, where they now make up about 20 percent of all students, and biology and business, where the genders are virtually on a par.[76]

But the numbers cited by critics just don't add up. For one thing, more *people* are going to college than ever before. In 1960, 54 percent of boys and 38 percent of girls went directly to college; today the numbers are 64 percent of boys and 70 percent of girls. Much of the gender disparity is actually what sociologist Cynthia Fuchs Epstein calls a "deceptive distinction," a difference that appears to be about gender but is actually about something else—in this case, class or race. The shortage of male college students is also actually a shortage of *nonwhite* males. The gender gap between college-age white males and white females is rather small, 51 percent women to 49 percent men. But only 37 percent of black college students are male and 63 percent are female, and 45 percent of Hispanic students are male, compared with 55 percent female.

Of course, boys do merit attention. In primary school, boys are more likely to be sent to child psychologists (by about four to one) and far more likely to be diagnosed with dyslexia and attention deficit disorder (ADD) than are girls. Throughout their schooling, boys receive poorer report cards; they are far more likely to repeat a grade. Nine times more boys than girls are diagnosed as hyperactive; boys represent 58 percent of those in special education classes for the mentally retarded, 71 percent of the learning disabled, and 80 percent of the emotionally disturbed. Nearly three-fourths of all school suspensions are of boys. By adolescence, boys are more likely to drop out, flunk out, and act out in class.[77]

But the recent research into the inner lives of boys indicates that the problem has far less to do with feminist-inspired educational reforms and far more to do with the very definitions of masculinity that these new boyhood defenders are defending. Young girls, assertive, confident, and self-aware, psychologist Carol Gilligan found, tend to "lose their voice" when they hit adolescence.[78] By contrast, boys become more confident, even beyond their abilities. Just at the moment that girls lost their voices, boys *find* one —but it is the inauthentic voice of bravado, of constant posturing, of foolish risk-taking and gratuitous violence. According to psychologist William Pollack, boys learn that they are supposed to be in power and thus begin to act like it. "Although girls' voices have been disempowered, boys' voices are strident and full of bravado," he observes. "But their voices are disconnected from their genuine feelings." Thus, he argues, the way we bring boys up leads them to put on a "mask of masculinity," a posture, a front. They "ruffle in a manly pose," as the poet William Butler Yeats put it, "for all their timid heart."[79]

It turns out that it is not the school experience that "feminizes" boys but rather the ideology of traditional masculinity that keeps boys from wanting to succeed. Boys see academic success itself as a disconfirmation of their masculinity. "Reading is lame; sitting down and looking at words is pathetic," commented one boy to a researcher.

"Most guys who like English are faggots," commented another. The traditional liberal arts curriculum is seen as feminizing by boys. "The work you do here is girls' work," one boy commented to a researcher. "It's not real work." Such comments echo the consistent findings of social scientists since James Coleman's path-breaking 1961 study that identified the "hidden curriculum" among adolescents in which good-looking and athletic boys were consistently more highly rated by their peers than were good students.[80] Or, as the feminist critic Catharine Stimpson put it sarcastically, "[R]eal men don't speak French."[81]

Those who suggest that feminist-inspired reforms have been to the detriment of boys believe that gender relations are a zero-sum game and that if girls and women gain, boys and men lose. But the reforms that have been initiated to benefit girls in class— individualized instruction, attention to different learning pathways, new initiatives, class-room configurations, teacher training, and more collaborative team-building efforts—have also been to the benefit of boys as well, as such methods would also target boys' specific experiences. And the efforts to make the classroom safer and more hospitable to girls have also redounded to boys' benefit. Take, for example, classroom decorum. In 1940, the top disciplinary problems identified by high-school teachers were (in order): talking out of turn, chewing gum, making noise, running in the hall, cutting in line, violating dress code, and littering. In 1990, the top disciplinary problems were (again, in order): drug abuse, alcohol abuse, pregnancy, suicide, rape, robbery, and assault.[82] Challenging stereotypes and having decreased tolerance for school violence and bullying enable both boys and girls to feel safer at school. Those who would simply throw up their hands in resignation and sigh that "boys will be boys" would have you believe that nothing can or should be done to make those classrooms safer. In my estimation, those four words, "boys will be boys," may be the most depressing words in educational policy circles today.[83] Consider instead an editorial in the Amherst College newspaper, *The Amherst Student*, when the school first debated coeducation at the turn of the twentieth century: "Every step in the advancement of women has benefited our own sex no less than it has elevated her."[84]

Angry Boys

Just because the right-wing rescuers of traditional masculinity and untrammeled boyhood have it entirely backward doesn't mean that boys are not in trouble. What many of the recent spate of books about boys has revealed is that the pressures to live up to the "boy code" leave many boys suppressing emasculating emotions like vulnerability, dependency, and compassion and effecting, instead, a hypermasculine unemotional pose.[85] Proving masculinity remains vitally important to young men, even as the opportunities to do so seem to be shrinking. Boys look to their fathers, public figures, athletes, and other media-created heroes, and they evaluate—constantly, relentlessly—each other's performance. Anyone who doubts one of this book's central arguments—that the testing and proving of masculinity is a "homosocial" experience, performed before and evaluated by the eyes of other men—need look no further than adolescent peer culture. And one of the central markers of American manhood has, for many decades, been the capacity for violence.

Recall the turn of the last century when fears of enervated and emasculated boyhood led to the promotion of rough-and-tumble boyhood, schoolyard fistfighting, and organized sports. Today, the capacity for violence is a marker of authentic masculinity (as in *Fight Club*), a test of manhood. Just about every boy and man in America has some experience with violence, either using it himself, having it used against him, or being threatened with its use if he steps out of line or crosses someone. American men learn from an early age to fight back and that there are few expressions more legitimate than retaliatory violence. Violence is immoral if you use it first, but it is redemptive if you use it second. Moral men don't get mad but get even; men don't start fights, but they are eager to finish them.

At no time in life is violence more prevalent than among boys and young men. Stated most baldly, young American men are the most violent group of people in the industrial world. The age group sixteen to twenty-four commits *most* of the violent crime in America. Our homicide rate is much higher than that of any other industrial country; in 1992, young men between fifteen and twenty-four had a homicide rate of 37.2 per 100,000. This is ten times higher than the next highest, that of Italy, and sixty times higher than Britain's. Take a look at this chart, which illustrates the relationship among gender and age and homicide.

And it's getting worse. Between 1985 and 1994, the number of homicides by fourteen- to seventeen-year-old males more than tripled. According to the California Highway Patrol, nine out of ten of those arrested for drunk driving are men; 84 percent of those jailed for fatal accidents resulting from drunk driving are men, and 86 percent of arson crimes are committed by men. Nationwide, nine of ten (nonparking) driving infractions are committed by men; 93 percent of all road rage accidents are caused by men.

One needn't look very far to see the real "boy crisis" in America. Ask any kid in middle school or high school anywhere in the country what is the most common putdown in his or her school. The answer is, "That's so gay." The fear of being tainted with homosexuality—the fear of emasculation—has morphed into a generic putdown. These days, "That's so gay" has far less to do with aspersions of homosexuality and far more to do with "gender policing," making sure that no one contravenes the rules of masculinity. Listen, for example, to that eminent gender theorist Eminem as he defended the constant homophobic references to "fags" in his raps. In an interview on MTV, he explained that

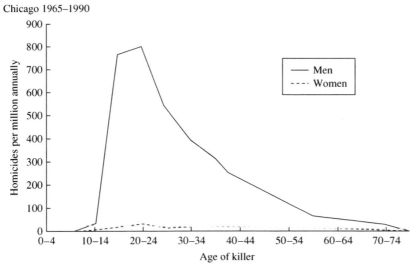

Figure 10.1 Homicide rates in Chicago, 1965–1990, by age and gender.
From "Darwinism and the Roots of Machismo," *Scientific American.*

the ubiquitous gay-baiting and calling other guys "faggots" were not slurs on their sexuality but a challenge to their masculinity. "The lowest degrading thing that you can say to a man . . . is to call him a faggot and try to take away his manhood. Call him a sissy. Call him a punk. 'Faggot' to me doesn't mean gay people. 'Faggot' just means taking away your manhood."[86]

High schools have become far more than academic testing grounds; they're the central terrain on which gender identity is tested and demonstrated. And unlike the standardized tests for reading and arithmetic, the tests of adequate and appropriate gender performance are administered and graded by your peers, by grading criteria known only to them. Bullying has become a national problem in high schools, in part because of the relentlessness and the severity of the torments. Verbal teasing and physical bullying exist along a continuum stretching from using hurtful language through shoving and hitting to criminal assaulting and school shootings. Harmful teasing and bullying happen to more than one million schoolchildren a year.

If bullying creates hostile high-school hallways, those homosocial preserves within the school can be even more terrifying. Locker rooms, sports teams, and even the school band are plagued by increasingly dangerous and harmful incidents of hazing. There were over one hundred hazing-related deaths on high-school and college campuses between 1995 and 2005. A national survey of high-school students found that hazing is ubiquitous. Nearly half (48 percent) of all students who belong to a group reported being subjected to hazing; 43 percent were subjected to humiliating activities and fully 30 percent performed possibly illegal acts as part of their initiation. Hazing was so universal that there were virtually no groups that were safe. One-fourth of all students involved in church groups were subjected to hazing. Substance abuse in hazing is prevalent in high school (23 percent) and increases in college, where over half of all hazing activities (51 percent) involve substance abuse.

Most of the kids who are targeted manage to cope; they're resilient enough or have enough emotional resources to survive reasonably intact. Many try valiantly, and often vainly, to fit in, to conform to these impossible standards that others set for them. Some carry psychological or even physical scars for the rest of their lives. Some withdraw and become depressed, alienated, or despondent. Some self-medicate with drugs or alcohol, and a few explode. As every adolescent knows, "doing a Columbine" means exploding in a murderous rage—and taking as many classmates and teachers as you can with you.

Since 1992, there have been twenty-eight case of random school violence in which a young boy (or boys) opened fire on classmates;[87] all twenty-eight were committed by boys. Contrary to many stereotypes, all but one of those cases took place in a rural or suburban school, not an inner-city school, and all but one of the shooters were white. Yet we seem to have missed this in all the discussion about these school shootings. We continue to call the problem "teen violence," "youth violence," "gang violence," "suburban violence," "violence in the schools." Just who do we think is doing it—girls? Imagine if the shooters in schools in Littleton, Colorado; Pearl, Mississippi; Paducah, Kentucky; Springfield, Oregon; and Jonesboro, Arkansas were instead black girls from poor families who lived in New Haven, Newark, Detroit, Compton, or South Boston. *Then* we'd notice race and class and gender! We'd likely hear about the culture of poverty, life in the inner city, and racial violence. Someone, I'd bet, would blame feminism for encouraging girls to become violent in vain imitation of boys.[88] Yet the obvious fact that these school killers were all middle-class white boys seems to have escaped almost everyone's notice.

More startlingly, though, is not that they were all middle-class white boys but that so many also had the same story. Virtually every single one of the shooters had a story about being targeted for gay baiting, bullied, and harassed—not every now and then but constantly, daily. Why? It was *not* because they were gay (at least there is no evidence to suggest that any of them were gay) but because they were *different* from the other boys—shy, bookish, academically talented, artistic, musical, theatrical, nonathletic, "geek-ish," or weird. It was because they were not athletic, were overweight or underweight, or wore glasses.

Take Luke Woodham, a bookish, overweight sixteen-year-old in Pearl, Mississippi. An honor student, he was part of a little group that studied Latin and read Nietzsche. Students teased him constantly for being overweight and a nerd and taunted him as "gay" or "fag." Even his mother called him fat, stupid, and lazy. Other boys bullied him routinely, and, according to one fellow student, he "never fought back when other boys called him names." On October 1, 1997, Woodham stabbed his mother to death in her bed before he left for school. He then drove her car to school, carrying a rifle under his coat. He opened fire in the school's common area, killing two students and wounding seven others. After being subdued, he told the Assistant Principal, "The world has wronged me." Later, in a psychiatric interview, he said, "I am not insane. I am angry . . . I am not spoiled or lazy; for murder is not weak and slow-witted; murder is gutsy and daring. I killed because people like me are mistreated every day. I am malicious because I am miserable."

Or recall Michael Carneal, a fourteen-year-old freshman at Heath High School in Paducah, Kentucky. Shy and skinny, Carneal was barely five feet tall and weighed about one hundred and ten pounds. He wore thick glasses and played in the high school band. He felt alienated, pushed around, picked on. Boys stole his lunch and constantly teased him. In middle school, someone pulled down his pants in front of his classmates. He was so sensitive and afraid that others would see him naked that he covered the air vents in the bathroom and was devastated when students called him a "faggot" and the school gossip sheet labeled him as "gay." On Thanksgiving 1997, he stole two shotguns, two semiautomatic rifles, a pistol, and seven hundred rounds of ammunition, and after a weekend of showing them off to his classmates, he brought them to school hoping that they would bring him some instant recognition. "I just wanted the guys to think I was cool," he said. When the cool guys ignored him, he opened fire on a morning prayer circle, killing three classmates and wounding five others. Now serving a life sentence in prison, Carneal told psychiatrists weighing his sanity, "[P]eople respect me now."[89]

At Columbine High School, the site of the nation's most infamous school shooting, this connection was not lost on Evan Todd, a 255-pound defensive lineman on the Columbine football team, an exemplar of the jock culture that Dylan Klebold and Eric Harris found to be such an interminable torment. "Columbine is a clean, good place, except for those rejects," Todd said. "Sure we teased them. But what do you expect with kids who come to school with weird hairdos and horns on their hats? It's not just jocks; the whole school's disgusted with them. They're a bunch of homos. . . . If you want to get rid of someone, usually you tease 'em. So the whole school would call them homos." Ben Oakley, a soccer player, agreed. "[N]obody liked them," he said. "[T]he majority of them were gay. So everyone would make fun of them." Athletes taunted them; they would throw rocks and bottles at them from moving cars. The school newspaper had recently published a rumor that Harris and Klebold were lovers.[90]

Actually, both appeared to be reasonably well-adjusted kids. Harris's parents were a retired Army officer and a caterer, decent well-intentioned people. Klebold's father was a geophysicist who had recently moved into the mortgage services business, and his mother worked in job placement for the disabled. Harris had been rejected by several colleges; Klebold was due to enroll at Arizona in the fall. But the jock culture was relentless. "Every time someone slammed them against a locker and threw a bottle at them, I think they'd go back to Eric or Dylan's house and plot a little more—at first as a goof, but more and more seriously over time," said one friend.[91]

The rest is now painfully familiar. Harris and Klebold brought a variety of weapons to their high school and proceeded to walk through the school, shooting whomever they could find. Students were terrified and tried to hide. Many students who could not hide begged for their lives. The entire school was held under siege until the police secured the building. In all, twenty-three students and faculty were injured and fifteen died, including one teacher and the perpetrators.

Of course, these explosions are rare; most bullying victims manage to survive reasonably intact. But what is pervasive, and what does seem to be notably elevated, is the level of anger expressed by and experienced by boys and young men. It's everywhere they turn. Older teenage boys spend countless hours blowing up the galaxy, graphically splattering their computer screens in violent video games. Teenage boys splay violent pornography everywhere in their dorm rooms; indeed, pornographic pictures are the most popular screen savers on their computers. They listen to imbecilically juvenile shock jocks on the radio when they aren't listening to hate-filled enraged musicians screaming venom at them; they're laughing at cable-rated T&A or guffawing to the sophomoric body-fluid humor of Beavis and Butthead. The Southern Poverty Law Center reports that racist hate activity among kids "has probably never been more widespread, or more violent." Racist graffiti, swastika tattoos, and Confederate T-shirts abound in American small-town and suburban high schools. And, as we've seen, they're learning all this from their fathers. Today's angry men are raising a generation of angry boys.

Sports Crazy

The world of sports has long been a masculine refuge, a pristine homosocial world of male bonding. At the turn of the last century, participation in sports was prescribed by those cultural observers who saw both American boyhood wracked by indolence and emasculated by overdominance of women and American manhood enervated into lassitude by office work and modern life.

So, too, it is with sports today, at least in part. While the professional ranks remain sex-segregated, it's also true that the increase in female participation and female competence has been extraordinary. Today, in every high school and college, there are plenty of girls who can run circles around many of the boys on soccer fields and tennis courts. Perhaps that's one reason for the increased popularity of football, as feminist writer and former Stanford basketball player Mariah Burton Nelson noted when she titled her first book *The Stronger Women Get, the More Men Love Football*. It may also be a reason for the exponential growth in one aspect of the sporting life. It's not *doing* sports that seems to have increased among guys because the ranks of American men are pretty divided, as we have been for some time, between ascetic, health-conscious jogging junkies and drinking and smoking coach potatoes. No, it's *talking* about sports that has ballooned into a steady stream of 24-7 television, radio, fantasy leagues, and Internet sites. Women may be doing sports almost as much as men are, but they don't like to talk about it very much. Maybe the stronger women get, the more men love *to talk about* football. In classrooms and around water coolers, men's sports talk is hardly harmless banter; it's a mechanism for the political exclusion of women. Like conducting business meetings at Hooters or local upscale strip clubs or hosting power breakfasts at 7 A.M., the emphasis on sports talk redraws the boundaries of sex segregation and keeps women out.

Not only do men talk about it with a vengeance, but they keep consuming ever more "extreme" sports, in some cases, extreme "sports" like professional wrestling, which offers hypermuscular caricatures of masculine icons locked in a timeless Manichean struggle between absolute good and absolute evil. (Professional wrestling, NASCAR races, and golf have moved into the top five sports on television, having edged baseball out.)

Perhaps one of the reasons sports has become contemporary American men's dominant institution is that it embraces all three strategies men have historically employed to prove their manhood. Participation in sports builds the body; it requires strength, skill, size, and stamina—and self-control. It's also, at least in principle, an all-male preserve, excluding those feminizing "others" from its hallowed fields. It's both the exclusion of others and a manly escape from them. Take, for example, the dramatic rise in golf among middle-class men. Their working world is increasingly heterogeneous; few can "escape" female colleagues, coworkers, supervisors, even bosses. Their home life is increasingly "androgynous": They have to cook, clean, and take care of the kids just like their working wives do. But on that golf course, that pristine field of masculine dreams, guys hang with other guys; it's a frat house and locker rook for middle-aged middle-class men. No wonder Hootie Johnson, Chairman of Augusta National, was so adamant about refusing to admit women. But, more importantly, no wonder so many otherwise sensible family men become apoplectically defensive about separate tee times for women and men. At least the golf course can remain a homosocial preserve, and the nineteenth hole a man's lair.

Another arena in which men's defensive anger is evident is the debate about the implementation of Title IX. When Title IX legislation was enacted by Congress as part of the 1964 Civil Rights Act, its intent was to alleviate the dramatic inequalities in educational opportunities afforded women and men. It's been especially useful in leveling the athletic playing field. No sooner was it implemented, though, than the backlash began. Several prominent universities (Brown, for example, among them) went to court to try and prevent full implementation, and several wrestling teams attempted to file federal sex discrimination suits with the Justice Department's Civil Rights Division, claiming "equal protection" violation. Once again, boys—white boys—were claiming to be the victims of reverse discrimination. (The Justice Department declined to take up any of these cases, since, as one of the department's lawyers explained it to me, "there is no constitutionally protected right to wrestle.")

From the Masculinity of Politics to Masculinity as Politics

Even before the terrorist attacks of 9-11, masculinity was intimately connected to American politics. Since the founding of the country, the electorate had always been assessing the manly strength and conviction of its leaders. A strong hand and firm resolve as well as virile restraint and a calm judiciousness, especially in the event of or the threat of war, have been seen as necessary to steer the ship of state. And while this has led, in part, to the exclusion of women from the pinnacles of power in the United States (compared to, for example, Israel, Britain, India, Pakistan, and other less bellicose nations), it has also enabled America to remain a beacon of hope to millions around the world.

That beacon had most often a decidedly parental (that is, a paternal) glow. It was not simply a man's guiding hand but that of an older man, a father figure, who could embody both comfort and strength. Ronald Reagan exuded those qualities in abundance and was perhaps the most popular president in the twentieth century. Even his more feckless successor, George H. W. Bush, while a bit more patrician than paternal, still projected a sagacious calm.

The election of 1992 proved a generational watershed as well as a changing of political parties. Just as John F. Kennedy had announced his administration as the first of a generation born "in this century," so too did Bill Clinton represent the first generation born after World War II, for whom Vietnam was the defining war and who grew up amid the unparalleled prosperity of the 1950s. Clinton's manhood was always in doubt and always on display. He didn't serve in the military, and his wife was hardly the subservient but gracious hostess we had come to expect from First Ladies; he expressed his feelings and felt our pain. Depicted by his enemies as alternately conniving and gay (in both cases, Hillary was depicted as a demonically masculinized hydra), he was also beloved by his admirers as deeply compassionate and politically astute. The revelations of a sexual liaison with Monica Lewinsky, a White House intern, seem to have confirmed rumors of his habitual skirt-chasing, and his subsequent impeachment trial was discrediting, if not dethroning.[92] Now satirized as a satyr, he had little political capital to spend on his successor and spent the campaign of 2000 on the sidelines.

That campaign featured two literal as well as symbolic sons. George W. Bush and Al Gore were both the namesake sons of venerated political fathers and had been carefully groomed for elective office. Yet Gore could not shake his image as a ruling-class wimp when compared to the equally preppy, equally Ivy League, and equally entitled Bush. No matter how Gore tried to "butch" it up and present the male toughness of an alpha male, as he was advised by feminist writer Naomi Wolf, he seemed officious, elite, and effete. It was as if Gore presented an image of the man who had never been a boy; Bush, by contrast, appeared as the boy who had never grown up, a good-time frat boy Peter Pan. And white men, who voted overwhelmingly for Bush, made clear whom they would rather have hanging out in the White House.

And yet Gore won the election—that is, he won the popular vote and probably would have won the Electoral College had not the Supreme Court intervened to stop the recount of the popular vote in Florida. Riddled with fraud, those votes were never counted, and Bush was crowned as president under a cloud of suspicion. America was deeply divided politically, but also about gender. Red states and blue states signified something important about images of masculinity as well: gun owners vs. gun controllers, aggressive military vs. conciliatory and diplomatic corps, environmentally rapacious policies vs. environmental stewardship, tax-cutting free marketeers who run up the debt vs. fiscal conservatives who are prudent in both taxation and spending.

Bush's first term of office steered the nation hard to the right. Already by September 11, 2001, there were policies to open wilderness to oil exploration and real estate development, to cut taxes and social services, and to curtail the rights of women, gays and lesbians, and other minorities. Bush's avowed religiosity harked back to the Muscular Christianity of the previous century. Gone was the forgiveness of Christian compassion; in its stead was the angry and vindictive God whose wrath was boundless against His enemies.

Masculinity and 9-11

September 11, 2001, changed America—and the world. Indeed, it is often hard to recall the America before we were attacked by terrorists. In the years following the terrorist attacks on New York City and Washington, D.C., masculinity—both "ours" and that of the terrorists—has been very much debated and discussed. In a constructed cartoon version of good versus evil, masculinity versus cowardice, masculinity has been bandied about in contradictory ways: The terrorists are cowardly and diabolical; American men are courageous but peace-loving. Both cultural critic Susan Sontag and television commentator Bill Maher were vilified for daring to suggest that whatever else they were, the terrorists of 9-11 were not cowardly. (The fact that Maher's show was called "Politically Incorrect" did not dissuade the Manichean calls for his hide.)

On September 10, 2001, you may recall, firefighters, police officers, and soldiers represented some of the last remaining resisters of gender equality. Firehouses especially were bastions of men behaving badly, citadels of unreconstructed chauvinism. Photos of the fire department's graduating class every year looked more like the graduating class at the Citadel in 1964. How had New York City's fire department come to resemble a southern military school on the eve of integration? It's not that firefighters were the "bad guys"—one always distinguishes between the actual individual firefighters and the structure of their organization—but they were hardly the swoon-at-their-feet heroes they became on September 12.

Witness the divided fortunes of the two musical genres I discussed earlier: country and rap. Since 9-11, country music's been "firemanized," with its celebration of police, firefighters, and soldiers and its near-hysterical promotion of war against all comers. But rap's lost its focus; its anger feels almost sacrilegious. Eminem's most recent album is demonstrably tamer; groups like Outkast, Kanye West, or even Twista present a musical style more lovable than dangerous.

The nation's White Wing was politically divided by September 11. On one side were those who saw nonwhites, aliens, attacking America; they proclaimed the moment of holy war to have arrived and urged their followers to pick up their weapons and start killing immigrants. On the other hand, others marveled at the blow struck against America's Zionist Occupied Government and the symbols of global capitalism and governmental corruption, the World Trade Center and Pentagon. "We could work with those Islamic guys," one Alabama Klansman told a journalist. They "all feel the same way we do about who controls the world." Some even said they admired the terrorists' "testicular fortitude." "It's a disgrace that in a population of at least 150 million White/Aryan Americans, we provide so few that are willing to do the same," bemoaned Rocky Suhayda, Nazi Party chairman from Eastpointe, Michigan. "A bunch of towel head/sand niggers put our great White Movement to shame."[93]

On the other side of the class divide, on September 10, the newly installed global image of corporate masculinity was still riding high, despite the bursting of the dot-com bubble and the economic plunge into recession and the complicity of some of its most prominent high flyers in corporate scandals, the scale of which make Teapot Dome look increasingly like a tempest in a teapot. This globalized businessman became recognizable as a type in the late 1980s, and by 2001 had become the dominant image of a new class of corporate men around the world. He's readily identifiable: He sits in first-class waiting rooms or in the lobbies of elegant business hotels the world over in a designer business suit, speaking English, eating "continental" cuisine, talking on his cell phone, plugging his laptop computer into any electrical outlet in the world while he watches CNN International on television. Temperamentally, he is increasingly cosmopolitan, with liberal tastes in consumption (and sexuality) and conservative political ideas of limited government control of the economy.

The events of 9-11 reversed the fortunes of both images of masculinity. The rehabilitation of heroic masculinity among the firefighters, police, and other rescue workers was immediate. A headline in *The New York Times* proclaimed "Heavy Lifting Required: The Return of Manly Men," and a photo of brawny rescue workers, police, and firefighters reminded readers that "the attacks of Sept. 11 have brought more than a few good men back into the cultural limelight." A "Calendar of Heroes" with beefcake-like pinups of real firefighters sold sensationally. Even those few writers and pundits who managed to notice that there were female firefighters, police, and rescue workers among the heroes of 9-11 trumpeted the revival of traditional masculinity. "A certain kind of woman is tired of the dawdlers, melancholics and other variants of genius who would not know what to do with a baseball mitt or a drill press," gushed one female journalist. Real men were back—and we were safer for it. Some even proclaimed the crisis of masculinity over.[94]

The global business class has fared less well. Just as he was reeling from the bursting dot-com bubble, his masculinity quotient seems to be tumbling alongside the NASDAQ. Still connected to transnational institutions like the global marketplace, the European Union, and the United Nations, he's now seen as a dandified slave to the fashion designers of "Old Europe" (Secretary of Defense Donald Rumsfeld's term from those EU nations that had the temerity to oppose the U.S. invasion of Iraq). It is suspected he may even speak French. Globalization's well-dressed *Homo economicus* has been pushed aside by the reemergence of *Homo Reaganomicus*—the recharged militarized masculinity that proudly proclaims the United States not only as the world's only true superpower but as the axis of an emerging global empire. Beholden to no one and accountable to no one, U.S. foreign policy can be summed up simply: "Our way or the highway."

President George W. Bush is the icon of this new-old masculinity, a cowboy iteration derived less from the real western frontier than from cinematic westerns. (His wife calls him a "windshield cowboy," since he doesn't ride horses and surveys his ranch from a pickup truck.) Bush and his advisors clearly understand how masculinity is a "social construction" and forgo few opportunities to construct their man as a real man. Recall, for example, the image of the president, in military flight fatigues, staging a photo op to announce the end of the war against Iraq. Not only was he the first president in the twentieth or twenty-first century to don military attire (even Eisenhower restrained himself, and he was a general!), but the entire event was a staged pseudo-event, taking place a mile off the San Diego coast with the boat positioned to obscure the view of the coastline. This charade, "a masculine drag performance," was widely ridiculed, especially by real generals such as Wesley Clark, who scoffed at Bush "prancing on the deck of an aircraft carrier." But he was the first president to become an action figure![95]

Others are equally iconic. New York's then-Mayor Rudy Guiliani's belligerent authoritarianism was suddenly transformed into a laudatory steadfastness in the face of danger. Secretary of Defense Rumsfeld and his coterie of battle-pristine hawks in control of American foreign policy (who have not one day of actual military service among them) swagger into battle. *People* magazine called Rumsfeld one of the "sexiest Americans alive," CNN called him "a virtual rock star," Fox News labeled him a "babe magnet," and the president even began to call him "Rumstud." With testosterone-drenched rhetoric, American policy makers strut like bullies through the halls of the middle school—pushing inferior wimps out of the way, flouting the law, ignoring the fact that no one especially likes them, defying teachers, and daring the administration to do something about it. And it's probably not the last we'll see of this. One senior official made clear that masculinity was wrapped up in this ever-escalating military escapade. "Anyone can go to Baghdad," he said. "Real men go to Tehran."[96]

The new American unilaterialism is pitted against Old Europe's reliance on cooperative institutions and its promotion of social welfare and peace. The invasion of Iraq, the prosecution of terrorism in places both real and imagined, and the stewardship of the economy have been the dominant political issues of the post-9-11 era. These issues dominated the presidential campaign of 2004, offering America a new choice of heroes.

Election of 2004 and Beyond

Rarely has a national election been more saturated with contested images of masculinity than the presidential election of 2004. Not since the election of 1840, when William Henry

Harrison wimp-baited President Martin Van Buren, had masculinity been the axis around which the election was to revolve. In that election, the handlers and operatives for Harrison, Van Buren's Whig opponent, crafted an entire campaign to avoid any political issues and focused instead on Van Buren's gendered shortcomings.

Although we have discussed this campaign earlier, it might be useful to refresh the memory. In 1840, political songs chastised "Little Van" the "used up man," who "wore corsets, put cologne on his whiskers, slept on French beds, and rode in a British coach." One Harrison supporter declared van Buren's White House to be staffed by "French cooks" who furnished the president's table with "massive gold plate and French sterling silver services." (It is true that Van Buren presided over the installation of indoor plumbing in the White House.) Davy Crockett, he of unimpeachable masculinity, declared that "it would be difficult to say," from Van Buren's appearance, "whether he was man or woman." And it was rumored that when Van Buren read about these scandalous attacks, "he burst his corset." Campaign posters depicted Harrison, his sleeves rolled up and spade in hand, in front of his log cabin. In fact, none of it was true. Van Buren was a capable administrator, the son of an upstate New York innkeeper; Harrison was an aristocratic scion, bred in a three-story manor on a Virginia plantation. But the campaign worked. Over 80 percent of the eligible white male voters turned out for the election, and Harrison won in a landslide.

As in 1840, in the campaign of 2004 an aristocratic blueblood—prep school, Ivy League, summers in Kennebunkport—cast himself as a virtual log-cabin-born Everyman who raised himself by his bootstraps. And he cast his opponent, a sage and sober bureaucrat, as soft and sensitive, under the thumb of an emasculating wife. Bush snickered as Kerry windsurfed and waffled. Arnold Schwarzenegger, our own contemporary Davy Crockett, calls Kerry a girlie man. What might have been seen as "manly reticence" was sneered at as "patrician aloofness." Kerry, we heard, "looks French." Kerry and John Edwards, his running mate, were called "the first metrosexual presidential hopefuls." Edwards's styled hair brought him the label "the Breck Girl."[97]

More than representing two contrasting masculine styles, Kerry and Bush also embodied two competing masculine visions. President Bush embodies an older version of nineteenth-century manhood, hale and hardy, more comfortable clearing brush than debating policy. He offers casual swagger coupled with obstinate certainty, a resolute resistance to accepting blame for failures—the buck stops somewhere else. You know where he stands, even if it's in quicksand. Bush's election was understood by one reporter as "one of the last convulsions of angry, real American men, fighting desperately (and well) to hold back the time and tide of the new—the un-white and the un-Christian, and girlie-men too, who sooner or later will be America."[98]

John Kerry fought bravely in a war and, following his experience in Vietnam, did the unthinkable for a man: He changed his mind. He then fought bravely against it. This was, of course, used against him, proof that he waffled and flip-flopped in a feminine way. (Rarely has an election so denigrated femininity as a liability.) On Memorial Day weekend, one New York tabloid published the fictitious menus of the two candidates. For Bush it was sausages and beer (nonalcoholic, of course), and for Kerry it was frogs' legs, chardonnay, and crème brulee. It was parodies like these, and not his meritorious service or economic policies, that seemed to resonate with white male voters, who turned out overwhelmingly for Bush. Former President Bill Clinton summed up this new collective gendered psychology when he observed that when people feel uncertain or afraid, "they'd rather have somebody who's strong and wrong than somebody who's weak and right."[99]

While some think of the Republicans as the "Daddy Party" and the Democrats as the "Mommy Party," it is probably more accurate to see them representing two different visions of paternal masculinity. What sort of American father do we want, asked the linguist George Lakoff, a "nurturing parent" or a "strict father"? Democrats such as Bill Clinton nurtured; they felt our pain. George W. Bush offered a harsher, punitive style but promised safety and security under his wing. (In this analysis, it may be that Al Gore's and John Kerry's fatal mistake was not that they were not strict enough but that they were not nurturing enough!) And ironically, despite their link to myriad corporate scandals, libelous attacks on their opponents and fudging of Bush's elusive military service record, the Republicans became associated with the party of "moral values" in their steadfast opposition to abortion, gay marriage, and stem cell research and other scientific advances. (Such a position is doubly ironic because morality itself has so long been associated with femininity; real men typically chafe at the constraints opposed by such girlie virtues as fairness and compassion.)

The long-noted and oft-studied gender gap in politics often misses the point because it is typically expressed as the gap in women's voting patterns between the two major parties, that is, as Republicans' inability to appeal to women. However, women's voting patterns are only part of the picture. As Everett C. Ladd of the Roper Center explained, "[W]omen are not really more Democratic than they were fifteen years ago." The real story is that "men have become more Republican."[100]

The election also witnessed a divergence in cultural trends. True to political form, Bruce Springsteen gathered a team of contemporary pop stars (James Taylor, R. E. M., Dixie Chicks, and Dave Matthews, among others) to tour swing states; Sean Combs (aka Puff Daddy, P. Diddy, and a gaggle of other monikers) mobilized the inner-city youth vote. Toby Keith penned a bevy of boosterish country songs, praising Bush, the war effort, and heartland values. One song, "Courtesy of the Red, White and Blue (The Angry American)" makes promises:

> This big dog will fight
> When you rattle his cage
> And you'll be sorry that you messed with the U.S. of A
> 'Cause we'll put a boot in your ass
> It's the American way.

Contrast this knee-jerk jingoism to Eminem's surprising campaign anthem, "Mosh" released just prior to the election. In it, the black-hooded rapper calls the president himself a "Weapon of Mass Destruction" and leads a growing army of multicultural discontents. He chants:

> Let him impress daddy that way
> No more blood for oil, we got our own battles to fight on our own soil
> No more psychological warfare to trick us to thinking that we ain't loyal

If we don't serve our country, we're patronizing our hero
Look in his eyes, it's all lies
The stars and stripes have been swiped
Washed out and wiped and replaced with his own face
Mosh now or die.[101]

In the end, Bush's election confirmed that his image of masculinity would remain the dominant image in the first decade of the new century. But it also left an America deeply divided over that legacy, a country in which half the population was left singing the blue state blues while the other half was seeing red in Iraq. The election contained some ironic twists. Bush's campaign rested on the reassertion of traditional masculinity as the best way to combat the terrorists who would impose traditional masculinity because they, the terrorists, believed that America had fallen prey to such secular and modern trends as female suffrage and employment! In a world being propelled forward so rapidly, the clash between these two fundamentalist ideals of masculinity seems to pivot on which version would move more quickly forward, into the past.

Epilogue
Toward Democratic Manhood

The old, recognized virtues have begun to lose their authority, they are no longer able to fulfill the religious, moral, intellectual and social demands of the contemporary soul. Man's soul seems to have grown bigger, it cannot fit any longer within the old molds. A pitiless civil war has broken out in the vitals of our age, has broken out, whether consciously or unconsciously in the vitals of every man abreast of his times—a civil war between the old, formerly omnipotent myth which has vented its strength, yet which fights desperately to regulate our lives awhile longer, and the new myth which is battling, still awkwardly and without organization to govern our souls.

—Nikos Kazantzakis (1971)[1]

There comes a moment when we stop creating ourselves.

—John Updike (1992)[2]

We, with love, shall force our brothers to see themselves as they are, to cease fleeing from reality and begin to change it.

—James Baldwin (1962)[3]

The presidential election of 2004 revealed a nation deeply divided about politics, war, and economic issues. Red and blue states possess different visions of what America is and what America should be. And it's equally true that there are two disparate visions of American masculinity. As this new century unfolds, the pace of change accelerates, and the world grows ever more integrated, it remains to be seen what ideals of manhood will prevail both in the short run and in the longer run.

Personally, I believe that in the twenty-first century, we need a different sort of manhood, a "democratic manhood." The manhood of the future cannot be based on obsessive self-control, defensive exclusion, or frightened escape. We need a new definition of masculinity in this new century: a definition that is more about the character of men's hearts and the depths of their souls than about the size of their biceps, wallets, or penises; a definition that is capable of embracing differences among men and enabling other men to feel secure and confident rather than marginalized and excluded; a definition that is capable of friendships based on more than common activities (what among toddlers is called "parallel play") or even common consumer aesthetics; a definition that centers on standing up for justice and equality instead of running away from commitment and engagement.

We need men who truly embody traditional masculine virtues, such as strength, a sense of purpose, a commitment to act ethically regardless of the costs, controlled aggression, self-reliance, dependability, reliability, responsibility—men for whom these are not simply fashion accessories but come from a deeply interior place. But now these will be configured in new and responsive ways. We need men who are secure enough in their convictions to recognize a mistake, courageous enough to be compassionate, fiercely egalitarian, powerful enough to empower others, strong enough to acknowledge that real strength comes from holding others up rather than pushing them down and that real freedom is not to be found in the loneliness of the log cabin but in the daily compromises of life in a community.

Recall again the postscript to that vicious campaign of 1840. Taking the oath of office on one of the most bitterly cold days in the entire nineteenth century, William Henry Harrison refused to wear a topcoat lest he appear weak and unmanly. He caught pneumonia, was immediately bedridden, and died one month later—the shortest term in office of any president in our history. Believing your own hype may be dangerous for your health let alone the health of the nation.

The deep divisions between red and blue America parallel the deep divisions in red and blue gender politics. On the one hand, it appears that about half the country subscribes to older, more traditional notions of masculinity; the other half subscribes to a version that is more protean and responsive to social change. While it's surely a caricature to suggest that one side swills burgers and beer (not microbrew) while watching NASCAR and the other sips chardonnay and nibbles imported brie, every cultural arena does present us with a variety of images from which to choose. The increased polarization of the nation does lead these images to equally become more polarized.

So, for example, where once Jimmy Stewart and Cary Grant could capture the same audiences as Humphrey Bogart and Robert Mitchum, today one is unlikely to find many fans of the fey Leonardo di Caprio or the earnest Toby Maguire at a film starring The Rock or Vin Diesel. Yet these new iterations of the last action hero are cartoons of hypermasculine inarticulateness; they make Arnold Schwarzenegger or Bruce Willis seem positively emotional. And their young male audiences are as likely to laugh at their verbal grunting as they are to marvel at the special effects.

One-half of the country supports traditional gender arrangements; the other supports gender equality. As a result, there are still pockets of opposition to women's entry into the public sphere (corporate boardrooms, military operations theaters) and men whose idea of gender equality at home is sharing the use of the remote control. On the other hand, nationally, men's share of housework and child care has steadily increased in recent decades. Just as the wage gap has narrowed, so too has the laundry and babysitting gap.

Equally true, one definition of masculinity finds renewed opposition to gay rights; opposition to gay marriage and efforts to undermine antidiscrimination policies have found recharged enthusiasm. Some of this is less a matter of gender and more a matter of age. For example, while 73 percent of Americans over age 65 oppose gay marriage, 61 percent of those under 30 favor it.[1] Gay marriage is as inevitable as was women's admission to VMI and the Citadel and is likely to be met with the same sort of casual indifference. If that's what they really want, who's to say they can't do it?

The discussions of metrosexuality are also deeply divided meditations about masculinity. Urban and urbane, metrosexuals are decidedly "blue;" their critics unabashedly "red." In the recent election, the proclamation of "moral values" by many red states' voters may have had less to do with the immorality of Janet Jackson's "wardrobe malfunction" or Ellen Degeneres's sexual orientation and more to do with the general "immorality" of Hollywood-inspired popular culture in general, a culture promoted by metrosexual masculinity.

We've seen all these trends before, of course, over the course of American history. When the going gets tough, some of the tough run away; some circle the wagons to prevent others from getting in, and some retreat to an earlier ideal of gender relationships, one bathed in the soft glow of nostalgic sentiment. All through American history, men have tried to resolve their problems by excluding others, by bulking up, or by running off to some pastoral Eden. And all through our history, those strategies have failed. One measure of that failure, in fact, is that we keep trying them over and over again.

But we're at the end of that line. Not only are these strategies eternally doomed to failure, but many men seem to have figured it out. That may be one reason why we're so angry instead of so anxious. Proving manhood in these time-tested ways is doomed to failure; many men feel they've been sold a bill of goods, defrauded into thinking they could have it all. I think it's now time for some new strategies, some new ideas to enable men to resolve this perpetual crisis and to live deeper, more emotionally resonant, meaningful lives. For two centuries, we've shipped out, run off, headed west in search of a new start and an opportunity to prove our manhood. We've circled the wagons, tossed "them" out, and barred "them" from entry. We've pumped up, worked out, and injected carcinogenic poisons into our systems to look bigger, tougher, stronger.

I have but two words for us: *come home!*

The past century has witnessed such a dramatic transformation in the lives of American women. Few of us can even remember when women couldn't vote, drive a car, serve on a jury, serve in the army, or become a doctor, a lawyer, a journalist, or an architect. The women's movement accomplished half a revolution; it freed women from the requirement that they only care for homes and children and should neither want nor have anything else in their lives. Today the majority of American women struggle to balance work and family life. But if women had been imprisoned in the home, men have been exiled from it.

I'm not proposing that all America's social problems can be laid at the foot of absent fatherhood, a dubious and empirically shallow proposition (and one we've unmasked in the previous chapter). Nor is this one of those disingenuous calls for tightening divorce laws as a way to keep marriages together. We need strong laws to keep men responsible, not to keep bad marriages together. Responsibility is more than a lifestyle option, but we need more than just responsibility; we need responsibility without entitlement.

Responsibility is both a red and a blue state value; it's one of the moral unifiers in our national culture. And responsibility is the way for men to live the lives they want— animated by close relationships with their wives, their partners, their children, their friends. Men can't have those lives by running off to the woods but by coming home and doing their share of the mundane chores that really constitute nurturing, sharing housework and child care. In short, we need more ironing Johns, not Iron Johns.

It's also about the lives we want for our children. As women work outside the home, our children, both boys and girls, will grow up to know that competence, ambition, and skill are qualities that *grown-ups* have, not something that men have and that women may sporadically exhibit. And if men share housework and child care, our children will grow up knowing that nurture is something that grown-ups do, not something that women do routinely and men do only at halftime on Sunday afternoon.

It's about the public sphere as well. Though we think of family-friendly workplace reforms—on-site child care, flextime, parental leave—as "women's issues," they are more accurately *parents'* issues. As men identify as parents, *we* must support them so that we all can be involved parents.

It's also about our own lives. For the past thirty years, psychologist John Gottman has been tracking what makes successful marriages work.[2] What he's found is revealing. When men share housework and child care, their children are healthier and happier and do better in school. This makes a certain intuitive sense; after all, with two involved parents, kids get a lot more nurturing and support. When men share housework and child care, their wives report much higher levels of marital satisfaction and have better physical and psychological health. That also makes a certain amount of intuitive sense, since they're not running themselves ragged trying to balance work and family all by themselves.

It's equally true, though, that when men share housework and child care, the men themselves are happier, with higher levels of marital satisfaction and fewer symptoms of depression. They're healthier: They reduce alcohol and tobacco use, have more preventive screenings, take better care of their health, and report far less psychological distress.

And—as if that were not reason enough—they also have more sex. This too makes a certain intuitive sense: If men share housework and child care, their wives are significantly less tired and significantly less resentful about having to do the entire "second shift." They have, as it were, both opportunity and motive!

I'm not suggesting, of course, that men should immediately embrace egalitarian parenthood and democratic manhood because it will help them get more sex. Well, not that alone, anyway. But I am suggesting that those advice books that suggest that men and women are from different planets, that we are "opposite" sexes engaged in a primordial and eternal "battle of the sexes," are a load of nonsense. We are all earthlings! We're neighboring sexes, and the very things that will enable women to live the lives they say they want to live are the very same things that men need to live the sort of lives they say *they* want to live. Gender equality is good for children, it's good for women, and, it turns out, it's good for men as well.

Thomas Jefferson envisioned democracy as a delicate balance between rights and responsibilities. American men have spent so much time and energy recently focusing on rights that they've forgotten it is the responsibility side of the equation that connects them to their communities, their friends, their families, and themselves. It is to that vision that this work is dedicated.

Notes

INTRODUCTION: Toward a History of Manhood in America

1. See, e.g., Joe Dubbert, *A Man's Place: Masculinity in Transition* (Englewood Cliffs: Prentice-Hall, 1979); Peter Filene, *Him/Her/Self: Sex Roles in Modern America* (Baltimore: The Johns Hopkins University Press, 1986); E. Anthony Rotundo, *American Manhood: Transformations in Masculinity from the Revolution to the Modern Era* (New York: Basic Books, 1993); Peter Stearns, *Be a Man! Males in Modern Society* (New York: Holmes and Meier, 1979); Mark E. Kann, *On the Man Question: Gender and Civic Virtue in America* (Philadelphia: Temple University Press, 1991); G. J. Barker-Benfield, *The Horrors of the Half-Known Life: Male Attitudes Towards Women and Sexuality in Nineteenth-Century America* (New York: Harper and Row, 1976); David Pugh, *Sons of Liberty: The Masculine Mind in the Nineteenth Century* (Westport, Conn.: Greenwood Press, 1984).

Some specific historical studies also place masculinity at the heart of their analysis, including Mark Carnes, *Secret Ritual and Manhood in Victorian America* (New Haven: Yale University Press, 1990); Mary Ann Clawson, *Constructing Brotherhood: Gender, Class and Fraternalism* (Princeton, N.J.: Princeton University Press, 1990); Michael Paul Rogin, *Fathers and Children: Andrew Jackson and the Subjugation of the American Indian* (New York: Vintage, 1975); Elliot Gorn, *The Manly Art: Bare-Knuckle Prize Fighting in America* (Urbana: University of Illinois Press, 1986); David Macleod, *Building Character in the American Boy: The Boy Scouts, YMCA and Their Forerunners* (Madison: University of Wisconsin Press, 1983); Robert Griswold, *Fatherhood in America: A History* (New York: Basic Books, 1993).

Several anthologies also develop a more gendered notion of men's experiences, most notably Mark Carnes and Clyde Griffen, eds., *Meanings for Manhood: Constructions of Masculinity in Victorian America* (Chicago: University of Chicago Press, 1990); J. A. Mangan and James Walvin, eds., *Manliness and Morality: Middle-Class Masculinity in Britain and America, 1800–1940* (New York: St. Martin's Press, 1987); Elizabeth Pleck and Joseph Pleck, eds., *The American Man* (Englewood Cliffs: Prentice-Hall, 1980).

Works in literary criticism are also taking note of the applicability of a gender perspective to men's lives. See, for example, Leslie Fiedler, *Love and Death in the American Novel* (New York: Stein and Day, 1970); "The Male Novel," in

Partisan Review 37(1), 1970; and "Come Back to the Raft Ag'in Huck Honey!" in *Partisan Review*, June 1948; David Leverenz, *Manhood and the American Renaissance* (Ithaca, N.Y.: Cornell University Press, 1989); "The Last Real Man in America: From Natty Bumppo to Batman," in *American Literary History* 3, 1991; and "Manhood, Humiliation and Public Life: Some Stories," in *Southwest Review* 71, Fall 1986; Michael Paul Rogin, *Subversive Genealogy: The Politics and Art of Herman Melville* (New York: Knopf, 1983).

2. Thirty years ago social scientists would have only listed "class"; "race" was added about twenty-five years ago.

3. Thomas Lacquer, *Making Sex: Body and Gender from the Greeks to Freud* (Cambridge: Harvard University Press, 1990), p. 22.

4. See Catharine Stimpson, *Where the Meanings Are: Feminism and Cultural Spaces* (New York: Methuen, 1988).

5. Natalie Zemon Davis, "Women's History in Transition: The European Case," *Feminist Studies* 3(3–4), 1976, p. 83.

6. Robert Bly, *Iron John* (Reading, Pa.: Addison-Wesley, 1990), p. 230.

7. Erving Goffman, *Stigma: Notes on the Management of Spoiled Identity* (Englewood Cliffs: Prentice-Hall, 1963), p. 128.

8. R. W. Connell, *Gender and Power* (Stanford, Cal.: Stanford University Press, 1987), passim.

9. John Steinbeck, *Of Mice and Men* (New York: Scribners, 1937) p. 57.

10. Cited in the *New York Times*, 3 January 1993.

11. Gen. S. L. A. Marshall, *Men Against Fire* (New York: Morrow, 1947); also cited in John Keegan, *The Face of Battle* (New York: Viking, 1976).

12. David Leverenz, "Manhood, Humiliation and Public Life: Some Stories," in *Southwest Review* 71, Fall 1986, p. 451.

13. David Leverenz, "Manhood, Humiliation and Public Life," p. 455.

14. Garry Wills, *Nixon Agonistes* (Boston: Houghton Mifflin, 1970), pp. 162–163.

CHAPTER 1: The Birth of the Self-Made Man

1. Royall Tyler, *The Contrast: A Comedy in Five Acts* (Boston: Houghton Mifflin, 1920). Some commentary on the play is offered in Ada Lou Carson and Herbert L. Carson, *Royall Tyler* (Boston: Twayne Publications, 1979). See also Alexander Saxton, *The Rise and Fall of the White Republic: Class Politics and Mass Culture in Nineteenth-Century America* (New York: Verso, 1990), pp. 110–113.

2. Tyler, *The Contrast*, I, 1, p. 27.

3. Ibid., I, 2, p. 35.

4. Ibid., I, 2, pp. 32–33, pp. 38–39.

5. Ibid., III, 2, pp. 79, 82.

6. Ibid., V, pp. 112, 114–115.

7. My typology of masculine archetypes relies on several earlier efforts to map this terrain. See, e.g., Charles Rosenberg, "Sexuality, Class and Role in Nineteenth-Century America," *American Quarterly* 25, 1976; E. Anthony Rotundo, "Body and Soul: Changing Ideals of American Middle-Class Manhood," *Journal of Social History* 16, 1983, and "Learning About Manhood: Gender Ideals and the Middle-Class Family in Nineteenth-Century America," in *Manliness and Morality: Middle-Class Masculinity in Britain and America, 1800–1940*, J. A. Mangan and James Walvin, eds. (New York: St. Martin's Press, 1987); David Leverenz, *Manhood and the American Renaissance* (Ithaca, N.Y.: Cornell University Press, 1989).

8. Cited in Rotundo, "Learning About Manhood," p. 36.

9. Rotundo, "Body and Soul," p. 29.

10. On this image, see, e.g., Jay Fliegelman, *Prodigals and Pilgrims: The American Revolution Against Patriarchal Authority, 1750–1800* (New York: Cambridge University Press, 1982), and David Pugh, *Sons of Liberty: The Masculine Mind in Nineteenth-Century America* (Westport, Conn.: Greenwood Press, 1983).

11. John Adams to Thomas Jefferson, 21 December 1819; in Cappon, ed., *The Adams-Jefferson Letters* 549(2), 1959.

12. Charles Brockden Brown, *Edgar Huntley* [1799], 1928, p. xxiii; Washington Irving, *A Tour on the Prairies* [1835], John Francis McDermott, ed. (Norman: University of Oklahoma Press, 1956).

13. Fliegelman, *Prodigals and Pilgrims*, 1982, p. 224; see also Geoffrey Gorer, *The American People: A Study in National Character* (New York: Norton, 1964), and Winthrop Jordan, *White over Black* (Baltimore: Penguin, 1969), pp. 304–306.

14. Cited in Arthur M. Schlesinger, *Learning How to Behave: A Historical Study of American Etiquette Books* (New York: Macmillan, 1947), p. 12; letter 3. See also Charles M. Wiltse, *The New Nation, 1800–1845* (New York: Hill and Wang, 1961), p. 124.

15. Cited in Theodore P. Greene, *America's Heroes: The Changing Models of Success in American Magazines* (New York: Oxford University Press, 1970), p. 43.

16. Rev. Enos Hitchcock, *The Farmer's Friend* (Boston, 1793). See also John Cawelti, *Apostles of the Self-Made Man* (Chicago: University of Chicago Press, 1965), p. 32. On Franklin, see *The Autobiography of Benjamin Franklin* [1791] (New York: Doubleday, 1916), p. 129.

17. Samuel Adams, *Writings*, vol. 4, pp. 236–238.

18. See Stephanie Coontz, *The Social Origins of Private Life* (New York: Verso, 1988), pp. 118, 168.

19. Nancy Cott, *The Bonds of Womanhood: Women's Sphere in New England, 1780–1835* (New Haven: Yale University Press, 1977), p. 3; Norman Ware, *The Industrial Worker, 1840–1860* (Boston: Houghton Mifflin, 1924), p. 37.

20. Hunt is cited in Arthur M. Schlesinger, Jr., *The Age of Jackson* (Boston: Little, Brown, 1953), p. 129. Thomas Low Nichols, *Forty Years of American Life* (New York, 1837), pp. 194–195. Cited in Nancy Cott, *The Bonds of Womanhood*, p. 60.

Ralph Waldo Emerson, "Ode, Inscribed to W. H. Channing," in *The Poems and Translations of Ralph Waldo Emerson* (New York: Library of America, 1994), p. 119. In his advice book, *The Young Man's Friend* (1855), Rev. Daniel C. Eddy, the pastor of the Harvard Street Church in Boston, compared human life to a racecourse "in which a countless number of persons are contending for the prize." The prize was, of course, wealth, which was not only not a sin but a positive virtue. "There is nothing wrong in the accumulation of property; there is nothing wrong in a desire to have our needs approved by our fellowmen." Eddy's only caution was that we not become "inordinately attached" to wealth. It is "the *love* of money, and not money itself [that is the] root of all evil." Other books, like Charles Seymore's *Self-Made Men* (1859) and J. W. Kasey's *Young Man's Guide to Greatness* (1858), made similar arguments. See Rev. Daniel C. Eddy, *The Young Man's Friend* (Boston: Wentworth, Hewes, 1855), pp. 58, 129, 130.

21. Anonymous, *How to Behave* (New York, 1856), p. 124; cited in Schlesinger, *Learning How to Behave*, p. 16. Webster is cited in Rotundo, "Body and Soul," p. 30. Francis Grund, *The Americans in their Moral, Social and Political Relations*, 2 vols. (London: Longman, Rees, 1837), vol. 1, p. 173.

22. Cited in Michael Paul Rogin, *Fathers and Children: Andrew Jackson and the Subjugation of the American Indian* (New York: Vintage, 1975), p. 65.

23. Francis Grund, *The Americans in their Moral, Social and Political Relations*, 2 vols. (London: Longman, Rees, 1837), vol. 2, pp. 1–2, 5.

24. Charles Dickens, *American Notes for General Circulation* [1842] (New York: Penguin, 1972), pp. 141, 285, 287.

25. Ibid., pp. 229, 289.

26. Alexis de Tocqueville, *Democracy in America* [1840], George Lawrence, trans. (New York: Anchor, 1969), vol. 1, p. 314.

27. Ibid., vol. 2, p. 536.

28. Ibid., vol. 2, pp. 538, 627.

29. Cited in Irvin G. Wyllie, *The Self-Made Man in America* (New Brunswick, N.J.: Rutgers University Press, 1954), p. 10.

30. Calvin Colton, *Junius Tracts*, no. 7 (New York, 1844), p. 15. Also cited in Sellers, *The Market Revolution*, p. 238.

31. Kenneth Wayne, *Building the Young Man* (Chicago: A. C. McClurg, 1912), p. 18; Sam Osherson, *Wrestling with Love: How Men Struggle with Intimacy, with Women, Children, Parents, and Each Other* (New York: Fawcett, 1992), p. 291.

32. Kim Voss, *The Making of American Exceptionalism: The Knights of Labor and Class Formation in the Nineteenth Century* (Ithaca, N.Y.: Cornell University Press, 1993), p. 36. See also Sellers, *The Market Revolution*, pp. 152, 238; and David Leverenz, "The Last Real Man in America: From Natty Bumppo to Batman," in *American Literary History* 3, 1991, p. 757.

33. Kathy Peiss, "Of Makeup and Men: The Gendering of Cosmetics," paper presented at a Conference on the Material Culture of Gender, Winterthur Museum, November 1989, p. 4.

34. Ralph Waldo Emerson warned that "[t]he world is full of fops who never did anything and who persuaded beauties and men of genius to wear their fop livery; and these will deliver the fop opinion, that it is not respectable to be seen earning a living; that it is much more respectable to spend without earning" (Ralph Waldo Emerson, *Works*, vol. 6, pp. 91–92).

35. See William R. Taylor, *Cavalier and Yankee: The Old South and the American National Character* (New York: George Braziller, 1961), p. 91; other quotes were cited in Bruce Curtis, "The Wimp Factor," in *American Heritage*, November 1989; and Mark Kann, *On the Man Question: Gender and Civic Virtue in America* (Philadelphia: Temple University Press, 1991), p. 246.

36. T. Walter Herbert, *Dearest Beloveds: The Hawthornes and the Making of the Middle-Class Family* (Berkeley: University of California Press, 1993), p. 33.

37. Schlesinger, *The Age of Jackson*, pp. 23, 167; S. C. Allen is cited on p. 153.

38. The poem is in *Longfellow's Complete Poems* (Cambridge: Riverside Press, 1898).

39. Sean Wilentz, *Chants Democratic: New York City and the Rise of the American Working Class, 1788–1850.* (New York: Oxford University Press, 1984), p. 102; Allan Trachtenberg, *The Incorporation of American Culture: Culture and Society in the Gilded Age* (New York: Hill and Wang, 1982); Daniel Rodgers, *The Work Ethic in Industrial America, 1850–1920* (Chicago: University of Chicago Press, 1978), p. 19.

40. Walsh, cited in Lott, *Love and Theft*, p. 129; Mercein, cited in Howard Rock, *Artisans of the New Republic: The Tradesmen of New York City in the Age of Jefferson* (New York: New York University Press, 1984), p. 137; the poet is cited in Wilentz, *Chants Democratic*, p. 84; Tocqueville, *Democracy in America*, vol. 2, p. 48.

41. See Orestes Brownson, "The Laboring Classess," *Boston Quarterly*, July 1840, pp. 358–395.

42. Rock, *Artisans*, pp. 129, 319.

43. See Wilentz, *Chants Democratic*, pp. 260–261.

44. Wilentz, *Chants Democratic*, p. 145; Paul Johnson, *A Shopkeeper's Millennium: Society and Revivals in Rochester, New York, 1815–1837* (New York: Hill and Wang, 1978), p. 6; Carroll Smith-Rosenberg, *Disorderly Conduct: Visions of Gender in Victorian America* (New York: Knopf, 1985), p. 83. See also Bruce Laurie, *Artisans into Workers: Labor in Nineteenth-Century America* (New York: Hill and Wang, 1989), esp. p. 38.

45. Johnson, *Shopkeeper's Millennium*, pp. 57, 60, and Norman Ware, *The Industrial Worker, 1840–1860* (Boston: Houghton Mifflin, 1924), p. xii.

46. Charles Sellers, *The Market Revolution: Jacksonian America, 1815–1846* (New York: Oxford University Press, 1992); Thomas Cochran and William Miller, *The Age of Enterprise* (New York: Harper and Row, 1961), esp. p. 26.

47. David Montgomery, *Citizen Worker: The Experience of Workers in the United States with Democracy and the Free Market During the Nineteenth Century* (New York: Cambridge University Press, 1994), p. 50.

48. Cited in Laurie, *Artisans into Workers*, p. 64. See also Christopher Lasch, *The True and Only Heaven: Progress and Its Critics* (New York: Norton, 1991), esp. p. 203.

49. The statistic and citation come from Alice Kessler-Harris, *Out to Work* (New York: Oxford University Press, 1982), pp. 47, 69. Labor historian Philip S. Foner notes that "[m]any skilled craftsmen saw the entrance of women into the job market as the major source of their problems." See *Women and the American Labor Movement* (New York: Free Press, 1982), p. 13. "As they saw it, the more women workers hired, the more the wages of the skilled male workers would suffer"; *Foner*, p. 12.

50. Ware, *Industrial Worker*, p. 10.

51. See, e.g., Dale Knobel, *Paddy and the Republic: Ethnicity and Nationality in Antebellum America* (Middletown, Conn.: Wesleyan University Press, 1986).

52. David Roediger, *The Wages of Whiteness: Race and the Making of the American Working Class* (New York: Verso, 1991), p. 13.

53. Eric Lott, *Love and Theft: Blackface Minstrelsy and the American Working Class* (New York: Oxford University Press, 1993), pp. 53, 137, et passim.

54. Frederick Jackson Turner, *The Frontier in American History* [1903] (New York: Holt, Rinehart and Winston, 1947), p. 253.

55. Bancroft, cited in Wilson Carey McWilliams, *The Idea of Fraternity in America* (Berkeley: University of California Press, 1973), p. 250; Tocqueville, *Democracy in America*, p. 278. See also Smith-Rosenberg, *Disorderly Conduct*, pp. 99, 101.

56. Cited in Ron Takaki, *Strangers from a Different Shore: A History of Asian Americans* (New York: Viking, 1989), p. 94.

57. David Pugh, *Sons of Liberty*, p. 18.

58. Gadsden and Jackson, both cited in Rogin, *Fathers and Children*, p. 199.

59. Jackson and Van Buren, cited in Rogin, *Fathers and Children*, pp. 287, 290–291. See also Marvin Meyers, *The Jacksonian Persuasion: Politics and Belief* (Stanford, Cal.: Stanford University Press, 1957), esp. p. 78.

60. Jackson, cited in Sellers, *The Market Revolution*, p. 308 (italics in original); cabinet as pimps cited in Pugh, *Sons of Liberty*, p. 28.

61. Schlesinger, *The Age of Jackson*, p. 291.

62. Cited in Robert Gray Gunderson, *The Log Cabin Campaign* (Lexington: University of Kentucky Press, 1957), pp. 102–105.

63. Crockett et al. cited in Gunderson, *The Log Cabin Campaign*, p. 114.

64. Cited in Pugh, *Sons of Liberty*, p. 28. All songs are cited in Irwin Silber, *Songs America Voted By* (Harrisburg, Penn.: Stackpole Books, 1988), pp. 34, 35, 36, 41.

65. Richard Slotkin, *The Fatal Environment: The Myth of Frontier in the Age of Industrialization* (New York: Atheneum, 1985), p. 125.

66. Cited in John Updike, *Memories of the Ford Administration* (New York: Knopf, 1992), p. 229.

67. George G. Foster, *New York by Gas Light: With Here and There a Streak of Sunshine* (New York: Dewitt and Davenport, 1849), p. 101.

68. Cited in *Account of the Terrific and Fatal Riot at the Astor Place Opera House* (New York: H. M. Ranney, 1849), p. 10. Other valuable sources on the Astor Place riots include Iver Bernstein, *The New York City Draft Riots* (New York: Oxford University Press, 1990), pp. 149–151.

69. *Account of the Terrific and Fatal Riot*, pp. 56–57.

70. "The Astor Place Riot," p. 227.

71. *Account of the Terrific and Fatal Riot*, p. 15.

72. On the B'hoys, see Peter Buckley, "To the Opera House," George Foster, *New York by Gas Light*; and Sean Wilentz, *Chants Democratic*.

73. For accounts of the events of the Astor Place riots, see Peter Buckley, "To the Opera House," *Account of the Terrific and Fatal Riot at the Astor Place Opera House*, Sean Wilentz, *Chants Democratic*; Harry Brinton Henderson III, "Young America and the Astor Place Riot"; and Iver Bernstein, *The New York City Draft Riots*.

74. *Account of the Terrific and Fatal Riot*, p. 19.

75. "The Astor Place Riot," p. 173; *Account of the Terrific and Fatal Riot*, pp. 24–28.

CHAPTER 2: Born to Run

1. Henry David Thoreau, *Walden* [1854] (New York: Signet, 1960), p. 10.

2. Charles Sellers, *The Market Revolution: Jacksonian America, 1815–1846* (New York: Oxford University Press, 1992), p. 246.

3. Such books were enormously popular. William Alcott's *The Young Man's Guide* (1833) ran through twenty-one editions by 1858. The first edition of Daniel Eddy's *The Young Man's Friend* sold ten thousand copies. In 1857 Albert Barnes noted "the unusual number of books that are addressed particularly to young men" and the way in which "our public speakers everywhere advert to their character, temptations, dangers and prospects with deep solicitude"; cited in Joseph Kett, *Rites of Passage* (New York: Basic Books, 1977), p. 95.

4. *Onania* and Tissot's *A Treatise on the Diseases Produced by Onanism* are both reprinted in *The Secret Vice Exposed!* Carroll Smith-Rosenberg and Charles Rosenberg, eds. (New York: Arno, 1974).

5. G. J. Barker-Benfield, *The Horrors of the Half-Known Life: Male Attitudes Toward Women and Sexuality in Nineteenth-Century America* (New York: Harper and Row, 1976), pp. 180–181; see also esp. chaps. 15–16.

6. Cited in G. J. Barker-Benfield, *The Horrors of the Half-Known Life*, p. 179.

7. John Todd, *The Student's Manual* (Boston: Lee and Shepherd, 1835), pp. 147–148. See also G. J. Barker-Benfield, "The Spermatic Economy," p. 173.

8. Sylvester Graham, *A Lecture to Young Men* (Providence: Weeden and Cory, 1834), pp. 25, 33–34, 39, 58, 73.

9. Graham, *A Lecture*, p. 25.

10. Gardner, cited in Barker-Benfield, *The Horrors*, pp. 272–273. See also John Haller and Robin Haller, *The Physician and Sexuality in Victorian America* (New York: Norton, 1977), p. 208. R. J. Culverwell, *Professional Records: The Institutes of Marriage, Its Intent, Obligations, and Physical and Constitutional Disqualifications* (New York, 1846), p. 75.

11. Other "remedies" are cited in Haller and Haller, *The Physician and Sexuality*, pp. 208–209.

12. Charles Dickens, *American Notes for General Circulation* [1842] (New York: Penguin, 1972), p. 292.

13. Cited in Sellers, *The Market Revolution*, p. 259.

14. Paul E. Johnson and Sean Wilentz, *The Kingdom of Matthias: A Story of Sex and Salvation in Nineteenth-Century America* (New York: Oxford University Press, 1994), p. 59; Sellers, *The Market Revolution*, p. 259.

15. James B. Finley, *Autobiography of Rev. James B. Finley; or, Pioneer Life in the West* (Cincinnati: Methodist Book Concern, 1854), pp. 310–311; William Rorabaugh, *The Alcoholic Republic* (New York: Oxford University Press, 1979), pp. 14–15.

16. William Rorabaugh, *The Alcoholic Republic*, p. ix. Bourne is cited on p. 146. See also Donald Horton, "The Function of Alcohol in Primitive Societies," *Quarterly Journal of Studies on Alcohol* 4, 1943, pp. 199–320.

17. Carroll Smith-Rosenberg and Charles Rosenberg, *The Female Animal*, 1973, p. 353.

18. Tocqueville, *Democracy in America*, p. 240, 603.

19. Ibid., p. 587, 588.

20. Ibid., p. 601.

21. T. Walter Herbert, *Dearest Beloveds*, p. 187. See also John Mack Farragher, *Women and Men on the Overland Trail* (New Haven: Yale University Press, 1979), pp. 1–3.

22. Ruth Schwartz Cowan, *More Work for Mother: The Ironies of Household Technology from the Revolution to the Present* (New York: Basic Books, 1983), p. 64. See also Carroll Smith-Rosenberg, *Disorderly Conduct*, p. 85.

23. See, e.g., David Rothman, *The Discovery of the Asylum: Social Order and Disorder in the New Republic* (Boston: Little, Brown, 1971).

24. John Demos, *A Little Commonwealth* (Boston: Little, Brown, 1970), pp. 177–178. See also Rogin, *Fathers and Children*, p. 63, and Cowan, *More Work for Mother*, pp. 66–67.

25. Cited in T. Walter Herbert, *Dearest Beloveds*, p. 14.

26. See Paul Johnson and Sean Wilentz, *The Kingdom of Matthias*, p. 106 and passim.

27. Buell, cited in Nancy Cott, *The Bonds of Womanhood*, p. 54.

28. See Cott, *The Bonds of Womanhood*, p. 63, Kessler-Harris, *Out to Work*, pp. 51, 71, and passim, and Kennedy, *If All We Did Was to Weep at Home*, p. 17.

29. Meyers, *The Jacksonian Persuasion*, p. 52; Ward, 1962, p. 193.

30. Barbara Welter, "The Cult of True Womanhood," *American Quarterly*, Summer 1966, and Smith-Rosenberg, *Disorderly Conduct*, p. 13.

31. Cited in Sellers, *The Market Revolution*, pp. 242, 245. See also Barbara Welter, "The Cult of True Womanhood," esp. p. 152, and passim; Cott, *The Bonds of Womanhood*, p. 92.

32. Cited in Francesca Cancian, *Love in America: Gender and Self-Development* (New York: Cambridge University Press, 1987), pp. 19, 21.

33. Judd is cited in Ann Douglas, *The Feminization of American Culture* (New York: Knopf, 1977), p. 102. Eliza Farnham, *Woman and Her Era* (New York, 1864), p. 95.

34. E. Anthony Rotundo, *American Manhood*, chaps. 2–4.

35. Cited in T. Walter Herbert, *Dearest Beloveds*, p. 261.

36. Herbert, *Dearest Beloveds*, pp. 261, 262.

37. Eric Lott, *Love and Theft: Blackface Minstrelsy and the American Working Class* (New York: Oxford University Press, 1993), p. 196.

38. Committee on Female Labor and Commons, *Documentary History*, cited in Robert Max Jackson, untitled MS, chap. 4, pp. 5–8.

39. Cited in Christine Stansell, *City of Women* (New York: Knopf, 1986), p. 137. Committee on Female Labor and Commons, *Documentary History*, cited in Jackson, chap. 4, pp. 5–8.

40. Bram Dykstra, *Idols of Perversity: Fantasies of Women and Sexuality in Fin de Siècle America* (New York: Oxford University Press, 1986), p. 209.

41. Garfield, cited in Douglas, *The Feminization of American Culture*, p. 59; other citations in Michael S. Kimmel, "Men's Responses to Women's Educational Equality, 1848–the Present," *Thought and Action* 8(2), 1993.

42. Todd, *Woman's Rights*, pp. 14, 26. Long cited in Susan B. Anthony, Elizabeth Cady Stanton, and Matilda Joslyn Gage, *History of Woman Suffrage* (New York: National Woman's Suffrage Association, 1887), vol. 1, pp. 853–854.

43. Pierce, cited in Cott, *The Bonds of Womanhood*, p. 120; E. Anthony Rotundo, "American Fatherhood: A Historical Perspective," *American Behavioral Scientist* 29(1), 1985, pp. 10, 13; Jay Fliegelman, *Prodigals and Pilgrims*, p. 200; Adams, cited in Dubbert, *A Man's Place: Masculinity in Transition* (Engelwood Cliffs: Prentice-Hall, 1979), p. 23; Abbott, cited in Mark Carnes, *Secret Ritual and Manhood in Victorian America* (New Haven: Yale University Press, 1989), p. 111.

44. Carroll Smith-Rosenberg, *Disorderly Conduct*, p. 88.

45. David Leverenz, *Manhood and the American Renaissance* (Ithaca, N.Y.: Cornell University Press, 1989), p. 165; Burroughs, cited in Cott, *The Bonds of Womanhood*, p. 64.

46. Henry David Thoreau, *Walden* [1854] (New York: New American Library, 1960).

47. Brownson converted to Catholicism because he felt it to be more manly and patriarchal. Brownson, cited in Barbara Welter, "The Feminization of American Religion, 1800–1860," in *Clio's Consciousness Raised*, Mary Hartman and Lois Banner, eds. (New York: Harper and Row, 1974), p. 139. See also Rotundo, "Learning About Manhood," p. 47.

48. A similar process was evidenced in Britain, where the percentage of clean-shaven men pictured in the *Illustrated London News* dropped sharply from 1840, when about 40 percent were clean shaven, to a nadir of less than 10 percent clean shaven by 1885. See Dwight Robinson, "Fashions in Shaving and Trimming of the Beard: The Men of the *Illustrated London News*, 1842–1972," *American Journal of Sociology* 81(5), 1976, pp. 1134 (quote) and 1136 (for chart of percentages).

49. Whitman and *Harper's Monthly*, cited in William Leach, *True Love and Perfect Union: The Feminist Reform of Sex and Society* (New York: Basic Books, 1980), p. 217. On men and spectacles, see Paul E. Johnson and Sean Wilentz, *The Kingdom of Matthias* (New York: Oxford University Press, 1994), p. 94. Oliver Wendell Holmes, "The Autocrat at the Breakfast Table," in *Atlantic Monthly* 1, May 1858, p. 881.

50. Turner, *The Frontier in American History*, p. 92.

51. Flint, cited in Adams, *The Great Adventure*, p. 25; Timothy Dwight, *Travels in New England and New York*, 4 vols. (New Haven, 1821), vol. 2, p. 441; Crèvecoeur, cited in Roderick Nash, *Wilderness and the American Mind* (New Haven: Yale University Press, 1967), p. 30.

52. Francis Parkman, *The Oregon Trail: Sketches of Prairie and Rocky Mountain Life* [1849] (Boston: Little, Brown, 1892). Cited also in George M. Frederickson, *The Inner Civil War: Northern Intellectuals and the Crisis of the Union* [1965] (Champaign: University of Illinois Press, 1993), p. 34.

53. Charles Webber, *Old Hicks, the Guide; or, Adventures in the Comanche Country in Search of a Gold Mine*, 2 vols. (New York, 1855), vol. 1, p. 311.

54. Paula Mitchell Marks, *Precious Dust: The American Gold Rush Era, 1848–1900* (New York: William Morrow, 1994), p. 23.

55. Richard Stott, "The Geography of Gender in Nineteenth-Century America: Youth, Masculinity, and the California Gold Rush," paper presented at the 1991 Annual Meeting of the Organization of American Historians, esp. p. 6; Rev. John Todd, 1871, pp. 44–45; C. W. Haskins, *The Argonauts of California* (New York, 1890), p. 73; Elisabeth Margo, *Taming the Forty-Niner* (New York, 1855), p. 8.

56. Stott, "The Geography of Gender," pp. 6, 8, 11; Marks, *Precious Dust*, p. 326.

57. Henry David Thoreau, *Walden*, pp. 10, 66. 216.

58. Thoreau, *Walden*, pp. 142, 211.

59. See Henry Nash Smith, *Virgin Land: The American West as Symbol and Myth* (Cambridge: Harvard University Press, 1950), p. 226; Turner, *The Frontier in American History*, John Mack Farragher, *Daniel Boone: The Life and Legend of an American Pioneer* (New York: Henry Holt, 1992), esp. pp. 6, 29, 66, 327–328.

60. Slotkin, *The Fatal Environment*, p. 374.

61. Michael A. Lofaro, "Riprorious Shemales: Legendary Women in the Tall Tale World of the Davy Crockett Almanacs," in *Davy Crockett at Two Hundred*, Michael Lofaro and Joe Cummings, eds. (Knoxville: University of Tennessee Press, 1989), p. 26.

62. Leslie Fiedler, *Love and Death in the American Novel* (New York: Stein and Day, 1966), p. 181.

63. Washington Irving, "Rip Van Winkle" [1820], in *Collected Stories of Washington Irving* (New York: Signet, 1963), pp. 43–57.

64. Fiedler, *Love and Death*, p. 214.

65. See Fiedler, *Love and Death*, p. 211 and passim.

66. Christopher Lasch, *The True and Only Heaven* (New York: Norton, 1991), p. 94.

67. D. H. Lawrence, *Studies in Classic American Literature* (New York: Grove Press, 1967), p. 59. David Leverenz, "The Last Real Man in America," p. 754 and passim. See also Henry Nash Smith, *Wilderness*, p. 256; Cawelti, *Apostles of the Self-Made Man*, p. 78.

68. Cooper, *Last of the Mohicans*, p. 26.

69. Cooper, *Last of the Mohicans*, p. 318.

70. Cooper, *Last of the Mohicans*, p. 356.

71. See Walt Whitman, *Leaves of Grass and Other Poems*. The phrase "athletic democracy" appears in "To Foreign Lands."

72. Cited in George Frederickson, *The Inner Civil War*, p. 30.

73. Leverenz, *Manhood and the American Renaissance*, pp. 279, 281.

74. Leverenz, *Manhood and the American Renaissance*, pp. 290, 294.

75. See, e.g., John Neal, "The Rights of Woman" (1843); Samuel May, "The Rights and Condition of Women" (1946); Theodore Weld, "Man's Disparagement of Woman in All Times and Climes" (1855)—all edited and reprinted in Kimmel and Mosmiller, eds., *Against the Tide*, pp. 82–93, 94–98, 297–299. See also William Thompson, *Appeal of One-Half of the Human Race* (New York, 1825), and *History of Woman Suffrage*, vol. 1.

76. Noyes linked slavery and women's sexual subordination explicitly in a short play, "Slavery and Marriage—A Dialog" [1850] (Woman's Rights Collection, Arthur and Elizabeth Schlesinger Library on The History of Women, Harvard University).

77. Walt Whitman, *Complete Poetry and Collected Prose*, Justin Kaplan, ed. (New York: Library of America, 1982), pp. 248, 1307; see also William Patrick Jeffs, " 'Man's Words' and Manly Comradeship: Language, Politics and Homosexuality in Walt Whitman's Works," *Journal of Homosexuality* 23(4), 1992.

78. William Lloyd Garrison, "Intelligent Wickedness," reprinted in Kimmel and Mosmiller, eds., *Against the Tide*, pp. 212–214. Italics added.

79. Cited in Arthur Schlesinger, "The Role of Women in American History," in *New Viewpoints in American History* (New York: Macmillan, 1922), p. 139.

80. Bennett is cited in Bertram Wyatt-Brown, "The Abolitionist Controversy: Men of Blood, Men of God," in *Men, Women and Issues in American History*, vol. 1, Howard Quint and Milton Cantor, eds. (Homewood, Ill.: Dorsey Press, 1975), p. 222. *New York Daily World*, 11 May 1866. *Baltimore Patriot* is cited in Nina Silber, *The Romance of Reunion: Northerners and the South, 1865–1900* (Chapel Hill: University of North Carolina Press, 1993), p. 22.

81. Phillips and Garrison are cited in Bertram Wyatt-Brown, "The Abolitionist Controversy," pp. 228, 233–234.

82. All cited in David Shi, *The Simple Life* (New York: Oxford University Press, 1985), pp. 150, 151, 152.

83. Cited in Nina Silber, *The Romance of Reunion: Northerners and the South, 1865–1900* (Chapel Hill: University of North Carolina Press, 1993), p. 25.

84. H. Ford Douglass, cited in Richard Yarborough, "Race, Violence and Manhood: The Masculine Ideal in Frederick Douglass's 'The Heroic Slave,'" in *Frederick Douglass: New Literary and Historical Essays*, edited by Eric Sundquist (New York: Cambridge University Press, 1990), p. 169.

85. Frederick Douglass, *Narrative of the Life of Frederick Douglass, an American Slave* [1845] (New York: New American Library, 1968), p. 117.

86. Frederick Douglass, *My Bondage and My Freedom*, p. 247; *Narrative of the Life of Frederick Douglass*, p. 105. "Self-Made Men," in Frederick Douglass papers, Library of Congress, vol. 29, microform reel 18; cited also in Rafia Zafar, "Franklinian Douglass: The Afro-American as Representative Man," in *Frederick Douglass*, Eric Sundquist, ed., p. 113.

87. Cited in Jon Cullen, "'I's a Man Now': Gender and African American Men," in Clinton and Silber, eds., *Divided Houses*, p. 85.

88. Douglass, cited in Lee Ann Whites, "The Civil War as a Crisis in Gender," in Clinton and Silber, eds., *Divided Houses*, p. 11. Two slaves are cited in Cullen, pp. 85, 91. Albery A. Whitman, *Not a Man, and Yet a Man* (Springfield, Ohio: Republic, 1877), p. 202.

89. Cited in Taylor, *Cavalier and Yankee*, p. 334.

90. Memminger, cited in Eugene Genovese, *The World The Slaveowners Made* (New York: Vintage, 1969), p. 195. Huntley, cited in William R. Taylor, *Cavalier and Yankee: The Old South and The American National Character* (New York: George Braziller, 1961), p. 97. W. J. Cash, *The Mind of the South* (New York: Vintage, 1960), p. ix.

91. Genovese, *The World the Slaveholders Made*, p. 158.

92. William R. Taylor, *Cavalier and Yankee: The Old South and American National Character* (New York: George Braziller, 1961), pp. 48, 334.

93. Hale, cited in Taylor, *Cavalier and Yankee*, p. 133.

94. "Jeff in Petticoats" is reprinted in Irwin Silber, ed., *Songs of the Civil War* (New York, 1960), p. 345. See Nina Silber, *The Romance of Reunion*, for a superb discussion of this event.

95. George Frederickson, *The Inner Civil War*, p. 183.

96. On the crisis see Peter Filene, *His/Her Self: Sex Roles in Victorian America* (Baltimore: The Johns Hopkins University Press, 1986), p. 78.

97. Mark Twain, *The Adventures of Tom Sawyer*, p. 65.

CHAPTER 3: Men at Work

1. Madison C. Peters, *The Strenuous Career; or, Short Steps to Success* (Chicago: Laird and Lee, 1908), p. 22; Orison Swett Marden, *Power of Personality* [1899] (New York: Thomas Y. Crowell, 1906), p. 7.

2. C. Wright Mills, *White Collar* (New York: Oxford University Press, 1953), p. 63; Bruce Laurie, *Artisans into Workers*, p. 16.

3. Richard Edwards, *Contested Terrain: The Transformation of the Workplace in the Twentieth Century* (New York: Basic Books, 1979), pp. 23–28.

4. Laurie, *Artisans into Workers*, p. 115.

5. Cited in Kett, *Rites of Passage*, p. 145.

6. H. L. Arnold and L. F. Faurote, *Ford Methods and the Ford Shops* (New York: Engineering Company Magazine, 1915), p. 328. Daniel Rodgers, *The Work Ethic in Industrial America, 1850–1920* (Chicago: University of Chicago Press, 1974), pp. 166–167.

7. Eliot, cited in Rodgers, *The Work Ethic*, p. 33; Greeley, cited in James F. Willard, *Union Colony at Greeley* (Denver: W. F. Robinson Printing Co., 1918), p. 1; Anthony Ludovici, "Women's Encroachment on Man's Domain," *Current History* 27, October 1927, pp. 21–22. The mechanic is cited in Kim Voss, *The Making of American Exceptionalism*, 1993, p. 82.

8. Cited in William Leach, *Land of Desire: Merchants, Power and the Rise of a New American Culture* (New York: Pantheon, 1993), p. 161.

9. Henry Adams, *The Education of Henry Adams* (New York: Modern Library, 1931), pp. 241, 247.

10. James Platt, *Business* (New York: G. P. Putnam's Sons, 1889), p. vii; Rev. Russell Conwell, *Acres of Diamonds* (New York: Harper and Row, 1943), pp. 18, 21.

11. Melvin Adelman, *A Sporting Time: New York City and the Rise of Modern Athletics, 1820–1870* (Champaign: University of Illinois Press, 1986), p. 21; Thomas Cochran and William Miller, *The Age of Enterprise* (New York: Harper and Row, 1961), p. 230; George Frank Lydston, *Diseases of Society and Degeneracy (The Vice and Crime Problem)* (Philadelphia: Lippincott, 1904); Ronald Takaki, *Strangers from a Different Shore: A History of Asian Americans* (New York: Viking, 1989); Homer Lea, *The Valor of Ignorance* (New York: Harpers, 1909), p. 343.

12. James R. Grossman, *Land of Hope: Chicago, Black Southerners and the Great Migration* (Chicago: University of Chicago Press, 1989). See also Stanley Coben, *Rebellion Against Victorianism: The Impetus for Cultural Change in 1920s America* (New York: Oxford University Press, 1991), p. 72.

13. Cited in Grossman, *Land of Hope*, p. 167; cited in Laurie, *Artisans into Workers*, p. 158.

14. See, among other sources, Cornelia Meigs, *What Makes a College? A History of Bryn Mawr* (New York: Macmillan, 1956), and Arthur Cole, *A Hundred Years of Mount Holyoke College: The Evolution of an Educational Ideal* (New Haven: Yale University Press, 1940).

15. Steven Seidman, *Romantic Longings: Love in America, 1830–1980.* (New York: Routledge, 1991), p. 68.

16. See Billington, 1967, p. 78; Daphne Spain, *Gendered Spaces* (Chapel Hill: University of North Carolina Press, 1992), p. 201.

17. John Andrews and W. D. P. Bliss, *A History of Women in Trade Unions*, vol. 10 of *Report on Conditions of Woman and Child Earners in the United States*, S.Doc. 645, 61st Cong., 2nd sess. (Washington, D.C.: U.S. GPO, 1911), p. 48. See also Angel Kwolek-Folland, *Engendering Business: Men and Women in the Corporate Office, 1870–1930* (Baltimore: The Johns Hopkins University Press, 1994), pp. 4, 30.

18. Frederick Jackson Turner, *The Frontier in American History* [1893] (New York: Holt, Rinehart and Winston, 1947), p. 32.

19. On Adams's germ theory, see Daniel Patrick Moynihan, *Pandaemonium* (New York: Oxford University Press, 1993), p. 13.

20. Turner, *The Frontier*, p. 169; Horace Porter, "The Philosophy of Courage," *Century Illustrated Monthly Magazine* 36, May–October 1888, p. 253.

21. Hamlin Garland, *Jason Edwards, An Average Man* (Boston: Arena Publishing, 1892), p. v.

22. Cited in R. W. B. Lewis, *The American Adam* (Chicago: University of Chicago Press, 1957), p. 168.

23. Cited in Donald Worster, *Under Western Skies: Nature and History in the American West* (New York: Oxford University Press, 1992).

24. Cited in Richard Hofstadter, *Social Darwinism in America* (Boston: Beacon Press, 1955), p. 51.

25. Charles Zueblin, *Democracy and the Overman* (New York: B. W. Huebsch, 1910).

26. Clemenceau is cited in George Frederickson, *The Inner Civil War: Northern Intellectuals and the Crisis of the Union* [1965] (Champaign: University of Illinois Press, 1993), pp. 192–193.

27. Eric Lott, *Love and Theft: Blackface Minstrelsy and the American Working Class* (New York: Oxford University Press, 1993), p. 122.

28. Lathrop Stoddard, *The Rising Tide of Color* (New York: Scribners, 1920), pp. 297–298. Madison Grant, *The Passing of the Great Race; or, the Racial Basis of European History* (New York: Scribners, 1916), pp. 68, 81; Homer Lea, *The Day of the Saxon* (New York: Harper Bros., 1912), pp. 71, 234; see also Homer Lea, *The Valor of Ignorance* (New York: Harper Bros., 1909).

29. St. Louis physician cited in John S. Haller, *Outcasts from Evolution: Scientific Attitudes of Racial Inferiority, 1859–1900* (Urbana: University of Illinois Press, 1971), p. 44, see also p. 117; anatomist cited in Stephen Jay Gould, *The Mismeasure of Man* (New York: Norton, 1981), p. 103.

30. Anatomist, cited in Stephen Jay Gould, *The Mismeasure of Man*, p. 103.

31. Donnelly, cited in Ronald Takaki, *Strangers from a Different Shore*, p. 249. Gompers is cited in Alexander Saxton, *The Indispensable Enemy: Labor and the Anti-Chinese Movement in California* (Berkeley: University of California Press, 1971), p. 276; Agassiz, cited in Stephen Jay Gould, *The Mismeasure of Man*, p. 49; editor, cited in Richard Slotkin, *The Fatal Environment*, p. 185.

32. See Alexander Saxton, *The Indispensable Enemy*, pp. 172, 272. English, cited in John Haller, *Outcasts from Evolution*, p. 51.

33. Joseph Alfred Conwell, *Manhood's Morning; or, "Go It While You're Young": A Book for Young Men Between 14 and 28 Years of Age* (Vineland, N.J.: Hominus, 1896), p. 148.

34. Cited in Alexander Saxton, *The Indispensable Enemy*, p. 59.

35. Editor cited in Richard Slotkin, *The Fatal Environment: The Myth of the Frontier in the Age of Industrialization* (New York: Atheneum, 1985), p. 469.

36. The document is printed in John C. Lester and David L. Wilson, *The Ku Klux Klan* [1884] (New York: Neale Publishing, 1905), p. 155.

37. *Prescript* is cited in Lester and Daniel Wilson, *Ku Klux Klan*, p. 155.

38. George Lydston, *Diseases of Society and Degeneracy*, p. 424.

39. California State Historical Library, San Francisco, MS. 2334.

40. Edward Clarke, *Sex in Education: or, A Fair Chance for The Girls* (Boston: Houghton, 1873), p. 128.

41. Zueblin, *Democracy and the Overman*, p. 96. Bok is cited in Vincent Vinikas, *Soft Soap, Hard Sell: American Hygiene in an Age of Advertisement* (Ames, Iowa: Iowa State University Press, 1992), p. 52.

42. Cited in Richard Slotkin, *The Fatal Environment*, p. 237.

43. Angel Kwolek-Folland, *Engendering Business*, pp. 167, 168.

44. Harry Thurston Peck, "The Woman of To-Day and To-Morrow," in *Cosmopolitan* 27, June 1899, p. 154.

45. Frederick Douglass, introduction to *The Reason Why the Colored American Is Not in the World's Columbian Exposition*, Ida B. Wells, ed. (Chicago, 1892), p. 12.

46. On 1850s gay male subculture, see Christine Stansell, *City of Women: Sex and Class in New York, 1789–1860* (New York: Knopf, 1986), pp. 90–92; George Lydston, *Diseases of Society and Degeneracy*, p. 319; Jonathan Ned Katz, *Gay American History* (New York: Crowell, 1976), and *Gay/Lesbian Almanac* (New York: Harper and Row, 1983); George Chauncey, "Christian Brotherhood or Sexual Perversion? Homosexual Identities and the Construction of Sexual Boundaries in the World War I Era," *Journal of Social History* 19, 1985, p. 190.

47. George Chauncey, *Gay New York: Gender, Urban Culture, and the Making of the Gay Male World, 1890–1940* (New York: Basic Books, 1994), pp. 133, 355.

48. *New York Medical Journal*, 1884, cited in Jonathan Ned Katz, *Gay/Lesbian Almanac*, p. 119; George Lydston, cited in Katz, p. 213; sailor cited in George Chauncey, "Christian Brotherhood . . . ," p. 192, and George Chauncey, *Gay New York*, p. 55. On psychiatric diagnosis see Elizabeth Lunbeck, *The Psychiatric Persuasion*, p. 237. See also M. W. Peck, "The Sex Life of College Men," *Journal of Nervous and Mental Disease* 62, 1925.

49. George Chauncey, *Gay New York*, p. 56.

50. Ibid., p. 57.

51. Ibid., p. 117. On the term "sissy" see Peter Stearns, *American Cool* (New York: New York University Press, 1994), p. 33.

52. Cited in George Chauncey, *Gay New York*, p. 179.

53. See, e.g., Roger Bruns, *The Damndest Radical* (Urbana: University of Illinois Press, 1988), on Ben Reitman. For contemporary discussions see Timothy Nonn, "Hitting Bottom: Homelessness, Poverty and Masculinity," in *Men's Lives*, M. Kimmel and M. Messner, eds. 3rd ed. (New York: Macmillan, 1994).

54. Henry Ward Beecher, *Twelve Lectures to Young Men* (New York: Appleton, 1888), p. 8; Albert Shaw, *The Outlook for the Average Man* (New York: Macmillan, 1907), p. 26; Bouck White, *The Book of Daniel Drew* (New York: Doubleday, 1910), p. 144.

55. See Orison Swett Marden, *Pushing to the Front* (New York: Thomas Y. Crowell, 1894); *Success* (Boston: W. A. Wile, 1897), *The Secrets of Achievement* (New York: Thomas Y. Crowell, 1898), *Character, The Greatest Thing in the World* (New York: Thomas Y. Crowell, 1899), *The Power of Personality* [1899] (New York: Thomas Y. Crowell, 1906), *The Young Man Entering Business* (New York: Thomas Y. Crowell, 1903), *Optimistic Life* (New York: Thomas Y. Crowell, 1907), *He Who Can Thinks He Can* (New York: Thomas Y. Crowell, 1908), *The Crime of Silence* (New York: Physical Culture Publishing, 1915), *How to Get What You Want* (New York: Thomas Y. Crowell, 1917), *Prosperity* (New York: Success Magazine, 1922).

56. Orison Swett Marden, *The Optimistic Life* (New York: Thomas Y. Crowell, 1907), p. 228; Marden, *Pushing to the Front* (New York: Thomas Y. Crowell, 1894), pp. 69, 105, 109.

57. Cited in Cindy Aron, *Ladies and Gentlemen of the Civil Service: Middle-Class Workers in Victorian America, 1840–1870* (New York: Oxford University Press, 1987), p. 188.

58. Angel Kwolek-Folland's fascinating study *Engendering Business*, pp. 87, 91, 173. The phrase "a nation of salesmen" is from Earl Shorris's book *A Nation of Salesmen* (New York: Norton, 1994).

59. Max Weber, *The Protestant Ethic and the Spirit of Capitalism* [1904] (New York: Scribners, 1970), pp. 41, 53.

60. Max Weber, *The Protestant Ethic*, pp. 181, 182.

61. Thorstein Veblen, *The Theory of the Leisure Class* [1899] (New York: New American Library, 1953).

62. Hitchcock, cited in Harvey Green, *Fit for America* (New York: Pantheon, 1986), p. 15; Homer Lea, *The Valor of Ignorance* (New York: Harper Bros., 1909), p. 9, 58.

63. Andrew Carnegie, cited in John Cawelti, *Apostles of the Self-Made Man* (Chicago: University of Chicago Press, 1965), p. 194.

64. James Weir, "The Methods of the Rioting Striker as Evidence of Degeneration," *Century* 48, October 1894, pp. 952–953.

65. James is cited in Richard Slotkin, *Gunfighter Nation: The Myth of the Frontier in Twentieth-Century America* (New York: Athenaeum, 1992), p. 153.

66. Letter to *Miner's Magazine* 6(74), 24 November 1904; letter to *Boston Labor Leader*, 19 February 1887; both cited in Andrew Neather, "'The Dignity and Grandeur of Perfect Manhood': American Workingmen's Gender and the Ideology of Organized Labor, 1885–1914," unpublished MS, Duke University, Department of History, 1992.

67. Cited In Christopher Lasch, *The True and Only Heaven*, p. 213; Larry Glickman, "A Living Wage: Political Economy, Gender and Consumerism in American Culture, 1880–1925" (Ph.D. diss., U. C. Berkeley, 1992); James Davis, *The Iron Puddler: My Life in the Rolling Mills and What Came of It* (Indianapolis, 1922).

68. Cited in William Wyckoff, *The Workers* (New York: Scribners, 1899), pp. 111–112.

69. James Grossman, *Land of Hope in Chicago: Black Southerners and The Great Migration* (Chicago: University of Chicago Press, 1989), p. 218; David Roediger, *The Wages of Whiteness: Race and the Making of the American Working Class* (New York: Verso, 1991); *Workingman's Advocate*, Chicago, January 1871, cited in Gerald Grob, *Workers and Utopia: A Study of Ideological Conflict in the American Labor Movement, 1865–1900* (Chicago: Quadrangle, 1969), p. 24.

70. Leon Fink, *Workingman's Democracy: The Knights of Labor and American Politics* (Urbana: University of Illinois Press, 1983), p. 23; Carroll Wright, "An Historical Sketch of the Knights of Labor," *Quarterly Journal of Economics* 1, 1887, pp. 137–168; Kim Voss, 1992; Bruce Laurie, *Artisans into Workers*, esp. chap. 4; Gerald Grob, *Workers and Utopia*; and Susan Levine, "Labor's True Woman: Domesticity and Equal Rights in the Knights of Labor," *Journal of American History* 70(2), 1983, pp. 330–331 and passim.

71. Steven Hahn, *The Roots of Southern Populism: Yeomen Farmers and the Transformation of the Georgia Upcountry, 1850–1890* (New York: Oxford University Press, 1983), p. 168.

72. *People's Party Paper*, cited in Hahn, *Roots of Southern Populism*, p. 282. See Bryan's "Speech Before the Democratic National Convention, Chicago, 1896," also known as the "Cross of Gold" speech, reprinted in *Life and Speeches of William J. Bryan*, edited by J. S. Ogilvie (New York: J. S. Ogilvie Publishing, 1896).

73. I trust that my reading does not slight Dorothy, that protofeminist heroine whose sole desire is to return to Kansas, to her Aunt Em and Uncle Henry. Of course,

Dorothy had the power to return the entire time, contained in her silver slippers, the new currency that Bryan claimed would help the farmers and workers retain their independence. I realize that there are feminist readings of *The Wizard of Oz* that stress the relationship between Dorothy and the various witches. Not only is Dorothy a feminist heroine, but the entire story has a feminist theme; it is, after all, her ambition and resolve that allows, enables, and encourages the men to undertake their quest in the first place. I trust that examining this redemptive quest for manhood by Dorothy's three friends can help to complete that picture.

74. William Morris, *Selected Writings*, G. D. H. Cole, ed. (London: Nonesuch Press, 1948), p. 659. See also E. P. Thompson, *William Morris* (New York: Pantheon, 1977).

75. Eileen Boris, *Art and Labor: Rusin, Morris and the Craftsman Ideal in America* (Philadelphia: Temple University Press, 1986), p. 165.

76. Cited in Alan Crawford, *C. R. Ashbee: Architect, Designer, and Romantic Socialist* (New Haven: Yale University Press, 1986), p. 37. For these reasons, though, Ashbee opposed women's entry into the guilds.

77. Cited in Boris, *Art and Labor*, p. 76.

78. See, e.g., "Furniture for Men," *American Homes and Gardens* 1(4), October 1905.

79. Lea, *The Valor of Ignorance*, p. 11.

80. Carl Schurz, "About War," in *Harper's Weekly* 42, 5 March 1898, p. 219.

81. William James, *The Varieties of the Religious Experience* (Boston, 1902).

82. Cited in Peter Filene, *His/Her Self: Sex Roles in Victorian America* (Baltimore: The Johns Hopkins University Press, 1986), p. 324.

83. Lester Frank Ward, "Our Better Halves" *Forum* 6, November 1888.

84. Lester Frank Ward, *Pure Sociology* (New York: Macmillan, 1903), p. 377; Lester Frank Ward, *Applied Sociology* (Boston: Ginn, 1906), p. 233.

85. On the rhetorics of support for feminism offered historically by profeminist men, see my introduction to *Against the Tide. Pro-Feminist Men in the United States, 1776–1990, A Documentary History.*

86. Max Eastman, *Enjoyment of Living* (New York: Harper, 1948), p. 310.

87. Floyd Dell, "Feminism for Men," *The Masses* 5(20), July 1917. The essay is reprinted in *Against the Tide*, pp. 361–364.

88. "What Do You Know About That!" *The Masses*, 1914, p. 7.

89. Dell, "Feminism for Men," in *Against the Tide*, p. 361.

CHAPTER 4: Playing for Keeps

1. Henry James, *The Bostonians* [1885] (New York: Modern Library, 1984), p. 293.

2. Ann Douglas, *The Feminization of American Culture* (New York: Knopf, 1977).

3. Elliot J. Gorn, *The Manly Art: Bare-Knuckle Prize Fighting in America* (Ithaca, N.Y.: Cornell University Press, 1986), p. 192.

4. E. Anthony Rotundo, "Body and Soul: Changing Ideals of American Middle-Class Manhood, 1770–1920," *Journal of Social History* 16(4), 1983, p. 32.

5. David Riesman, *The Lonely Crowd* (New Haven: Yale University Press, 1950).

6. Roberta J. Park, "Physiologists, Physicians, and Physical Education: Nineteenth-Century Biology and Exercise, Hygienic and Educative," in *Sport and Exercise Science*, J. W. Berryman and R. J. Park, eds. (Urbana: University of Illinois Press, 1992), p. 141.

7. Bernarr Macfadden, "An Open Letter to President Roosevelt," *Physical Culture*, vol. 18, 1907, p. 75. Frank Lloyd Wright, cited in Herbert Muschamp, *Man About Town: Frank Lloyd Wright in New York City* (Cambridge: M.I.T. Press, 1983), p. 13.

8. Percentages of women teachers were even higher in major cities, such as New York (89%), Philadelphia (91.4%), Boston (89%), and Chicago (93.3%). See G. J. Barker-Benfield, *The Horrors of the Half-Known Life: Male Attitudes Towards Women and Sexuality in Nineteenth-Century America* (New York: Harper and Row, 1976), p. 21, and Earl Barnes, "The Feminizing of Culture," *Atlantic Monthly* 109, 1912, p. 772.

9. Alfred Cleveland, "The Predominance of Female Teachers," *Pedagogical Seminary* 12, September 1905, pp. 301, 303; A. Chadwick, "The Woman Peril," *Educational Review* 47, February 1914, pp. 115–116, 118.

10. See John Higham, *Strangers in the Land: Patterns of American Nativism, 1860–1925* (New York: Atheneum, 1970), pp. 78–79; Merwin, 1897, p. 838; O. S. Fowler, *Private Lectures on Perfect Men, Women and Children in Happy Families . . .* (Sharon Station, N.Y.: privately printed by Mrs. O. S. Fowler, 1883), p. 5.

11. Rafford Pyke, "What Men Like in Men," *Cosmopolitan* August 1902, pp. 405–406. Stillé, cited in Morris Fishbein, *A History of the American Medical Association* (Philadelphia: Saunders, 1947), pp. 82–83.

12. See George Chauncey, *Gay New York: Gender, Urban Culture and the Making of the Gay Male World, 1890–1940* (New York: Basic Books, 1994).

13. See Kathy Peiss, "Of Makeup and Men: The Gendering of Cosmetics," paper presented at a Conference on Gender and the Material Culture, Winterthur Museum, 1989, p. 7; *Decorum* (New York, 1877), p. 320.

14. See William Leach, "Transformations in a Culture of Consumption: Women and Department Stores, 1890–1925," *Journal of American History* 71, September 1984; and also William Leach, *Land of Desire: Merchants, Power and the Rise of a New American Culture* (New York: Pantheon, 1993).

15. Orison Swett Marden, *Pushing to the Front*, p. 9; Kenneth Wayne, *Building the Young Man* (Chicago: A. C. McClurg, 1912), pp. 95–96, 167.

16. See George Chauncey, *Gay New York*, p. 80; see also Leonard Ellis, "Men Among Men: An Exploration of All Male Relationships in Victorian America," unpublished Ph.D. diss., Columbia University, 1982.

17. Elizabeth Lunbeck, *The Psychiatric Persuasion: Knowledge, Gender and Power in Modern America* (Princeton, N.J.: Princeton University Press, 1994), p. 245, also p. 248; Richard Stivers, *A Hair of the Dog: Irish Drinking and American Stereotype* (University Park, Pa.: Pennsylvania State University Press, 1976).

18. Ted Ownby, *Subduing Satan: Religion, Recreation and Manhood in the Rural South, 1865–1920* (Chapel Hill: University of North Carolina Press, 1991).

19. Cited in MacLean, 1994, p. 100. Cited in Barbara Franco, "The Ritualization of Male Friendship and Virtue: Nineteenth-Century Fraternal Organizations," paper presented at Winterthur Conference on The Gender of Material Culture, 9–11 November 1989, p. 8. See also Leonard Ellis, "Men Among Men," p. 168; and David Healy, *The Individual Delinquent: A Text-Book of Diagnosis and Prognosis for All Concerned in Understanding Offenders* (Boston, 1915).

20. L. Pierce Clarke, "A Psychological Study of Some Alcoholics," *Psychoanalytic Review* 6, 1919, pp. 270–271; Otto Juliusberger, "Psychology and Alcoholism," *Psychoanalytic Review* 1, 1913, p. 469; Karl Abraham, "The Psychological Relations Between Alcoholism and Sexuality," *International Journal of Psychoanalysis* 7, 1926, p. 4. See also Ellis, "Men Among Men," pp. 168–169.

21. See George Chauncey, *Gay New York*, p. 81.

22. George Ruskin Phoebus, "Civilization—Physical Culture," *Physical Culture* 3, 1900, pp. 21–22.

23. Hall, cited in Michael C. C. Adams, *The Great Adventure: Male Desire and the Coming of World War I* (Bloomington: Indiana University Press, 1990), p. 38.

24. Cited in James Whorton, "Eating to Win: Popular Concepts of Diet, Strength and Energy in the Early Twentieth Century," in *Fitness in American Culture*, Kathryn Grover, ed. (Amherst: University of Massachusetts Press, 1990), p. 111.

25. See, e.g., Harvey Green, *Fit for America: Health, Fitness, Sport and American Society* (New York: Pantheon, 1986). See also Harvey Green, *Fit for America*, and Christopher Lasch, *The Culture of Narcissism* (New York: Norton, 1979).

26. Orison Swett Marden, *The Crime of Silence* (New York: Physical Culture Society, 1915), p. 48. On jealousy see Peter Stearns, *Jealousy: The Evolution of an Emotion in American History* (New York: New York University Press, 1989), esp. pp. 39–43, 154.

27. Joseph Alfred Conwell, *Manhood's Morning; or, "Go It While You're Young": A Book for Young Men Between 14 and 28 Years of Age* (Vineland, N.J.: Hominis, 1896), p. 197; O. S. Fowler, *Private Lectures on Perfect Men . . .* , p. 173; Bernarr Macfadden, *The Virile Powers of Superb Manhood: How Developed, How Lost, How Regained* (New York: Physical Culture Publishing, 1900), pp. 22, 29.

28. G. Douglas, "Social Purity," in *Official Report of the 12th International Christian Endeavor Convention* (New York, 1900), p. 254; Winfield Hall, *From Youth to Manhood* (New York: Association Press, 1900), p. 54. See also Martin Peck, "The Sex Life of College Men," *Journal of Nervous and Mental Disease* 62, 1925; and Albert Stearne, "Effects of Lascivious Conversations, Books and

Companions in the Causation of Sexual Excess," *American Journal of Dermatology and Genito-Urinary Disease* 11, 1907.

29. See J. H. Kellogg, *Man the Masterpiece; or, Plain Truths Plainly Told About Boyhood, Youth and Manhood* (Burlington, Iowa: I. F. Segner, 1886), pp. 445–453; see also J. H. Kellogg, *Plain Facts for Old and Young, Embracing the Natural History and Hygiene of Organic Life* (Burlington, Iowa: I. F. Segner, 1888); Joseph Kett, *Rites of Passage* (New York: Basic Books, 1977), p. 165; John Money, *The Destroying Angel* (Buffalo: Prometheus Books, 1985); and T. J. Jackson Lears, *No Place of Grace*, p. 14.

30. Among the physical indicators Kellogg listed premature development, rounded shoulders, weak backs, stiffness in the joints, paralysis, awkward gait, lack of female breast development, paleness, acne, heart palpitation, epilepsy, and cold, clammy hands. Behaviors and attitudes that might be indicators included general debility, sudden change in disposition, lassitude, sleeplessness, mental lapses, fickleness, untrustworthiness, love of solitude, bashfulness, boldness, mock piety, confusion, nail-biting, capricious appetite, eating slate pencils, use of tobacco, hysteria, bed-wetting, unchastity of speech.

31. For girls Kellogg's remedies were equally gruesome. He claimed that he had found "the application of pure carbolic acid to the clitoris and excellent means of allaying the abnormal excitement, and preventing the recurrence of the practice in those whose willpower has become so weakened that the patient is unable to exercise entire self-control."

32. Henry Guernsey, M. D., *Plain Talks on Avoided Subjects* (Philadelphia, 1882). Cited in Haller and Haller, pp. 208–209.

33. Cited in Kevin Mumford, "Lost manhood Found: Sexual Impotence and the Contradictions of Victorian Culture," unpublished MS, Stanford University, 1991, pp. 24–25.

34. Herman Adler, "Unemployment and Industry—a Study of Psychopathic Cases," *Mental Hygiene* 1, 1917.

35. Jarvis, cited in Barker-Benfield, *The Horrors of the Half-Known Life*, p. 29; Bryce, cited in John Starrett Hughes, "The Madness of Separate Spheres: Insanity and Masculinity in Victorian Alabama," in *Meanings for Manhood: Constructions of Masculinity in Victorian America*, M. Carnes and C. Griffen, eds. (Chicago: University of Chicago Press, 1991), p. 60; Philip Hamerton, *The Intellectual Life* (Boston: Roberts Bros., 1873), p. 5. See also Martin A. Berger, "Negotiating Victorian Manhood: Thomas Eakins and the Rowing Works," *masculinities* 2(4), 1994.

36. Cited in Spiller, 1990, p. 80.

37. Elaine Showalter, *The Female Malady: Women, Madness, and English Culture, 1830–1980* (New York: Pantheon, 1985), pp. 172, 175, and 170–175 passim.

38. George Beard, *American Nervousness*, 1881, p. 138; see also Tom Lutz, *American Nervousness, 1903: An Anecdotal History* (Ithaca, N.Y.: Cornell University Press, 1991); Edward Wakefield, "Nervousness: The National Disease of

America," *McClure's* 2, February 1894; and Albert J. Underhill, "Sexual Neurasthenia in Men," *Journal of the American Medical Association* 60, 1913.

39. John Starrett Hughes, "The Madness of Separate Spheres," p. 57; see also John Haller and Robin Haller, *The Physician and Sexuality in Victorian America* (New York: Norton, 1977), esp. p. 217.

40. Sander Gilman, *Freud, Race and Gender* (Princeton, N.J.: Princeton University Press, 1993), p. 95.

41. See E. Anthony Rotundo, "Body and Soul," p. 28; Leon Fink, *Workingmen's Democracy: The Knights of Labor and American Politics* (Urbana: University of Illinois Press, 1983), p. 9; Delaware ad, cited in Kenneth Jackson, *Crabgrass Frontier* (New York: Oxford University Press, 1985), p. 138; John Muir, cited in David Shi, *The Simple Life: Plain Thinking and High Thinking in American Culture* (New York: Oxford University Press, 1985), p. 197; George Evans, "The Wilderness," *Overland Monthly* 43, January 1904, p. 33.

42. Roosevelt and Grinnell, 1893, pp. 14–15; Kent is cited in Roderick Nash, *Wilderness and the American Mind* (New Haven: Yale University Press, 1967), p. 153.

43. Woods Hutchinson, *Instinct and Health* (New York: Dodd and Mead, 1909).

44. Sargent, cited in Joe Dubbert, *A Man's Place: Masculinity in Transition* (Englewood Cliffs: Prentice-Hall, 1979), p. 169. Fiske is cited in Donald Mrozek, *Sports and American Mentality* (Knoxville: University of Tennessee Press, 1983), p. 207. British paper, cited in Melvin Adelman, *A Sporting Time: New York City and the Rise of Modern Athletics, 1820–1870* (Champaign: University of Illinois Press, 1986), p. 284.

45. Walker and Wesleyan *Bulletin*, cited in Louise Knight, "The 'Quails': The History of Wesleyan University's First Period of Coeducation, 1872–1912," B.A. honors thesis, Wesleyan University, 1972. New York newspapers, cited in Melvin Adelman, *A Sporting Time*, p. 277. See also George Frank Lydston, *Diseases of Society and Degeneracy (The Vice and Crime Problem)* (Philadelphia: Lippincott, 1904), p. 582.

46. Frederic Paxson, "The Rise of Sport," *Mississippi Valley Historical Review* 4, September 1917, p. 146. See also Melvin Adelman, *A Sporting Time*, p. 83.

47. Cited in David Chapman, *Sandow the Magnificent: Eugen Sandow and the Beginnings of Bodybuilding* (Urbana: University of Illinois Press, 1994), p. 190.

48. Harvey Green, *Fit for America*, p. 215. On boxing, football, and baseball, see also Ellis, "Men Among Men," pp. 443–491, 491–542, 543–603, respectively. Boxing fan is cited in Michael C. C. Adams, *The Great Adventure*, p. 41.

49. Elliot Gorn, *The Manly Art: Bare-Knuckle Prize Fighting in America* (Ithaca, N.Y.: Cornell University Press, 1986), p. 138 and passim.

50. Ibid., p. 247.

51. Others included running, rowing, football, boxing, wrestling, shooting, riding, and mountain climbing.

52. Marshall, cited in Albert Spalding, *America's National Game* (New York: American Sports Publishing, 1911), p. 534. William McKeever, *Training the Boy*

(New York: Macmillan, 1913), p. 91. Zane Grey, "Inside Baseball," *Baseball Magazine* 3(4), 1909. Much of the material in this section is condensed from my "Baseball and the Reconstitution of American Masculinity, 1880–1920," *Baseball History* 3, 1990.

53. Cited in Melvin Adelman, *A Sporting Time*, p. 173.

54. Gunther Barth, *City People: The Rise of Modern City Culture in Nineteenth-Century America* (New York: Oxford University Press, 1980), pp. 190, 191.

55. Taft here clearly refers to the solitary vice, as well as other feminizing indoor activities. Charles Murphy, "Taft, the Fan," *Baseball Magazine* 9(3), 1912, pp. 3–4.

56. Peter Filene, *Him/Her Self: Sex Roles in America* (Baltimore: The Johns Hopkins University Press, 1986), p. 139.

57. Richard Slotkin, *The Fatal Environment*, p. 363.

58. James Robertson, "Horatio Alger, Andrew Carnegie . . . ," p. 251.

59. On this see Marcus Klein, *Easterns, Westerns and Private Eyes: American Matters, 1870–1900* (Madison: University of Wisconsin Press, 1994), p. 13.

60. Alger subtitle is from *The Spider and the Fly* (1873); others from Marcus Klein, *Easterns, Westerns and Private Eyes*, p. 52.

61. Horatio Alger, *Luke Larkin's Luck*.

62. Stephen Crane, *The Red Badge of Courage* [1895] (New York: Penguin, 1983).

63. W. Churchill Williams, "Red Blood in Fiction," *The World's Work* 6(1), May 1903, p. 3694; Carman cited in T. J. Jackson Lears, *No Place of Grace*, p. 106. Leslie Fiedler claims that at the turn of the century, the male audience "reasserted itself." Leslie Fiedler, "The Male Novel," *Partisan Review* 37(1), 1970, p. 81.

64. Cited in Larzer Ziff, *The American 1890s: Life and Times of a Lost Generation* (New York: Viking, 1966), pp. 251, 252.

65. Frank Norris, *McTeague* [1899] (New York: New American Library, 1964), p. 7.

66. Frank Norris, *Vandover and the Brute* (Garden City, N.Y.: Doubleday, 1914), p. 309.

67. Frank Norris, *A Man's Woman*.

68. William Dean Howells, *The Rise of Silas Lapham* [1885] (New York: Harper and Row, 1958).

69. On Henry James see Alfred Habegger, *Gender, Fantasy, and Realism in American Literature* (New York: Columbia University Press, 1982), p. 255.

70. On Eakins see David Lubin, *Acts of Portrayal* (New Haven: Yale University Press, 1985), and Martin A. Berger, "Negotiating Victorian Manhood: Thomas Eakins and the Rowing Works," *masculinities* 2(4), 1994.

71. Ives, cited in Henry Cowell and Sidney Cowell, *Charles Ives and His Music* (New York: Oxford University Press, 1955), p. 10. See also David Noble, *The Progressive Mind, 1890–1917* (New York: Rand McNally, 1970), p. 131; and Rupert Wilkinson, *American Tough: The Tough-Guy Tradition and American Character* (New York: Harper and Row, 1986), p. 103.

72. Vincent Scully, *Modern Architecture* (New York: George Braziller, 1974), p. 18; see also Robert Twombly, *Louis Sullivan: His Life and Work* (New York: Viking, 1986).

73. Johnson is cited in Henry Nash Smith, *The Virgin Land*, p. 122.

74. Wallace Stegner, cited in Ben Merchant Vorpahl, *My Dear Wister: The Frederic Remington–Owen Wister Letters* (Palo Alto: American West Publishing, 1972), p. ix. James Robertson, "Horatio Alger, Andrew Carnegie, Abraham Lincoln and the Cowboy," *Midwest Quarterly* 20, 1979, p. 253.

75. Frontier Days handbill and program, American Heritage Center, University of Wyoming Library, Laramie, W994-t-ch-fd, 1925. E. M. Bond, "The Cowmen's Carnival," *Sunset* 23(2), August 1909, p. 173.

76. Bond, "the Cowmen's Carnival," p. 176; Jimmy Walker, "Rodeo Killers," *True West*, 1958; article in scrapbook at American Heritage Center, University of Wyoming, Laramie, Ro 614. See also *Saturday Evening Post*, 29 November 1919.

77. The cowboy is a man "in flight from his ancestors, from his immediate family, and from everything that tied him down and limited his freedom of movement," writes cultural critic Christopher Lasch, *The True and Only Heaven: Progress and its Critics* (New York: Norton, 1991), p. 39. To the cowboy, as Wallace Stegner puts it, civilization "meant responsibility, meant law, meant fences and homesteads, and water rights and fee-simple land ownership, meant women" (Stegner cited in Ben Merchant Vorpahl, *My Dear Wister*, p. ix). Robert Warshow put it most succinctly when he wrote that "the true enemy of the cowboy is the schoolmarm"; cited in Marcus Klein, *Easterns, Westerns, and Private Eyes*, p. 101.

78. Wright is cited in Mark Gerzon, *A Choice of Heroes* (Boston: Houghton Mifflin, 1983), p. 77.

79. The unattributed quotations above are all from Owen Wister's letters to his friend Frederic Remington and from an essay "The Evolution of the Cow Puncher" (1893), all in Ben Merchant Vorpahl, *My Dear Wister*, pp. xi, 81, 93, 94, and passim.

80. Owen Wister, *The Virginian* [1902] (New York: New American Library, 1979).

81. Cited in G. Edward White, *The Eastern Establishment and the Western Experience* (New Haven: Yale University Press, 1968), p. 124.

82. Jane Tompkins, *West of Everything: The Inner Life of Westerns* (New York: Oxford University Press, 1992), p. 136.

83. Donald Worster, *Under Western Skies: Nature and History in the American West* (New York: Oxford University Press, 1992), p. 80; Will J. Wright, *Six-Gun Society* (Berkeley: University of California Press, 1975), p. 152; Robert Murray Davis, *Playing Cowboys: Low Culture and High Art in the Western* (Norman: University of Oklahoma Press, 1992), p. 13.

84. Louise Levathes, "Remington: The Man and the Myth," *National Geographic*, August 1988, p. 226.

85. Remington, cited in Richard Slotkin, *The Fatal Environment*, p. 97; letter from Frederic Remington to Owen Wister, cited in Nixon O. Rush, *Frederic Remington and Owen Wister: The Story of a Friendship, 1893–1909* (Tallahassee: privately printed, 1961), p. 30; at University of California, Berkeley, Bancroft Library.

86. Louise Levathes, "Remington: The Man and the Myth," p. 226.

87. Jack London, *The Call of the Wild* [1903] (New York: Signet, 1975), p. 75.

88. Jack London, *The Sea Wolf* [1904] (New York: Bantam, 1963), p. 13. See also Madonne Miner, "'It Will Be the (un)Making of You': Manhood Besieged in Jack London's *The Sea Wolf*," *Jack London Newsletter* 21, 1990.

89. Edgar Rice Burroughs, *Tarzan of the Apes* [1912] (New York: Signet, 1966).

90. Burroughs, *Tarzan*, p. 243. See also David Leverenz, "The Last Real Man in America," p. 759.

91. Cited in Jane Tompkins, *West of Everything*, pp. 33, 167.

CHAPTER 5: A Room of His Own

1. See E. Anthony Rotundo, "Boy Culture: Middle-Class Boyhood in Nineteenth-Century America," in *Meanings for Manhood: Constructions of Masculinity in Victorian America*, M. Carnes and C. Griffen, eds. (Chicago: University of Chicago Press, 1991), p. 32.

2. Cited in Dolores Hayden, *A Grand Domestic Revolution: A History of Feminist Design for American Homes, Neighborhoods, and Cities* (Cambridge: M.I.T. Press, 1981), p. 16.

3. Samuel Fraser, "What Are You Going to Do November Second?" addresses before the Livingston County Granges, Geneseo, New York, 1914 (Buffalo and Erie County Historical Society Library, Buffalo, New York), p. 2. Watson, is cited in Mintz and Kellogg, *Domestic Revolutions*, p. 108; see also Robert Griswold, "Divorce and the Legal Redefinition of Victorian Manhood," in *Meanings for Manhood*.

4. J. Jill Suitor found that husbands began attending the births of their children in the 1830s and continued until hospital births became common in the 1910s. J. Jill Suitor, "Husbands' Participation in Childbirth: A Nineteenth-Century Phenomenon," *Journal of Family History*, Fall 1981, p. 284 and passim.

5. Margaret Marsh, "Suburban Men and Masculine Domesticity, 1870–1915," *American Quarterly* 40, June 1988, p. 166.

6. Margaret Marsh, "Suburban Men," pp. 176 and esp. 181. Masculine domesticity was actually a form of resistance, a reaction against women's putative control over domestic life.

7. This led to the conclusion of "blue for girls." See "Pink or Blue?" *Infants' Department*, June 1918; "What Color for Your Baby?" *Parents*, March 1939. The best contemporary historical account of children's clothing is in Jo Paoletti, "The Gendering of Infants' and Toddlers' Clothing in America," paper presented at the Conference on Gender and Material Culture, Winterthur Museum of American Culture, Wilmington, 1989.

8. E.g., Alfred Carleton Gilbert invented the Erector set, that conglomeration of girders and screws, because, as he put it, "I know what boys like"; cited in Paula Petrick, "The Self-Made Boy and the Scientific Capitalist: Gender and the Toy Industry, 1890–1920," paper presented at the Berkshire Conference on the History of Women, June 1990, p. 8.

9. J. Adams Puffer, *The Boy and His Gang* (Boston: Houghton Mifflin, 1912), p. 91.

10. Hall is cited in Peter Stearns, *American Cool* (New York: New York University Press, 1994), p. 31.

11. Albert Beveridge, *The Young Man and the World* (New York: Appleton, 1905). Dana cited in John Curtis Crandall, "Images and Ideals for Young Americans: A Study of American Juvenile Literature," 1825–1860, Ph.D. diss., University of Rochester, 1957, p. 92.

12. Rev. William Forbush, *The Boy Problem: A Study in Social Pedagogy* (Boston: Pilgrim Press, 1901), p. 47. See also J. H. Tufts, "Feminization," *School Review* 17, January 1909.

13. G. Stanley Hall, *Adolescence: Its Psychology and Its Relations to Physiology, Anthropology, Sociology, Sex, Crime, Religion and Education*, 2 vols. (New York: Appleton, 1904). See also "How and When to Be Frank with Boys," *Ladies' Home Journal*, 1907; "The Awkward Age," *Appleton's Magazine*, August 1900, for more of Hall's thoughts on adolescence. See also his essays "Some Dangers in Our Educational System and How to Meet Them," *New England Magazine* 41, February 1907, and "Coeducation in the High School," *Addresses and Proceedings of the National Educational Association*, 1903, for his perspective on coeducation.

14. G. Stanley Hall, *Adolescence*, vol. 2, p. 562. See also G. Stanley Hall, "Flapper American Novissima," *Atlantic Monthly* 129, June 1922.

15. Hall, *Adolescence*, vol. 2, p. 532; Hall, "How and When to Be Frank with Boys."

16. Hall, "The Awkward Age," p. 154. Even bullying other boys was understandable, Hall argued. "The boy's bullying is the soul-germ of the man's independence," he wrote, before citing approvingly one boy who was "over-bearing and cruel" to his sister, whom he had "perfectly terrorized," and another boy who forced his younger sister to kneel before him. Bullying helped boys develop manly independence, esp. if they bullied girls.

17. J. Adams Puffer, *The Boy and His Gang*, pp. 83, 142; Albert Beveridge, *The Young Man and the World*, p. 101.

18. Cited in Gail Bederman, Ph.D. diss., p. 30.

19. Although several colleges and universities were founded as coeducational, the great push for coeducation came in the decades after the Civil War, when the provisions of the Morrill Act prompted the founding of many of the nation's large state universities and also when other colleges and universities took up the question of women's admissions and educational and social segregation. See Rosalind Rosenberg, *Beyond Separate Sphere: Intellectual Roots of Modern Feminism* (New Haven: Yale University Press, 1982), and "The Limits of Access: The

History of Coeducation in America," in *Women and Higher Education in American History*, J. Faragher and F. Howe, eds. (New York: Norton, 1988).

20. Wesleyan University Libraries, MS coll. 31, pp. 31–35. See also Louise Knight, " 'The Quails': The History of Wesleyan University's First Period of Coeducation, 1872–1912," B.A. honors thesis, Wesleyan University, 1972; Charles Emerick, "College Women and Race Suicide," *Political Science Quarterly* 24, June 1909.

21. Wesleyan University *Argus* is cited in Knight, " 'The Quails' "; Hamilton is cited in Thomas Woody, *A History of Women's Education in the United States*, 2 vols. (New York: Science Press, 1929), vol. 1, p. 268.

22. Wesleyan remained all-male until 1970. Both cited in Louise Knight, " 'The Quails,' " pp. 50, 51.

23. Cited in Thomas Woody, *A History of Women's Education*, vol. 2, p. 281.

24. Eliot, letter to Lindley C. Kent, 30 March 1880; Schlesinger Library, A/K37 Lindley Kent.

25. University of California papers, cited in Lynn Gordon, *Gender and Higher Education in the Progressive Era* (New Haven: Yale University Press, 1990), p. 70. On Columbia see also Rosalind Rosenberg, *Beyond Separate Spheres*; Helen Lefkowitz Horowitz, *Alma Mater: Design and Experience in the Women's Colleges from their Nineteenth-Century Beginnings to the 1930s* (New York: Knopf, 1984), p. 134; Frederick Barnard, "Should American Colleges Be Open to Women As Well As to Men?" a paper presented to the twentieth Annual Convocation of the University of the State of New York at Albany, July 12, 1882; published by the Proceedings of the Convocation (Albany, 1882); Morgan Dix et al., "To the Trustees of Columbia College: A Report of the Select Committee on the Subject of Admission of Women to the College," 23 April 1884 (MS coll., Columbia University Library); Alice Duer Miller and Susan Myers, *Barnard College: The First Fifty Years* (New York: Columbia University Press, 1939).

26. TR to GSH, 29 November 1899; Hall papers, Clark University, box 25, folder 18.

27. "The notion that our splendid women teachers are making mollycoddles of their boy students is utterly absurd. Why, women themselves are anything but mollycoddles in these days of basket-ball and athletic 'stunts' without number! They'd be the first to despise the 'feminine' boy—instead of petting him into being"; cited in Woody, *A History of Women's Education*, Vol. 2, p. 514; See John Dewey, "Is Coeducation Injurious to Girls?" *Ladies' Home Journal* 28, 1911; "Education and the Health of Women," *Science* 6, 1885; and "Health and Sex in Higher Education," *Popular Science Monthly* 28, 1886.

28. On the coeducation debate see my *Against the Tide: Pro-Feminist Men in the United States, 1776–1990* (with Tom Mosmiller), part II. Dewey's comment about men who oppose coeducation is in a letter to President William Raney Harper of the University of Chicago, 25 July 1902 (University of Chicago Library, President's Papers, 1899–1925).

29. Joseph Kett, *Rites of Passage: Adolescence in America, 1790–the Present* (New York: Basic Books, 1977), p. 203; Gulick, cited in J. Adams Puffer, *The Boy and His Gang*, p. 127.

30. George Bird Grinnell and Charles Sheldon, *Hunting and Conservation: The Book of the Boone and Crockett Club* (New Haven: Yale University Press, 1925), pp. 534–535.

31. Rev. William Forbush, *The Boy Problem*, pp. 98, 140.

32. Baden-Powell, cited in Allen Warren, "Popular Manliness: Baden Powell, Scouting and the Development of Manly Character," in *Manliness and Morality: Middle-Class Masculinity in Britain and America, 1800–1940*, J. A. Mangan and J. Walvin, eds. (New York: St. Martin's Press, 1987), p. 203.

33. "My aim was to make a man," wrote Seton in *The History of the Boy Scouts*. "Baden-Powell's was to make a soldier"; cited in Betty Keller, *Blackwolf: The Life of Ernest Thompson Seton* (Vancouver: Douglas and McIntyre, 1984), p. 169.

34. Frederick Jackson Turner, *The Frontier in American History* (New York: Holt, Rinehart and Winston, 1947), p. 358. Daniel Beard, *The Boy Scout Handbook* [1914] (Boy Scouts of America Publication, 1955), p. 12.

35. Cited in Robert MacDonald, *Sons of the Empire*, p. 142.

36. Seton cited in Keller, *Blackwolf*, p. 161.

37. Cited in Betty Keller, *Blackwolf*, p. 189.

38. Seton, cited in Macleod, *Building Character*, p. 49; *Boy Scout Handbook*, p. 38.

39. Francis Shepardson, *The Beta Book: The Story and Manual of Beta Theta Pi* (published by Beta Theta Pi, 1927), p. 23.

40. Henry Sheldon, *Student Life and Customs*, p. 219.

41. W. S. Harwood, "Secret Societies in America," *North American Review* 164, May 1897. See also Noel Gist, "Secret Societies: A Cultural Study of Fraternalism in the United States," *University of Missouri Studies* 15, October 1940.

42. James P. Carnahan, *Pythian Knighthood* (Cincinnati: Pettibone Manufacturing Co., 1909); also cited in Barbara Franco, "Fraternal Organizations and Industrial Society," p. 6.

43. Mary Ann Clawson, *Constructing Brotherhood*, p. 146.

44. Beharrell, cited in Carnes, *Secret Ritual and Manhood*, p. 84; A. B. Grosh, *The Odd Fellows Improved Manual* (Philadelphia, 1871).

45. Gage is cited in Mark Carnes, *Secret Ritual*, p. 80.

46. On racial exclusion see Noel Gist, "Secret Societies," pp. 128–131; on the Klan in the 1910s and 1920s, see Kathleen Blee, *Women of the Klan: Racism and Gender in the 1920s* (Berkeley: University of California Press, 1991).

47. Jeffrey Charles, *Service Clubs in American Society: Rotary, Kiwanis, and Lions* (Champaign: University of Illinois Press, 1993), p. 7.

48. Club member, cited in G. Edward White, *The Eastern Establishment and the Western Experience* (New Haven: Yale University Press, 1968), p. 27.

49. The Bohemian Club still runs a weeklong drunken revel for America's ruling elite at its Sonoma County retreat (although their homosocial intimacy was reportedly lubricated by the availability of prostitutes at local inns). See G. William

Domhoff, *The Bohemian Grove and Other Ruling-Class Retreats* (New York: Harper and Row, 1974),

50. On the decline of fraternalism, see Gist, "Secret Societies," esp. pp. 42–43; see also Carnes, *Secret Ritual*, and Clawson, *Constructing Brotherhood*. The quote about men being less anxious after World War I is from Mark Carnes, *Secret Ritual*, p. 153.

51. Ann Douglas, *The Feminization of American Culture* (New York: Knopf, 1977), pp. 17, 97, 101, 113.

52. Cited in Douglas, *The Feminization of American Culture*, p. 91.

53. Cited in Ted Ownby, *Subduing Satan: Religion, Recreation and Manhood in the Rural South* (Chapel Hill: University of North Carolina Press, 1991), p. 14.

54. Norman Vance, *The Sinews of the Spirit: The Ideal of Christian Manliness in Victorian Literature and Religious Thought* (Cambridge: Cambridge University Press, 1985), p. 29.

55. Thomas Wentworth Higginson, "Saints and Their Bodies," *Atlantic Monthly* 1, 1858, pp. 584, 587. See also his "Barbarism and Civilization," *Atlantic Monthly* 7, 1861, pp. 51–61, and "Gymnastics" in *Atlantic Monthly* 7, 1861, pp. 283–302. See also "Muscular Christianity," *North Carolina Presbyterian*, 2 January 1867.

56. Carl Case, *The Masculine in Religion* (New York, 1906); R. W. Conant, *The Manly Christ, a New View* (Chicago, 1904); Harry Emerson Fosdick, *The Manhood of the Master* (New York, 1911); Thomas Hughes, *The Manliness of Christ* (Boston: Houghton Mifflin, 1880); Jason Noble Pierce, *The Masculine Power of Christ; or, Christ Measured as a Man* (Boston: Pilgrim Press, 1912); Kenneth Wayne, *Building the Young Man* (Chicago: A. C. McClurg, 1912); Bouck White, *The Call of the Carpenter* (New York: Doubleday, 1913).

Interestingly, just as American Protestants were creating Muscular Christianity, Viennese Jews were experimenting with Muscular Jewry. Max Nordau, the widely read literary critic and novelist, summoned Jewish men to the Bar Kokhba Gymnastic Clubs in 1903 in the name of "Muskeljudentum," or Muscular Jewry. See Paul Breines, *Tough Jews: Political Fantasies and the Moral Dilemma of American Jewry* (New York: Basic Books, 1990).

57. Kenneth Wayne, *Building the Young Man*, pp. 168, 169.

58. White, *The Call of the Carpenter*, pp. 36, 38, 110, 171.

59. White, *The Call of the Carpenter*, pp. 182, 333–334.

60. Citations from the Ku Klux Klan are from Nancy MacLean, *Behind the Mask of Chivalry*, p. 161.

61. Gail Bederman, "'The Women Have Had Charge of the Church Work Long Enough': The Men and Religion Forward Movement of 1911–1912 and the Masculinization of Middle-Class Protestantism," *American Quarterly* 41, 1989; *Delaware Republican*, 27 February 1915; cited in Paula Baker, *The Moral Frameworks of Public Life: Gender, Politics and the State in Rural New York, 1870–1930* (New York: Oxford University Press, 1991), p. 171; Alfred Stearns et al., *The Education of the Modern Boy* (Boston: Houghton Mifflin, 1928),

p. 105; Roger A. Bruns, *Preacher: Billy Sunday and Big Time American Evangelism* (New York: Norton, 1992), p. 15.

62. William A. Sunday, "Why I Left Professional Baseball," *Young Men's Era* 19(30), 27 July 1893, p. 1. See also William T. Ellis, *Billy Sunday: The Man and His Message* (Philadelphia: Universal Book and Bible House, 1914) for long passages from Sunday's sermons. Quote from journalist is from Roger Bruns, *Preacher*, p. 137; see also p. 110. Other important secondary works on Billy Sunday include Lyle Dorsett, *Billy Sunday and the Redemption of Urban America* (Grand Rapids, Mich.: Eerdmans, 1991); William G. McLaughlin, *Bill Sunday Was His Real Name* (Chicago: University of Chicago Press, 1955).

63. Quotes from Sunday are cited in William McLaughlin, *Billy Sunday Was His Real Name*, pp. 141, 179; Bruns, *Preacher*, p. 15.

64. Cited in Bruns, *Preacher*, pp. 16, 121, 122, 138, 284. McLaughlin, *Billy Sunday Was His Real Name*, p. 175.

65. Cited in McLaughlin, *Billy Sunday Was His Real Name*, pp. 141, 142, 177.

66. Cited in Bruns, *Preacher*, p. 15.

67. Not everyone was enamored with Sunday, however. Emma Goldman denounced him as a "frothing, howling huckster," and Carl Sandburg denounced him in a poem, "To a Contemporary Bunkshooter" (1915), as a "bughouse peddlar of second-hand gospel . . . tearing your shirt . . . yelling about Jesus."

68. Henry Rood, "Men and Religion," *Independent* 71, 1911, p. 1364; Fred Smith, *A Man's Religion* (New York, 1913). See Gail Bederman, " 'The Women Have Had Charge of the Church Work Long Enough,' " and Gary Scott Smith, "The Men and Religion Forward Movement of 1911–1912: New Perspectives on Evangelical Social Concern and the Relationship Between Christianity and Progressivism," *Westminster Theological Journal* 49(1), Spring 1987.

69. Quote from Gary Scott Smith, "The Men and Religion Forward Movement," p. 100; Gail Bederman, " 'The Women Have Had Charge of Church Work Long Enough,' " p. 22.

70. David Leverenz, "The Last Real Man in America: From Natty Bumppo to Batman," *American Literary History* 3, 1991, p. 763.

71. Herman Hagedorn, *A Boy's Life of Theodore Roosevelt* (New York: Harper, 1918). One of the best-selling boys' books of all time, *A Boy's Life* made Roosevelt's journey a template for twentieth-century American men.

72. Tom Lutz, *American Nervousness* (1903), p. 79.

73. Roosevelt thought he looked smashing in his "sombrero, silk neckerchief, fringed buckskin shirt, sealskin chaparajos or riding trousers, and alligator hide boots" and with his "pearl-hilted revolver and beautifully finished Winchester rifle," he felt "able to face anything," as he wrote to his sister, cited in Donald Day, ed., *The Hunting and Exploring Adventures of Theodore Roosevelt* (New York: Dial, 1955), p. 47. See also G. Edward White, *The Eastern Establishment and the Western Experience*, p. 83, and John Eliot, "TR's Wilderness Legacy," *National Geographic*, September 1982, p. 344.

74. *Autobiography*, p. 76.

75. Tom Lutz, *American Nervousness (1903)*, p. 28.

76. Theodore Roosevelt, *The Works of Theodore Roosevelt*, vol. 13, pp. 322–323, 331.

77. Thorstein Veblen, *The Theory of the Leisure Class*, p. 168.

78. Joseph Dana Miller, "Militarism or Manhood?" *Arena* 24, October 1900, pp. 385, 386–388.

79. Amy Hardwicke, "A Woman's Idea of the Physical Culture Man," *Physical Culture* 4, 1901. Charlotte Perkins Gilman, *Women and Economics* [1899] (New York: Harper and Row, 1966), pp. 119, 126.

80. See "Muster Out Roll," reprinted in Roosevelt, *The Rough Riders*, pp. 238–269. *Santa Fe New Mexican*, 11 May 1898. These journalistic reports are cited in G. Edward White, *The Eastern Establishment*, p. 155.

81. Theodore Roosevelt, "The American Boy," 1900. Roosevelt's comment on continental expansion is from the foreword to the 1900 edition of *The Winning of the West*, vol. 1, pp. x–xi.

82. The quote is from George Frederickson, *The Inner Civil War: Northern Intellectuals and the Crisis of the Union* (Champaign: University of Illinois Press, 1993), p. 166. TR's boys' books, *The Wilderness Hunter* (1894), *American Big Game Hunting* (1894), and *Hunting in Many Lands* (1896), were written for the Boone and Crockett Club and became part of boy culture in the early twentieth century. As one of the founders of the American Museum of Natural History, Roosevelt linked Darwinian evolution, eugenics, and racism into a potent blend that the historian of science Donna Haraway ingeniously calls "Teddy Bear Patriarchy." See Donna Haraway, *Primate Visions: Gender, Race and Nature in the World of Modern Science* (New York: Routledge, 1989), chap. 3.

83. William Davison Johnson, *TR: Champion of the Strenuous Life*, pp. 126–127, 138.

84. See Kathleen Dalton, "Theodore Roosevelt," p. 11.

85. Gail Parker, *Mind Cure in New England: From the Civil War to World War I* (Hanover, N.H.: University Press of New England, 1973), p. 34.

CHAPTER 6: Muscles, Money, and the M–F Test

1. Hemingway's letter is cited in Mark Spilka, *Hemingway's Quarrel with Androgyny* (Lincoln: University of Nebraska Press, 1990), p. 329.

2. George W. Henry, "Psychogenic Factors in Overt Homosexuality," *American Journal of Psychiatry* 93, p. 904.

3. See Elizabeth Lunbeck, *The Psychiatric Persuasion: Knowledge, Gender, and Power in Modern America* (Princeton, N.J.: Princeton University Press, 1994), p. 253; Aaron Rosanoff, "A Study of Hysteria, Based Mainly on Clinical Material Observed in the U.S. Army Hospital for War Neuroses at Plattsburgh Barracks, N.Y.," *Archives in Neurology and Psychiatry* 2, 1919; Karl Menninger, "Hysteria

in a Male as a Defense Reaction: A Case Report," *Boston Medical and Surgical Journal* 180, 1919.

4. Robert Lynd and Helen Lynd, *Middletown* [1929] (New York: Free Press, 1955); Robert Lynd and Helen Lynd, *Middletown in Transition* [1937] (New York: Free Press, 1966).

5. Clarence Darrow, "Salesmanship," *American Mercury*, August 1925.

6. Frederick Payne Millard, *What a Man Goes Through* (Boston: Christopher Publishing House, 1925), p. 108.

7. Suzanne LaFollette quote and "These Modern Husbands," letter to the editor of the *Nation*, 12 January 1927, p. 39; both cited in Kevin White, *The First Sexual Revolution*, p. 178.

8. Labor Force Statistics, Series D 85–86: Unemployment, 1890–1970.

9. Henry H. Goddard, "Mental Tests and the Immigrant," *Journal of Delinquency* 2, 1917, p. 252; Carl C. Bingham, *A Study of American Intelligence* (Princeton, N.J.: Princeton University Press, 1923), pp. 111, 162; see also p. 180.

10. Cited in Ronald Takaki, *Strangers from a Different Shore: A History of Asian Americans* (New York: Viking, 1989), pp. 324–331.

11. Alexander Goldenweiser, "Prehistoric KKKs," *World Tomorrow* 7, March 1924, p. 81. See also F. Bohn, "Ku Klux Klan Interpreted," in *American Journal of Sociology* 30, 1925.

12. Devere Allen, "Substitutes for Brotherhood," *World Tomorrow* 7, March 1924, pp. 74, 75. Charles Merz provided the estimate of 800 secret societies in "Halt! Who Comes There?" *New Republic* 35, 1923, and in "Sweet Land of Secrecy," *Harper's Magazine* 154, 1927.

13. See Stanley Coben, *Rebellion Against Victorianism*, p. 138.

14. Bruce Barton, *The Man Nobody Knows* (New York and Indianapolis: Bobbs-Merrill, 1924), pp. 31, 43, and passim.

15. David Nye, *Image Worlds: Corporate Identities at General Electric, 1890–1930* (Cambridge: M.I.T. Press, 1985), p. 96.

16. Newcomer, 1959, pp. 10–36.

17. Frederick Payne Millard, *What a Man Goes Through: Friendly Chats About the Battle of Life* (Boston: Christopher Publishing House, 1925), p. 66.

18. H. L. Mencken, *In Defense of Women* (New York: P. Goodman Company, 1918), p. 135.

19. Sherwood Anderson, *Perhaps Women* (New York: Horace Liveright, 1931), pp. 42, 142.

20. Quoted in Steven Mintz and Susan Kellogg, *Domestic Revolutions: A Social History of American Family Life* (New York: Free Press, 1988), p. 138.

21. Cited in Robert Griswold, "Fatherhood and World War II," paper presented to the Organization of American Historians annual meeting, April 1989, p. 2.

22. Cousins is cited in Alice Kessler-Harris, *Out to Work* (New York: Oxford University Press, 1982), p. 256.

23. Cited in Warren Sussman, *Culture as History: The Transformation of American Society in the Twentieth Century* (New York: Pantheon, 1984), p. 195.

24. Mirra Komorovsky, *The Unemployed Man and His Family* (New York: Dryden Press, 1940), pp. 74–75.

25. Komorovsky, *The Unemployed Man and His Family*, 355, 357.

26. Lurine Pruette, *The Parent and the Happy Child* (New York: Henry Holt, 1932), p. 32.

27. Roy Dickerson, *Growing into Manhood* (New York: Association Press, 1933), p. 21.

28. Sinclair Lewis, *Babbit* [1922] (New York: Signet, 1961), p. 97.

29. See Peter Filene, *Him/Her Self: Sex Roles in Modern America*, 2nd ed. (Baltimore: The Johns Hopkins University Press, 1986), p. 46, and Stephanie Coontz, *The Way We Never Were: American Families and the Nostalgia Trap* (New York: Basic Books, 1992).

30. John B. Watson, *Psychological Care of Infant and Child* (New York: Norton, 1928), pp. 5, 6, 12, 86, and esp. chap. 3.

31. Joseph Collins, *The Doctor Looks at Love and Life* (New York: Doran, 1926), p. 73; Clement Wood, *Manhood: The Facts of Life Presented to Man* (Kansas City: Haldeman-Julius, 1924).

32. "Masculine Women! Feminine Men!" written by Monaco and Leslie, 1925; first recorded by Frank Harris in 1926 (Okeh Records, 40593). I am grateful to Jonathan Ned Katz for first bringing this song to my attention.

33. See George Chauncey, *Gay New York: Gender, Urban Culture and the Making of the Gay Male World, 1890–1940* (New York: Basic Books, 1994), pp. 354, 559–560.

34. Jodi Vandenberg-Daves, "Pursuing a Partnership Between the Sexes: The Debate over Programs for Women and Girls in the Young Men's Christian Association, 1914–1933," unpublished paper, University of Minnesota, 1991; William Allen White, *Boys—Then and Now* (New York: Macmillan, 1926), pp. 42–43.

35. See Thomas Woody, *A History of Women's Education in the United States* (New York: Science Press, 1929) vol. 2, p. 451.

36. Geoffrey Gorer, *The American People: A Study in National Character* (New York: Norton, 1964), pp. 48–49.

37. See the discussion of this film in George Chauncey, *Gay New York*, p. 325.

38. Lewis Terman and Catherine Cox Miles, *Sex and Personality* (New York: Russell and Russell, 1936), p. 3.

39. Joseph Pleck, *The Myth of Masculinity* (Cambridge: M.I.T. Press, 1981), p. 159, and passim.

40. For more about Terman and the M-F test, see Henry L. Minton, "Femininity in Men and Masculinity in Women: American Psychiatry and Psychology Portray Homosexuality in the 1930s," *Journal of Homosexuality* 13(1), Fall 1986.

41. To score this section, give yourself a minus (–) for every answer in which you said that the thing caused "a lot" of the emotion—except for the answer "being a Bolshevik," which was obviously serious enough for even men to get very emotional about. On all the others, though, and through the entire test, high levels of emotion—regardless of the cause or the emotion—were scored as feminine.

42. The original sample upon which this MMPI was based, incidentally, was 54 male soldiers, 67 female airline employees, and 13 male homosexuals. See Joseph Pleck, *The Myth of Masculinity* (Cambridge: M.I.T. Press, 1981), p. 37. On the Strong Vocational Interest Blank, see Edward K. Strong, "Interests of Men and Women," *Journal of Social Psychology* 7, 1936, and Edward K. Strong, *Vocational Interests of Men and Women* (Stanford, Cal.: Stanford University Press, 1943). On the Guilfords' temperament survey, see J. P. Guilford and Ruth P. Guilford, "Personality Factors S, E, and M and Their Measurement," *Journal of Psychology* 2, 1936.

43. See Miriam Lewin, "'Rather Worse Than Folly?' Psychology Measures Femininity and Masculinity, Part 1: From Terman and Miles to the Guilfords," in Miriam Lewin, ed., *In the Shadow of the Past: Psychology Portrays the Sexes*, p. 164.

44. Terman and Miles. *Sex and Personality*, p. 320.

45. See, e.g., George W. Henry, "Psychogenic Factors in Overt Homosexuality," *American Journal of Psychiatry* 93, 1937, and *Sex Variants: A Study of Homosexual Patterns*, vol. 1 (New York: Hoeber, 1941). See also Henry L. Minton, "Femininity in Men and Masculinity in Women: American Psychiatry and Psychology Portray Homosexuality in the 1930s," *Journal of Homosexuality* 13(1), 1986. On subsequent measures see Lewin, "'Rather Worse Than Folly?'"

46. So significant is the development of the M-F test that Joseph Pleck places the emergence of the contemporary male sex-role paradigm in 1936. See Joseph Pleck, *The Myth of Masculinity*, and "The Rise and Fall of the Male Sex Role, 1936 to the Present," in *The Making of Masculinities*, Harry Brod, ed. (Boston: Unwin Hyman, 1987).

47. M. Zolotow, "You Too Can Be a New Man," *Saturday Evening Post* 214, 7 February 1942, p. 59. See also "Muscle Makers," *Time*, 22 February 1937.

48. Robert Lewis Taylor, "I Was Once a 97-Pound Weakling," *New Yorker*, 3 January 1942, p. 25.

49. Cited in Zolotow, "You Too Can Be a New Man," p. 60.

50. Ibid., p. 21.

51. Jules Feiffer, *Great Comic Book Heroes* (New York: Dial Press, 1965), p. 19.

52. James Thurber, "The Secret Life of Walter Mitty," *New Yorker*, 18 March 1939.

53. Raymond Chandler, *The Simple Art of Murder* (New York: Norton, 1968).

54. Wexman, p. 27. Cited in Frank Krutnik, *In a Lonely Street: Film Noir, Genre, Masculinity* (New York: Routledge, 1991), pp. 42–43.

55. Leslie Fiedler, *Love and Death in the American Novel* (New York: Stein and Day, 1970), pp. 316–317. Sandra Gilbert and Susan Gubar, *No Man's Land: The Place*

of the Writer in the Twentieth Century, vol. 1 (New Haven: Yale University Press, 1988), p. 36. D. H. Lawrence is cited in Mark Spilka, *Hemingway's Quarrel with Androgyny* (Lincoln: University of Nebraska Press, 1994), p. 179.

56. Quotes are from Ernest Hemingway, *The Sun Also Rises* (1927).

57. Sinclair Lewis, *Babbit*, [1922] (New York: Signet, 1961), p. 155.

58. John Cawelti, *Apostles of the Self-Made Man* (Chicago: University of Chicago Press, 1965), p. 230.

59. F. Scott Fitzgerald, *The Great Gatsby* (New York: Scribners, 1925), pp. 99, 174.

60. John Steinbeck, *Of Mice and Men* [1937] (New York: Penguin, 1974), p. 104.

61. The phrase is Jim Hoberman's from his review of the film *Of Mice and Men* in the *Village Voice*.

62. John Lahr, "Waiting for Odets," *New Yorker*, 26 October 1992, p. 122.

63. See Clifford Odets, *Waiting for Lefty*, in *Three Plays by Clifford Odets* (New York: Random House, 1935).

64. Gold is cited in David Savran, *Communists, Cowboys and Queers: The Politics of Masculinity in the Work of Arthur Miller and Tennessee Williams* (Minneapolis: University of Minnesota Press, 1992), p. 25.

65. See Joan Mellon, *Big Bad Wolves: Masculinity in American Film* (New York: Pantheon, 1977), p. 29.

CHAPTER 7: "Temporary About Myself"

1. See Sonya Michel, "Danger on the Home Front: Motherhood, Sexuality, and the Disabled Veterans in American Postwar Films," *Journal of the History of Sexuality* 3(1), 1992; and Kaja Silverman, "Historical Trauma and Male Subjectivity," in *Psychoanalysis and Cinema*, E. Ann Kaplan, ed. (New York: Routledge, 1990).

2. Cited in Michael C. C. Adams, *The Best War Ever: America and World War II* (Baltimore: The Johns Hopkins University Press, 1994), pp. 150, 151.

3. Adams, *The Best War Ever*, p. 112.

4. Raymond Sobel, "The Battalion Surgeon as Psychiatrist," *Bulletin of the U.S. Army Medical Department*, suppl., November 1949, p. 38.

5. Stephen Ranson, "The Normal Battle Reaction: Its Relation to the Pathologic Battle Reaction," *Bulletin of the U.S. Army Medical Department*, suppl., November 1949, p. 6.

6. Cited in Frank Krutnik, *In a Lonely Street: Film Noir, Genre, Masculinity* (New York: Routledge, 1991), p. 210.

7. Cited in Griswold, "Fatherhood and World War II," p. 11.

8. See Daniel Boone, "No Substitute for Father," *Rotarian* 65, August 1944, and Robert Griswold, "Fatherhood and World War II," paper presented at the Organization of American Historians annual meeting, April 1989.

9. Cited in Griswold, "Fatherhood and World War II," pp. 5–6.

10. Ada Hart Arlitt, "How Separation Affects the Family," *Marriage and Family Living* 5, February 1943, p. 21.

11. Talcott Parsons, "Certain Primary Sources and Patterns of Aggression in the Social Structure of the Western World," in *Essays in Sociological Theory* (New York: Free Press, 1963), p. 309.

12. E.g., Arnold Green argued in 1946 that it was the sons of permissive and punishment-shunning mothers who turned out to have neurotic dispositions, not the sons of authoritarian and punitive parents. See Arnold Green, "The Middle-Class Male Child and Neurosis," *American Sociological Review* 11, 1946.

13. Philip Wylie, *A Generation of Vipers* (New York: Farrar and Rinehart, 1942); David Levy, *Maternal Overprotection* (New York: Columbia University Press, 1943); and Edward Strecker, *Their Mothers' Sons* (Philadelphia: Lippincott, 1946).

14. Philip Wylie, *A Generation of Vipers*, pp. 187–188.

15. Margaret Mead, *And Keep Your Powder Dry* (New York: Morrow, 1942), pp. 68–69.

16. Ibid., pp. 142, 151, 157.

17. Richard Wright, *Native Son* (New York: Harper and Row, 1940), pp. 12, 273, 280. See also Richard Wright, "The Man Who Was Almost a Man," in *Eight Men* (Cleveland: World Publishing, 1961), p. 18.

18. Cited in James Greenberg, "In Film Noir, the Past Is Present and Perfect," *New York Times*, 6 February 1994, H9.

19. Arthur Miller, *Death of a Salesman* [1949] (New York: Penguin, 1986), p. 36.

20. Ibid., p. 73.

21. Ibid., p. 23; other citations from pp. 22, 54, 65.

22. Ibid., pp. 132, 138.

23. Chafe is cited in Wini Breines, *Young, White and Miserable: Growing Up Female in the Fifties* (Boston: Beacon Press, 1992), p. 8.

24. Sen. Wherry is quoted in Max Lerner in the *New York Post*, 17 July 1950; both the Lerner article and McCarthy are cited in David Savran, *Cowboys, Communists and Queers: The Politics of Masculinity in the Work of Arthur Miller and Tennessee Williams* (Minneapolis: University of Minnesota Press, 1992), pp. 4–5. McCarthy's aide is cited in David Caute, *The Great Fear: The Anti-Communist Purge Under Truman and Eisenhower* (New York: Simon and Schuster, 1978).

25. Ruth Hartlet, "Sex Role Pressures and the Socialization of the Male Child," *Psychological Reports* 5, 1959, p. 468.

26. J. D. Salinger, *The Catcher in the Rye* (Boston: Little, Brown, 1951), pp. 198, 204.

27. Erich Fromm, *Escape from Freedom* (New York: Holt, Rinehart and Winston, 1941); Erich Fromm, *Man for Himself* (New York: Rinehart, 1947). See also Erich Fromm, *The Sane Society* (New York: Rinehart, 1955).

28. C. Wright Mills, *White Collar* (New York: Oxford University Press, 1953), pp. ix, xii.

29. Ibid., pp. 108–109.

30. Ibid., pp. xvii, 110, 111, 353.

31. David Riesman, *The Lonely Crowd* (New Haven: Yale University Press, 1950), p. 47.

32. Frank Tannenbaum, *A Philosophy of Labor* (New York: Knopf, 1951).

33. Vance Packard, *The Status Seekers* (New York: McKay, 1959); Vance Packard, *The Hidden Persuaders* (New York: McKay, 1957).

34. Peale was influenced by Muscular Christianity and condemned "sissy religion" in his effort to reshape the American personality. See Carol V. R. George, *God's Salesman: Norman Vincent Peale and the Power of Positive Thinking* (New York: Oxford University Press, 1992).

35. William Whyte, *The Organization Man*, pp. 12, 144, 147.

36. Sloan Wilson, *The Man in the Gray Flannel Suit* (New York: Simon & Schuster, 1955).

37. Norman Mailer, "The White Negro" (San Francisco: City Lights Books, 1957), cited in Breines, *Young, White and Miserable*, p. 144.

38. Cited in Elaine Tylor May, *Homeward Bound* (New York: Basic Books, 1988) p. 147.

39. Albert Cohen, *The Culture of the Gang* (New York: Free Press, 1955), pp. 163, 164. See also Joseph Pleck, *The Myth of Masculinity* (Cambridge: M.I.T. Press, 1981), pp. 96–106.

40. Walter Miller, "Lower-Class Culture As a Generating Milieu of Gang Delinquency," *Journal of Social Issues* 14, 1958, p. 9.

41. See J. Rohrer and M. Edmonson, *The Eighth Generation* (New York: Harper, 1960), p. 163; cited in Pleck, *The Myth of Masculinity*, p. 97.

42. Theodor Adorno et al., *the Authoritarian Personality* (New York: Harper and Row, 1950), pp. 405, 428.

43. Talcott Parsons, "The Social Structure of the Family," in *The Family: Its Functions and Destiny*, Ruth Nanda Ashen, ed. (New York: Harper Bros., 1959), p. 271.

44. See Harvey Levenstein, *Paradox of Plenty: A Social History of Eating in Modern America* (New York: Oxford University Press, 1993), p. 105.

45. Psychiatrist is cited by Elaine Tylor May, *Homeward Bound: American Families in the Cold War Era* (New York: Basic, 1988), p. 143. *Esquire Handbook for Hosts* is cited in Levenstein, *Paradox of Plenty*, p. 132,

46. Spock is cited in Barbara Ehrenreich and Deirdre English, *For Her Own Good: 150 Years of Experts' Advice to Women* (New York: Anchor Books, 1975), p. 239. Morris Zelditch, "Role Differentiation in the Nuclear Family: A Comparative Study," in *Family, Socialization and Interaction Process*, Talcott Parsons and Robert F. Bales, eds. (New York: Free Press, 1955), p. 339. *Parents'*

magazine offered articles like "Men Make Wonderful Mothers" to reassure men. See Peter Filene, *Him/Her/Self: Sex Roles in Modern America* (Baltimore: The Johns Hopkins University Press, 1986), pp. 172–173.

47. Elaine Tylor May, *Homeward Bound*, p. 148.

48. Cited in Elaine Tylor May, *Homeward Bound*, p. 149.

49. Mark Crispin Miller, "Dads and Their Discontents," *Village Voice*, 25 November 1986, p. 45. See also Mark Crispin Miller, "Prime Time: Deride and Conquer," in *Watching Television*, Todd Gitlin, ed. (New York: Pantheon, 1986), p. 199. Ozzie Nelson is cited in Gerard Jones, *Honey I'm Home* (New York: St. Martin's Press, 1992), p. 92.

50. Gerard Jones, *Honey I'm Home*, pp. 124–125.

51. John Cawelti, *The Six-Gun Mystique* (Bowling Green, Ohio: Bowling Green University Popular Press, n.d.), pp. 2, 83.

52. See Jenni Calder, *There Must Be a Lone Ranger: The American West in Film and Reality* (New York: Tapplinger, 1974).

53. Martin Nussbaum, "Sociological Symbolism of the 'Adult Western,'" *Social Forces* 39, October 1960, p. 26.

54. On the Wayne iconography, see "John Wayne as the Last Hero," *Time*, 8 August 1969.

55. Joan Mellon, *Big Bad Wolves: Masculinity in American Film* (New York: Pantheon, 1977), p. 259.

56. Cited in Myron Brenton, *The American Male*, p. 30.

57. Barbara Ehrenreich, *The Hearts of Men: American Dreams and the Flight from Commitment* (New York: Anchor Books, 1983), p. 42.

58. Philip Wylie, *A Generation of Vipers*, pp. 48, 88, 192, 207.

59. Myron Brenton, *The American Male* (London: George Allen and Unwin, 1967), p. 80.

60. Barbara Ehrenreich, *The Hearts of Men*, pp. 50, 51.

61. Philip Wylie, "The Womanization of America," *Playboy*, September 1958; *Playboy* panel, "The Womanization of America," *Playboy*, June 1962.

62. Wylie, "The Womanization of America," pp. 52, 77, 78.

63. Ibid., pp. 77, 79.

64. *Playboy* panel, "The Womanization of America," pp. 47, 134.

65. Ibid., p. 142.

66. Cited in Ehrenreich, *The Hearts of Men*, pp. 38, 51.

67. Sloan Wilson, *The Man in the Gray Flannel Suit*.

CHAPTER 8: The Masculine Mystique

1. Betty Friedan, *The Feminine Mystique* [1963] (New York: Dell, 1983), p. 386. The citation is from the epilogue, published in 1973.

2. Arthur Schlesinger, Jr., "The Crisis of American Masculinity," *Esquire*, November 1958.

3. Friedan, *The Feminine Mystique*, pp. 15, 19, 32.

4. Leslie Fiedler argued in "The New Mutants" that the hippies wanted to become "not only more Black than White but more female than male." Cited in Mark Gerzon, *A Choice of Heroes: The Changing Faces of American Manhood* (Boston: Houghton Mifflin, 1982), p. 95.

5. Robert Blauner, *Alienation and Freedom* (Chicago: University of Chicago Press, 1964).

6. W. Lloyd Warner and James Abegglen, *Big Business Leaders in America* (New York: Atheneum, 1963), p. 83.

7. Cited in Myron Brenton, *The American Male* (London: George Allen and Unwin), p. 197.

8. Cited in Barbara Ehrenreich, *The Hearts of Men: American Dreams and the Flight from Commitment* (New York, Anchor, 1983), p. 83.

9. See Jack Nichols, *Men's Liberation* (New York: Penguin, 1975), p. 170.

10. Paul Goodman, *Growing Up Absurd* (New York: Vintage, 1960), p. 14. See also Philip Slater, *The Pursuit of Loneliness* (Boston: Beacon Press, 1970);

11. Charles Reich, *The Greening of America* (New York: Simon and Schuster, 1970).

12. Students for a Democratic Society, "The Port Huron Statement" (1962) is reprinted in James Miller, *Democracy Is in the Streets* (New York: simon and Schuster, 1988).

13. Quoted in the *New York Times*, 17 July 1960.

14. Tom Wolfe, *The Right Stuff* (New York: Farrar, Straus and Giroux, 1979), pp. 284, 303, 367.

15. Cited in Marc Feigen Fasteau, *The Male Machine* (New York: McGraw-Hill, 1975), p. 162.

16. Halberstam, *The Best and the Brightest*, p. 531.

17. Moyers is cited in Marc Feigen Fasteau, *The Male Machine*, pp. 172–173.

18. Bruce Mazlish, *In Search of Nixon* (New York: Basic Books, 1972), p. 116.

19. James Baldwin, *The Fire Next Time* (New York: Dell, 1962), p. 132.

20. Eldridge Cleaver, *Soul on Ice* (New York: Delta, 1968).

21. Baraka is quoted in bell hooks, *Black Looks* (Boston: South End Press, 1991), p. 98.

22. Eldridge Cleaver, *Soul on Ice*, pp. 188–189.

23. National Organization for Women, "Statement of Purpose," 1966.

24. Myron Brenton, *The American Male*, p. 165; see also p. 188.

25. Norman Mailer, "The Prisoner of Sex," first appeared in *Harper's* magazine in 1971 and later appeared as a book (see pp. 43, 45, 56 in the magazine version).

26. Steven Goldberg, *The Inevitability of Patriarchy* (New York: Morrow, 1973).

27. George Gilder, *Sexual Suicide* (New York: Quadrangle, 1973), pp. 11, 62.

28. Gilder, *Sexual Suicide*, p. 10.

29. Cited in David Pugh, *Sons of Liberty: The Masculine Mind in Nineteenth-Century America* (Westport, Conn.: Greenwood, 1984), p. 134.

30. Patricia Cayo Sexton, *The Feminized Male: Classrooms, White Collars and the Decline of Manliness* (New York: Random House, 1969), pp. 4, 12, 39. See also Patricia Cayo Sexton, "How the American boy Is Feminized," *Psychology Today* 3(23), January 1970.

31. Sexton, *The Feminized Male*, pp. 55, 97.

32. Hans Sebald, *Momism: The Silent Disease of America* (Chicago: Nelson-Hall, 1976), pp. 3,15, 65, 86.

33. Ardrey is cited in Sebald, *Momism*, p. 169.

34. Ron Bishop, "The Big Squeal," *True*, January 1974, p. 28.

35. Lionel Tiger, *Men in Groups* (New York: Vintage, 1969), pp. 262–265.

36. Tom Wolfe, "Honks and Wonks," in *Mauve Gloves and Madmen, Clutter and Vine, and Other Stories, Sketches, and Essays* (New York: Farrar, Straus and Giroux, 1976), p. 222.

37. Philip Roth, *Portnoy's Complaint* (New York: Random House, 1967), p. 36.

38. The two quotes from Arthur Koestler are from *Promise and Fulfillment: Palestine, 1917–1949* (New York: Macmillan, 1949), p. 67, and *Thieves in the Night* (New York: Berkley Books, 1960). Uris is cited in Paul Breines, *Tough Jews*, p. 54.

39. Friedan is cited in Steven Seidman, *Romantic Longings*, p. 137. See also Patricia Cayo Sexton, *The Feminized Male*, p. 200, and Hans Sebald, *Momism*, pp. 140, 170.

40. Peter Wyden and Barbara Wyden, *Growing Up Straight: What Every Thoughtful Parent Should Know About Homosexuality* (New York: Trident Press, 1968).

41. Some gay lib theorists continued to argue for the sissy as an alternative role model for American manhood. See, e.g., Kenneth Pitchford, "The Effeminist Manifesto," and also Frank Rose, "Sissyhood Is Powerful," *Village Voice*, 15 November 1976.

42. For more on the birth of gay masculinity, see Seymour Kleinberg, "The New Masculinity of Gay Men," in *Alienated Affections* (New York: St. Martin's Press, 1980).

43. On the proportion of gay men who were clones, see Alan Bell and Martin Weinberg, *Homosexualities: A Study of Diversity Among Men and Women* (New York: Simon and Schuster, 1978).

44. See Jack Sawyer, "On Male Liberation," *Liberation* 15 (6–8), August–October 1970; Warren Farrell, *The Liberated Man* (New York: Random House, 1974); Marc Feigen Fasteau, *The Male Machine* (New York: Delta, 1975); Herb Goldberg, *The Hazards of Being Male* (New York: Nash, 1976) and *The New Male* (New York: New American Library, 1979); Jack Nichols, *Men's Liberation* (New York: Penguin, 1975); Deborah David and Robert Brannon, eds., *The*

Forty-Nine Percent Majority (Reading, Mass.: Addison-Wesley, 1976); and Joseph Pleck and Jack Sawyer, eds., *Men and Masculinity* (Englewood Cliffs, Prentice-Hall, 1974).

45. Pleck is cited in Barbara Katz, "Women's Lib Auxiliaries?" *National Observer*, 29 December 1973, p. 8; Berkeley Men's Center Manifesto (1973) is reprinted in Pleck and Sawyer, *Men and Masculinity*.

46. Herb Goldberg, *The New Male*, pp. 17, 45.

47. Robert Brannon, "The Male Sex Role—and What It's Done for Us Lately," in *The Forty-Nine Percent Majority*, p. 5.

48. Myron Brenton, *The American Male*, pp. 14, 15; Jack Nichols, *Men's Liberation*, p. 122; Robert Gould, "Measuring Masculinity by the Size of a Paycheck," *Ms.*, June 1973, p. 98.

49. Arthur Shostak, "Blue Collar Work," in *The Forty-Nine Percent Majority*, pp. 101, 103.

50. Alan Alda, "What Every Woman Should Know," *Mr.*, 1975; Feigen Fasteau, *The Male Machine*, p. 21; Herb Goldberg, *The Hazards of Being Male*, p. 118.

51. Thomas Hearn, "Jesus Was a Sissy After All," *Christian Century* 87(40), October 1970, p. 1192; see also Leonard Swidler, "Jesus Was a Feminist," *Catholic World* January, 1971.

52. Herb Goldberg, *The Hazards of Being Male*, pp. 104, 143, 151.

53. Warren Farrell, *The Liberated Man.*

54. Marc Feigen Fasteau, *The Male Machine*, p. 60; Glenn Bucher, ed., *Straight/White/Male* (Philadelphia: Fortress Press, 1976), p. 111.

55. Joseph Pleck, "My Male Sex Role—and Ours," *WIN*, 11 April 1974; Joseph Pleck, "Men's Power with Women, Other Men, and Society: A Men's Movement Analysis," in *Women and Men: The Consequences of Power*, D. Hiller and R. Sheets, eds. (Cincinnati: Office of Women's Studies, University of Cincinnati, 1977).

56. Pleck, "My male Sex Role, " p. 15.

57. Joan Mellers, *Big Bad Wolves: Masculinity in American Film* (New York: Pantheon, 1977).

58. James Dickey, *Deliverance* (New York: Dell, 1970), p. 62.

59. See Carolyn Heilbrun, "The Masculine Wilderness of the American Novel," *Saturday Review*, 29 January 1972.

60. Norman Mailer, *Why Are We in Vietnam?* (New York: Putnam, 1967), p. 179.

61. Geoffrey Wolff, *The Duke of Deception* (New York: Avon, 1979), p. 7; Leonard Michaels, *The Men's Club* (New York: Farrar, Straus and Giroux, 1978).

CHAPTER 9: Wimps, Whiners, and Weekend Warriors

1. See Mark Gerzon, *A Choice of Heroes* (Boston: Houghton Mifflin, 1982). Gerzon makes the process seem entirely voluntary, as if individual men could come to the table of heroes and choose as one would choose dishes at a buffet.

2. Tsongas is cited in Sam Osherson, *Finding Our Fathers: How a Man's Life Is Shaped by His Relationship with His Father* (New York: Fawcett, 1987), p. 172.

3. The quote from John Lennon is from an interview in *Newsweek*, October 1978.

4. For an example, see Alan Alda's writing in support of feminism in *Ms.* magazine, especially his "Why Should Men Care?" and "What Women Should Know About Men." The former essay is reprinted in Michael S. Kimmel and Thomas E. Mosmiller, eds. *Against the Tide: Pro-Feminist Men in the United States, 1776–1990* (Boston: Beacon Press, 1992).

5. George Stade in the *New York Times Book Review*, 1984.

6. Quotes are from Curt Suplee, "The Dawn of the Wimp," *Miami Herald*, 16 September 1984.

7. Janet Maslin, "The New Man in Films," *New York Times*, 1988.

8. All these were in columns in the *New York Times Magazine*, which launched its "About Men" column in 1983.

9. Bruce Feirstein, *Real Men Don't Eat Quiche* (New York: Warner Books, 1982).

10. *Economist*, 30 May 1992, p. 32.

11. Barbara Ehrenreich, "The Warrior Culture," *Time*, 15 October 1990, p. 88.

12. See Katherine Newman, *Falling from Grace: The Experience of Downward Mobility in the American Middle Class* (New York: Free Press, 1988), and Barbara Ehrenreich, *Fear of Falling: The Inner Life of the Middle Class* (New York: Pantheon, 1989).

13. Lloyd Cohen, "Fear of Flirting," *New York Times*, 12 October 1991.

14. This trend was noted by countless observers during the 1994 political campaign. See, e.g., Susan Estrich, "The Last Victim," *New York Times Magazine*, 18 December 1994; Todd Gitlin, "Republicans Told White Guys: You *Can* Get It Up Again," *New York Observer*, 3 December 1994; and Rick Wartzman, "Clinton Is Still Struggling to Get Message Across to 'Angry White Males' Who Have Tuned Out," *Wall Street Journal*, 24 January 1995.

15. Ray Raphael, *The Men from the Boys* (Omaha: University of Nebraska Press, 1988), p. 167; Richard Haddad, "Feminism Has Little Relevance for Men," in *To Be a Man: In Search of the Deep Masculine*, Keith Thompson, ed. (Los Angeles: Jeremy Tarcher, 1991), p. 100; C. H. Freedman, *Manhood Redux* (Brooklyn: Samson Publications, 1985), p. 109.

16. "The Chaplain's Lament," letter to the editor of the *New York Times*, 12 June 1992.

17. These arguments are summarized conveniently in Warren Farrell, *The Myth of Male Power* (New York: Simon and Schuster, 1993).

18. Nicholas Davidson, *The Failure of Feminism* (Buffalo, N.Y.: Prometheus, 1987).

19. Michael Levin, *Feminism and Freedom* (New Brunswick, N.J.: Transaction, 1987), pp. 2, 3, 300.

20. Asa Baber, *Naked at Gender Gap* (New York: Birch Lane Press, 1992), pp. 27, 50, 112.

21. Ibid., pp. 79, 92, 109, 138, 156, 169, 218.

22. Warren Farrell, "We Should Embrace Traditional Masculinity," in *To Be a Man: In Search of the Deep Masculine*, Keith Thompson, ed. (Los Angeles: Jeremy Tarcher, 1991); Farrell, interviewed in *Christian Science Monitor*, 29 February 1988, p. 24. Jerry Boggs, review of Davidson's *The Failure of Feminism*, *Transitions* 10(2), March/April 1990, pp. 9, 10.

23. Farrell's *The Myth of Male Power*. Ibid., pp. 293, 298.

24. Farrell, *The Myth of Male Power*, pp. 298, 301.

25. Ibid., p. 310; Farrell at First International Men's Conference, Austin, Texas, October 1991.

26. See Herb Goldberg, *The New Male-Female Relationship* (New York: William Morrow, 1983), *The Inner Male* (New York: New American Library, 1987), and *What Men Really Want* (New York: Signet, 1991).

27. Richard Doyle, *The Rape of the Male* (St. Paul: Poor Richard's Press, 1986); Marcy Sheiner, "What Do Men Really Want . . . and Why Should We Care?" *East Bay Express*, 10 July 1992, p. 11.

28. Jon Conine, *Fathers' Rights: The Sourcebook for Dealing with the Child Support System* (New York: Walker, 1989), p. 2.

29. Quoted in Daniel Gross, "The Gender Rap," *New Republic*, 16 April 1990, p. 13.

30. Terrence Rafferty, "Woman on Top," *New Yorker*, December 1994, p. 107.

31. Cited in Sam Keen, *Fire in the Belly: On Being a Man* (New York: Bantam, 1991), p. 66.

32. Charles Nicholl, *Borderlines* (New York: Viking, 1989); P. J. O'Rourke, *Holidays in Hell* (Boston: Atlantic Monthly Press, 1989); Tim Cahill, *A Wolverine Is Eating My Leg* (New York: Vintage, 1988); Nick Danziger, *Danziger's Travels: Beyond Forbidden Frontiers* (New York: Vintage, 1988); Stuart Stevens, *Malarian Dreams* (Boston: Atlantic Monthly Press, 1989).

33. Michael Pakaluk, "War Games," *Crisis*, October 1991; Susan Jeffords, *The Remasculinization of America* (Bloomington: Indiana University Press, 1989) and *Hard Bodies: Hollywood Masculinity in the Reagan Era* (New Brunswick, N.J.: Rutgers University Press, 1993).

34. Brian Mitchell, *Weak Link: The Feminization of the American Military* (Washington: Regnery Gateway, 1990); Philip Caputo, *A Rumor of War* (New York: Holt, Rinehart and Winston, 1977).

35. Carol Flake, *Redemptorama: Culture, Politics and the New Evangelism* (New York: Viking, 1984), p. 93.

36. Jerry Falwell is quoted in Frances Fitzgerald, *Cities on a Hill* (New York: Simon and Schuster, 1986), p. 166; Leon Podles, "Men Not Wanted," *Crisis*, November 1991.

37. William G. Thompson, "Men and the Gospels," *Catholic World*, May 1992, p. 105; Podles, "Men Not Wanted," p. 20.

38. Laurie Beth Jones, *Jesus CEO: Using Ancient Wisdom for Visionary Leadership* (New York: Hyperion, 1994).

39. See *San Francisco Chronicle*, 15 August 1989; David Leon Moore, "Ballplayers Putting Faith in Christ," *USA Today*, 27 July 1991. Eaton is quoted in *Esquire*, January 1993, p. 67.

40. See Sharon Mazer, "The Power Team: Muscular Christianity and the Spectacle of Conversion," *Drama Review* 38(4), Winter 1994, pp. 162, 169.

41. Dotson Rader, "Against Coeducation," *Playboy*, January 1976.

42. William F. Buckley, "The Clubhouse," *About Men*, p. 256.

43. Keith Thompson, "A Man Needs a Lodge," in *To Be a Man*, p. 254.

44. See G. William Domhoff, *The Bohemian Grove and Other Ruling Class Retreats* (New York: Harper and Row, 1974), p. 23 et al.; other quotes from Reed M. Powell, *Race, Religion and the Promotion of the American Executive* (Columbus: College of Administrative Science Monographs, no. AA-3, Ohio State University, 1969), p. 50.

45. Quotes from Bliss are from Kenneth Guentert, "Returning to the Wound—an Interview with Shepherd Bliss," *Festivals* 7(1), February 1988, p. 7.

46. R. W. Connell, "Drumming Up the Wrong Tree," *Tikkun* 7(1), 1991, p. 33.

47. Sam Keen, *Fire in the Belly*, pp. 208, 209.

48. Robert Moore and Douglas Gillette, *King, Warrior, Magician, Lover* (New York: HarperCollins, 1990). See also their *The King Within* (New York: William Morrow, 1992), *The Warrior Within* (New York: William Morrow, 1992), *The Magician Within* (New York: William Morrow, 1993), and *The Lover Within* (New York: William Morrow, 1994).

49. Jill P. Baumgaertner, "The New Masculinity or the Old Mystification?" *Christian Century*, 29 May 1991, p. 596.

50. See Nina Silber, *The Romance of Reunion: Northerners and the South, 1865–1900* (Chapel Hill: University of North Carolina Press, 1993), p. 130.

51. "Male bonding is not a vehicle for male-male emotional relationships, but rather a substitute for them," notes psychologist Joseph Pleck in *The Myth of Masculinity* (Cambridge: M.I.T. Press, 1981), p. 150.

52. Springsteen is quoted in the *New York Times*, 9 August 1992.

CHAPTER 10: From Anxiety to Anger Since the 1990s

1. See, for example, Paul Starobin, "The Angry American," in *Atlantic Monthly*, January/February 2004, pp. 132–136.

2. See Richard Goldstein, "Butching Up for Victory," in *The Nation*, January 26, 2004; available at http://thenation.com/doc.mhtml?i=20040126&s=goldstein.

3. Norman Mailer, "The White Man Unburdened," in *New York Review of Books*, 50(12), July 17, 2003; available at http://www.nybooks.com/articles/16470.

4. Cited in Starobin, "The Angry American," p. 132.

5. Barbara Ehrenreich, *Nickel and Dimed* (New York: Metropolitan Books, 2002); Mailer, "White Man Unburdened"; Jonathan Mahler, "Commute to Nowhere," in *New York Times Magazine*, April 13, 2003, pp. 44–49, 66, 70, 75.

6. Dale Maharidge, *Journey to Nowhere* (New York: Hyperion, 1996), and *Homeland* (New York: Seven Stories Press, 2004).

7. Susan Faludi, *Stiffed: The Betrayal of the American Man* (New York: William Morrow, 1999), pp. 40, 31.

8. See Terrence Real, *I Don't Want to Talk About It* (New York: Scribner, 1998); Eric Ramirez-Ferrero, *Troubled Fields: Men, Emotions and the Crisis of American Farming* (New York: Columbia University Press, 2005).

9. Chuck Palahniuk, *Fight Club* (NY: Owl, 2004).

10. Arlie Hochschild, "Let the Eat War" alternet.org, October 2, 2003; available at http://www.alternet.org/story.html?StoryID=16885. Bruce Springsteen, "The Promised Land" (1979).

11. See David Brooks, "The Return of the Pig," in *Atlantic Monthly*, April 2003; available at www.theatlantic.com/issues/2003.

12. This is, of course, statistically impossible; it is simply the flip side of Lake Wobegon, where, as Garrison Keilor reminds us, everyone is above average.

13. Cited in Stephen J. Ducat, *The Wimp Factor: Gender Gaps, Holy Wars and the Politics of Anxious Masculinity* (Boston: Beacon Press, 2004), p. 54.

14. See Bruce Handy, "The Viagra Craze," in *Time*, May 4, 1998, pp. 50–57; Christopher Hitchens, "Viagra Falls," in *The Nation*, May 25, 1998, p. 8; see also Meika Loe, *The Rise of Viagra: How the Little Blue Pill Changed Sex in America* (New York: New York University Press, 2004).

15. Cited in Susan Bordo, *The Male Body* (New York: Farrar Straus, and Giroux, 2000), p. 61. Loe, *The Rise of Viagra*, pp. 59, 78. There is actually some evidence of Viagra-related violence against women and a sort of sexual "road rage."

16. See Susan Bordo, *The Male Body*.

17. Harrison Pope, Katharine Phillips, and Roberto Olivardia, *The Adonis Complex: The Secret Crisis of Male Body Obsession* (New York: Free Press, 2000).

18. Cited in Richard Morgan, "The Men in the Mirror," in *Chronicle of Higher Education*, September 27, 2002, p. A 53.

19. Gina Kolata, "With No Answers on Risks, Steroid Users Still Say 'Yes,'" in *New York Times*, December 2, 2002, pp. A-1, 19.

20. The average flaccid penis is about 3.5 inches long; erect, it's about 5.1 inches long. In one of the few studies that rely on data and not anecdotal evidence and thrilled testimonials, psychologist Randy Klein found that the average penile length before surgery was 2.6″ (flaccid) and 5.4″ (erect); after the surgery, penile length was 3.8″ (flaccid) and 5.7″ (erect). The only significant difference in length was when the penis was flaccid. See Sam Fields, "Penis Enlargement Surgery," at www.4-men.org/penisenlargementsurgery.html; Randy Klein,

"Penile Augmentation Surgery," in *Electronic Journal of Human Sexuality* 2, March 1999, Chapter 2, p. 1, and Chapter 5, pp. 8–9.

21. Testimonial letters to Dr. E. Douglas Whitehead; available at www.penile-enlargement-surgeon.com/diary.html.

22. Robin Finn, "Public Lives: The Queer Brown Behind Queer Eye" New York Time, November 21, 2003, B-2.

23. Lillian Rubin, *Families on the Fault Line* (New York: HarperCollins), p. 186.

24. This section is part of an ongoing research project on masculinity and the extreme right. See "Globalization and Its Mal(e)contents: The Gendered Moral and Political Economy of Terrorism," in *International Sociology*, 18(3), September 2003. Some of this material is based on collaborative research with Abby Ferber; see, especially, our "'White Men Are This Nation!' Right Wing Militias and the Restoration of Rural American Masculinity," in *Rural Sociology*, 2000. I am grateful to the Carnegie Foundation for their continued support of this research.

25. *Intelligence Report*, Spring 2002.

26. Mark Hamm, *In Bad Company: America's Terrorist Underground* (Boston: Northeastern University Press, 2002), p. 287.

27. Of course, these movements are not entirely populated by men. Some older established groups have auxiliary functions for women, while in some of the newer groups, women skinheads are equally eager to engage in violence. But virtually all groups venerate a traditional family in which the breadwinner father returns to his "castle" where housewife and children await the benevolent patriarch; see, for example, Kathleen Blee, *Women of the Klan* (Berkeley: University of California Press, 2001).

28. William Pierce, *The Turner Diaries* Hillsboro, VA: National Vanguard, 1978, p. 33.

29. Betty Dobratz and S. Shanks-Meile, *The White Separatist Movement in the United States: White Power! White Pride!* (Baltimore: Johns Hopkins University Press, 2001), p. 271. See also J. Coplon, "The Roots of Skinhead Violence: Dim Econmic Prospects for Young Men," in *Utne Reader*, May/June 1989.

30. Lyrics from Toby Keith, "American Soldier." See also McKusker and Pecknold, *A Boy Named Sue* (Oxford: University Press of Mississippi, 2004).

31. It often appears that the most virulent misogyny and homophobia occur as the rap artist is beginning to make his reputation. Several notable rappers, such as Nelly and 50 Cent, have toned down their vicious lyrics as they have become more famous; Snoop Dogg has become positively cuddly in his portrayals in advertising.

32. Anthony Bozza, *Whatever You Say I Am: The Life and Times of Eminem* (New York: Crown, 2004), p. 31. My own interpretation of Eminem's meaning and importance has been greatly influenced by conversing with Steven Zyck and reading his "Undressing Eminem: Intersection and Abjection in the Formation of a Cultural Icon," BA conors thesis, Dartmouth College, June 2004.

33. Bozza, *Whatever You Say I Am*, p. 30.

34. Ibid., p. 34.

35. Cited in Randy Thornhill and Craig T. Palmer, "Why Men Rape," in *The Sciences*, January 2000, p. 33.

36. Richard Dawkins, *The Selfish Gene* (New York: Oxford Univ. Press, 1990), pp. 153, 162.

37. Robert Wright, *The Moral Animal* (New York: Vintage, 1995), p. 71.

38. Randy Thornhill and Craig T. Palmer, *A Natural History of Rape: Biological Bases of Sexual Coercion* (Cambridge: MIT Press, 1999); quote from Thornhill and Palmer, "Why Men Rape," p. 30.

39. Thornhill and Palmer, *A Natural History of Rape*, p. 53.

40. Ibid., p. 142.

41. Thornhill and Palmer, "Why Men Rape," pp. 32, 34.

42. George Gilder, *Men and Marriage* (Gretna, La.: Pelican, 1993). The current edition comes with a ringing endorsement from Rush Limbaugh.

43. Ibid., p. 5.

44. Ibid., pp. 11, 45.

45. Ibid., p. 39.

46. Ibid., pp. 39, 62.

47. Ibid., p. 5.

48. Ibid., p. 73.

49. Charles Murray, *The Emerging British Underclass* (London: IEA Health and Welfare Unit, 1990), cited in Richard Collier, *Masculinities, Crime and Criminology* (London: Sage Publications, 1998), p. 129; Christina Hoff Sommers, comment at Symposium on "Reconnecting Males to Liberal Education," (Morehouse College, April 4–5, 2001; David Popenoe, *Life Without Father* (New York: Free Press, 1996), p. 12.

50. Popenoe, *Life Without Father*, p. 4.

51. David Blankenhorn, *Fatherless America* (New York: Basic Books, 1995).

52. Ibid., p. 96.

53. Ibid., p. 102.

54. Ibid., p. 122.

55. Harvey Mansfield, "Why a Woman Can't Be More Like a Man," in *Wall Street Journal*, November 3, 1997, p. A 22.

56. Lionel Tiger, *The Decline of Males* (New York: Golden Books, 1999), p. 90.

57. In one of his more bizarre arguments, Tiger suggests that women's use of barbiturates during pregnancy in the 1950s and 1960s caused the spike of male homosexuality in the 1960s and 1970s. "The sons of women using barbiturates are much more likely to be 'feminized,' to display bodies and behavior more typically female than male. Millions of American mothers of boys, an estimated

eleven million in the 1950s and 60s, used barbiturates, and millions still do. A compelling thought is that this may have something to do with the evident increase in the number, or at least prominence, of male homosexuals" (p. 95). Although there is not a scintilla of evidence that those same women who took barbiturates had gay sons, nor even a correlation between barbiturate use and *having* a gay son, Tiger goes even further than a simple "correlation does not imply causation" fallacy. He thinks barbiturates explain not only the cause but the "prominence" of gay men. One can only imagine that causal reasoning: Gay sons of barbiturate-using mothers support liberalized drug laws, which bring them into public policy arenas and make them more prominent?

58. Schlessinger has no formal training as a psychologist; her degree is in kinesthesiology. And Columbia Pacific University, where Gray received his graduate "training," was a correspondence school offering degrees via what is called "distance learning," in which students receive course packets, read the materials, and then take open-book exams and receive degrees—until it was shut down, that is, by California's Department of Consumer Affairs, which called it a "giant scam" and a "diploma mill." See *San Francisco Chronicle*, March 14, 2001.

59. Laura Schlessinger, *Ten Stupid Things Women Do to Mess Up Their Lives* (New York: HarperCollins, 1995); *Ten Stupid Things Men Do to Mess Up Their Lives* (New York: HarperCollins, 1998); and *Ten Stupid Things Couples Do to Mess Up Their Relationships* (New York: HarperCollins, 2001).

60. Schlessinger, *Ten Stupid Things Men Do to Mess Up Their Lives*, pp. 194, 273.

61. Susan Goodman, "Dr. No," in *Modern Maturity*, September–October 1999, p. 68.

62. John Gray, *Men Are from Mars, Women Are from Venus* (New York: HarperCollins, 1992), p. 5.

63. John Gray, *Men, Women, and Relationships* (New York: HarperCollins, 1993), p. 53.

64. Ibid., pp. 52, 84.

65. Ibid., p. 95.

66. Ibid., pp. 27, 246.

67. Gray, *Men Are from Mars*, p. 68.

68. Ibid., pp. 146, 148, 78.

69. Ellen Fein and Sherrie Schneider, *The Rules: Time-Tested Secrets for Capturing the Heart of Mr. Right* (New York: Warner Books, 1995).

70. Ibid., p. 14.

71. Ibid., p. 167.

72. Ibid., pp. 7, 9, 28, 127, 157.

73. Ibid., p. 90.

74. This section summarizes the case I make in "'What About the Boys?' What the Current Debates Tell Us—and Don't Tell Us—About Boys in School," in *Michigan Feminist Studies*, 14, 1999–2000.

75. Christine Hoff Sommers, *The War Against Boys* (New York: Scribners, 1999). Sommers, cited in Debra Viadero, "Behind the 'Mask of Masculinity,'" in *Education Week*, May 13, 1998; Thompson cited in Margaret Combs, "What About the Boys?" in *Boston Globe*, Jule 26, 1998. For more of this backlash argument, see Michael Gurian, *The Wonder of Boys* (New York: Jeremy Tarcher/Putnam, 1997) and Judith Kleinfeld, "Student Performance: Male Versus Female," in *The Public Interest*, Winter 1999. For dissenting opinions, see my review of Gurian, "Boys to Men," in *San Francisco Chronicle*, January 12, 1997, and R. W. Connell, "Teaching the Boys," in *Teachers College Record*, 98(2), Winter, 1996.

76. Brendan Koerner, "Where the Boys Aren't," in *U.S. News & World Report*, February 8, 1999; Tamar Lewin, "American Colleges Begin to Ask, Where Have All the Men Gone?" in *New York Times*, December 6, 1998; Michael Fletcher, "Degrees of Separation," in *Washington Post*, June 25, 2002; Jamilah Evelyn, "Community Colleges Start to Ask, Where Are the Men?" in *Chronicle of Higher Education*, June 28, 2002; Ridger Doyle, "Men, Women and College," in *Scientific American*, October 1999.

77. See, for example, William Pollack, *Real Boys: Rescuing Our Sons from the Myths of Boyhood* (New York: Random House, 1998).

78. Carol Gilligan, *In a Different Voice*; Lyn Mikel Brown and Carol Gilligan, *Meeting at the Crossroads* (New York: Ballantine, 1992).

79. Pollack, cited in Debra Viadero, "Behind the Mask."

80. Martain Mac an Ghaill, *The Making of Men: Masculinities, Sexualities and Schooling* (Buckingham: Open University Press, 1994), p. 59; David Gillborne, *Race, Ethnicity and Education* (London: Unwin Hyman, 1990), p. 63; James Coleman, *The Adolescent Society* (New York: Harper and Row, 1961).

81. Wayne Martino, "Masculinity and Learning: Exploring Boys' Underachievement and Underrepresentation in Subject English," in *Interpretation*, 27(2), 1994; "Boys and Literacy: Exploring the Construction of Hegemonic Masculinities and the Formation of Literate Capacities for Boys in the English Classroom," in *English in Australia*, 112, 1995; "Gendered Learning Experiences: Exploring the Costs of Hegemonic Masculinity for Girls and Boys in Schools," in *Gender Equity: A Framework for Australian Schools* (Canberra: Publications and Public Communications, Department of Urban Services, ACT Government, 1997). Catharine Stimpson, quoted in Tamar Lewin, "American Colleges Begin to Ask, Where Have All the Men Gone?" in *New York Times*, December 6, 1998.

82. From the American Psychological Association, "All That Violence Is Numbing"; available at www.apa.org; statistics first appeared in 1992 in *U.S. News & World Report*.

83. "Boys will be boys" are, not so incidentally, the last four words of Hoff Sommers's antifeminist creed.

84. Cited in Michael S. Kimmel, "The Struggle for Gender Equality: How Men Respond," in *Thought and Action: The NEA Higher Education Journal* 8(2), 1993.

85. See, for example, William Pollack, *Real Boys* (New York: Henry Holt, 1998); Dan Kindlon and Michael Thompson, *Raising Cain* (New York: Ballantire, 2000, 1999); Eli Neuberger, *The Men They Will Become* (Cambridge: Perseus, 1999); and Paul Kivel, *Boys Will Be Men* (Philadelphia: New Society Press, 1999).

86. Cited in Richard Kim, "Eminem—Bad Rap?" in *The Nation*, March 13, 2001, p. 4. It's also true that in *8 Mile*, Eminem goes out of his way to defend a gay man from a gay-bashing assault, as if to undermine the charges of homophobia.

87. This section draws on Michael Kimmel and Matthew Mahler, "Adolescent Masculinity, Homophobia, and Violence: Random School Shootings, 1982–2001," in *American Behavioral Scientist*, 46(10), June 2003, pp. 1439–1458.

88. Actually, somebody did. Tom DeLay, the Texas Congressman, blamed day care, the teaching of evolution, and "working mothers who take birth control pills." See "The News of the Weak in Review," in *The Nation*, November 15, 1999, p. 5.

89. J. Adams and J. Malone, "Outsider's Destructive Behavior Spiraled into Violence," in *Louisville Courier Journal*, March 18, 1999; J. Blank, "The Kid No One Noticed," in *U.S. News & World Report*, December 16, 1998, p. 27.

90. N. Gibbs and T. Roche, "The Columbine Tapes," in *Time*, December 20, 1999, p. 40; D. Cullen, "The Rumor That Won't Go Away," in *Salon*, April 24, 1999; available at http://www.salon.com/news/feature/1999/04/24/rumors/index.html.

91. Eric Pooley, "Portrait of a Deadly Bond," in *Time*, May 10, 1999, pp. 26–7.

92. His impeachment trial came because he was accused of lying to the Special Prosecutor of the case when he said that he "did not have sexual relations with that woman." However, it appears that President Clinton and Monica Lewinsky's sexual trysts involved "everything but" sexual intercourse and instead were based on other sexual acts. In a survey published by the *Journal of the American Medical Association*, most Americans apparently agreed with him, saying that "sex" is defined only by penile-vaginal intercourse. Therefore, it appears that he was telling the truth, at least according to public opinion, if not according to the spirit of the law (cf. Stephanie A. Sanders and June Machover Reinisch, "Would You Say You 'Had Sex' If . . . ?" in *JAMA*, 281, 1999, pp. 275–277.

93. Cited in James Ridgeway, "Osamas' New Recruits": *The Village Voice*, November 6, 2001, p. 41.

94. Richard Goldstein, "Neo-Macho Man," in *The Nation*, March 24, 2003; available at http://www.thenation.com/doc.mhtml?i=20030324&s=goldstein. The *American Enterprise* magazine trumpeted their return in a special issue: "Real Men, They're Back"; Patricia Leigh Brown, "Heavy Lifting Required: The Return of Manly Men," in *New York Times*, October 28, 2001, section K, p. 5. Some cheerleaders were just silly; see, for example, Charlotte Allen's paean to real guys in "Return of the Guy," in *Women's Quarterly*, 30, Winter 2002, pp. 9–11. Let me be clear: I share the reverence for those people who were willing to run into burning and collapsing skyscrapers to save others; they did behave heroically. But heroic actions in one arena should not blind us to unheroic behavior in other arenas.

95. See, for example, David Ford, "Shrinking Bush: S. F. Psychologist Argues That Hyper-Masculinity Is Undermining the American Political Culture," in *San Francisco Chronicle*, September 17, 2004; Lexington, "It's a Man's World," in *The Economist*, August 7, 2004, p. 28. The costuming was also noted by gay columnists such as Richard Goldstein; see "Bush's Basket," in *Village Voice*, May 21–27, 2003; available at http://www.villagevoice.com/print/issues/0321/Goldstein.php.

96. See, for example, www.ruminatethis.com/archives/001256.html accessed 6/25/05.

97. Front page headline in *New York Sun*, July 13, 2004; see also Katha Pollitt, "The Girlie Vote," in *The Nation*, September 27, 2004, p. 12; Kenneth Walsh, "What the Guys Want," in *U.S. News & World Report*, September 20, 2004, pp. 22–23; Frank Rich, "How Kerry Became a Girlie-Man," in *New York Times*, September 5, 2004, section 2, pp. 1, 18.

98. Richard Reeves, "The Chosen People," in *New York*, September 25, 2004, p. 26.

99. Cited in Richard Goldstein, "Neo-Macho Man." See also Frank Rich, "How Kerry Became a Girlie-Man"; Kenneth Walsh, "What the Guys Want."

100. Cited in Stephen J. Ducat, *The Wimp Factor*, p. 174.

101. Eminem, "Mosh" lyrics available at http://www.sing365.com.

EPILOGUE: Toward Democratic Manhood

1. Nikos Kazantzakis, *Report to Greco* (New York: Bantam, 1971).

2. John Updike, *Memories of the Ford Administration* (New York: Alfred Knopf, 1992), p. 362.

3. James Baldwin, *The Fire Next Time* (New York: Dell, 1962), p. 21.

4. Ben Smith, "Gay Marriage Issue Divides Generations," in *New York Observer*, October 25, 2004, p. 5.

5. John Gottman, *Why Marriages Succeed or Fail* (New York: Simon and Schuster, 1995); John Gottman and Nan Silver, *Seven Principles for Making Marriages Work* (New York: Three Rivers Press, 2000). See also Janet Shibley Hyde, John D. DeLamater, and Erri Harris, "Sexuality and the Dual Earner Couple: Multiple Roles and Sexual Functioning," in *Journal of Family Psychology*, 12(3), 1998, pp. 354–368.

Index

Note: C refers to endnote chapter, *n* refers to endnote number.

Lightning Source UK Ltd.
Milton Keynes UK
16 May 2010
154209UK00006B/1/P